From Deficit to Dialect

OXFORD STUDIES IN SOCIOLINGUISTICS

General Editors:
Brook Bolander
Monash University
Adam Jaworski
University of Hong Kong

RECENTLY PUBLISHED IN THE SERIES:
*Sustaining the Nation: The Making and Moving of Language and Nation*
Monica Heller, Lindsay A Bell, Michelle Daveluy, Mireille McLaughlin, and Hubert Noel

*Style, Mediation, and Change: Sociolinguistic Perspectives on Talking Media*
Janus Mortensen, Nikolaus Coupland, and Jacob Thogersen

*Reimagining Rapport*
Zane Goebel

*Elite Authenticity: Remaking Distinction in Food Discourse*
Gwynne Mapes

*In Pursuit of English: Language and Subjectivity in Neoliberal South Korea*
Joseph Sung-Yul Park

*Choreographies of Multilingualism: Writing and Language Ideology in Singapore*
Tong King Lee

*From Deficit to Dialect: The Evolution of English in India and Singapore*
Devyani Sharma

# From Deficit to Dialect

*The Evolution of English in India and Singapore*

Devyani Sharma

# OXFORD
UNIVERSITY PRESS

Oxford University Press is a department of the University of Oxford. It furthers
the University's objective of excellence in research, scholarship, and education
by publishing worldwide. Oxford is a registered trade mark of Oxford University
Press in the UK and certain other countries.

Published in the United States of America by Oxford University Press
198 Madison Avenue, New York, NY 10016, United States of America.

© Oxford University Press 2023

All rights reserved. No part of this publication may be reproduced, stored in
a retrieval system, or transmitted, in any form or by any means, without the
prior permission in writing of Oxford University Press, or as expressly permitted
by law, by license, or under terms agreed with the appropriate reproduction
rights organization. Inquiries concerning reproduction outside the scope of the
above should be sent to the Rights Department, Oxford University Press, at the
address above.

You must not circulate this work in any other form
and you must impose this same condition on any acquirer.

Library of Congress Cataloging-in-Publication Data
Names: Sharma, Devyani, 1976– author.
Title: From deficit to dialect / Devyani Sharma.
Description: New York, NY : Oxford University Press, [2023] |
Series: Oxford studies sociolinguistics series |
Includes bibliographical references and index.
Identifiers: LCCN 2023006289 (print) | LCCN 2023006290 (ebook) |
ISBN 9780195307504 (hardback) |
ISBN 9780197696415 (epub) | ISBN 9780197698624
Subjects: LCSH: English language—Dialects—India. |
English language—Dialects—Singapore. |
English language—Social aspects—India. |
English language—Social aspects—Singapore.
Classification: LCC PE3502.I694 S54 2023 (print) |
LCC PE3502.I694 (ebook) | DDC 427/.954—dc23/eng/20230506
LC record available at https://lccn.loc.gov/2023006289
LC ebook record available at https://lccn.loc.gov/2023006290

DOI: 10.1093/oso/9780195307504.001.0001

Printed by Integrated Books International, United States of America

# CONTENTS

*List of Figures*     *xi*
*List of Tables*     *xiii*
*Acknowledgments*     *xv*

1  Introduction     *1*
   1.1  Dialect Birth in Multilingual Settings     *2*
   1.2  Deficit or Dialect?     *3*
   1.3  Goals and Questions     *5*
   1.4  Outline of the Book     *6*
   1.5  Methods Used     *8*
   1.6  Data for Indian English     *10*
   1.7  Data for Singapore English     *14*

**PART I:  English in India**
2  Histories of English in India     *19*
   2.1  Social Histories of English in India     *20*
      2.1.1  Phase I: Early Colonial Contact     *20*
      2.1.2  Phase II: The British Raj     *21*
      2.1.3  Phase III: The Independence Movement     *29*
      2.1.4  Phase IV: Contemporary India     *31*
   2.2  Common Features of Indian English     *35*
      2.2.1  Retention of Historical British English Forms     *35*
      2.2.2  Transfer from Indian Languages     *38*
      2.2.3  Independent Innovations     *44*
   2.3  Indian English as "decreasingly imperfect" Over Time?     *46*
   2.4  Phase 3, Phase 4, or Phase 5?     *49*
3  Errors or Innovations?     *52*
   3.1  The Problem of Nativeness     *53*
   3.2  Models for Studying Variation in New Englishes     *55*
      3.2.1  Second Language Acquisition     *56*
      3.2.2  Native Dialect Variation     *59*
      3.2.3  Language Contact and Creolization     *61*

3.3 Modeling New Englishes as a Usage Cline    62
   3.3.1 Bilingual Continua    62
   3.3.2 Implicational Scaling    62
3.4 The Usage Cline of Indian English    64
   3.4.1 Grammatical Features    64
   3.4.2 The Indian English Usage Cline    65
   3.4.3 Learner Features    69
   3.4.4 New Dialect Features    70
   3.4.5 Correspondence to Social Factors    72
3.5 Implications    74
   3.5.1 IndE and Other Continua    74
   3.5.2 Why Are Some Features More Dialect-Like than Others?    77

4 The Article System    79
4.1 Differences between Hindi and English    80
4.2 Predicted Types of Grammatical Change    82
   4.2.1 Hypothesis 1: Indo-Aryan Positional Marking of Discourse Familiarity    82
   4.2.2 Hypothesis 2: Indo-Aryan Specificity Marking    83
   4.2.3 Hypothesis 3: Universal Prototypes    84
   4.2.4 Hypothesis 4: Discourse Status    84
4.3 Methodology    85
4.4 Results for Hypotheses 1–3    90
   4.4.1 Hypothesis 1: Transfer of L1 Positional Marking of Topicality    91
   4.4.2 Hypothesis 2: Transfer of L1 Form Contrasts    92
   4.4.3 Hypothesis 3: Universal Prototypes    94
4.5 Results for Hypothesis 4    94
   4.5.1 Modeling Givenness    95
   4.5.2 Multivariate Analysis of Article Omission    98
4.6 Discussion: Pragmatic Reanalysis in Contact Settings    99
   4.6.1 Corroboration across Studies    102
   4.6.2 Implications: Contact Varieties and Discourse-Driven Restructuring    104

5 The Verbal System    106
5.1 Differences between Hindi and English    107
5.2 Predicted Types of Grammatical Change    110
5.3 Methodology    112
   5.3.1 Data    112
   5.3.2 Analytic Approach for Four Hypotheses    112
   5.3.3 Detailed Coding Criteria    113

5.4 Past Tense (Hypothesis 1)  *116*

5.5 Progressive (Hypothesis 2)  *118*

5.6 A Unified Account of Tense-to-Aspect Shift in IndE  *120*

5.7 The Past Perfect (Hypothesis 3)  *123*

5.8 Modality (Hypothesis 4)  *127*

    5.8.1 The Semantics and Pragmatics of *Will* and *Would*  *127*

    5.8.2 *Will* and *Would* in IndE  *128*

    5.8.3 Explaining *Will/Would* Variation in IndE  *130*

5.9 Discussion: An Indic Perfective-Imperfective System in English  *132*

6 Dialect Identity  *135*

6.1 Background  *136*

    6.1.1 Acceptance of Indian English  *136*

    6.1.2 Predictions: Contact and Accommodation  *136*

6.2 Quantitative Patterns in Grammar and Accent  *137*

    6.2.1 The Proficiency Cline: Grammar and Acquisition  *137*

    6.2.2 Beyond Proficiency: Accent as Identity?  *139*

6.3 Personal Responses to Dialect Contact  *143*

6.4 "Grammar" versus "Accent"  *146*

    6.4.1 How Aware Are Participants of Their Syntax and Phonology?  *146*

    6.4.2 Language Ideologies: Correct Grammar and Personal Accent  *148*

6.5 Discussion: Language Ideologies in Indigenizing Groups  *150*

**PART II: Comparing India and Singapore**

7 Rates of Change  *155*

7.1 English in India: A Recap  *156*

7.2 Social Histories of English in Singapore  *158*

7.3 Common Features of Singapore English  *164*

    7.3.1 British-Derived Retentions  *165*

    7.3.2 Substrate Structures  *165*

    7.3.3 Independent Innovations  *167*

7.4 Mechanisms of Change: Ecology and Policy  *168*

8 Grammatical Universals?  *171*

8.1 Methodological Preliminaries  *172*

    8.1.1 Data: Comparing Like with Like  *172*

    8.1.2 Hypotheses: Universals of New Englishes?  *173*

    8.1.3 Methods for Comparing Englishes: Frequencies, Constraints, and Sources  *175*

8.2 Article Use  *176*

8.3 Past Tense    *180*
    8.3.1 Substrate Grammars for IndE and SgE    *181*
    8.3.2 Past Tense Omission in IndE and SgE    *183*
8.4 Progressive    *185*
8.5 Copula Absence    *190*
8.6 Modality    *192*
8.7 Mechanisms of Change: Substrate Typology    *194*

9 The Role of Input    *197*
9.1 Variation versus Stabilization    *198*
9.2 Shifting the Focus from Product to Process    *199*
9.3 The Subset Principle    *201*
9.4 The Interface Hypothesis    *205*
    9.4.1 The Interface Hypothesis in SLA and Language Contact    *205*
    9.4.2 Applying the Model to Long-Term Outcomes in IndE and SgE    *206*
9.5 Input as a Core Factor    *207*
9.6 Input Is Not the Only Factor    *209*
9.7 Mechanisms of Change: The Dynamic Learner    *211*

10 Style Range and Attitudinal Change    *212*
10.1 Style Range in India    *213*
    10.1.1 Conservatism in IndE    *214*
    10.1.2 Ongoing Supraregionalization and Vernacularization of IndE Styles    *215*
    10.1.3 Limited Style Range    *220*
10.2 Style Range in Singapore    *222*
    10.2.1 Continuum and Diglossia Models of SgE Lectal Range    *222*
    10.2.2 Colloquial SgE    *224*
    10.2.3 Intraspeaker and Intrasituational Code-Switching    *225*
10.3 Comparing Style Ranges across New Englishes    *227*
    10.3.1 Style Ranges in English    *227*
    10.3.2 Style Range across a Speaker's Languages    *229*
10.4 Ideologies of New Englishes    *230*
    10.4.1 IndE: "Correctness" and Incipient Dialect Confidence    *231*
    10.4.2 SgE: Robust Dialect Confidence and Vestigial Insecurity    *236*
10.5 Mechanisms of Change: Style, Ideology, and Language Change    *239*

11 Summary and Implications    *241*
    11.1 Summary    *242*
    11.2 Mechanisms of Change in Bilingual Settings    *243*
    11.3 Feedback Loops between the Linguistic and the Social    *245*
    11.4 Implications for Method    *246*
    11.5 Implications for Theory    *247*
    11.6 Implications for Public Understanding    *250*

*Appendix: Use of Imperfective Forms in English and Chinese Languages*    *253*
*References*    *263*
*Index*    *289*

# FIGURES

2.1. Early development of independent classed varieties    *47*

2.2. Distribution of subvarieties in contemporary India    *48*

3.1. SLA and New Englishes    *58*

3.2. Cumulative rates of nonstandardness for learner features    *70*

3.3. Cumulative rates of nonstandardness for dialect features    *71*

3.4. Social and grammatical features of a bilingual continuum    *76*

4.1. English article system    *81*

4.2. Hindi article system    *81*

4.3. Taxonomy of Assumed Familiarity (Prince 1981)    *89*

4.4. Percentage omission of indefinite articles by proficiency group    *93*

4.5. Percentage omission of definite articles by proficiency group    *93*

4.6. Omission of articles according to relative givenness    *97*

5.1. Tense and aspect time relations in English (adapted from Reichenbach 1947)    *116*

5.2. Meanings associated with *had* + V-*ed* by percentage    *125*

6.1. Cumulative percentage rates of use of IndE grammatical features by speaker    *138*

6.2. Cumulative percentage rates of use of AmE phonetic features by speaker    *140*

8.1. Mandarin and Hindi article systems    *177*

8.2. Omission of indefinite article in IndE and SgE according to specificity    *178*

8.3. Omission of definite article in IndE and SgE according to modification    *178*

8.4. Past tense use according to clausal aspect in IndE and SgE    *184*

8.5. Past tense use according to clausal aspect in IndE and SgE    *189*

8.6. Copula absence by predicate type    *191*

9.1. Rates of nonstandardness among more proficient speakers of IndE and SgE    *199*

9.2. Subset and superset grammars in acquisition    *202*

10.1. Sociolinguistic variation in three English varieties    *228*

11.1. Dynamics of new dialect formation in postcolonial settings    *244*

# TABLES

1.1. Participants' social characteristics (US data set)   *12*

1.2. Participants' social characteristics (Delhi data set)   *13*

3.1. Types of English   *56*

3.2. Percentage rates of nonstandardness by speaker (Delhi data set)   *66*

3.3. Percentage rates of nonstandardness by speaker (California data set)   *67*

3.4. Participants' social characteristics   *73*

4.1. Article omission according to clause position and topicality of NP   *91*

4.2. Null article use with definite and indefinite NPs   *92*

4.3. Article use according to predicted universal tripartite system   *94*

4.4. Null article use according to familiarity status of NP   *96*

4.5. Multivariate regression results for omission of definite article   *100*

4.6. Multivariate regression results for omission of indefinite article   *101*

5.1. Morphological tense-aspect markers in standard English   *107*

5.2. Morphological tense-aspect markers in Hindi   *108*

5.3. Lexical aspect   *114*

5.4. Past tense marking according to sentential aspect   *117*

5.5. Multivariate regression results for overt past tense marking   *117*

5.6. Functions of progressive forms   *119*

5.7. Verbal morphology in Hindi, Indian English, and British English   *121*

5.8. Morphology used for imperfective subtypes   *122*

5.9. Use of imperfective forms in Hindi, British English, Indian English   *122*

5.10. Use of *will* 130

5.11. Use of *would* 130

5.12. IndE TMA features in relation to the Indo-Aryan and English systems 133

6.1. Proficiency factors in nonstandard use of four syntactic features 138

6.2. Proficiency factors in use of American phonetic variants 142

6.3. Attitudinal factors in use of American phonological variants 145

7.1. Factors and outcomes in Indian and Singapore English 169

8.1. Tense marking in Hindi, Mandarin, and English 181

8.2. Tense-aspect marking in Singaporean languages 182

8.3. Past tense marking according to sentential aspect in IndE ($N = 702$) 183

8.4. Past tense marking according to sentential aspect in SgE ($N = 8725$) 183

8.5. Functions of progressive forms ($N = 339$) 186

8.6. Use of main verbs *having* and *knowing* in ICE-India and ICE-Singapore 187

8.7. Copula systems in substrate languages 190

8.8. IndE and SgE features in relation to substrates 194

9.1. Subset Principle predictions for IndE TMA 203

9.2. IndE grammatical features and input demand 208

9.3. SgE grammatical features and input demand 209

10.1. Contracted forms in the press registers of three corpora 214

10.2. Average sentence length (words per sentence) in three corpora 215

10.3. Available codes in IndE and SgE 227

10.4. Preferred models of English among Indians across three decades 235

# ACKNOWLEDGMENTS

This book brings together studies of New Englishes conducted over two decades, which were informed and improved over years of learning from friends, collaborators, and colleagues. I am particularly indebted to John Rickford, Rajend Mesthrie, Rakesh Bhatt, Bao Zhiming, Lionel Wee, Claudia Lange, Penny Eckert, and Marianne Hundt for their insights and inspiration in the study of language contact and variation. Earlier collaborations with John Rickford and Ashwini Deo formed part of the work in Chapters 5 and 8. To better understand the context of Singapore, I was extremely fortunate to have Lionel Wee's invaluable and generous support for a sabbatical visit to the National University of Singapore, and additional expert input from Bao Zhiming, Yosuke Sato, Mie Hiramoto, and E-Ching Ng. I am especially grateful to Lisa Lim for extensive discussions of the contemporary and historical situation in Singapore. E-Ching Ng and Lavanya Sankaran kindly helped me to find native speakers, who offered crucial input for understanding details of grammatical usage in the languages of Singapore. These consultants were Huang Zhipeng, Amanda Cheung, Youping Han, Jiang Dan, Lim Chey Cheng, Huifong Chen, and Dorothy Tan. Sincere thanks to the Oxford University Press team, in particular Meredith Keffer, for their patience, encouragement, and guidance through all stages of producing this book. And finally, very special thanks to Erez Levon, Claudia Lange, Adam Jaworski, and Chris Tyson for intellectual inspiration and personal motivation to see this project through.

# CHAPTER 1

# Introduction

In April 2010, Google issued this release: "With Google Mobile App for iPad speak your queries in American, British, Indian or Australian English accents." Soon after, the Google Apps website listed the following English language options: UK, US, Australia, India, New Zealand, and Singapore.[1] A decade earlier, Nuance's voice recognition software Dragon Naturally Speaking was designed to work with five English dialects: UK, US, Australian, Indian and Southeast Asian. And more recently, virtual assistants such as Apple's Siri and Amazon Alexa have developed Indian English and Hinglish capabilities.

It is no accident that the tech industry has identified Indian English (IndE) and Singapore English (SgE) as the newest dialects worthy of attention and investment. These two varieties stand out as two of the most recognizable New Englishes on the block: Singapore is a global center for international trade and finance, and India is home to a growing English-speaking market several times the size of Great Britain. Seeing these new varieties listed alongside familiar native dialects suggests a coming of age, a recognition of new speech communities. This recognition was new for Australia and New Zealand a hundred years earlier. It is now new for IndE and SgE, and still controversial.

This book explores how early nonnative encounters with colonial British English evolved into established new dialects with millions of native speakers in these two regions. What forces—in the minds of speakers and in their social environments—caused particular ways of speaking to emerge? And why has English transformed so much more radically in Singapore, when it has been embedded in India for twice as long?

---

*From Deficit to Dialect.* Devyani Sharma, Oxford University Press. © Oxford University Press 2023.
DOI: 10.1093/oso/9780195307504.003.0001

## 1.1. DIALECT BIRTH IN MULTILINGUAL SETTINGS

An English as a foreign language (EFL) instructor in the United States once asked me why Indian students never signed up for English language support classes, as Chinese or Korean students did. When I replied that they probably thought their English was fine, she lamented, "Sure, they can speak, but their accents are horrible!" A remark of this kind is no longer made about speakers of Irish or Welsh English, which emerged out of similar bilingual histories. Even if an Irish English speaker's accent were challenging for an American, they would rarely be advised to seek EFL pronunciation classes. They have come to be ratified as legitimate native speakers of English, and responsibility for understanding their accent lies as much with the hearer as the speaker. By contrast, this well-intentioned instructor was struggling to reconcile Indian English speakers' native-like self-confidence and indifference to corrective input with her conception of them as nonnative or EFL learners.

The exchange reveals a mismatch between self-perception and others' perception of speakers of postcolonial Englishes, or New Englishes.[2] These new and globally mobile styles of speaking are receiving ever more popular recognition, but their newness also attracts skepticism, even hostility. Their speakers can neither be pigeonholed as foreign language learners nor simply accepted as native speakers. To some, these varieties embody an empowering process of democratization and reappropriation; to others, they signal failed mimicry, poor education, even cultural betrayal.

Some of these tensions derive from a natural lag between the fast-changing reality of young speakers' usage and outdated perceptions of their communities. In other cases, genuine differences in attitude are involved: some people are conservative about language; others are not. Finally, terms such as "Indian English" or "Singapore English" are also used to refer to very different kinds of speech and speakers, leading to confusion in both public discourse and scholarly work.

Any simple stance—"Indian English is a dialect just like British English!" or "Indian English is just a collection of errors!"—shoehorns enormous diversity into a one-size-fits-all ideology. Dialect birth in bilingual settings is a collection of diverse, uneven, sometimes even contradictory processes. This book examines these many component pieces empirically, to better capture the complex states of new dialects in postcolonial regions, and how they came about.

New dialect formation has been studied more in regions where English speakers settled, such as New Zealand, and some aspects of those processes apply equally to cases like India and Singapore. For example, the birth of a new dialect, whether among monolinguals or bilinguals, is always the result of an interplay between cognitive and social change, with new usage becoming attached to a shared identity. However, bilinguals add complexity

[2]  *From Deficit to Dialect*

to this process—they participate in multiple language groups, they layer languages over one another, and they challenge simple notions of nativeness. This can significantly complicate the task of describing dialect birth. Sankoff (2002: 640) acknowledged this challenge:

> [T]he dominant trend in language contact studies has been SLA [second language acquisition], and the dominant trend in sociolinguistics has been the study of monolingual speech communities. [Language contact] research has been difficult to assimilate into the mainstream of sociolinguistics partly because the variability found in bi- and multi-lingual speech communities is more extensive than that found in monolingual and majority language communities.

This book triangulates a range of data and methods for this task. In multilingual regions, we cannot focus solely on processes of internal change, diffusion, historical origins, and universals (e.g., Trudgill 2004; Chambers 2004). New English speakers are also subject to transfer of linguistic structures from other languages, limited exposure to the target variety, second language learning effects, and distinctive bilingual ideologies. In addition to these processes in the individual, we also need to bear in mind broad historical conditions. India and Singapore experienced uneven contact with native varieties of English during the colonial period as well as changing national ideologies about English after independence.

The study of postcolonial dialect formation thus calls for particular attention to how macrolevel (historical, societal) and microlevel (interactional, cognitive) processes conspire in language change.

## 1.2. DEFICIT OR DIALECT?

The title of this book invokes a long-standing ideological tension in both research and public discourse. The contemporaneous statements below typify two extremes:

> No one should underestimate the problem of teaching English in such countries as India and Nigeria, where the English of the teachers themselves inevitably bears the stamp of locally acquired deviations from the standard language. (Quirk 1990: 8)

> It is to be hoped that native speakers of Indian English will more thoroughly investigate . . . the grammar of Indian English. For it indubitably now is a bona fide dialect of English (not some other dialect, spoken with lots of mistakes), and it deserves to be provided with a comprehensive descriptive grammar. (Dixon 1991: 447)

This ideological divide was first articulated in an exchange between Randolph Quirk and Braj Kachru in *English Today*. Quirk (1990) set out a case for a native standard English norm for all nonnative speakers of English globally. In his view, nonnative English usage is noninstitutionalized and therefore should be exonormative, taking native varieties as a guiding pedagogical standard. Kachru (1991) characterized Quirk's position as a classic "deficit" model, assuming a failure to attain a standard native target for acquisition. Kachru questioned Quirk's conflation of ESL (English as a second anguage) and EFL varieties, in opposition to English as a native language (ENL) varieties, suggesting that in fact indigenized postcolonial Englishes possess distinctive linguistic and sociolinguistic characteristics and emergent indigenous norms and innovations. Quirk's writing is frequently taken to represent a *unicentric* approach, and Kachru's work a *pluricentric* one.

It was at this time that Kachru set out his well-known three circles model of Englishes, with native and settler varieties comprising the Inner Circle, new postcolonial varieties the Outer Circle, and countries with recent EFL usage the Expanding Circle. These categories have had a lasting impact on the framing of research on New Englishes, despite being superseded by newer models, in particular Schneider's (2003, 2007) Dynamic Model, discussed later. The circles model allowed Kachru to draw the three-way distinction he favored, but it imposed a static reification of national and historical boundaries that do not always correspond well to linguistic and social processes. The circles model is not used in the present book, but Kachru's associated concept of a bilingual cline is relevant to the usage cline of IndE presented in Chapter 3.

The legacy of Kachru's work was a wholesale shift in the field from deficit to difference or dialect in the treatment of New Englishes, hence the title of this book.

However, this shift too is not without its problems. Pennycook (2010), citing Canagarajah (1999), identified one risk of the Kachruvian ideology of World Englishes as the "smoothing" of diverse communities of users into a single entity based on the educated elite variety in that country, even though Kachru himself was careful to acknowledge internal heterogeneity. Just as "deficit" was a broad-brush mischaracterization of complex and changing situations, the ideological turn toward "dialect" characterizations risks being equally totalizing. As Snell (2013: 110) warns, "a key assumption that both deficit and difference approaches share [is] that there exist discrete varieties of English."

Sridhar and Sridhar (1992) first appealed for a rapprochement between these extremes, to bridge a "paradigm gap" between second language acquisition (SLA) and New Englishes. Later work continued this effort to move beyond totalizing ideological stances and instead deconstruct the opposition by revealing elements of both views in dynamic, incremental stages of change (Sharma 2005a; Mukherjee and Hundt 2011). Van Rooy (2011), for example,

[4]   *From Deficit to Dialect*

distinguishes innovations from errors in terms of grammatical stability and social acceptability, noting that errors occur and gain acceptance in monolingual language change too (Croft 2000).

Like stills taken from a film reel, deficit and dialect views of New Englishes are to some extent an artifact of where an analyst chooses to focus their lens. The present study shows that certain speakers are more native-like than others, and certain linguistic features too are more native-like in their patterning than others. But it also shows that if this heterogeneous mix starts to move toward language shift over time, with a community abandoning one language in favor of another—as in Irish English and, increasingly, Singapore English—then learner-like elements of language variation recede, replaced by a process of dialect focusing (LePage and Tabouret-Keller 1985) and patterns of variation characteristic of native dialects.

For this reason, despite robust critiques of the term, we cannot dismiss the question of nativeness altogether. We know very well that English occupies dramatically different roles in individual multilingual repertoires, and we cannot simply redefine errors as innovations and nonnative speakers as native without losing fundamental insights about cognitive and sociolinguistic change.

The present work therefore avoids characterizing IndE and SgE as native or nonnative, as deficit or dialect, and instead aims to look closely at patterns of variable use to identify the main social and cognitive forces that shaped, and continue to shape, English in India and Singapore. Chapter 3, for example, uses conversational recordings to show that IndE is certainly not a collection of learner errors, but that learner-like features can also be found in the cline of IndE speakers. Chapters 6 and 10 also show that, although IndE speakers identify with their own speech styles, as the EFL instructor in the opening vignette discovered, they also exhibit elements of linguistic insecurity and restricted style ranges more reminiscent of learners rather than native speakers.

Almost 20 years ago now, Bamgbose (1998: 22) asked, "[t]he main question with innovations is the need to decide when an observed feature of language use is indeed an innovation and when it is simply an error?" This distinction has since been seen as trivial, irrelevant, or disenfranchising. But if we accept that language change involves the grammatical stabilization and social uptake of new forms, this uncertainty lies at the heart of language change and new dialect formation. Only solid empirical evidence can move us closer to understanding when, how, and why dialects coalesce in multilingual communities.

## 1.3. GOALS AND QUESTIONS

As dialect variation in these communities is notoriously messy, the first step is to describe it as carefully as possible. Only with this in hand can we try to explain the shape and extent of language change in each community. The present volume addresses these sets of questions:

1. Describing New Englishes
   a. Can we distinguish between learner errors and innovations, either structurally or socially? Do both exist in the cline of IndE speakers?
   b. How similar are New Englishes in terms of grammatical structures, linguistic history, and social practices?
2. Explaining New Englishes
   a. Do universal forces give rise to similar processes and outcomes across regions?
   b. Or do local languages and histories determine the shape of English in each region?
   c. Why have some linguistic innovations stabilized more than others in each variety?

The questions in (1) address Bamgbose's puzzle, namely, the descriptive challenge of identifying *types* and *degrees* of variation subsumed under generic rubrics such as "Indian English," "Singapore English," or indeed "New Englishes." This includes variation within grammatical systems, across grammars, across speakers, and across styles.

Once we document variation, we are faced with the puzzle of explanation. McMahon (1994: 248) argues that the "real actuation question" asks "why some of these innovations die out and others catch on, spreading through the community, or why certain instances of variation become changes and others don't." This question—why some new uses caught on more than others historically, in a given community—is a major question in historical linguistics but not often addressed in accounts of New Englishes.

The second challenge in this book is therefore to account not only for variable use in the present day, but also for why only a subset of those forms has taken root in the community. Questions (2a) and (2b) evaluate competing predictions that either substrate languages (e.g., Filppula 2004; Bao 2015) or universals (e.g., Kortmann and Szmrecsanyi 2004) are the basis of New English grammars. And question (2c) responds to McMahon's real actuation question, accounting for why only some features of these new grammars stabilize over time, out of a wider pool of variation.

## 1.4. OUTLINE OF THE BOOK

Some of these questions can be answered by looking at a single case study, but others require a comparison.

[6]   *From Deficit to Dialect*

Part I of this book therefore first focuses on a single case study—Indian English. It explores three dimensions of how the language and its speakers have gradually converged toward new norms: social history (Chapter 2), language structure (Chapters 3–5), and social identity (Chapter 6).

Part II explores the same three forces from a comparative perspective, setting the cases of India and Singapore side by side (Chapters 7–10).

Together, the two parts offer the following answers to the core questions posed above:

1. Describing Englishes

    *Social history*: Despite some similarities in colonial policy and institutions, English was inserted into very different sociohistorical conditions in India and Singapore. In each nation, English grew out of multiple "rhizomatic" histories, developing very differently in diverse sub-communities of users, giving rise to the ranges of use we see today. (Chapters 2, 7)

    *Errors*: A usage cline across more and less competent users in IndE shows two different types of variation: learner-like variation for some language traits and stable use for others, with the latter shared more stably across all users. (Chapter 3)

    *Innovations*: Quantitative comparisons of more stable grammatical features show robust and distinct innovations in the two varieties, IndE and SgE. (Chapters 4, 5, 8)

    *Social identities*: Attitudes show a steady shift toward endonormative orientation in both regions, but to different degrees. The regions face prescriptive resistance to vernacularization, again to different degrees, and different types of linguistic insecurity. The style range of SgE speakers has expanded such that it now dramatically exceeds that found in British English, whereas the style range of IndE speakers, who are less nativized than the SgE community as a whole, is much narrower. (Chapters 6, 10)

2. Explaining Englishes

    *Social histories*: It is primarily the factors of demographics, type of contact, and postindependence policy that have led to very different degrees of language change, dialect focusing, and nativization in India and Singapore. (Chapter 7)

    *Language structure*: Substrate languages are a much stronger influence than universals on contact outcomes. However, the new English system is rarely an exact copy of the substrate. New Englishes often develop "third grammars" that derive from L1-driven inferences or discourse-based solutions to the challenge of mapping L1 meanings to surface forms in English. (Chapters 4, 5, 8)

*Dialect stabilization*: The greater entrenchment of some substrate-based features than others is accounted for by appealing to the additional factor of *input demand*. As IndE and SgE both involved a historical reduction of British English input, SLA models prove very relevant and remind us that language acquisition is at the heart of dialect birth in postcolonial settings. (Chapter 9)

In the concluding chapter, I draw together these diverse mechanisms of change—historical, cognitive, and social—and discuss feedback cycles between the three. New linguistic forms derive from the wider ecology of language use, while social awareness acts as a filter on the use or avoidance of this new pool of innovative forms.

The volume highlights the importance of New English scenarios for mainstream questions in sociolinguistics, SLA, and linguistics more widely, including the role of L1s, universals, input, and ideology in language change. It aims to move beyond common disciplinary divisions that separate SLA, language contact, World Englishes, and quantitative sociolinguistics, for an integrated account of incremental language change in contact settings.

## 1.5. METHODS USED

Methods for studying New Englishes have diversified dramatically since the early debates in applied linguistics. I offer a brief overview here before outlining the methods adopted in the present study.

Much early work relied on isolated or informal examples (Kachru 1983; Platt et al. 1984; Sridhar 1985; Williams 1987). Early quantitative analysis favored error analysis or contrastive analysis, which were current in applied linguistics at the time (e.g., Selinker 1974; Sahgal and Agnihotri 1985). While scholars have been broadly united in leaving behind deficit and fossilization models, which focus on a failure to acquire a standard native variety, some have continued to draw on acquisition research and methods to make an empirically grounded case for a fairly central role for individual SLA in the development of New Englishes (e.g., Mesthrie 1992; Hilbert 2008; Davydova 2011; Mukherjee and Hundt 2011; Sharma 2012; Meriläinen and Paulasto 2014). Indeed, few would deny that language transfer—a hallmark of SLA—is a major source of new forms in new Englishes.

Other early work used creative new methods, for example, Sridhar's (1991) elicitation study of the pragmatics of IndE, and methodologies from neighboring fields were increasingly brought into World Englishes research. Mesthrie (1992) pioneered the integrated use of methods from quantitative sociolinguistics, Creole studies, and language acquisition to account for the structures of South African Indian English. Ho and Platt (1993) similarly

[8]   *From Deficit to Dialect*

employed quantitative methods from Creole studies, for example, implication scaling to model individual differences across speakers and within grammars, alongside methods from the variationist sociolinguistic tradition, such as statistical examination of multiple factors influencing variation. Both of these landmark studies also chose to include a full range of proficiency and nativeness in their data sample, often with distinct lects identified through quantitative comparison of subgroups. The present study adopts many of these decisions.

Some more recent studies of new Englishes have adopted a quantitative sociolinguistic approach (e.g., for IndE, Khan 1991; Y. Kachru 2003; Sharma 2005a; Chand 2010; R. Sharma 2010; Davydova 2011). This is particularly true for research that focused on more proficient speakers and established norms, setting aside some of the complexity of clines of nativeness and variable proficiency. This approach allows group data to be aggregated, following the variationist assumption of relative homogeneity across the speech community. With New English populations it is not always clear that homogeneity can be assumed, so scholars need to resort to careful and restrictive sampling or include distinct subgroups.

Perhaps the most significant methodological shift in the field has been the use of large-scale corpus methods, and the creation of large corpora for comparative analysis of English varieties such as the International Corpus of English (ICE) corpora. Corpus studies of IndE (e.g., Hoffmann et al. 2011; Balasubramanian 2009; Sedlatschek 2009; Lange 2012) exemplify how the sophisticated use of corpus methods can generate insightful generalizations about New English usage. Corpus methods benefit from the same high-level aggregation and generalization of variationist methods and so run the same risk of losing sight of individual heterogeneity, a particular concern in bilingual communities.

As Mesthrie (1992) noted early on, the nature of bilingual continua requires insights from SLA and contact linguistics to account for subparts of variation found across the continuum. Other studies of contact varieties have been similarly eclectic in how they capture diverse processes in bilingual dialect formation (e.g., Ho and Platt 1993; Silva-Corvalán 1994; Filppula 1999; Newman 2010).

The present study also combines several methods. As both internal (linguistic) and external (social) explanations are of interest, variationist sociolinguistic methods are used where relevant. However, as the study is also interested in variation across more and less proficient or regular users of these varieties of English, methods from SLA and language contact research are used to track and explain individual differences. Finally, because the core data consist of sociolinguistic interview recordings, I do not use large public corpora except where tokens are sparse or to furnish specific comparisons with SgE in Part II.

INTRODUCTION [9]

This range of methods is adopted in individual chapters as follows:

In Part I ("English in India"), Chapter 2 reviews the linguistic history of the region in terms of multiple genealogies (Foucault 1969) rather than a single narrative. The resulting diversity in variety types is described quantitatively in Chapter 3 using implicational scaling, a tool developed in SLA and Creole studies that facilitates a global picture of individual differences. Chapters 4 and 5 adopt multivariate analysis—a methodology more typical of variationist sociolinguistics—to examine the detailed nature of grammatical variation in IndE. However, unlike standard variationist work, the analyses keep speakers from different ends of the usage cline (identified in Chapter 3) separate, avoiding too much group aggregation and bearing in mind distinct levels of proficiency. These chapters also include qualitative syntactic and semantic analysis. Chapter 6, which turns to social change in IndE, returns to a quantitative, variationist methodology and a qualitative consideration of individuals' evaluative stances.

In Part II ("Comparing India and Singapore"), the findings for IndE are compared with SgE. Chapter 7 describes the two linguistic ecologies and associated differences in language outcomes. Chapter 8 uses quantitative comparisons of grammatical structures in IndE with SgE. Chapter 9 highlights some limitations of the approach used in Chapter 8 and introduces a new perspective from SLA theory. And Chapter 10 returns to sociolinguistic methods to review differences in style range and attitudes in IndE and SgE.

## 1.6. DATA FOR INDIAN ENGLISH

To track different processes of variation and change in different parts of the grammar and in different parts of the community, the sample of IndE speech used must cover as wide a spectrum of speakers as possible.

The IndE data set therefore covers a full bilingual range of IndE speakers (cf. Kachru's 1965 "cline of bilingualism"), from heavily L1-dominant individuals with limited use of English to balanced bilinguals with equal or even more use of English than their L1s.

Two similar sets of IndE data were collected from a total of 24 individuals born and raised in India. Twelve individuals are still resident in India (Delhi), whereas the other 12 migrated to the United States (California) as adults and were recorded there. Both subgroups span the full range of IndE proficiency and use. As will be seen in Chapter 3, these two independent data sets are almost identical in terms of distribution of grammatical features across speakers and can be combined for grammatical analysis. In fact, the arrestingly similar patterning of grammatical forms between two independent data sets increases the validity and reliability of many of the claims in this volume.

[10]   *From Deficit to Dialect*

The California data also permit a subinvestigation of how IndE speakers behave in a situation of contact with a native English environment. Chapter 6 looks at self-image and degree of adoption of American English among these 12 individuals and explores degrees of indigenization of IndE in terms of speaker ideologies and insecurity.

As the present study aims to characterize the natural development and use of new dialect features, both sets of audio recordings were collected through casual sociolinguistic interviews that ranged in duration from 40 minutes to two hours. These interviews were designed to elicit naturalistic speech data through casual conversation and personal narratives but also served to establish personal biographies, migration experiences where relevant, attitudes toward language and dialects, cultural practices, and patterns of cultural contact. The full corpus of 24 sociolinguistic interviews represents 40 hours and approximately 100,000 words.

Tables 1.1 and 1.2 list participant details for the two data sets. All names are pseudonyms, and speaker codes are used in later chapters to remind the reader of basic demographic information about the speaker's gender (F/M, e.g., M1, M2 . . . Mn), English level (L/H), and location of recording (cal/del). L (lower proficiency) and H (higher proficiency) are used to indicate whether individuals are in the lower or upper half of the overall proficiency cline described later in Chapter 3.

The California data in Table 1.1 were gathered in 2001 in two Indian neighborhoods: the East Bay (Berkeley) and the South Bay (San Jose) regions of San Francisco's Bay Area. The core of the East Bay community consisted of merchant businesses run by North Indians, the dominant Asian ethnicity in the East Bay since the first Punjabi farmers migrated in the early 20th century. The South Bay Indian population, by contrast, tended to have migrated more recently from the technological and commercial centers of South India, due to the sudden increase in Silicon Valley recruitment of South Asian software engineers, accompanied by an increase in associated workforces for food services and commercial businesses.

All individuals in the California data set acquired English in India, many but not all in Hindi-speaking regions like Delhi. They emigrated as adults to the United States and for the most part maintained their multilingual repertoires in the United States, mostly working in small shops or businesses. In this data set, only Kumar, Sujit, and Nalin can be considered balanced bilinguals, and only Nalin is English dominant, using English in more contexts than Hindi.

The Delhi data in Table 1.2 were gathered in 2005 in South Delhi, as an extension of the existing California data set of 12 individuals. As in most major metropolitan centers in India, bilingualism with English is common in Delhi, particularly among the middle and upper classes. Punjabi and Hindi are the dominant L1s of Delhi residents: Hindi due to the regional location of the city and Punjabi due to postpartition migration in the mid-20th century.

INTRODUCTION [11]

**Table 1.1.** PARTICIPANTS' SOCIAL CHARACTERISTICS (US DATA SET)

| Speaker | Code | English education | Daily use of English | Age | Sex | Years in US | Occupation | First languages |
|---|---|---|---|---|---|---|---|---|
| Kapil | M1Lcal | 0 | 0 | 34 | M | 2 | shop owner | Gujarati |
| Shalu | F1Lcal | 0 | 0 | 38 | F | 18 | shop owner | Punjabi, Hindi |
| Chandan | M2Lcal | 0 | 0 | 67 | M | 17 | shop owner | Gujarati, Hindi |
| Ronnie | M3Lcal | 1 | 1 | 26 | M | 2 | waiter | Tamil |
| Rahul | M4Lcal | 1 | 1 | 48 | M | 17 | shop owner | Gujarati, Hindi |
| Kavita | F2Lcal | 1 | 2 | 54 | F | 25 | housewife | Gujarati, Hindi |
| Kishore | M5Hcal | 2 | 2 | 62 | M | 39 | shop owner | Punjabi, Hindi |
| Gopal | M6Hcal | 2 | 1 | 35 | M | 0.5 | software engineer | Kannada |
| Ram | M7Hcal | 2 | 2 | 29 | M | 0.5 | shop staff | Hindi |
| Kumar | M8Hcal | 2 | 3 | 67 | M | 40 | shop owner | Hindi |
| Sujit | M9Hcal | 2 | 3 | 23 | M | 0.7 | shop staff | Hindi |
| Nalin | M10Hcal | 2 | 3 | 24 | M | 2 | software engineer | Hindi |

*Note:*

English education:
0 (*no English medium education*)
1 (*some, e.g., higher education in English*)
2 (*mostly English medium education*)

Daily use of English:
0 (*minimal*),
1 (*at work*),
2 (*work and some friendships/younger relatives*),
3 (*work, friendships, home*)

Participants were selected based on their length of residence in Delhi and their relative use of English, in order to sample a bilingual range comparable to the California data set collected earlier. Their class status ranges from lower to middle class, broadly indicated in the Occupation column. All participants were active bilinguals. In this data set, only Aman and Prashant can be considered balanced bilinguals, but use slightly more Hindi in their daily repertoire than English.

Notice that the more regular English users at the bottom of both tables are Hindi speakers. The Hindi speakers in both groups are from the heavily Hindi-English bilingual urban area of Delhi, which, like other urban areas, has a higher proportion of regular users of IndE, reflecting the importance of Hindi in particular as a primary substrate language for IndE.

This 100,000-word corpus is a typical size for a data set of personally gathered sociolinguistic interviews but is small with respect to present-day corpora. Smaller, self-created sociolinguistic corpora have two main advantages over publicly available larger corpora. First, the researcher is able to gather detailed information about social background, biography, and English proficiency and use for each participant, which supports the interpretation of variable patterns. Second, the researcher can design the interviews in parallel, to gather the same range of speaking styles as well as specific content such as attitudes to varieties and experiences of migration. The data sets are thus

[12] *From Deficit to Dialect*

***Table 1.2.*** PARTICIPANTS' SOCIAL CHARACTERISTICS (DELHI DATA SET)

| Speaker | Code | English education | Daily use of English | Age | Sex | Years in Delhi | Occupation | First languages |
|---|---|---|---|---|---|---|---|---|
| Alok | M11Ldel | 1 | 1 | 66 | M | 45 | shop owner | Hindi |
| Bhanu | M12Ldel | 0 | 1 | 32 | M | 17 | shop salesman | Garhwali, Hindi |
| Mona | F3Ldel | 0 | 1 | 30 | F | 30 | street stall seller | Tamil, Hindi |
| Bharat | M13Ldel | 0 | 1 | 59 | M | 54 | shop owner | Punjabi, Hindi |
| Rani | F4Ldel | 1 | 1 | 84 | F | 32 | retired | Dogri, Punjabi, Hindi |
| Gagan | M14Ldel | 1 | 1 | 33 | M | 33 | street stall owner | Hindi |
| Mohit | M15Hdel | 1 | 1 | 23 | M | 8 | shop salesman | Maithili, Hindi |
| Deepa | F5Hdel | 2 | 2 | 23 | F | 23 | shop saleswoman | Hindi, Gujarati |
| Balram | M16Hdel | 2 | 2 | 59 | M | 42 | govt. area manager | Hindi, Punjabi |
| Reema | F6Hdel | 2 | 2 | 72 | F | 50 | retired | Punjabi, Hindi |
| Aman | M17Hdel | 2 | 3 | 35 | M | 35 | hospital manager | Hindi |
| Prashant | M18Hdel | 2 | 3 | 29 | M | 29 | architect | Hindi |

*Note:*
English education:
0 (*no English medium education*)
1 (*some, e.g., higher education in English*)
2 (*mostly English medium education*)

Daily use of English:
0 (*minimal*),
1 (*at work*),
2 (*work and some friendships/younger relatives*),
3 (*work, friendships, home*)

small but well designed for sociolinguistic analysis and large enough for the broad analyses of variable grammar conducted here.

The disadvantage of a smaller data set is, of course, sparsity of less frequent linguistic features. For this reason, in a few places, larger corpus data are used to bolster numbers for low-frequency features. In the examination of past perfect constructions in Chapter 5, for example, the Kolhapur Corpus of Indian English was used. As a corpus of written English, it included more uses of the past perfect, for example, in news writing. The corpus also facilitated comparisons, not presented in this book, to parallel corpora of American and British English (the Brown Corpus and the Lancaster-Oslo-Bergen Corpus, respectively).

Corpora are also used in places for comparison between Indian and Singapore, as described in the next section. The use of corpus data is limited to these necessary uses. Both the Kolhapur Corpus and ICE-India are slightly skewed toward standard IndE and so do not lend themselves well to many of the questions investigated here. Furthermore, as noted, corpus data lack the extensive ethnographic information available for participants in my primary data set, which is crucial for the analysis of external (social) factors. The emphasis throughout is therefore on the primary IndE sociolinguistic data set.

## 1.7. DATA FOR SINGAPORE ENGLISH

To compare IndE with SgE data in Part II, I use secondary sources and corpus data. The main secondary sources used here for SgE are Ho and Platt (1993), Platt (1979), Wee and Ansaldo (2004), and Leimgruber (2008a, 2013). These studies are particularly well matched to the present one, as their SgE samples and quantitative results can be directly compared with the analyses in Part I of the primary IndE data (e.g., the use of articles, copula omission, and tense marking). The studies include detailed social information about individuals as well, more so than is typically found in corpus data. For example, Ho and Platt (1993) use a database of conversational interviews with 100 ethnically Chinese speakers of SgE, stratified into five educational levels. In the comparison, these levels can be matched fairly well to the parallel points on the bilingual cline of IndE users. Similarly, Leimgruber (2008a) provides details of situational variation across 36 individuals that can be compared to style variation in IndE speakers.

Corpus data are used in a limited way in Part II, to support broad comparisons of the ICE-Singapore and ICE-India corpora. Each ICE corpus consists of one million words of English produced after 1989, with 300 transcripts of spoken recordings and 200 written texts designed for direct comparison across dialects. In the case of ICE-Singapore, some previous subcorpora were integrated into the main corpus, for example, the Grammar of Spoken Singapore English Corpus (GSSEC), which represents a mesolectal or moderate level of vernacularization.

In keeping with the present research goal of accounting for changes in spoken usage, the use of both ICE corpora is restricted to informal spoken recordings. The ICE corpora do not provide speaker information, which slightly limits their use for comparative analysis in Part II, but Chapter 8 offers a brief description of how a comparable subset of ICE-Singapore individuals was identified for comparison with the IndE sociolinguistic interviews.

A final point worth noting is heterogeneity across these SgE data sets. ICE-Singapore data date from the 1990s, but Ho and Platt's speakers date from two decades earlier. Because Mandarin became compulsory for ethnically Chinese students only after 1980, Ho and Platt's participants are less likely to be native speakers of Singapore English or of Mandarin (Ansaldo 2004; Lim 2007). Importantly, this may also mean that Ho and Platt's data are in some ways more analogous to the current situation with IndE, with fewer native speakers and more diverse L1 influences.

These complex historical changes in the substrate languages in Singapore mean that it is also important to verify the actual linguistic systems of Singapore Mandarin (rather than assuming that it is identical to mainland Chinese Mandarin) and other languages in Singapore. I therefore conducted independent consultations with eight Singaporeans to establish details of

[14]   *From Deficit to Dialect*

their substrate grammars: Hokkien, Malay, Cantonese, and Singaporean Mandarin. These are described in more detail in the relevant chapters.

The diverse methods and data of this book all support a single question: How and why do emerging Englishes develop as they do? The combination of methods and data allows linguistic factors (properties of the substrates, language universals, input demand) and social factors (sociohistory, policy, ideology, repertoire) to be evaluated. It also helps us keep individual differences visible where necessary, while also allowing group convergence toward stable new norms to emerge in the data.

In the next chapter, we begin our investigation of IndE in Part I, starting with an exploration of the historical conditions under which it emerged.

PART I

*English in India*

CHAPTER 2

# Histories of English in India

Dialects are often described informally as evolving in some direction over time, diverging from a parent variety or converging on a new norm, implying a linear transformation from an earlier to a later stage. However, framing large-scale change as a single historical trajectory can favor a selective or dominant narrative, when in fact multiple historical processes may be present in distinct discourses and subject positionings (Foucault 1969).

Rather than assuming a classical tree model of the development of cultures and history, it is worth exploring interactions and connections across many parallel tracks—rhizomes (Deleuze and Guattari 1980)—sustaining hybridity and multiplicity within apparently unitary structures. Historical linguistics cannot dispense with genetic models, but these alternative perspectives should guard against an overly linear record of a language as heterogeneous and historically and regionally contingent as Indian English (IndE).

In this chapter, I describe how a number of subcommunities of users of English evolved over time in India. After a summary of historical phases and linguistic outcomes, I assess recent claims about the variety's stage of evolution. Rather than a single entity moving unidirectionally toward or away from a single norm, IndE is better conceived of as a series of overlapping domains of use, arising out of specific moments and shifts in power and social relations. The term "Indian English" is shown to be a weakly defined supraregional abstraction that classes together quite distinct subcommunities of users, at different stages of nativization.

*From Deficit to Dialect.* Devyani Sharma, Oxford University Press. © Oxford University Press 2023.
DOI: 10.1093/oso/9780195307504.003.0002

## 2.1. SOCIAL HISTORIES OF ENGLISH IN INDIA

British India can be divided into four broad chronological phases for the purposes of examining cultural and linguistic change:

I. Early colonial contact and the British East India Company (1600–1857)
II. Direct British rule and the British Raj (1858–1947)
III. The independence movement (1905–1947)
IV. Independent India (1947–present)

These dates correspond to major historical events rather than specific linguistic developments. For instance, the Indian Mutiny of 1857 (followed in 1858 by the imposition of direct rule by the British crown) is a key historical marker for the start of Phase II, but a more important boundary for India's linguistic history is 1835, when an ordinance by the Governor-General of India redirected funding to English medium education in India, with a profound and lasting impact on language, culture, and education in the region. Similarly, the Partition of Bengal in 1905 marks the start of Phase III, with the *swadeshi* (economic self-sufficiency) and *swaraj* (home rule) movements, but the seeds of independence, and of divergence from British English (BrE), were sown before this time.

For each broad phase discussed next, I trace how cultural contact led to particular linguistic developments in that period.

### 2.1.1. Phase I: Early Colonial Contact

English was established in India with Queen Elizabeth I's Royal Charter of 1600, granting the East India Trading Company exclusive rights to pursue trade in the Indian subcontinent for two decades. This led to two centuries of economic and military expansion by the Company, culminating in the assumption of direct British rule in 1858.

In the early years of British India, the main domains of English use were trade, military, and missionary work. In all of these, the initial practice was for men to take up temporary posts in India without their families. They were frequently encouraged to learn local languages in order to communicate with local groups. At first, then, contact between speakers of English and of local languages was functional, each group incompletely acquiring fragments of the other's language for trade, revenue collection, and other officialdom. Only later did missionary schools, established from the early 18th century onward (Sailaja 2009), become the first institutionalized source of diffusion of English into the indigenous population.

It is worth noting that, even at this early stage, particularly prior to the arrival of British women in greater numbers, some British military men started

[20]   *English in India*

relationships with Indian women and established the earliest small communities of Anglo-Indian ancestry and of early nativized English use. One of the world's oldest schools still in operation, the English medium St. George's Anglo-Indian School and Orphanage in Chennai, Tamil Nadu, was founded 300 years ago, in 1715, for children of the Anglo-Indian community. This community is important in the history of IndE and discussed further in Phase II.

Aside from these very small groups, bilingualism among Indians was limited in the 17th and 18th centuries. The systematic "Indianization" of English (Kachru 1983) began later. Superficial English use among Indians did give rise to Butler English (Hosali 2005), also called Bearer English or Kitchen English, a pidginized variety used between Indian domestic staff and their British employers. This variety is likely to have arisen by the 18th century (Schuchardt, cited in Hosali 2005, describes it as declining in 1891). The example in (1) is from a 67-year-old who worked under the British.

(1)   Working the bearer . . . just I going six month ago – dining-hall . . . attend after the drink – any sahibs coming. Morning-morning's 8 to 4. One time one week like that. One one week night. (Hosali 2005: 36)

The extract uses the British Indian terms *sahib* and *bearer* and some typical IndE features (reduplication with distributive meaning: *one one*; progressive with habitual meaning: *sahibs coming*) but also many strikingly non-IndE features (null copula: *I going*; noun reduplication: *morning-morning*; lack of plural marking: *six month*). A number of these features are shared with other English pidgins.

### 2.1.2. Phase II: The British Raj

During the 18th century the expansion of the East India Company created a base of power for British dominion, including increased monopolistic control of trade and revenue (e.g., the Treaty of Allahabad, 1765, which designated the Company as chief revenue collector of the weakened Mughal emperor's Eastern provinces) and greater military command of Indian provinces (e.g., the Battle of Plassey, 1757, in which the Company gained control over Bengal through military conquest). The resulting tensions culminated in the Indian Mutiny of 1857 and the immediate assumption of direct rule by the British crown in 1858, with continued central administration by the East India Company.

Colonial policies were profoundly affected by this elaboration of British rule, which now extended much deeper into intellectual and cultural dominion. Colonial language ideologies grew more complex, crystallizing into an opposition between what were termed Orientalist and Anglicist stances.

The term Orientalist applied to the styles of engagement favored by British governors and scholars during the 18th and early 19th century. These tended to condone the retention of indigenous knowledge structures and languages rather than Western learning and English. Pennycook (1994) suggests that despite their apparent support for local cultures, Orientalists were as concerned with the superiority of Western culture and with colonial control as Anglicists. While it is certainly the case that many Orientalists condoned both the introduction of Western learning and the retention of indigenous structures, any attempt to define a single moral stance among Orientalists is misguided: motivations ranged widely from pure colonial strategy to intellectual interest. Warren Hastings, the first British Governor-General of India (1773–1785), promoted a tactical acceptance of existing commercial, judicial, military, and cultural systems in order to better cooperate with intermediaries. He was known to express respect for Indian culture and ancient scripture; he spoke Bengali fluently and founded the Calcutta Madrassa on the old Persian Islamic model. Hastings brought other Orientalist scholars to India, most notably William Jones, founder of the Royal Asiatic Society of Bengal, who famously, in 1786, hypothesized a shared origin for Indo-Aryan languages, Greek, and Latin. This Aryan link formed the foundation of a particular strain of Orientalist affection for Indic study that tended to resist the infiltration of the English language and Western education into India.[1]

By contrast, the second Governor-General, Charles Cornwallis (1786–1793), continued the Orientalist practice of leaving internal social structures broadly in place, but for a very different ideological reason. A mere five years before his arrival in India, Cornwallis had been personally humiliated in the British surrender at Yorktown in the American War of Independence. So, his very different strain of Orientalism was based in a fear that Western education and the English language would foment a similarly dangerous rationality and autonomy among other Indian overseas subjects.

In the early 19th century, a new, countervailing Anglicist ideology promoting Western cultural and linguistic intervention emerged. Two domestic developments in British political and religious philosophy drove this change: the evangelical movement and utilitarianism. As the evangelical movement gained momentum in Britain, it fought to strengthen missionary work in British India and forge a new moral obligation: the "enlightenment" of native populations. The English language played a pivotal role in these ideals. Charles Grant, evangelist chairman of the East India Company (1746–1823), saw the imposition of English as a means to "silently undermine, and at length subvert, the fabric of error" in Hindu culture (Zastoupil and Moir 1999: 6). Nineteenth-century advocates of utilitarianism arrived at a similar colonial policy, seeing rational socioeconomic progress rather than Christian faith as the modernizing and civilizing force to be imposed.

Both of these movements, for divergent reasons, favored cultural intervention. The provision of modest funds by the Charter Act of 1813 for "the revival and improvement of literature, and the encouragement of the learned natives of India, and for the introduction and promotion of a knowledge of the sciences" (Zastoupil and Moir 1999: 91) ignited a protracted Orientalist–Anglicist debate to define this mission. The Orientalists argued for the indigenous revival of traditional learning, and the Anglicists for exogenous renewal with Western learning. The Anglicist view that ultimately prevailed was implemented in an ordinance passed by the Governor-General Lord Bentinck in 1835, redirecting funds to English education and decreeing that English be the medium of all higher education in India. The ordinance was based on a recommendation by an ardent evangelist, Thomas Babington Macaulay (member of the Supreme Council of India, 1835–1839). Macaulay's opinion, entitled *Minute on Indian Education*, illustrates the dramatic reversal in attitudes to Indian intellectual and linguistic history among 19th-century British colonists:

> What then shall that language be? One-half of the Committee maintain that it should be the English. The other half strongly recommend the Arabic and Sanscrit. The whole question seems to me to be, which language is the best worth knowing?
>
> I have no knowledge of either Sanscrit or Arabic,—I have never found one among them [Orientalists] who could deny that a single shelf of a good European library was worth the whole native literature of India and Arabia. . . . It is, I believe, no exaggeration to say, that all the historical information which has been collected from all the books written in the Sanscrit language is less valuable than what may be found in the most paltry abridgments used at preparatory schools in England . . .
>
> We have to educate a people who cannot at present be educated by means of their mother-tongue. We must teach them some foreign language. The claims of our own language it is hardly necessary to recapitulate. It stands preeminent even among the languages of the West . . .
>
> We must at present do our best to form a class who may be interpreters between us and the millions whom we govern; a class of persons, Indian in blood and colour, but English in taste, in opinions, in morals, and in intellect.
>
> (Macaulay, 1835, in Zastoupil and Moir 1999: 166)

Although he is widely cited, Macaulay was not the originator of these views. The striking failure of several expert and brilliantly persuasive Orientalist rebuttals suggests that the tide of British missionary zeal was already with Macaulay, and his personal standing in British social circles simply sealed the transition (Cutts 1953; Phillipson 1992). Furthermore, the Indian response was not one of monolithic resistance. A number of Hindu intellectuals, most notably Raja Rammohun Roy, adopted the view that Western learning and the English language could be beneficial in such areas as political and religious reform (Pennycook 1994; Zastoupil and Moir 1999).

Governor-General Bentinck's order in support of Macaulay's position, issued in March 1835, initiated a shift in the allocation of funds exclusively to English education in medium and content:

> First, His Lordship in Council is of opinion that the great object of the British Government ought to be the promotion of European literature and science among the natives of India; and that all the funds appropriated for the purpose of education would be best employed on English education alone.
>
> Second, But it is not the intention of His Lordship in Council to abolish any College or School of native learning, while the native population shall appear to be inclined to avail themselves of the advantages which it affords. . . . But his Lordship in Council decidedly objects to the practice which has hitherto prevailed of supporting the students during the period of their education. He conceives that the only effect of such a system can be to give artificial encouragement to branches of learning which, in the natural course of things, would be superseded by more useful studies and he directs that no stipend shall be given to any student that may hereafter enter at any of these institutions . . .
>
> Fourth, His Lordship in Council directs that all the funds which these reforms will leave at the disposal of the Committee be henceforth employed in imparting to the native population a knowledge of English literature and science through the medium of the English language; and His Lordship in Council requests the Committee to submit to Government, with all expedition, a plan for the accomplishment of this purpose. (Zastoupil and Moir 1999: 194)

This ordinance led to an increase in English-medium teaching throughout the education system, which continues to the present day. The establishment of several new universities in 1857 led to a rapid rise in secondary school education, often designed specifically as preparation for English-medium universities. In conjunction with subsequent educational recommendations favoring English primary school education (the Hunter Commission in 1883), this led to a trickle-down effect in primary school language choice that even now remains contentious. British government policy also explicitly favored English-educated applicants for government service in India, creating an early (and lasting) instrumental motivation to acquire English for occupational advancement.

As a consequence, the 19th century witnessed a significant expansion of English in India, through an expansion of convent schools, the imposition of English in education, and further employment of Indians under the British.

It was at this time that the distinctive variety of Anglo-Indian English, mentioned earlier, became firmly established. The Anglo-Indian community, which still exists in India today albeit in declining numbers, had mixed Indian and European ancestry and were mostly Christian. The British explicitly targeted the progeny of European soldiers in India with favorable access to employment and education in the hope of gaining a loyal indigenous group. However, this special status, and the increasing taboo of intermarriage as more British women settled with their husbands in India, meant Anglo-Indians were often not fully accepted by either Indian or British society. Although they are among the very few Indians who count English as their native language, their language and community faced stigmatization from both the British and Indian communities. A derogatory term at the time for this variety was Chee-Chee English (Coelho 1997: 568), possibly from the Hindi term of disapproval or disgust *chhi*.

In more recent times, the variety has lost these negative associations. Indeed, it may have had a unique settler or founder (Mufwene 1996) effect. Anglo-Indians typically received a convent education and were often recruited into service professions such as teaching, nursing, and administration (Maher 2007). In the postindependence period Anglo-Indians continued to succeed in these areas, in part due to their education and English ability.

The prominent role of Anglo-Indian and wider Christian communities, all associated with greater native use of English, in teaching has made them an important source of established features of wider IndE. This influence is rarely noted in descriptions of IndE but is clearly observable. Anglo-Indian English retains certain elements of 19th-century British dialects, due to early native acquisition and greater British input. For instance, the variety retains h-dropping and r-lessness from BrE. It also reserves [oː] for words in the FORCE lexical set, including *four*, *bored*, *course*, *force*, *pork*, and [ɔː] for words in the NORTH lexical set, including *north*, *stork*, and *fork*. Modern BrE speakers no longer distinguish between these lexical sets but did so until recent decades. (See Coelho 1997 for a detailed analysis.) The [oː/ɔː] lexical distinction can today be found among many IndE speakers. Similarly, the second-person plural pronouns *you-all* and *y'all*, once characteristically Christian and Anglo-Indian, is now found across many IndE users.

As schools are a major route of acquisition of English for most Indians, the status of teachers from Anglo-Indian and Christian communities—as well as, anecdotally, the covert prestige of native English-speaking Anglo-Indian peers within convent schools—may have led to widespread uptake of elements of their speech styles, including indigenous innovations by adolescents.

In addition to this founder effect on wider IndE, Christian communities continue to have some of the most distinctive and native use of IndE. Kurzon

(2004: 67) suggests, for instance, that the gap created by a decline in use of Konkani within the family has been filled by English in Christian communities along the Goa/Karanataka coast.

This more advanced nativization predicts greater differentiation of styles (Schneider 2007). Though not yet fully documented, the Bandra district of Mumbai offers one such example. During Phase II, in the 19th century, this area was home to a traditionally Catholic community. In the present day, their long-standing native use of English and Westernized culture has given rise to an enregistered (i.e., socially recognized and named; Agha 2003) Bandra speech style and identity. Bandra Boy memes circulate on the Internet, and a website dedicated to "You know you're a Bandra boy when . . . " lists several typically Anglo-Indian and Christian linguistic features, including "You say 'Aks' instead of 'Ask'" and "Every other sentence you speak ends in "men" (NOT "man")."[2]

A commenter on the list parodies Anglo-Indian speech (discourse markers, distinctive pronunciation, grammar, swearing) and cultural signifiers (Catholicism, Western dress, names, locations) in further detail:

> What you have in your bloddy cupboard men. I am guessing you have that tight red sequins frock. When Philomina Aunty sees that no she will be making you go to mass and say 200 Hail Marys. Also bugger why you dont have any girlfriends. You bloddy are always going out with that Francis fellow from Danda men. What you are pataoing him or what.

Locally distinctive traits can similarly be noted in the English of other Christian communities across India, e.g., in Goa, the Konkan Coast (Mangalore, Karanataka), Kerala, and across the Northeast.

Christian communities are thus an example of Phase 5 differentiation in India, in Schneider's terms, and therefore also an important source of diffusion of stable new dialect forms in India, via their role in teaching and their status as native speakers. We return to this in Section 2.4.

A second Indian variety of English that may have developed as early as the 18th century but that is characteristic of the 19th century was derogatorily termed Babu English. This is sometimes wrongly conflated with Butler English and Bearer English, described earlier, but was a term specifically used to describe the ornate bureaucratic style of English used by lower- or middle-class Indians, such as junior clerks (Widdowson 1979; Hosali 2005). Its old-fashioned flavor persists in IndE today, and the term is still occasionally used to describe any IndE of intermediate proficiency. The following 19th-century British parody plays up the excessive use of idiomatic language and classical vocabulary, along with performed educatedness and prescriptive language ideology on the part of the Babu character:[3]

[26] *English in India*

(2a)  Since my sojourn here, I have accomplished the laborious perusal of your transcendent and tip-top periodical, and, hoity toity! I am like a duck in thunder with admiring wonderment at the drollishness and jocosity with which your paper is ready to burst in its pictorial department. But, alack! when I turn my critical attention to the literary contents, I am met with a lamentable deficiency and no great shakes, for I note there the fly in the ointment and *hiatus valde deflendus*—to wit the utter absenteeism of a correct and classical style in English composition.

(from F. Anstey, *Baboo Jabberjee, BA*. London: Dent,1897, cited in Mehrotra 1998: 41)

As Sailaja (2009: 113) notes, Anstey's parody of Babu English fails to incorporate a number of elements of grammatical divergence, alongside idiomatic and formal style, that for many characterized Babu English. The authentic example in (2b) more accurately captures the style.

(2b)  PERPETUAL MOUSE TRAP: Always it requires no failing, and catches continually so long any remains. (c. 1890, Sailaja 2009: 150)

Butler English and Babu English are linguistically and socioeconomically distinct varieties. The example of Butler English given earlier in (1) showed resemblances to pidginization processes; Babu English, by contrast, shows substantial familiarity with standard English morphology, lexicon, and syntax and clearly resembles later stages of second language acquisition (SLA) rather than pidginization.

In the colonial British textual record, including popular literature (Anstey 1897; Steel 1900), letters, and interviews (e.g., Allen 1975), a nostalgic fondness is frequently articulated for the speakers of Butler English—ayahs, bearers, butlers—and a more cruel condescension toward speakers of Babu English, as in (2a) above. The fondness sometimes derives from personal domestic childhood relationships with speakers of Butler English, for example, in Charles Allen's interviews in the 1970s, but it may also mark British colonial comfort with a nonthreatening, low-status variety, as compared with the social aspiration and upwardly mobile claims on the language marked by Babu English. The pejorative response to the latter possibly grafts aristocratic Victorian distaste for Britain's own middle classes onto parallels in the Indian context (Cannadine 2001).

A final variety worth mentioning from this period represents a *settler* variety, not an indigenous variety, to use Schneider's (2007) distinction. This BrE variety was used by British residents in 19th-century India. It mixed fragments of Hindi into BrE in a style that became recognized and also much parodied among the domestic British public.[4] Lewis (1991: 13) describes this variety as a "frontier language," constructed on the fly in superficial interactions and never even approaching expert ability in the foreign code. Its users were the *qui-his*, "the popular distinctive nickname of the Bengal Anglo-Indian, from the usual manner of calling servants in that Presidency, viz. 'Koi hai?' 'Is anyone there?'" (Yule and Burnell 1886: 750; "Anglo-Indian" is used here with its other meaning of British residents in India).

A turn-of-the-century novel parodies this colonist style, mixing working-class British dialect markers with inexpert, fragmented use of Hindi (Steel 1900, cited in Lewis 1991). Although a fictional monologue, the early date suggests that the extract in (3a) draws on personal familiarity with this style.

(3a)   *Decko*, you want this *admi abhi*, but you ain't goin' to get 'im. *Tumhara nahin*. He's mine, *mehra admi, sumja*? If you want to *lurro*, come on. You shall have a bellyful, and there'll be plenty of you to *phansi*. But wot I say is don't be a *pargul soors*. I don't do your temples 'arm. It's *durm shester ram-ram* an' *hurry ganga*, so far's I care. But this man's my guv'nor. You don't touch 'im *kubbi nahin*. I'm a *nek admi, burra ussel*, when I'm took the right way, contrariwise I'm *zulm* an' *ficker* an *burra burra affut*? (Steel 1900 in Lewis 1991: 12, italics added)

   [Word translations of Hindi forms being attempted: *dekho* 'look,' *aadmi* 'man,' *abhi* 'now,' *tumhara* 'yours,' *nahin* 'not,' *mera aadmi* 'my man,' *samjha* 'understood,' *laro* 'fight,' *phansi* 'noose,' *pagal* 'crazy,' *soor* 'pig, *dharma* 'faith,' *shastra* 'sacred text,' Ram-Ram, *hari* 'praise,' *Ganga* 'Ganges,' *kabhi nahin* 'never,' *nek aadmi* 'virtuous man,' *bara asal* 'very sincere,' *zulm* 'tyrant,' *fikar* 'trouble,' *bara bara aafat* 'big big misfortune']

The example in (3b) is from Charles Allen's interviews with survivors of the British Raj for a popular BBC radio series and book in the 1970s. He describes the extract as a "well-known admonition," so again an artificial but informed parody of the style.

(3b)   You *dekko*ed me *giro* in the *peenika pani* and you *cooch-biwani*ed. You *soono*ed me *bolo. Iswasti* I'll *gurrum* your *peechi*. (Allen 1975: 273, italics added)

   [Word translations of Hindi forms being attempted: *dekho* 'look at,' *giro* 'fall,' *peene ka pani* 'drinking water,' *cooch bhi nahin* 'nothing at all,' *suno* 'hear,' *bolo* 'speak,' *iswaste* 'hence,' *garam* 'warm,' *peechhe* 'back(side).']

[28]  *English in India*

Finally, the period extract in (3c) expresses a typical 19th-century Anglicist view. It indicates clearly that a smattering of Hindi was used by many colonists as a pejorative and intentionally inexpert "other" code for issuing orders and scoldings.

(3c)    He said he'd see the natives hung
        Before he'd learn their lingo;—
    If he'd his way, the British tongue
        He'd teach them all, by Jingo!
    His Hindostanee words were few—
        They couldn't well be fewer—
    As "Jeldy jao!" and "Deckho, do!"
        And "Kupperdar, you soor!"

[Word translations of Hindi forms being attempted: *jaldi jao* 'go quickly,' *dekho* 'look,' *do* 'give,' *khaberdar* 'don't you dare,' *soor* 'pig.']

(Walter Yeldham, "The Wonderful Shikaree" in *Lays of Ind*,
Bombay: Thacker, Vining and Co. 1907, cited in Sadaf 2007: 75)

In an 1837 letter, this activity of berating workers is even referred to as "Hindustani-ing the syces [horse grooms]" (Sadaf 2007).

IndE bears an extraordinary imprint of this moment in history. The imperative suffix *-o* is now the standard verbal template for Hindi loans into IndE (see example [9] later). This is likely due to the overwhelming use of Hindi imperative verb forms to issue orders in colonial 19th-century usage—*decko, sunoo, bolo, jao, lurro* above. The form even found its way, via working-class British military men in colonial India, into Cockney (*decko* 'have a look').

### 2.1.3. Phase III: The Independence Movement

The comprehensive implementation of English in India via Macaulay's Minute was a transformative moment in India's linguistic history. The 19th century witnessed a steady increase in English use in education, press, printing, and bureaucracy. However, particularly after World War I, the National Swadeshi ('self-reliance') Movement emerged as an opposing force, bringing with it ideologies of vernacular resistance and Gandhi's argument that "real education is impossible through a foreign medium" (Mehrotra 1998: 5).

Gandhi used English to make the case for independence to British and Indian audiences but always promoted vernacular medium education as central to his policies of noncooperation and self-rule:

The only education we receive is English education . . . I hold it to be as necessary for the urban child as for the rural to have the foundation of his development laid on the solid work of the mother tongue. It is only in unfortunate India that such an obvious proposition needs to be proved. (Gandhi cited in Ramanathan 2006: 236).

Nevertheless, embodying the impact of a hundred years of English education since Macaulay's Minute, Nehru's landmark words at the moment of Indian independence in August 1947 were spoken in English, even using the metaphor of speech for freedom: "A moment comes, which comes but rarely in history, when we step out from the old to the new, when an age ends, and when the soul of a nation, long suppressed, finds utterance."

Gandhi's and Nehru's personal biographies also exemplify the conflicted place of English in early 20th-century India. Gandhi, born in a small Gujarati town in 1869, initially struggled with English at school and in early public speaking. Studying law in London, he recognized the political benefits of a command over English rhetoric and style and began to take elocution lessons and read widely; in fact, his voracious consumption of radical literature and philosophy, partly as a means to acquiring fluency in the language, forged a close link between his political convictions and the English language (Khilnani 2003: 136–137). Gandhi's first book, *Hind Swaraj* (1909), was written in Gujarati en route to South Africa but translated by Gandhi into English (*Indian Home Rule*) and published in 1910. An immediate British ban on grounds of sedition remained in place until 1938, but this and subsequent writings by Gandhi—some in English, some in Gujarati, and some translated—nevertheless formed the key texts for the independence movement in the intervening period.

Nehru, born 20 years after Gandhi into a powerful family in the colonial administrative center of Allahabad, received English tuition very early and spent years at Harrow and Cambridge. Unlike Gandhi's works, Nehru's three major books and collections of letters were all written in English (in prison). Writings by these two leaders, more than any other in the independence movement, represent the transformed role of English in India by the 20th century: "English made the empire, but they [Gandhi and Nehru] showed how it could be used to unmake it—how the language could be a tool of insubordination and, ultimately, freedom" (Khilnani 2003: 136).

The political equivocation over whether a new nation should eschew or exploit the colonial language was apparent in the final decades of the independence movement. During the 1920s and 1930s a critical stance was widely adopted, and Gandhi amended the Indian National Congress party constitution in 1925 to reduce the role of English. Nehru too suggested that continued reliance on the language would cause Indians to "remain slaves to British thought" (Mehrotra 2003: 154). However, once independence (which

[30]  *English in India*

came in 1947) was imminent, more pragmatic views resurfaced, with Gandhi acknowledging "the rule of the English will go because it was corrupt, but the prevalence of English will never go" (Khilnani 2003: 154).

Despite this persistence of English, by the mid-20th century many Indians no longer aspired to a British acrolectal standard. Endonormative stabilization (Phase 4; Schneider 2007, see Section 2.4) was already underway before independence. Detailed historical analyses dating the origins of IndE features do not yet exist and are complicated by second language variability; however, Mehrotra (1998) shows that many contemporary IndE features appear in 19th-century letters and other texts. By the late 19th and early 20th century these forms are evident and increasingly unmarked, even in written registers. In an article from July 1950, for example, a leading English-language newspaper, *The Hindu*, still used quotation marks to signal a loan in the headline *A general "hartal" was observed in the town to-day*, but later states *A hartal was being observed in the town markets to-day*, dispensing with quotation marks around the word hartal ('strike'), a word used freely in IndE today.

### 2.1.4. Phase IV: Contemporary India

English is now embedded within a complex multilingual hierarchy of local, state, regional, and national languages in India. Estimates of the number of languages in India range from 462 (*Ethnologue*, Simons and Fennig 2018) to 860 (Ganesh Devy's *People's Linguistic Survey of India*, Pathak 2013), with Hindi and English functioning as the two major languages of wider communication in the country, albeit with vastly different numbers of native speakers.

The Indian Constitution, written in 1950 with subsequent amendments, currently lists 22 official major regional languages and designates Hindi as the official language of central government with English as a co-official language. The Northeastern states of Meghalaya, Manipur, and Nagaland designate English as their state language. The Constitution lists slightly different official roles for Hindi and English. For instance, both are official languages of parliamentary proceedings and national administration, but English is the official language of the Supreme Court and of laws. Extensive provisions for exceptions and translation are provided, and states are given the authority to regulate official language designations at the state level.

Immediately after independence in 1947, Indian languages were initially favored as the medium of instruction, and the Congress party supported efforts to reintroduce them at the university level. English was seen as a necessary presence, but one that might soon be phased out, as implied in the formulations in (4).

HISTORIES OF ENGLISH IN INDIA [31]

(4)    a.    The English language shall continue to be used for a period of 15 years from the commencement of this Constitution for all official purposes of the Union for which it was being used immediately before such commencement. (Indian Constitution, 1950, Article 343)

       b.    It shall be the duty of the Commission to make recommendations to the President as to: (i) the progressive use of the Hindi language for the official purposes of the Union; (ii) restrictions on the use of the English language for all or any of the official purposes of the Union. (Indian Constitution, 1950, Article 344)

Salman Rushdie's *The Moor's Last Sigh* captures this awkward positioning of English, voiced through a drunken monologue at the moment of Indian independence: "bleddy Macaulay's minutemen! . . . Bunch of English-medium misfits, the lot of you. Minority group members. Square-peg freaks. You don't belong here" (1995: 165–166).

However, pragmatic and political concerns arose almost immediately. In pragmatic terms, ceasing widespread English use in newspaper production, universities, and government was unfeasible. Politically, the choice of the Northern lingua franca Hindi as a national language was far from neutral. Opposition to the imposition of Hindi and its ensuing benefits for Hindi speakers was fierce, particularly in the South, where Dravidian languages are spoken. This culminated in language riots in Tamil Nadu in the 1960s, in which 70 people were killed and Hindi and English were both temporarily banished from the state (Kachru 1983: 90). The government was forced early on to offer a more generous reinterpretation of the postindependence role of English:

(5)    We do not recommend that any restriction should be imposed for the present on the English language for any of the purposes of the Union. . . It is not suggested that English be rejected merely because it is a foreign language for we entirely agree that a language is not the property of any particular nation, and obviously it belongs to all who can speak it. *Report of the Official Language Commission* 1956 (Kher 1957)

In the field of education, distinct pressure groups emerged early in the debate, variously championing English, Hindi, or regional languages. The Council for Secondary Education (1956) ultimately settled on a three-language formula for education, still in place today, whereby non-Hindi speakers would learn Hindi, English, and their mother tongue, while Hindi speakers would learn Hindi, English, and another Indian language. A modified version in 1966 proposed that the mother tongue or regional language would be studied for

[32]   *English in India*

10 years, the official language (Hindi or English) for a minimum of 6 years, and a modern Indian or foreign language for a minimum of 3 years.

Ambiguities in the three-language formula were left open to determination by each state, and these have been resolved very differently. Hindi states frequently fill the modern Indian language slot with Sanskrit, while some non-Hindi states (e.g., West Bengal) have sometimes replaced the Hindi slot with Sanskrit. In contentious non-Hindi regions, the three-language formula has often been reduced to two languages or even one. In others, in which minority languages are not identical to the regional language, there is an effective four-language policy in place (see Khubchandani 1978).

Overall in the country, Hindi-medium schooling is far more extensive than English-medium, accounting for approximately half of Indian schools. Although English-medium schooling is far more limited, figures have risen sharply in recent years. One estimate cites a 274% increase between 2003 and 2011, but with enrollment in such schools still below 10% of overall school enrolment.[5] Some regions have actively encouraged the trend. The government of the new state of Telangana, formed in 2014, supported English-medium primary schooling and triggered extensive uptake by parents. This in turn sparked serious concerns about the quality of education provided by primarily Telugu-speaking teachers, and loss of the cognitive benefits of mother tongue education. English-medium school enrollment shows enormous variation regionally: it can be as high as 90% in the Northeast, where English has been adopted as the official language in some states, and absent in other regions.

Aside from perceived economic benefits, English-medium schools are sought after as preparation for university study, which is largely in English. English is taught as a subject in almost all schools, and English-medium education exists in private schools as well as via government initiatives in state schools. State governments change English-medium teaching provisions regularly; for example, West Bengal abolished English-medium teaching in government schools in 1984 but was forced through popular protest to bring back and expand the provision from 1992 onward. The Karnataka government similarly recently entered into a dispute over the enforcement of a 1994 state law requiring Kannada-medium education in primary schools. The government's move against widespread English-medium teaching in the state aligns with resentment among local Kannada speakers toward English-speaking migrants who feed the new, expanding IT industry of the state. For example, the CEO of Infosys, the largest business in Karnataka, advocated English medium schools to foster growth in IT.

Along with other major languages such as Hindi and Tamil, English now dominates domains such as administration, law, national politics, the armed forces, business, entertainment, mass media, and publishing. English language newspaper production is a long-standing institution, beginning in Calcutta in the 1780s, at the same time that newspapers were first being established in Britain. The current top-selling English daily in India, *The Times of India*, was founded in 1838. Figures for print media have shifted in recent decades: in 1978, out of 16,000 newspapers and magazines, 27% were Hindi and 20% English (Mehrotra 1998:10). In 2006, the Registrar of Newspapers for India (RNI) recorded 62,000 registered newspapers and magazines; of the 2,130 daily newspapers, 44% were Hindi and 9% English.

These figures indicate the central position of the two languages in India, but also the faster growth of Hindi. Despite its popularity, English has not displaced indigenous languages extensively yet. In 1971, the Indian census reported 192,000 mother tongue speakers for English and 202 million for Hindi. Thirty years later, the 2001 census reported a similar absolute number for English—227,000—but a doubled figure of 422 million for Hindi. As the population of India also doubled during this time, the relative proportion of Hindi speakers has remained steadily close to 40%, with a doubling in the absolute number of speakers. Bhatt and Mehboob (2008) make the important point that despite claims of the voracious spread of English (Phillipson 1992), it is in fact indigenous languages of wider communication such as Hindi that are at present replacing minor regional languages in India.

By contrast, the lack of change in absolute numbers of native English speakers suggests an actual decrease in reporting of English as a native language. These figures almost certainly underreport real rates of English use, which are likely to have increased steadily, at least in urban areas (Pathak 2013).

At present, English in India is best described as existing alongside other languages playing an awkward, functional role. Certainly at this stage Hindi is a greater threat to minority languages than English. However, census figures belie the dramatic change taking place in urban areas such as Delhi and Bombay, where intensive use of Hinglish (see Chapter 10) by balanced bilinguals has become the norm among many segments of the younger generation (Sailaja 2009; Punnoose 2017), possibly foreshadowing language shift for some. English has thus become an indigenized presence—an Indian language—yet still remains an alien code at the very top of the scale, supporting class inequalities (Dasgupta 1993).

Social class broadly determines an individual's mode of acquisition of English. This may range from exclusively formal educational settings to exclusively informal spoken interaction, or a combination. The prominence of British-influenced school curricula and the high prestige of functional literacy in English (without language shift) sustains a conservative, formal style, spelling pronunciations, and widespread prescriptivism in IndE. The high prestige of BrE in relation to American English (AmE) has waned slightly in recent years, however, with evidence of American features (e.g., rhoticity and idioms) in popular media, call centers, and younger speech (Cowie 2007, 2018; Chand 2010; Sailaja 2009; Sedlatschek 2009; Starr and Balasubramaniam 2019).

[34]  *English in India*

As English has filtered into informal genres, the range in bilingual competence and indigenized uses has continued to expand. Contemporary newspapers reflect some of these changes, incorporating extensive use of loanwords and IndE grammatical forms. Despite this continuing indigenization of the variety, pedagogical norms for the type of English taught in schools remain conservative except in pronunciation, where indigenous norms have prevailed for decades. These complex practices and attitudes are explored in Chapters 6 and 10.

Summarizing the current Indian linguistic ecology, Gargesh (2006: 92) delineates a number of distinct functions of English: auxiliary (passive knowledge used strictly for access to information), supplementary (limited, semiroutinized interactions, e.g., with non-Indians in commercial settings), complementary (regular interactions involving different first language backgrounds, e.g., in the workplace), and equative (balanced bilinguals). These uses are distributed unevenly; for instance, there are far fewer equative users of English than other users.

## 2.2. COMMON FEATURES OF INDIAN ENGLISH

The sociohistory outlined above has led to a slow gestation of English in India. English was introduced into speech repertoires primarily via top-down institutional channels—education and employment—though informal modes of acquisition are on the rise. Adoption of English was also limited by the long-standing presence of many indigenous lingua francas such as Hindi and Urdu. This has given IndE a characteristic form: a general absence of Creole-like or highly radical adaptations in structure (except in particular historical subcommunities, e.g., Butler English), and a tendency toward formality and conservative, even archaic, style.

In this section, I briefly describe a few linguistic outcomes of this history of English in India. Excellent overviews of features of IndE are now abundantly available (e.g., Bhatt 2008; Sailaja 2009; Sedlatschek 2009; Balasubramanian 2009; Schilk 2011; Lange 2012), and I do not aim for a comprehensive overview here. Instead, I use a few examples to illustrate three dominant historical sources of distinctively IndE traits: Colonial British dialects, contact with Indic languages, and independent innovations.

In all three areas, we see the relative structural conservatism of IndE, a striking contrast to the radically restructured SgE described later in Part II.

### 2.2.1. Retention of Historical British English Forms

As the parent variety for IndE, it is not surprising that some characteristics of Northern IndE derive from BrE. In some cases, particularly lexical and idiomatic usage, the form in question has become obsolete or rare in contemporary British usage. This has been referred to as "colonial lag" (Marckwardt 1958: 80; Hundt 2009; among others).

### Phonetics and Phonology

The list in (6) shows a few examples of BrE influence in IndE phonetics and phonology.

(6)    a.   split in pronunciation of words in TRAP/BATH lexical sets[6]
        b.   nonrhoticity in educated varieties
        c.   h-dropping in Anglo-Indian English
        d.   split in FORCE/NORTH lexical sets in Anglo-Indian English

The TRAP/BATH split, (6a), refers to the phonological system in which words with the vowel in TRAP differ from those with the vowel in BATH; this feature represents a clear case of retaining the Southern British phonological split. Domange (2015) points to a number of further lexical class effects in the speech of native and near-native IndE speakers that may be long-term historical retentions from British input varieties. The case of rhoticity, (6b), is more complicated, as it tends to be most typical of higher prestige urban varieties of IndE. Many other varieties of IndE are variably rhotic, with influence from substrates and possibly AmE (Chand 2010). The dropping of word-initial /h/, (6c), as in words such as *house, have,* and *hello,* is not common in IndE but is found in Anglo-Indian English. The same is true for (6d)—a difference in the pronunciation of FORCE and NORTH lexical sets, found in traditional varieties of BrE. The higher presence of these and other British features in Anglo-Indian English (Coelho 1997) is linked to the greater input from British speakers in that community, nativization, and relative social isolation.

### Lexicon

IndE is well known for early British influence in its lexicon. The examples in (7) were actively used in British colonial English in Company or military outposts but are now seen as archaic or obsolete within contemporary BrE. They nevertheless remain in active use in India.[7]

(7)    *beseech, respected* (address term), *thrice, stepney* ('spare tyre'), *fortnight, evil-doers, dastardly deeds, donkey's (y)ears, out of station, hill station*

[36]   *English in India*

### Syntax

A preference for cliticizing auxiliaries to the subject rather than cliticizing negation to the auxiliary—that is, a tendency to use the forms in (8) rather than *I haven't, I have to,* and *you won't,* respectively—is noticeable in the speech of fluent English-speaking Indians in the present data set; all the examples in (8) were uttered by Nalin (M10Hcal). This parallel to British and Irish dialects may again point to early dialect influence.[8]

(8)    Auxiliary and negative contraction:
   a.  I've not really met very many people like that over here.
   b.  I've to do my laundry.
   c.  Don't you worry that you'll not come back?

Fuchs (2022) shows convincingly that the conjunction *and that too* in IndE is very likely also an instance of colonial lag in IndE.

Perhaps the most surprising British-derived structure in North and South IndE is the standard loan verb template V-*o* (Hindi imperative suffix) for inserting Hindi verbs into IndE. An example is given in (9). As noted earlier in relation to (2), the use of Hindi imperatives by British colonists to order Indian subjects is the likely source of this usage.

(9)    'College principal gheraoed.' (*ghera-o* 'surround,' *The Hindu*, January 12, 2008)

### Discourse Pragmatics

Finally, IndE discourse styles have also long been influenced by BrE-oriented conservatism, and IndE written registers favor either a dense bureaucratic style or a highly elaborated style.

The bureaucratic style favors acronyms, passives, nominalizations, and the omission of function words, as in (10a). The centrality of government in historical, and even contemporary, English use in India has led to seepage among registers such that this bureaucratic style has influenced genres like journalism, as in (10b), and even spoken usage.

(10)   a.  CT3 certificate is required to be obtained from the Range Superintendent of Central Excise. (*Indian government tax website*)
   b.  The Gautam Budh Nagar district Congress has demanded CID enquiry. (*Hindustan Times*, September 4, 1998)

The highly elaborated, florid style of writing, also often noted for IndE (Parasher 1983; Mehrotra 1998; Sailaja 2009), is marked by a lack of contracted forms, frequent Latinization (e.g., *demise* rather than *death*), and florid phrasing (e.g., *most respected sir, for your kind attention, your good self*). This may derive from the bookish prescriptivism and conservatism of historic Babu English styles, which perhaps overaccommodated to earlier forms of BrE. However, the style may also draw on traditional Indian textual genres that involve elaborate politeness and honorific marking. In the past decade, AmE has begun to make inroads into IndE registers and style, particularly among balanced bilinguals, so these registers may change rapidly in coming years.

### 2.2.2. Transfer from Indian Languages

Indian languages are the most substantial source for the distinctive qualities of IndE. In fact, substrate languages have even influenced whether the BrE forms just discussed were lost or retained. A BrE form that is shared with an Indian substrate is more likely to be retained. For example, the Southern BrE BATH lexical set was retained in IndE, as noted above, but this may be in part because of the presence of the [ɑ:] vowel in Indian languages. The [ɒ] vowel in words such as *doctor* and *office* is not found in many Indian languages, and so these words are often produced with the same vowel as the BATH set.

The Indian subcontinent is a classic "linguistic area" or "sprachbund," in which linguistic convergence across genetic boundaries over millennia has given rise to many parallel or comparable structures across language families such as Indo-Aryan and Dravidian (Emeneau 1956; Gumperz and Wilson 1971). This congruence across substrate languages encourages the retention of those overlapping forms and systems in the offspring variety (Croft 2000; Mufwene 2001; Ansaldo 2009).

#### *Phonetics and Phonology*

Phonetic features of IndE take markedly different forms according to region and are very sensitive to first language systems, as has been shown for variation in the realization of consonantal and vocalic forms (Nihalani et al. 1979; Bansal 1990; Wiltshire and Harnsberger 2006; Maxwell and Fletcher 2010; Wiltshire 2014).

Many typical phonetic characteristics of Northern IndE derive from Indo-Aryan areal features at different levels of phonological structure, as in (11).

[38] *English in India*

(11)  a.   inventory substitutions (e.g., substitution of retroflex consonants
           for the alveolar series, monophthongs for diphthongs, dental stops
           for interdental fricatives, trilled /r/ for approximant or silent /r/)
      b.   phonemic differences (e.g., lack of phonemic distinction between
           /v/ and /w/)
      c.   phonotactic differences (e.g., repair of sC- clusters with vowel ep-
           enthesis, e.g., [ɪskul] 'school')
      d.   addition or loss of allophonic rules (e.g., absence of stop aspira-
           tion, absence of /l/-velarization)
      e.   absence of neutralization of vowels in unstressed positions
      f.   prosodic differences (e.g., syllable-timed rather than stress-timed
           prosody, or lower nPVI, a measure of durational contrast)

South Indian Englishes are characterized by a different set of features, influenced by Dravidian substrates such as Tamil and Malayalam. Examples include
glide epenthesis in vowel-initial words (e.g., [jɛvəri] 'every') and replacement
of voiceless interdental fricatives with unaspirated stops (e.g., [t̪ɜːd] as opposed to North Indian [t̪ʰɜːd] for BrE [θɜːd]). Similar regional effects arise elsewhere; for example, the phonology of Bengali leads to phonemic replacement
of English /v/ variably with /bʰ/ in Bengal, but /w/ in Delhi.

Rhoticity in IndE illustrates the potential for complex interactions among
substrate and other sources. Standard Northern IndE, spoken by balanced
bilinguals in urban centers, has tended to be nonrhotic on the model of BrE in
the first half of the 20th century, while more regional and nonstandard varieties exhibit variable rhoticity deriving from dominant L1s of the speakers, for
example, a trilled form rather than the American approximant variant (Sharma
2005a; see also Chapter 6). Hirson and Sohail (2007) confirm these associations, finding that British Asians who identify more with being Asian than
British have higher rates of rhoticity. Sahgal and Agnihotri (1988) and Chand
(2010) report that younger women in their study were more associated with
r-less pronunciation, relating perhaps to the prestige of BrE. However, Chand
(2010) interestingly also reports a rise in rhoticity among younger speakers in
urban centers, which might be attributable to a recent rise in prestige of AmE
or to regional in-migration. Hindi could itself be shifting toward higher rates
of approximant /ɹ/, resulting in two variants within the substrate feeding into
IndE. Variable and even contradictory outcomes in IndE can result from these
complex influences on rhoticity across class, proficiency, and L1.

### Lexicon

Many, though by no means all, distinctive IndE lexical forms are drawn from
Indian languages. Kachru (1986: 42, 152–153) noted categories such as

register-specific loans (*lathi* 'stick, police baton,' *bandh* 'strike,' lit. 'closed'), hybrid loans (*lathi charge* 'armed charge for mob control,' *policewala* 'police person'), loan translations or calques (*open hair* 'hair worn down or untied,' *to stand on someone's head* 'to supervise closely'), and reduplicated forms (*acting-wakting* Hindi reduplication template, *court-kacheri* hybrid reduplication similar to Old English-Norse doublets such as *kith and kin* or *time and tide*). Balasubramanian (2009) offers a wide-ranging empirical description of lexical variation in IndE, including some forms that are not divergent in form but in meaning (*stay in X place* 'live in X place,' *keep it* 'put it,' *catch it* 'hold it').

Lexicon can of course vary regionally (e.g., *military hotel* 'restaurant' in South India) or culturally (e.g., *zikr* 'invocation' in Muslim communities). English in South India has undergone an independent process of indigenization, with quite distinct substrate-influenced forms. Tamil English examples from Krishnaswamy (2009) include *da/de* 'friend, man, dude' and *put* + V as the template for loan verbs. One of the richest illustrations of substrate influence in Tamil IndE ('Tamlish') at all structural levels, as well as of the global appeal of New Englishes generally, can be observed in the global hit song 'Why this Kolaveri, Di?' (released in 2011, CNN's Top Song 2012).

### Syntax

IndE morphosyntax also shows extensive influence from Indian languages. Several grammatical subsystems are analyzed in detail in later chapters and therefore not listed here, including article use, marking of tense and aspect, and use of modals.

A salient features of IndE syntax is flexible word order, modeled on word order in Indian languages. This often involves the fronting of topicalized constituents, as in (12), but can take different forms.

(12) Word order:
    a. Always Hindi and Gujarati and Marathi you can use in   [M1Lcal]
       Bombay.
    b. Not so much adjustment I have to make.   [F2Lcal]
    c. Minimum one month you have to wait.   [M6Hcal]
    d. Actually, this part I have not been.   [M7Hcal]

Another common feature of IndE, resumption, also takes a variety of forms. The examples in (13) show instances of fixed expressions as in (a), and insertion of copy prepositions, as in (b), or pronouns, as in (c) and (d).

[40] *English in India*

(13)  Resumptive forms:
    a.  I don't think <u>so</u> there's such a thing as Indian     [M9Hcal]
        English.
    b.  Depending upon <u>from</u> what status you are coming     [M8Hcal]
        from . . .
    c.  A person living in Calcutta, <u>which he</u> didn't know     [M16Hdel]
        Hindi earlier, when he comes to Delhi . . . he has to
        learn English.
    d.  My old life I want to spend <u>it</u> in India.     [F1Lcal]

Some of these constructions may indicate a difference in processing, whereby a narrow syntactic domain—based on the substrate system—is taken to be the boundary beyond which explicit forms are needed for reconstructing anaphoric relations. But other forms may relate more closely to information structural preferences.

Lange (2012) links the two features described above—word order variation and resumption—through a deeper analysis of change in IndE toward topic prominence rather than subject prominence (see also Leuckert 2019). Her analysis links an entire set of related structures—including left dislocation, topicalization, noninitial existentials, resumption—all of which shift as part of a deep process of pragmatic restructuring. Her approach moves the study of substrate influence in New Englishes beyond the level of individual features, toward a more robust typology of language change in New Englishes.

Another common substrate influence on IndE syntax, also discourse related, is prodrop. The forms in (14), which show prodrop across grammatical functions and thematic roles, directly parallel optional argument omission in Hindi.

(14)  a.  Noninitial subject: When you are working for some-     [F2Lcal]
        body, Ø don't get so much vacations.
    b.  Direct object (transitive verbs): We have two tailors     [F1Lcal]
        who can make Ø for us.
    c.  Direct object (psych verbs and stative verbs): In old age     [F1Lcal]
        we can go and enjoy Ø. If my husband agree. He don't
        like Ø. He like Ø here more.
    d.  Direct object with 'give': And I say, no he didn't give     [F1Lcal]
        me Ø.
    e.  Indirect object with 'give': Yesterday you gave Ø that,     [M3Lcal]
        no? Give me that again!

f.  PP object or reanalysis of P as phrasal verb: I mean,  [M8Hcal]
    amazing if you look at _Ø_ comparatively.
g.  Relativizer: Those people _Ø_ are coming from Bombay,  [F2Lcal]
    they speak fluently English.

IndE has been noted for its curious behavior with respect to interrogative inversion (Bhatt 2000; Hilbert 2008), illustrated in (15).

(15)  a.  Uninverted matrix wh-question: Which part you are  [M2Lcal]
          from?
      b.  Inverted embedded question: I don't know how long  [M8Hcal]
          have you been here but . . .

Rather than being eliminated, English inversion rules appear to reversed in (15). This does not quite mimic the substrate systems, as Indian languages tend to have no interrogative inversion, so (15a) may correspond broadly to Hindi syntax, but (15b) does not. Hilbert (2008) argues convincingly that SLA plays a part in the development of these structures. An interaction of substrate grammars with acquisitional factors is found in the analyses in later chapters too.

Additional grammatical features that may derive directly from substrate systems but that did not occur robustly in the data include invariant tags and reduplication, shown in (16).

(16)  a.  invariant tags (_You're English, isn't it?_)
      b.  reduplication with meanings of distributivity or intensity (_We had four four mangoes._ 'We had four mangoes each.' _Bring hot hot tea._ 'Bring very hot tea.')

Regional variation in substrate effects can also be seen in the domain of morphosyntax, although less clearly than in phonetic variation. One example is that the demonstratives _this, that,_ and _some_ are used in place of English articles _a_ and _the_ more frequently by South Indian speakers in the current data set, as Dravidian languages use demonstrative and quantifier forms in these contexts.

### Pragmatics

Some, but not all, aspects of IndE pragmatic constructions (e.g., _Will you give me water?_ with polite rather than direct meaning, Sridhar 1991) can

[42]  _English in India_

be traced to a mapping from parallel constructions in the first languages of speakers.

IndE has a number of innovative pragmatic markers. The examples in (17) illustrate one such form, focus marking with *only* (Lange 2007, 2012; Parviainen 2012; Nayak et al. 2016).

(17)  a.  Yeah, they [parents] are in Madras <u>only</u>.  [M3Lcal]
       b.  [How did you meet them?] In the church <u>only</u>.  [M3Lcal]
       c.  Like that <u>only</u> I got my license.  [M3Lcal]
       d.  So before coming to U.S. <u>only</u> we got stamped.  [M6Hcal]
       e.  So you buy ticket there <u>only</u> yeah? On the train?  [M6Hcal]
       f.  So he told, like, *Bhai, mai yahii pe rehna chahta huun*
           [brother I here-FOC in live want-PROG AUX]. I want to
           live over here <u>only</u>.  [M7Hcal]

In none of the utterances in (17) does *only* perform the standard English exclusivity-marking function. It is used to mark focus. A close equivalent in meaning to the sentence in (17b) would be 'It was actually *in the church* that I met them' not 'I only met them in the church (and nowhere else).' Like most Indo-Aryan and Dravidian languages, Hindi has a focus-marking morpheme *hii* on which this extension of *only* is modeled. The excerpt in (17f) is a nice illustration of this, as the speaker first states the sentence in Hindi, using *hii*, and then repeats it in English using *only*.

Although IndE speakers with many different L1s use this form in the present data, the most frequent users in the present data set are Dravidian language speakers. This could derive from higher average rates of use of the Tamil (and other Dravidian) focus forms *daan* and *ee* relative to Hindi *hii*. Alternatively, as noted elsewhere in this volume, it may be that Christian South Indians (two of the three South Indian language speakers in the full data set) may speak a more focused and nativized subvariety of IndE.

IndE also shows adaptation in the use of other pragmatic forms, for example, *itself* (Lange 2007), *also* (Parviainen 2012), and *still*,[9] via analogy with Hindi discourse markers such as *bhi* ('also'), *tak* ('until'), and *phirbhi* ('nevertheless'), suggesting a broader mapping of Hindi information structural morphology to English scopal and scalar adverbs in IndE.

Lange (2012) follows Matras (2009) in noting that pragmatic forms such as tag questions often involve heavy direct borrowing of forms as well as functions from local languages (both MATTER and PATTERN, Matras and Sakel 2007). The adjunct position and distinctive pragmatic force of such forms make them more easily detached from a language and shared across codes: Lange (2012: 234) finds a high use of not just indigenized IndE tags (*no, isn't it*) but also of Hindi tags in IndE (*na*).

### 2.2.3. Independent Innovations

As IndE continues to vernacularize, an increasing number of its innovations derive neither from BrE nor from L1s. In some cases, these are simplifications to reduce cognitive processing load or to increase transparency or regularity in the system and thus might be found across many indigenized Englishes (Kortmann and Szmrecsanyi 2004; Filppula et al. 2009). In other cases, changes result from ongoing speaker creativity in usage or social prestige valuations of forms, just as in native dialect variation and change. A few examples of each kind are briefly noted here.

In phonology, some speakers of IndE extend the British BATH lexical set, for example, *romance* by analogy with *dance*. This process is neither L1 based nor a founder effect of BrE; it derives from general processes of analogy, possibly triggered by social prestige, namely, a tendency to hypercorrect words with [æ] toward the saliently British BATH target vowel. Some IndE patterns of lexical stress, notoriously difficult to account for (Pandey 1994; Wiltshire and Moon 2003), may also arise more from selective processes of analogy and regularization than from substrate transfer.

By contrast, other phonetic processes documented in recent work are more like processes of change typically found in native dialects of English. Domange (2020) has documented lowering of TRAP and DRESS vowels that intriguingly resembles similar shifts in unrelated native varieties. Similarly, Chand (2010), Cowie (2018), and Starr and Balasubramaniam (2019) report shifts to American-style rhoticity and TRAP/BATH usage based on global networks and transnational circulation of speech styles. And Maxwell, Payne, and Billington (2018) show convergent patterns in prosody, with only weak L1 influence, across IndE, also suggesting the emergence of a coherent core system. Such findings represent crucial evidence that IndE is starting to behave like a socially differentiated variety that is undergoing the same processes of sociophonetic change found in monolingual native varieties.

In syntax, some nonstandard phrasal verb constructions can be strikingly similar across New Englishes (Tongue 1979; Mehrotra 1982; Hartford 1996), again possibly due to parallel regularization processes, for example, the use of prepositions to increase semantic transparency, as in (19).

(19) Nonstandard phrasal verbs
    a.  He had <u>requested for</u> a Hindi teacher.                [M7Hcal]
    b.  I used to give it to my brother, because he used to     [M7Hcal]
         <u>take out</u> some use of it.
    c.  This particular business is <u>confined with</u> the Indian   [M2Lcal]
         community.
    d.  So you have to <u>stick onto</u> the mother tongue.         [M9Hcal]

[44] *English in India*

A related process of increased semantic transparency is the "de-bleaching" or un-fixing of idiomatic constructions in the absence of British native speaker usage in the environment. The example in (20) shows the idiomatic *give X the slip* construction being grafted onto the nonidiomatic *give NP to NP* construction.

(20)   In a bid to give a slip to the police party, the alleged criminal hurled a bomb onto the police jeep. (*The Hindu*, Trousdale 2008: 61)

A loss of mass/count distinctions in the nominal domain has also been widely observed in indigenized Englishes (Lowenberg 1986: 5), including in the present data set, and also involve regularization of the system. In some cases, for example, *I washed my hairs*, a substrate difference in countability is identifiable, but other examples, as in (21), are less directly attributable to substrates. They arise in most New Englishes, likely due to the lack of sufficient target variety input to maintain the distinction.

(21)   Loss of mass/count distinction:
       a.   Because lots of Indian <u>populations</u> are here.            [M3Lcal]
       b.   After A. R. Rahman comes to the field, all the <u>musics</u>     [M3Lcal]
            are very good.
       c.   He think, well, this is <u>a</u> menial work.                 [M5Hcal]
       d.   You open merchant business wherever there is <u>a</u> foot     [M8Hcal]
            traffic.

At the lexical level too, we find innovation, as in (22), that derive from natural processes of coinage and semantic shift in speech communities, rather than BrE or Hindi.

(18)   Lexical innovations and semantic shift:
       a.   North: *eve-teasing* ('euphemism for sexual harassment'), *prepone* ('bring forward'), *timepass* ('idle entertainment')
       b.   South: *feeling* (adjective, 'emotionally moving,' Krishaswamy 2009)

This creative process is not restricted to the lexicon. Young urban speakers of IndE have developed a well-articulated informal style, indicating a comfortable, nativized role for English in their multilingual repertoire (Bhatt 2008; Sailaja 2009). This style is characterized by code-switching ('Hinglish'), discussed in detail with further examples in Chapter 10.

In summary, we can point to three sources of structural change in IndE: retentions from the founder dialects of BrE, transfer from Indian L1 systems, and cognitively motivated or other independent innovations. The first accounts for less regionally variable traits that are shared across varieties of IndE. The second accounts for regional differences in IndE. And the third accounts for other types of natural change, sometimes shared with unrelated dialects of English. Interactions among these processes are the subject of detailed analysis in later chapters.

## 2.3. INDIAN ENGLISH AS "DECREASINGLY IMPERFECT" OVER TIME?

In the final two sections, we will assess recent characterizations and models of the evolution of IndE.

In an excellent review of the relationship between New Englishes and other contact language types, Mesthrie and Bhatt (2008: 177) offer the following suggestive parallel to Mufwene's (2001) characterization of Creoles: "A Creole involves increasingly imperfect replication over time; whereas the indigenised variety involves decreasingly imperfect replication over time, as education and adoption of English by local elites makes the TL [target language] more and more available."

This describes the emergence of an educated English-using elite in regions such as India, but this focus is rather narrow, as is the description of Creoles. The depiction of Creoles above favors the view that their initial state was often more akin to second language acquisition (SLA) and developed under a higher colonist-to-slave ratio, with the wider lectal range growing out of a later process of basilectalization with changes to demographic proportions (Mufwene 1996; Chaudenson 2001). While this process is historically attested, other processes have also been evidenced and debated. Decreolization can lead Creoles to converge with, rather than diverge from, native varieties. Even individual scholars have shifted their position on this question (e.g., Bickerton 1984 vs. 1986). Furthermore, the life-cycle of a Creole could involve starting points at both ends of a continuum, with the *intermediate* lects developing later (Hall 1966), or it could involve all lects existing from the outset, with changes over time in the balance of use and competences rather than in the continuum itself (Alleyne 1980; Rickford 1987).

The same uncertainty regarding directions of change historically arises in relation to the origins of African-American Vernacular English and whether its distance from Standard AmE increased or decreased over time (Fasold et al. 1987; Myhill 1995; Singler 1998).

Two similar concerns can be noted with a linear characterization of change in New Englishes as becoming "decreasingly imperfect."

The first relates to directionality, and the claim that educated usage will expand over time. Even if an increase in education and elite use has occurred in absolute terms, demographic proportions of overall use in the country must also be factored in, to assess the relative impact of elite users on the variety as

[46]   *English in India*

a whole. As discussed in Section 2.1, much of the early introduction of English into India was via the education of elites, whom the British explicitly designed to serve as "interpreters" between themselves and the masses they governed. At first this educated elite represented a large proportion of Indian users of English. Today, the users of English in India are much more numerous and heterogeneous, so even if we do see an increase in English education and elite use, this does not necessarily entail a proportional increase, driving a move toward a "less imperfect" variety. On the contrary, one could argue that English has spread to far *more*, not less, heterogeneous and informal modes of acquisition and use in recent times. In any case, a linear description relies on a static target, whereas varieties such as IndE are known to involve a moving target for acquisition, with increasingly endogenous norms of use.

The second concern relates to treating varieties as unified entities. The development of English in India involves too diverse a collection of speech styles to be easily described as a single object moving in any one direction. The process is better described as an incremental growth of spheres of use in distinct but intersecting speech communities—"clusters of varieties of English, comprising several registers and dialects" (Balasubramanian 2009: 4), or "Indian Englishes" (Dasgupta 1993).

Some parts of the vast array of communities in India are indeed focusing (i.e., converging on stable norms; Le Page and Tabouret-Keller 1985) toward new norms in urban areas, but others are not.

Section 2.1 has shown how, over centuries of class-stratified interaction with British colonists, a range of types of English developed among subcommunities in India. A few of these varieties are shown in Figure 2.1: the pidgin-like variety of Butler English, the influential native variety of Anglo-Indian

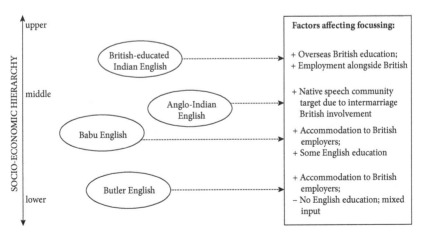

**Figure 2.1.** Early development of independent classed varieties. (+/− indicates positive or negative conditions for a shared norm to emerge.)

English, and various educated second language (L2) varieties of English, such as Babu English and elite IndE.

The precise point of origin of some of these varieties remains unclear, but many were contemporaneous. Figure 2.1 thus depicts *simultaneous* emergence of varieties at different social strata. We do not see linear change over time but, rather, numerous independent "rhizomes" (Deleuze and Guattari 1980) in the context of contact between two highly stratified and regulated class systems, British and Indian (Cannadine 2001).

Figure 2.1 also lists factors that supported (+) or inhibited (–) convergence among groups of speakers toward a shared norm. The target variety for speakers, and certainly the target for accommodation, was initially BrE. The gradual removal of BrE as either a target variety or a target for accommodation has allowed diverse indigenous target varieties to develop over time, leading to greater diversity in usage, with "defocusing" as well as "refocusing" in recent decades.

Figure 2.2 sketches some of these changes in the more contemporary subvarieties of IndE. Unlike in Figure 2.1, where the convergent norm tended to be BrE, in this figure "+" indicates focusing toward a range of new norms, mostly not BrE.

Defocusing has occurred with the loss of a narrow exogenous (BrE) target variety and a linking up of the social space between traditional usage spheres. There is more widespread, regional L2 use of English, leading to heavy admixture with first languages (L1s). However, refocusing has also taken place. In many places homogeneous subcommunities of English users have become oriented to endogenous (local, Indian) rather than exogenous (foreign, British) norms. This process is on the rise in urban contexts, particularly among

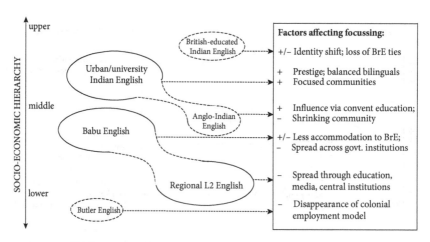

**Figure 2.2.** Distribution of subvarieties in contemporary India. (+/– indicates positive or negative conditions for a shared norm to emerge.)

university students, giving rise to a new, highly proficient, and urban, but clearly Indian, variety of English.

The erstwhile communities of British-educated and British-employed elites (upper class), Anglo-Indian English speakers (lower middle and middle class), and Butler English users (lower class), have dwindled in contrast to these expanding English-using middle and upper middle classes. Interestingly, as discussed in Section 2.1, the small but distinctive community of Anglo-Indians may have left a substantial founder effect on contemporary IndE.

A useful pair of concepts to capture these recent developments are "supra-regionalization," or leveling toward a more standard-like norm, and "vernacularization," or movement away from a standard-like norm (Hickey 2004). One can argue that both are occurring in different subcommunities in India. This is discussed further in Chapter 10 in relation to style range and variation in IndE.

An important element to note here is that Figures 2.1 and 2.2 describe shifts in community network structures and relative proportions, not necessarily massive changes in absolute demographics. Even though English use has spread more broadly across users, India is still not a region experiencing rapid language shift to English (unlike Singapore), with the possible exception of middle-class urban residents and the influence of recent changes in schooling (Punnoose 2017). Later chapters will highlight the implications of this complex landscape of IndE use for the language structures that we find.

## 2.4. PHASE 3, PHASE 4, OR PHASE 5?

Seeing IndE in this way—as a cluster of parallel developments—complicates the idea of a mass of initially unfocused L2 speech moving steadily toward more focused dialect status. Early stages of English in India showed focusing of English some speech communities, and historical and political change has meant that we are now seeing focusing in different directions and other locations.

Schneider's (2007) model of the development of New Englishes does not assume a linear direction of focusing; instead, it proposes an ordered set of phases that involve different norm orientations. The five phases Schneider proposes—foundation, exonormative stabilization, nativization, endonormative stabilization, and internal differentiation—trace the development of postcolonial Englishes from their initial contact setting, through their orientation to external, colonial norms followed by a shift to structural change and emergent endogenous norms, and ultimately an expanded local dialect range.

Schneider's use of the term stabilization at both Phase 2 and Phase 4 suggests that norm orientation (stage of evolution) and degree of focusing should be treated as separate properties. The kind of stabilization Schneider describes for Phase 4 is what dialectologists have termed focusing toward shared local norms. Differentiation in Phase 5 is not a loss of that focusing but, rather, the development of multiple focused subvarieties. An example is the development of focused subvarieties over time in the United States, first in the older Eastern states and more recently in the West.

Schneider (2007: 162–172) suggests that India spans Phase 3 and Phase 4, as "an endonormative attitude as such is definitely gaining ground, but it is also far from being generally accepted" (p. 171). There is wide agreement on this description of IndE as having entered the phase of endonormative identification (Phase 4) since the postindependence period of the 1960s (Kachru 1994: 526; Mukherjee 2007: 163; Lange 2012: 22; Balasubramanian 2009: 228).

Schneider broadly associates the onset of Phase 4 with independence, a typical case of a triggering "Event X" in his model. However, the degree to which independence is truly causal is often unclear, as independence frequently coincides with other changes, for example, institutional practice and educational policy. In a detailed study of the emergence of Hong Kong English, Evans (2014) shows that it was educational policy, not simply identity and independence, that initiated endonormative shifts in language use.

Although Schneider's model avoids a purely linear history, there is still a sense in which it looks for unified shifts. Figures 2.1 and 2.2 complicate such a narrative.

Several communities around India do not conform to the placement of IndE as transitioning from Phase 3 to Phase 4. As described earlier, the Anglo-Indian and wider Christian communities in India have long been associated with native English use. Although this has not yet been documented systematically, Section 2.1 noted clear evidence of enregistered dialect differentiation in these communities, pointing to the final phase of Schneider's model (differentiation, Phase 5).

Focusing past the stage of Phase 4 is likely to have already occurred in the 19th century for these communities, also complicating the role of Event X. Due to a tendency to focus on generalized urban usage, IndE is rarely (though cf. Mukherjee 2007: 170) described as occupying Phase 5 despite these important and influential subvarieties.

Elite IndE in the preindependence period was also quite focused and near native, but it was oriented toward BrE norms and so might have been classified at Phase 2, despite considerable focusing. Contemporary elite IndE orients to endogenous norms but remains distinct from the new speech style common among young urban middle-class groups, again suggesting a degree of differentiation among native (bilingual) English users in India akin to Phase 5.

Further back in time too, although the degree of focusing in historical varieties such as Butler English and Babu English is much more difficult to ascertain, their enregisterment as named and recognized varieties in the 19th

[50]   *English in India*

century should again warn us not to treat early IndE as an unstructured set of incomplete L2 before later shifts to endonormativity.

In sum, placing IndE at Phase 3/4 of Schneider's model reifies just one highly visible process in urban India and risks erasing the stories of many subvarieties. These subvarieties are not simply a case of uneven diffusion of change across a unified speech community. They represent entirely distinct histories, cultures, and trajectories. At every stratum of society and at different points in time, specific class-related varieties have developed with different degrees of focusing, and those groups have continued to be reconfigured, with both defocusing and refocusing occurring in different places. At present we can certainly find Phase 3/4 speakers, but also incipient Phase 5 behavior in urban contexts as well as in historical communities.

In the next chapter, we begin our investigation of these different subgroups of speakers with a snapshot of the overall grammars of the 24 IndE speakers in this study.

# CHAPTER 3

# Errors or Innovations?

The diverse histories and uses of Indian English (IndE) in Chapter 2 have shown that, in order to understand the origins and trajectory of the variety, we need to start with a wide lens, capturing more than just the speech of more proficient or English-educated speakers.

In this chapter, I start with the basic descriptive challenge of all New Englishes: Do new features of IndE behave like errors or dialect innovations? Is it even possible to draw such a distinction?

Choice of methods is crucial here, as the wrong choice can obscure key patterns in the data. Early World Englishes scholars called for research to be grounded in real data and close linguistic analysis rather than anecdotalism or ideology (Bamgbose 1998; Singh 1996; Kandiah 1991; Dixon 1991). Dasgupta (1993: 130) encouraged a "move away from a naturalistic taxonomy of facts and wonders towards a well-founded linguistics of Indian English, a well-founded account of its linguistic and cultural context, and a set of independently motivated principles linking the two."

Although much recent work has addressed these concerns, New Englishes do not fit into existing methodologies easily, and researchers have varied considerably in their choices. A number of approaches are potentially relevant to the question of errors and innovations: those that assume that an underlying acquisitional process is at play (second language acquisition [SLA]), those that recognize the stable social setting (sociolinguistics), and those that combine the two (contact studies). I briefly review these paradigms and select implicational scaling—used in SLA and contact studies—as a particularly appropriate tool for the initial analysis in this chapter.

I develop a *usage cline* to tackle the question of errors and innovations. The cline brings together two notional ends of a proficiency continuum. Several grammatical features are examined for all 24 individuals, and their patterns

---

*From Deficit to Dialect.* Devyani Sharma, Oxford University Press. © Oxford University Press 2023.
DOI: 10.1093/oso/9780195307504.003.0003

of use can be broadly divided into two different types along the continuum of speakers: learner-like traits and dialect-like traits. The hybrid picture that emerges shows clearly the transitional status of IndE and hence reasons why competing "deficit" and "dialect" ideologies have circulated, with studies selectively focused on one or another end of the usage cline.

A second important property of the usage cline is that focusing—that is, the convergence toward shared norms typical of a dialect community—has occurred only at the more "proficient" end of the scale. This is in contrast to Creoles, monolingual dialects, and rapidly nativizing varieties such as Singapore English (SgE), which are more symmetric in terms of focused norms at both ends of the continuum.

The broad usage profile developed for 24 IndE speakers in this chapter forms the basis for in-depth analysis in later chapters.

## 3.1. THE PROBLEM OF NATIVENESS

Any discussion of innovation and change in bilingual settings must start with a consideration of the question of (non)nativeness. Although the native speaker is privileged in almost all fields of linguistics, it is a surprisingly indeterminate concept. Nativeness can be defined in linguistic or social terms, including shared grammaticality judgments, mode of acquisition, amount of use, test performance, language dominance, type of variation, social group membership, historical status, or perception by others.

The study of World Englishes has challenged some of these conceptualizations within linguistics. Common assumptions about nativeness falter in these settings (Ferguson 1983; Kachru 1983; Paikeday 1985; Rampton 1990; Kandiah 1998; Davies 2003; Schneider 2007; Hackert 2009, 2012; Agnihotri and Singh 2012)—it is unremarkable in India to find people who pass one but not another "test" of nativeness. A person might have used English every day for most of their life and affiliate with it as one of their dominant languages yet have highly variable grammatical structures and intuitions. Or they might have stable or standard grammatical structures and intuitions but only one register and relatively little daily use. They might have a default code that mixes Hindi and English, so that they sound like native speakers in both but may be unable to speak either language on its own. Parents might transmit English to their children as their primary language while nevertheless retaining a host of highly variable phonetic and grammatical forms. The reality of these complexities complicates any simple categorization of IndE speakers as nonnative or native.

Singh's (1994: 370) definition of a native speaker relied on the standard sociolinguistic definition, namely, convergent intuitions held by speech community members: "Linguistically speaking, a native speaker of a language is a person who has relatively stable and consistent grammaticality judgements, which he shares with some other speakers, regarding structures alleged to be from his language." For this reason, he rejected the term "non-native variety of English" as oxymoronic, since "variety" implies shared use by users, and therefore nativeness. Singh (1972) made a related critique of an idealized conceptualization of nativeness in linguistics, which imagines a perfectly consistent and invariant native competence in contrast to unsystematic nonnative divergences and erases the reality of variability within native competence.

Singh (2012: 28) proposed that "speakers of at least the varieties that can be shown to have their own norms, such as Indian English and Singapore English, must be classified as native speakers of English by virtue of the fact that they are native speakers of their respective varieties."

This definition presupposes that IndE and SgE have their own norms. Singh's reasoning is valid, but the empirical facts presented in this chapter show that IndE diverges from his assertions in three ways:

(i) Analysis of nine grammatical features will show that only a subset conforms to shared norms of use across the full sample of IndE speakers.
(ii) One end of the continuum of speakers has high rates of use of features that have *not* converged toward an IndE norm. These features instead exhibit a learner-like S-curve of acquisition across the group, suggesting that some of the variation does not conform to a group norm but, rather, resembles learner stages.
(iii) SgE, discussed in Part II, shows many linguistic and social indicators of a greater degree of stability and focusing than IndE, so the two cannot be grouped as equally native simply due to the presence of some norms of use.

Singh (2007: 40) acknowledges that "what is being transmitted today may well have been coloured yesterday by the mother tongues of those who learnt it as a second language before transmitting it to the next generation as its first language." Peculiarly, this statement does not appear to allow that millions of Indians still do learn the language as a second language. Singh is presumably referring only to proficient or balanced bilingual speakers of IndE.

This focus on the proficient end of IndE users is common in recent work, reviewed in Section 3.2.2. This work is very welcome in recognizing and investigating the most stable and focused of IndE users and is certainly justified in assuming relatively native-like behavior. However, by setting aside other IndE speakers, we also set aside some of the main challenges and explanations in accounting for dialect birth. Less proficient users of IndE—by far the majority—are equally instrumental in the degree of variability and focusing in the variety. Including them in an analysis also forces us to ask why some linguistic forms more than others are shared across the full range of speakers in the IndE complex.[1]

[54]  *English in India*

In contrast to Singh's grouping of New Englishes together as native on principle, Mukherjee (2007: 182) offers an empirically based model of IndE as "semiautonomous," caught between the pull of conservative (exonormative) and innovating (endonormative) forces. He notes a characteristic self-critical stance—which surfaces later in Chapters 6 and 10 in discourses about both IndE and SgE—that suggests a lingering anxiety about correctness in varieties experiencing nativization.

The usage cline in the present chapter supports a need for intermediate distinctions in "how native" New Englishes are. Chapter 6 will show even finer intermediate patterns, namely, that native-like acceptance is more apparent in IndE phonology than grammar. And Chapter 10 will show differing degrees of dialect confidence between IndE and SgE, again pointing to *degrees* of nativeness.

We are left with the vexing question of what terminology to use when discussing New English usage. It is much easier to critique the notion of nativeness than to know what to replace it with. Rampton (1990: 97) observes that the terms *native speaker* and *mother tongue* "seem to be very resilient, and efforts to modify them just end up testifying to their power." Singh too warns that although "it is instructive to deconstruct certain construals of native speaker/user, not much is to be gained by throwing the baby out with the bath water " (2012: 22). He argues that nativeness still taps into some valid contrasts that are quite indispensable for linguistic and social analysis.

Paikeday (1985: 87) proposed the use of *proficient user of a specified language* instead. Rampton (1990) suggests *language expertise*, *language inheritance*, and *language affiliation* as alternatives. These and other proposals accept notions of language ability and social grouping as valid, indeed central, objects of study; they simply propose that none of these concepts are absolute or objective, nor are they always copresent in an individual.

Thus, setting aside simplistic, prepackaged notions of the native speaker does not mean we set aside the central notions of expertise, ability, use, variation, focusing, social grouping, and affiliation. These are key to understanding how and why IndE varies as it does. In the analysis that follows, I attempt to use terms more specific than native/nonnative to steer a path through the analysis of different IndE speakers. Inevitably, nativeness arises at times, but where possible nuances are clarified.

## 3.2. MODELS FOR STUDYING VARIATION IN NEW ENGLISHES

Numerous methodologies exist for studying variation in the grammars of the 24 individuals in the IndE data set. In this section, I briefly review methods used in three subfields, each with potential insights to offer the study of New Englishes.

**Table 3.1.** TYPES OF ENGLISH

| Type | Main native languages | Primary role of English | Examples |
|------|----------------------|-------------------------|----------|
| 1. | Non-English languages | foreign language | Japan, Switzerland |
| 2. | Non-English languages, lingua franca | second language | India, Kenya |
| 3. | Non-English languages, lingua franca | second language (and lexifier of local pidgin) | Ghana, Nigeria |
| 4a. | Non-English languages, lingua franca | nativizing via language shift | Singapore |
| 4b. | English | native via language shift | Ireland |
| 5. | English, English-based Creole | native language | Jamaica, Trinidad |
| 6. | English | native language | UK, USA |

The typology in Table 3.1 outlines a wide array of English linguistic ecologies. As with many traditional descriptions of English in the world, this summary initially distinguishes among English as a native language (ENL), as a second language (ESL), and as a foreign language (EFL).

The table is an expanded version of a typology presented in Platt et al. (1984: 9), which only included Types 2, 3, and 5 to describe New Englishes. Table 3.1 adds Types 1 and 6 to contextualize these within the full range of Englishes. It also adds Types 4a and 4b as a reminder that dynamic processes produce these varieties, and inner circle varieties may not always have been native. Platt et al. (1984) grouped Singapore with India and Kenya, but now, half a century on, it has moved further along in terms of language shift.

Certain defining characteristics set New Englishes apart from classroom SLA and from native dialects (Platt et al. 1984: 2):

(i) Broad range of social functions
(ii) "Localised" or "nativized" in structure
(iii) Initial absence of language shift; use as a secondary language through heterogenous modes of acquisition, combining education and informal use
(iv) Some evidence of community focusing of norms

This intermediate status means that elements from processes of SLA, creolization, and native dialect variation may all be applicable to some extent.

### 3.2.1. Second Language Acquisition

Early links were drawn between SLA and New Englishes but were then critiqued for overlooking important distinctions. More recently the relevance of SLA for New Englishes has been rehabilitated to some extent.

[56] *English in India*

SLA models have traditionally been concerned with classroom or other clearly foreign language learning, placing speakers on a trajectory toward a fixed, usually idealized, native target system. Thus, theories from the 1960s and 1970s such as contrastive analysis (Lado 1957) and error analysis (Corder 1967) focused on notions of interference, errors, and interlanguage at different stages or orders of learning. Community use that diverged systematically from the target was acknowledged but nevertheless seen as a fossilized, incomplete stage. Selinker (1974: 218) explicitly cited IndE as one such example:

> [N]ot only can entire interlanguage competences be fossilized in individual learners performing in their own interlingual situation, but also in whole groups of individuals, resulting in the emergence of a new dialect (here Indian English), where fossilized IL competences may be the normal situations.

Some early treatments of New Englishes therefore took a pedagogical and corrective stance (e.g., Quirk 1990). This work also generated some of the most detailed early quantitative work on IndE and SgE (e.g., Agnihotri and Khanna 1994). Ho and Platt's (1993: 27) early account of complex individual variation in SgE was primarily in terms of learner stages, with education (a proxy for exposure to and use of English) as the core explanatory factor of interest.

But scholars soon countered that the full cognitive and social life of these communities could not be depicted simply as failed SLA (Kachru 1983; Sridhar 1985; Lowenberg 1986; Williams 1987; D'Souza 2001). Sridhar and Sridhar (1992) pointed to the absence of a native target, heterogeneous modes of transmission among nonnative speakers, and a stable, functional role for English in a multilingual setting. Unlike classroom SLA, the original (colonial) native target is generally absent in new English contexts, and transmission proceeds from one local (often L2) speaker to another. This allows features that may have originated as transitory individual SLA features to become dialect features over time.

Weinreich (1953: 83) was among the first to observe that "when a group of some size brings two languages into contact, idiosyncrasies in linguistic behavior tend to cancel each other, while socially determined speech habits and processes characteristic of the group as a whole become significant." In India, and especially in Singapore, this is dramatically visible when individual ethnic backgrounds are "trumped" by the new dialect. Platt et al. (1984) cite the example of older Indian Singaporeans, who retain Indian features in their speech, in contrast to the younger generation of Indian Singaporeans who, according to an identification study, were indistinguishable from other Singaporeans. In other words, younger Indian Singaporeans acquire a dialect with Chinese-derived features whether or not they speak Chinese themselves. By this stage, language transfer is historical, not in the individual.

**Figure 3.1.** SLA and New Englishes.

Figure 3.1 shows the increasing divergence of New Englishes from SLA as English comes to be transmitted indigenously. This does not rule out SLA effects, but it represents a qualitatively different social and cognitive process.

The widespread rejection of a simple SLA model initially led to some overassertion of the native-like status of New Englishes. In fact, postcolonial regions still involve a mix of speakers. For some (most, in the case of India), English is still very much a second language, and individuals can be placed at a range of typical SLA stages, albeit with a local English as the target variety. Others exhibit increasing community-level cohesion ("group second language acquisition," Winford 2003). And some may have reached a stage of language shift or at least have English as a dominant language. Especially in this last group, L1 transfer may be retained from an earlier historic phase but is now acquired as a dialect feature, rather than being actively generated from their L1.

After an initial rejection of SLA accounts of New Englishes, recent work has again begun to explore these factors, but in a more nuanced way. Hilbert (2008), examining interrogative inversion in IndE and SgE, finds robust parallels to intermediate stages of L2 acquisition, including a reliance on formulaic chunks and strikingly similar preferences for (non) inversion with different auxiliaries. She suggests provocatively, but with sound support, that arguments for the distinctiveness of new Englishes such as social factors cited by Sridhar and Sridhar (1986) may account more for quantity than quality of divergence from other varieties, a point that relates to the empirical findings presented later in this chapter.

Mesthrie (2001) also showed the presence of each developmental stage claimed for L1 and L2 acquisition of English negation in an elegant analysis of a subsample of Black South African English. And van Rooy (2011) has similarly identified stabilizing innovations in Black South African English that may have originated as SLA errors. Other studies have similarly taken SLA effects in New Englishes seriously (Davydova 2011; Meriläinen and Paulasto 2014; Mukherjee and Hundt 2011). And in a meta-analysis of English varieties, Kortmann and Szmrecsanyi (2009) find a cline of grammatical variation that relates in part to mode of acquisition and learner principles such as transparent word–meaning correspondences (analyticity).

Unlike early uses of SLA, these studies are nuanced in their adoption of SLA concepts. They acknowledge the distinctive historical and social conditions of New Englishes but still take into account the undeniable presence of acquisitional dynamics: high degrees of intraspeaker variation, the need to track these differences, and the structural impact of the first language. These concerns are central to the usage cline I develop here too and are also factored into considerations of proficiency and input in later chapters.

### 3.2.2. Native Dialect Variation

SLA was associated with Type 1 situations in Table 3.1. At the other end of the typology are Type 6 situations, namely, native dialect variations. These too are relevant to the later life stages of New Englishes.

Kachru (1965) was among the first to characterize IndE as a variety in its own right, labeling it a nonnative institutionalized variety. At the same time, Fishman (1967) described access to English in India as being reserved for urban elites, citing it as a case of diglossia without (societal) bilingualism. Thomason and Kaufman (1988: 129) similarly focused on elite usage:

> [E]specially where use of the target language is confined to educated people who write it regularly, interference is very slight or nonexistent in the morphosyntax but more extensive in the phonology. . . . The English spoken by Indians in India is a classic example, with Standard English syntax but phonological features . . .

These depictions of IndE as a dialect grew in number as opposition to simple SLA models of New Englishes grew (Kachru 1983; Platt et al. 1984; Sridhar 1985; Lowenberg 1986; Williams 1987; Sridhar and Sridhar 1992; Singh 1994; and many others). Like Thomason and Kaufman, Y. Kachru (2003: 505) described one end of the IndE lectal continuum as nativelike:

> [I]nstitutionalized varieties of English are not the same as learner varieties. . . . They are not "interference varieties" as Quirk et al. (1985) characterize them. . . . If we take the acrolectal varieties of English, there may be very little difference between them [and American English].

The shift toward nativelike models has thus been associated with an increased interest in proficient IndE speakers. Corpus studies, for instance, have tended to develop and analyze acrolectal corpora (e.g., Balasubramanian 2009; Sedlatschek 2009; Lange 2012). When sampling more narrowly from educated

English users, these studies are certainly justified in assuming that the sample is sufficiently homogeneous to license aggregated, dialect-like analysis.

Attitudinal changes toward endonormativity in IndE over three decades, presented in Chapter 10, suggest the interesting possibility that the academic move away from error analysis has actually accompanied a real-time shift in the status of the variety in the eyes (ears) of its users—a "deficit to dialect" shift among both analysts and speakers themselves!

There are a number of benefits to focusing on the acrolectal or high-proficiency minority of IndE users. First, this is the group that is currently focusing toward the most stable indigenous norm, one that is increasingly treated throughout South Asia as a new standard norm. Second, and more controversially, one can argue that this is the main crucible of IndE identity formation, the community that is most strongly identified with English as its own language. Finally, this group is most likely to show stability in their variation, as they are regular users of English. This allows researchers to investigate systematicity using well-established, standard methods and to set aside complications such as learner heterogeneity and highly divergent attitudes.

For these reasons, in addition to the wealth of recent corpus linguistic studies, a number of studies have started to use standard variationist methods to study IndE (e.g., Khan 1991; Sharma 2005b; R. Sharma 2009; Chand 2010). Chand (2010) makes a particularly strong case for this approach, suggesting that "studying native speakers offers a counterpoint to L1 contact explanations for IndE stabilization and evolution in the postcolonial context" (p. 1). She takes an entirely native speaker view of the group and states that the study "is not seeking to explain r-pronunciation as caused by L1 influence" (p. 5). As with Domange (2020), this type of work opens up a fresh perspective, treating New Englishes as dialects in their own right for purposes of analysis. Chand (2010) goes so far as to omit the factor of language use in her analysis, in line with monolingual studies. Other studies retain such measures because of the focus on active bilinguals, but the factor can be relatively weak, a result that supports the autonomy of a new speech style from direct bilingual influence (e.g., Sharma and Sankaran 2011). Finally, recent work has used new computational methods to further demonstrate stability and focused use across age groups in IndE (Chand et al. 2017).

These mainstream sociolinguistic and corpus methodologies are a welcome and long overdue development in the study of New Englishes. Later chapters in the present study also employ variationist methods to assess multiple factors simultaneously.

However, despite growing parallels to native dialects, it remains the case that proficient English users are a small minority in the IndE complex. As an account of dialect birth, this study cannot set aside the majority of English users in India, who also participate daily in English-based institutional or

[60]   *English in India*

informal interactions with other bilingual speakers, all with varying degrees of competence, use, and social valuation of English (D'Souza 2001).

This volume therefore only adopts variationist methods selectively in later chapters. In this chapter, I examine individual differences and first establish the extent to which we can assume homogeneity in the data set for any given feature.

### 3.2.3. Language Contact and Creolization

New Englishes are a prime case of language contact, and the challenge of reconciling acquisition and native use. Mufwene (1994, 2001) proposes that differences between pidgins and Creoles and New Englishes are only a question of degree, not "different kinds of linguistic change, restructuring, or adaptation, only different outcomes due to different values borne by variables of the same language contact equation" (1994: 25).

In their extended discussion of the range of types of English-based contact languages and dialects, Foley et al. (1998: 20) similarly note that both pidgins and Creoles and New Englishes show parallel influences from Universal Grammar in the areas of morphology and word order. Winford (2003) links the two via the social process of group SLA, and Thomason and Kaufman (1988) suggest that the main difference between pidgins, Creoles and New Englishes is between "normal" and "interrupted" transmission, focusing again on degrees of restricted access.

In contrast to these views, Baker (1998) treats Creole genesis as qualitatively different from second language learning in terms of the motivation of participants in the change, with a medium for interethnic communication (MIC) initially arising through mutual construction by lexifier and substrate speakers, *not* through the incomplete acquisition of the lexifier by substrate speakers. Creole genesis, according to this view, did not occur because non-European groups were trying to acquire the European language as a second language, but because the modified input contributed by European speakers (of the lexifier language) was used to coconstruct a new, functionally motivated variety. Other researchers have drawn similar distinctions between Creole genesis and second language learning by associating the former with "successful creation" and "creative co-construction" based on divergent motivation, as opposed to "failed acquisition," based on limited access (e.g., McWhorter 1999).

Parkvall (2000:197) mediates between these views, noting that many linguistic and extralinguistic factors would have to be examined to establish which depiction is more appropriate for a given contact situation. The present chapter takes this view. Even if deeper cognitive processes are shared across these language types, it is crucial not to assume that the mere presence of some usage (e.g., null copula) implies deep similarity. A single grammatical feature may indeed be part of a stable new system—for example, in Irish English or in a Creole—or it may arise as part of a transitional stage of learning. The quantitative analysis in this chapter teases apart these differences.

## 3.3. MODELING NEW ENGLISHES AS A USAGE CLINE

### 3.3.1. Bilingual Continua

Half a century ago, Kachru (1965: 393–396) proposed a *cline of bilingualism* in New Englishes. His goal was to capture variable competence in the community across different dimensions: acquisition, function, and context of situation (Kachru 1992: 66). Acquisition refers to varying performance levels, for instance in rural as opposed to urban education and through daily use. Function may vary according to whether English is being used for personal functions, instrumentally as a national link language, or as an international mode of communication. And context of situation may vary considerably according to regional, cultural, or occupational practices and norms. At one end of the cline are speakers who consider English a native language and at the other, speakers who only command a restricted subset of instrumental uses for English.

Kachru's concept, and its precise relationship to grammatical structures in conversational speech, was not modeled quantitatively. Subsequent studies have tended to examine one or the other end of the proficiency continuum, often with a focus on just one or two linguistic features.

The *usage cline* of IndE presented in this chapter shows quantitative evidence of Kachru's cline, with distinct continua of SLA and dialect-like variation across the 24 individuals. We will see consistency across speakers and across grammatical features, but also crucial differences in the *type* of variation found across the cline.

Given the characteristic heterogeneity of New Englishes, the cline suggests strongly that we should initially avoid grouping speakers together (as is common in corpus and sociolinguistic studies) and instead begin with a bottom-up, microanalysis of individual grammars. This approach is common in acquisition research but has also garnered some interest in recent third-wave variation research in sociolinguistics (Eckert 2012). These approaches avoid assumptions of homogeneity in a sample of speakers and instead examine the behavior of individual forms in relation to situated users.

### 3.3.2. Implicational Scaling

To compare individual grammars across several syntactic features, I use implicational scaling, commonly used in SLA and Creole studies.

[62]   *English in India*

Unlike multivariate analysis, which aggregates individuals into groups, implicational scaling offers a more transparent picture of variation in each individual. It privileges individual differences in order to identify incremental variation across grammatical features and across speakers (Rickford 2002). The two-dimensional array lists quantitative differences in either discrete (presence or absence) or continuous (raw figures or percentages) terms. The analyst arranges features and speakers in such a way as to identify the maximal implicational relationships in each dimension, that is, to maximize a linear pattern of increasing or decreasing use in each dimension. When such patterns emerge, they predict a greater likelihood of use of a particular feature relative to other features, or a greater likelihood of use by a particular speaker relative to other speakers.

Under an implicational organization of data in a given table, a [+] value in one cell predicts or implies [+] values in columns to the left of and above that cell. The reverse is predicted for [–] values. These predictions restrict the degree and type of variation a given speech community is expected to display. If a binary contrast of [+] and [–] is used, a threshold must be set, above which a feature is assumed to be present in the grammar. Alternatively, actual frequencies of forms can be reported. I follow the latter convention, despite the potential for greater instances of ordering violations, as it offers a more precise and transparent representation of data.

Implicational scaling was adopted early as a methodology in the study of Creoles (DeCamp 1968; see Rickford 2002 for a summary) and has been used in SLA research to examine orders of acquisition of individual features and stages of acquisition among individual learners (e.g., Andersen 1978; Pienemann and Mackey 1993; Bayley 1999).

The method is particularly well suited to bilingual data. Zentella (1997) used implicational scaling of over a dozen tense-mood-aspect constructions across five individuals to illustrate (a) increasing degrees of language attrition across the five speakers and (b) relative difficulty of certain Spanish constructions for Spanish-English bilinguals. Gal (1978) and W. Li et al. (1992) used implicational scaling to model not specific grammatical constructions, but variation in the overall use of one or another language across different speaker types in a bilingual setting.

New Englishes have also been modeled this way. Platt (1979) and Ho and Platt (1993), inspired by Creole studies, showed systematic incrementation of grammatical traits across SgE speakers with different educational attainment. Several studies in the Agnihotri and Khanna (1994) collection on IndE used implicational scaling, though with an SLA and pedagogical orientation. Sharma (2005a) examined a small portion of the present data set of IndE speakers using this methodology, and Newman (2010), building on this work, applied the same technique to Puerto Rican English speakers in New York to similarly investigate the degree of focusing in the speech community.

Although legitimate concerns over the usefulness of a strict reliance on scaling for both second language data (Huebner 1983; Hudson 1993) and Creoles (see Rickford 2002) have been raised, I adopt this approach simply to first assess the degree, if any, to which IndE variation is systematic and/or homogeneous, and whether different types of variation and different degrees of focusing are evident.

One of the great advantages of this method is that it generates a *relative* measure of individual grammars, rather than an *absolute* contrast to a fixed standard variety that may or may not be the actual target for speakers. This obviates the need for fixed measures of proficiency, or language expertise, to use Rampton's (1990) term. As we will see, proficiency emerges through the correlation between the emergent grammars and the background social factors associated with them.

## 3.4. THE USAGE CLINE OF INDIAN ENGLISH

### 3.4.1. Grammatical Features

Nine grammatical features are examined for the 24 individuals. These are listed in (1).

(1)　　a.　copula omission
　　　　b.　past tense omission
　　　　c.　absence of subject–verb agreement
　　　　d.　definite article omission
　　　　e.　omission of specific indefinite articles
　　　　f.　omission of nonspecific indefinite articles
　　　　g.　stative uses of progressive *-ing*
　　　　h.　use of *only* with focus meaning
　　　　i.　extended use of the modal *would*

The first seven features have been noted as common in New Englishes and have been studied extensively in English SLA too (Dulay and Burt 1974; Wolfram 1985; Bayley 1994; R. Hawkins 2001). The last six have been noted as particularly characteristic of IndE (e.g., Kachru 1983; Platt et al. 1984; Agnihotri et al. 1984; Williams 1987; Jenkins 2003; Melchers and Shaw 2003; Lange 2007; Schneider 2007; Trudgill and Hannah 2008; Sailaja 2009; Sedlatschek 2009; Balasubramanian 2009; Parviainen 2012).

For the present analysis, I simply examine levels of nonstandard use of these variants across the continuum of 24 speakers. Nonstandardness here is defined in relation to standard British English use, as the historical input variety and a continuing reference variety for grammatical usage. In later

[64]　*English in India*

chapters I examine and account for the grammatical systems that underpin these features.

The copula was treated as null in cases of morphological absence of forms of *be* that were used with nominal (e.g., *She a teacher*), adjectival (e.g., *She lazy*), locative (e.g., *She at home*), and verbal (e.g., *She leaving*) predicates. In other words, the categories of copular and auxiliary uses were not separated for the analysis.

Past tense marking was considered absent if either a past tense suffix or an irregular past tense form was absent (e.g., *I stay in San Francisco last year*). Overgeneralization of the past tense suffix *-ed* to irregular stems was rare but was included as a form of past marking. Ambiguity between an unmarked past and a bare present form was usually resolvable from context (using narrative context, topic, adverbials, surrounding tense); when completely ambiguous, the token was excluded from the analysis.

Subject-verb agreement was treated as nonstandard if there was a mismatch in either number or person (e.g., *Our prices is cheaper*).

The definite article was treated as null if, in a standard context, the article *the* would have been required (e.g., *I asked bus driver which way to go*). Contexts involving optional definite marking (e.g., *Students who arrived late were locked out* vs. *The students who arrived late were locked out* or *taxation of income* vs. *the taxation of income*) were excluded.

Nonspecific indefinite articles were treated as null in contexts where standard native varieties would require the article *a* with nonspecific reference, that is, in which the real-world referent is not specified by the speaker (e.g., *I'm looking for job*). Similarly, specific indefinite articles were treated as null when standard native varieties require the article *a* with an intended specific reference (e.g., *I met friend of yours*).

The three remaining grammatical forms occur less frequently in the data, so I simply note the presence or absence of these features for a given speaker. Progressive *-ing* use was classified as having stative meaning based on a number of semantic tests (e.g., *She was knowing the answer*). Similarly, the meaning of *only* was checked for standard exclusivity meaning or innovative focus meaning (e.g., *I met her there only* with the meaning of 'the only place I met her was there' as opposed to 'I met her there, in the place we were just talking about'). Finally, the modals *will* and *would* were examined for interchangeable use (e.g., *V. would be coming to receive you on 15th*). Further details of coding for article use and tense and aspect are provided in Chapters 4 and 5.

### 3.4.2. The Indian English Usage Cline

Tables 3.2 and 3.3 present levels of nonstandard usage of the nine grammatical features by each speaker. These tables initially list the data from the Delhi

**Table 3.2.** PERCENTAGE RATES OF NONSTANDARDNESS BY SPEAKER (DELHI DATA SET)

| Speaker | L2 learning features | | | Stabilizing features | | | | | |
|---|---|---|---|---|---|---|---|---|---|
| | A | B | C | D | E | F | G | H | I |
| | no past marking | no copula | agreement mismatch | no indefinite article non-specific) | no definite article | no indefinite article (specific) | stative progressive | focus *only* | *will/would* variation |
| Alok | 53 | 31 | 9 | 67 | 31 | 30 | + | + | |
| Bhanu | 43 | 22 | 5 | 88 | 47 | 54 | + | | + |
| Mona | 57 | 18 | 4 | 56 | 55 | 32 | + | + | + |
| Bharat | 42 | 8 | 9 | 100 | 54 | 100 | + | + | + |
| Rani | 38 | 3 | 7 | 67 | 40 | 19 | + | + | + |
| Gagan | 36 | 2 | 8 | 50 | 38 | 14 | + | + | + |
| Mohit | 11 | 1 | 3 | 28 | 47 | 20 | + | + | + |
| Deepa | 2 | 2 | 0 | 50 | 27 | 4 | + | + | + |
| Balram | 0 | 1 | 0 | 64 | 18 | 28 | + | + | + |
| Reema | 0 | 0 | 0 | 20 | 27 | 23 | + | | + |
| Aman | 0 | 0 | 0 | 25 | 18 | 18 | + | + | + |
| Prashant | 0 | 0 | 0 | 38 | 16 | 13 | | + | |
| Total *N* | 758 | 1437 | 1730 | 239 | 602 | 297 | | | |

(Total *N* = total number of expected contexts.)

*Vertical scalability*, i.e., *relative rates across speakers*:
L2 features, columns A–C: 87.9% (within 1% range: 93.9%). Stabilizing features, columns D–F: 57.6%.

*Horizontal scalability*, i.e., *relative rates across grammatical features*:
L2 features, columns A–C: 79.1% (within 1% range: 87.5%). Stabilizing features, columns D–F: 79.1%.

**Table 3.3.** PERCENTAGE RATES OF NONSTANDARDNESS BY SPEAKER (CALIFORNIA DATA SET).

| | L2 learning features | | | Stabilizing features | | | | | |
|---|---|---|---|---|---|---|---|---|---|
| | A | B | C | D | E | F | G | H | I |
| Speaker | no past marking | no copula | agreement mismatch | no indefinite article non-specific) | no definite article | no indefinite article (specific) | stative prog. | focus *only* | *will/would* variation |
| Kapil | 70 | 24 | 6 | 82 | 58 | 50 | + | + | |
| Shalu | 70 | 21 | 16 | 84 | 34 | 50 | + | | + |
| Chandan | 47 | 23 | 9 | 67 | 38 | 45 | + | | |
| Ronnie | 28 | 16 | 3 | 58 | 48 | 31 | + | + | + |
| Rahul | 20 | 5 | 11 | 57 | 53 | 46 | + | | |
| Kavita | 22 | 5 | 8 | 47 | 30 | 23 | + | + | |
| Kishore | 7 | 15 | 4 | 65 | 27 | 30 | + | + | + |
| Gopal | 3 | 2 | 0 | 51 | 36 | 21 | + | + | + |
| Ram | 0 | 0 | 0 | 44 | 40 | 20 | + | + | |
| Kumar | 0 | 0 | 0 | 29 | 20 | 21 | + | | + |
| Sujit | 0 | 0 | 0 | 25 | 16 | 36 | + | + | + |
| Nalin | 0 | 0 | 0 | 9 | 3 | 0 | | | |
| Total *N* | 926 | 1147 | 1372 | 380 | 403 | 274 | | | |

(Total *N* = total number of expected contexts.)

*Vertical scalability*, i.e., *relative rates across speakers*:
L2 features, columns A–C: 84.8%. Stabilizing features, columns D–F: 66.7% (within 1% range: 69.7%).

*Horizontal scalability*, i.e., *relative rates across grammatical features*:
L2 features, columns A–C: 87.5%. Stabilizing features, columns D–F: 79.2% (within 1% range: 83.3%).

data set and the California data set separately, simply to show how remarkably parallel the two samples are. This similarity strengthens the reliability of the overall claims regarding variation across the IndE cline of usage and justifies a combined scaling of the data in the remainder of the chapter and in later analyses.

In both tables, the columns list syntactic features, and the rows indicate each speaker's rate of nonstandardness for each feature. These values are ordered to maximize implicational relations, with columns decreasing in nonstandardness from left to right, and rows decreasing in nonstandardness across speakers from top to bottom.

Implicational predictions in the horizontal dimension (across grammatical features) have been argued to carry slightly greater weight than implicational predictions in the vertical dimension (across speakers). This is because relationships among features in a single speaker's grammar may be more predictable than the exact distance between different speakers' rates of nonstandardness (Rickford 2002). Nevertheless, both dimensions are of interest here. Variation across speakers can tell us whether the group is homogeneous, sharing a single dialect system. Variation across features can tell us whether some grammatical features are more divergent than others.

To start with, I focus on the numerically quantified features, as these can be subjected to the scalability measures presented with each table. I temporarily set aside the three rightmost features in each table.

The first step in deriving an implicational scale is to identify the organization of the data that best fits a predicted ordering. In this case, we establish a prediction that values will decrease as we move downward and rightward in the table.

Next, the relative scalability of each dimension can be measured. The scalability of an implicational distribution represents the closeness of fit between the data and the predicted model. It is calculated by dividing the number of correctly predicted relationships between two adjacent values by the total number of such relationships. So, for instance in Table 3.3, for "L2 learning features" there are 33 predicted relationships between values in the vertical dimension, as there are 11 relationships between neighboring speakers for three different features. Twenty-eight of these conform to the predicted pattern. An example of a violation is the rate for Kavita and Kishore for copula omission, which should decrease as we move downward, but the difference is an increase of 10%. (Note that the least scalability is 50%, not 0%, as the latter would imply perfect reverse ordering.)

The high rates of scalability in both dimensions in both tables demonstrate firstly that IndE is clearly structured in some respects despite considerable variation across speakers. Particularly in the horizontal dimension (the comparison across grammatical features) there are very clear incremental differences in *how* nonstandard IndE is for different grammatical traits.

[68]   *English in India*

The data show a number of previously unobserved relationships among IndE traits. In both groups, subject-verb agreement exhibits the most standard usage, resembling standard native varieties of English. By contrast, omission of articles shows high rates for most speakers, even those who otherwise have completely standard use of features such as subject-verb agreement, copula, and past marking.

Perhaps the most important feature of Tables 3.2 and 3.3 is the clear division of variables that emerges. The initial goal was to generate a single ordering. However, unlike most implicational representations, the present data needed to be divided into *two* distinct scales. There is no single ordering for all six columns together whereby the requirements of implicational relations in both dimensions can be maintained.

For instance, in Table 3.3, Column F (null indefinite specific article) does have lower values than Column A (past marking), but only for the first three individuals. If we mutually reorder those two columns, we simply reverse the problem: an implicational relation now holds for Ronnie and below but is violated for the first three speakers. Exactly the same is true for Column E (null definite article) relative to Column A: a declining implication order holds for the first three speakers but is reversed for the others.

The fundamental problem in attempting a unified ordering is the presence of two different *types of variation* in the data. Certain nonstandard forms are spread much more evenly and broadly across speakers than others. These two types of variation have been classified here as learner features and stabilizing dialect features. Let us consider this difference more closely.

### 3.4.3. Learner Features

When the three features on the *left* side of Tables 3.2 and 3.3—subject-verb agreement, past marking, and the copula—are grouped by speaker, as in Figure 3.2, we see that they approach native-like use fairly quickly and are used standardly by nearly half of the speakers. The cumulative percentage for these features per speaker is also relatively low across the board.

I make no claim here regarding the relative ordering of these three features, some of which are examined in later chapters. The implicational order may reflect an acquisitional sequence driven by the relative complexity of learning each separate grammatical system. For now, I do not claim that this emergent order is universal in any way. In fact, the ordering of these three features is different from universal orders of acquisition proposed for English (Dulay and Burt 1974).

What is most relevant here is that these features show a qualitatively different pattern from the remaining six features. They never appear in the speech of some individuals, and they correlate much more closely with an

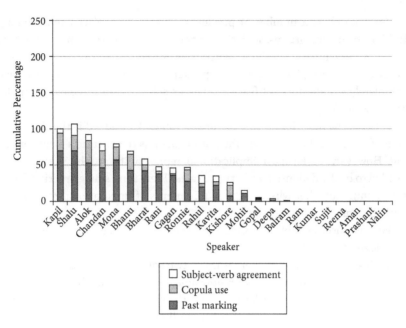

**Figure 3.2.** Cumulative rates of nonstandardness for learner features, columns A–C (combined data sets).

individual's English education and use of English than the other set of features, examined in the next subsection. This correlation, and the rapid drop-off in use across the cline, points more to an acquisitional S-curve than shared dialect forms.

### 3.4.4. New Dialect Features

Unlike the three learner features, the features on the *right* side of Tables 3.2 and 3.3 do not show a sharp decline and are instead shared across less and more proficient speakers alike. Figure 3.3 shows this very different distribution of the remaining three quantified features.

The two striking properties of Figure 3.3 are that (i) overall rates of use are higher for each speaker as compared with the learner features, and (ii) these variants continue to appear in the speech of interviewees long after learner features have been acquired. They have come to be generalized to the extent that they appear in the speech of otherwise more or less standard speakers such as Aman, Prashant, and Nalin.

This is confirmed by the clearly lower vertical scalability reported for columns D–F in Tables 3.2 and 3.3. These values mean that the strong implicational ordering of speakers for learner features does not hold for article use.

*English in India*

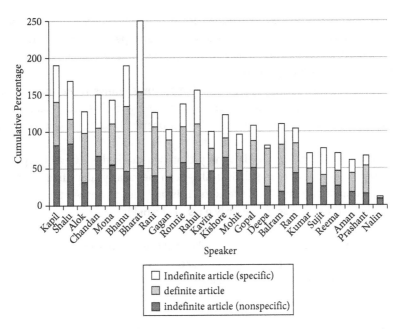

**Figure 3.3.** Cumulative rates of nonstandardness for dialect features, columns D–F (combined data sets).

The features in columns D–F extend right across all 24 speakers, with a much less predictable or complete decline across them.

The major difference between Figures 3.2 and 3.3 suggests that speakers have begun to share, converge on, and indigenously transmit certain new grammatical subsystems, such as a new article system and new aspectual usage. This is still weakly sensitive to individual proficiency, as discussed in the section that follows, but not as straightforwardly as learner features, whose trajectory ends with a system identical to native varieties of English.

An argument could be made that Figure 3.3 simply reflects late L2 acquisition of English articles, particularly as a speaker such as Kapil, who has very high rates of nonstandardness elsewhere, also has some of the highest rates of article absence. Even if IndE article use derives from late-stage SLA, at least two aspects of the new usage suggest that it has become a relatively stable system.

First, the more proficient speakers in the continuum show little evidence of being at intermediate stages of learning, and so the contrast between their article absence rates and lack of other SLA features is quite stark. The next section will show that a few of these individuals have grown up using English at home and consider it to be at least on an equal footing with their other languages, in some cases their dominant language.

Second, later chapters will show that speakers share a strikingly similar system of principles for article use, as well as for the other stable

ERRORS OR INNOVATIONS? [71]

dialect features—stative progressives, focus *only*, and *will/would* alternation. Recently, Nayak et al. (2016) have shown through a perception study that educated IndE speakers consistently share a subtle semantics for focus *only* that is unavailable to AmE speakers.

Ultimately, this subset of more stable features comes to be more widespread and thus more available for loading with sociolinguistic meaning in later stages of dialect stabilization. Whether positively or negatively, covertly or overtly, these are the traits that come to index IndE.

The key observation here is simply that two markedly different types of variation—learner-like and dialect-like—can be clearly identified within a single group of bilingual IndE speakers. This provides an answer to a question posed by Ayo Bamgbose in the early days of the field:

> The main question with innovations is the need to decide when an observed feature of language use is indeed an innovation and when it is simply an error? . . . If innovations are seen as errors, a non-native variety can never receive any recognition. (1998: 2)

The present analysis has shown a way to draw this distinction, with the validity of the method reinforced by the closely parallel result for two independent samples of speakers. This strongly argues for the need to avoid an ideological rejection of either type of variation when studying New Englishes. The cline of usage supports both recent work that has focused on proficient IndE speakers, to examine more established and stable norms, and studies that have pointed to SLA effects among some subgroups.

### 3.4.5. Correspondence to Social Factors

Why did this particular ordering of speakers emerge in the implicational scalings? Table 3.4 indicates some potential social underpinnings. It lists all 24 IndE speakers *in the order* that emerged in Figures 3.2 and 3.3, along with potentially relevant social factors for each speaker (see Chapter 1, Tables 1.1 and 1.2).

Table 3.4 shows informally that the ordering of speakers corresponds particularly closely to two of the four social factors listed: daily use of English and amount of English education. This correspondence is not at all surprising, as these two factors are measures of informal and formal acquisition and use, respectively—in other words, a clear influence of social ecology and acquisitional context.

This implies that a model of IndE must incorporate current, not just historic, SLA effects in many strata of IndE use. When referring to the speech community and the variety as a whole, it would be inaccurate to claim that

[72] *English in India*

*Table 3.4.* PARTICIPANTS' SOCIAL CHARACTERISTICS

| Speaker | English education | Daily use of English | Age | Sex |
|---|---|---|---|---|
| Kapil | 0 | 0 | 34 | M |
| Shalu | 0 | 0 | 38 | F |
| Alok | 1 | 1 | 66 | M |
| Chandan | 0 | 0 | 67 | M |
| Mona | 0 | 1 | 30 | F |
| Bhanu | 0 | 1 | 32 | M |
| Bharat | 0 | 1 | 59 | M |
| Rani | 1 | 1 | 84 | F |
| Gagan | 1 | 1 | 33 | M |
| Ronnie | 1 | 1 | 26 | M |
| Rahul | 1 | 1 | 48 | M |
| Kavita | 1 | 2 | 54 | F |
| Kishore | 2 | 2 | 62 | M |
| Mohit | 1 | 1 | 23 | M |
| Gopal | 2 | 1 | 35 | M |
| Deepa | 2 | 2 | 23 | F |
| Balram | 2 | 2 | 59 | M |
| Ram | 2 | 2 | 29 | M |
| Kumar | 2 | 3 | 67 | M |
| Sujit | 2 | 3 | 23 | M |
| Reema | 2 | 2 | 72 | F |
| Aman | 2 | 3 | 35 | M |
| Prashant | 2 | 3 | 29 | M |
| Nalin | 2 | 3 | 24 | M |

English education: 0 (*no English medium education*), 1 (*some [e.g., higher] education in English*), 2 (*mostly English medium education*).
Daily use of English: 0 (*minimal*), 1 (*at work*), 2 (*work and some friendships/younger relatives*), 3 (*work, friendships, home*).

IndE has established norms exactly as BrE or other inner circle varieties do (cf. Singh 2012). At least some grammatical features do not conform to a speech community norm at all across adult use; they are simply present due to diverse stages of L2 English use in the community.

The lack of an age pattern points to a lack of systematic change-in-progress, and the lack of a gender pattern points to a stronger role for acquisitional context than native-like sociolinguistic processes of change. Typical variationist age and gender patterns are more likely to surface in the study of variation within the group of very proficient speakers, as observed in recent phonetic studies by Domange (2020) and Cowie (2018).

A counterargument in favor of seeing IndE as on a par with native dialects may argue that a cline analysis of a broad sample of BrE speakers would similarly show some features dropping off in usage across the cline (e.g., working class or vernacular features) and others being more widely shared. Crucially, however, such a distribution would correlate with social factors such as class or region, not with degrees of use and exposure to the language. One could counter that this is in fact parallel, namely, that speakers of working class or regional varieties of BrE have indeed had less exposure to the standard variety and so to an extent are affected by acquisition-like factors just as the IndE speakers are. That would be an interesting and important revision of how native varieties are currently dealt with in sociolinguistics (which tends to omit any role for acquisition; see Sharma 2018). However, it would involve the *introduction* of acquisition as a factor in native BrE style variation, not the elimination of such a factor from the IndE cline. The relevance of acquisition in the present analysis is not refuted by such an argument.

While this sort of scaling has the advantage of laying bare the complexities, but also regularities, of dimensions of variation in New Englishes, it is worth bearing in mind that it does not incorporate many other dimensions of variation. Phonetic features have been omitted for now, as have social factors of identity and attitude. Chapter 6 will contextualize these effects within a more multidimensional perspective.

Chapter 9 returns to the two types of variation found here for a more theoretically motivated model of why certain features stabilize more than others.

## 3.5. IMPLICATIONS

Despite the bewildering diversity of English use in India, this chapter has uncovered a relatively orderly landscape of variation, with distinct factors operating in different social spaces. But this picture offers only a superficial snapshot. In the chapters that follow, I explore the precise structure of, and explanations for, these innovations in greater depth.

Here, I consider two final questions that this initial picture raises:

(i) How does this IndE scaling compare with other dialect continua or clines?
(ii) Why have specific features stabilized more than others?

### 3.5.1. IndE and Other Continua

This formalization of Kachru's cline of bilingualism adds multidimensionality to theoretical representations of new Englishes in the same way that constructs such as the wave model (Bailey 1973) and the Creole continuum (DeCamp 1968; Rickford 1987) originally aimed to represent different dimensions of

[74] *English in India*

variation in Creoles. So how similar is this continuum to other dialect and Creole continua? Let us briefly consider three well-studied examples.

In DeCamp's (1968) continuum for Jamaican Creole, more Creole features are prevalent at the more basilectal end and fewer at the acrolectal end. Speakers recognize *both* ends of the continuum as representing functional, native lects used by segments of the community for a range of functions, and employed by other groups intermittently for temporary functions such as interactional accommodation or indexing of stances such as informality, vernacular voice, or localness (Rickford 1987; Sidnell 1999).

The nativized Irish English dialect continuum (Hickey 2007) similarly exhibits a more nonstandard end that comprises more Irish-influenced features and a more standard end of the continuum. A similar correspondence to social status but also potential for style shifting in both directions exists in the continuum.

Finally, the partially nativized case of Singaporean English has also been described as forming a diglossic continuum, with Colloquial Singaporean English constituting one end of the range and Standard Singaporean English the other (Pakir 1991; Gupta 1994; Bao and Hong 2006). Again, speakers recognize both ends of the continuum as the vernacular of particular social groups and shift between them in order to index a variety of social stances (Leimgruber 2013).

All three of these continua are thus relatively *symmetric* in terms of stability, each end of the continuum involving a focused set of variants associated with a subvariety. Style shifting in individuals may not be entirely symmetric, but it *can* occur upward *or* downward in all of these continua, based on recognition of both ends as established speech varieties, whether through overt or covert prestige.

The IndE continuum does not have this lectal symmetry. The non-English-dominant end of the continuum (left side of Figures 3.2 and 3.3) does not represent a focused, recognized variety, and there is essentially no shifting by more proficient speakers into that lect for social or stylistic reasons. As discussed further in Chapter 10, with comparisons with SgE, balanced Hindi-English bilinguals have some range in their formal and informal styles, but the informal style is distinct from the nonproficient end of the cline presented here.

Newman's (2010) implicational scaling for New York Latino English bears some resemblance to IndE, in showing indicators that the variety has not focused entirely yet, with different degrees of systematicity across speakers. However, he does not find exposure and use of the two languages to correlate strongly with the variation found, and so New York Latino English may be slightly less SLA driven than IndE.

All continua arguably incorporate some asymmetry, but the IndE continuum shows a more dramatic lack of focusing, vernacular stability, and

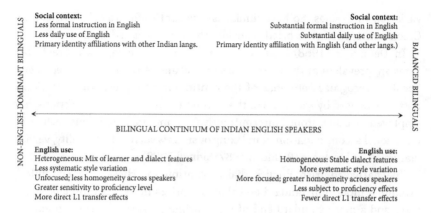

Figure 3.4. Social and grammatical features of a bilingual continuum.

covert prestige at the less proficient end of the continuum. In short, unlike fully native continua, the IndE continuum is comprised of a relatively unfocused set of SLA stages, and a more focused range of dialect-like usage.

Figure 3.4 maps out these distinct social and linguistics properties of the bilingual continuum. In Gargesh's (2006: 92) terms, more *auxiliary* functions are associated with the non-English-dominant end, and more *equative* functions with the balanced end.

This should not be mistaken for a return to fossilization explanations of variation (Selinker 1974; Quirk 1990). None of these speakers are *necessarily* at fossilized stages, and none are treated as cases of incomplete SLA of British English. Nor are the less English-dominant speakers here considered to be identical to classroom learners in terms of attitudes. Indeed, Chapter 6 will show evidence from phonetic variation that the entire continuum of speakers, even the learner-like end, has begun to perceive themselves as speakers of a valid, indigenous variety of English. Nevertheless, it is reasonable to suggest that some of the less proficient speakers are in fact aiming for a more standard IndE (endogenous, not exogenous) target that they have not yet attained.

Proficiency and SLA thus influence grammatical structures and types of variation, but at the same time—and quite independent of individual proficiency—the entire population is undergoing a robust identity shift away from exonormativity. This can lead to L2 features being recast as dialect features. This has not taken place across all grammatical forms in IndE, but this and later chapters show strong indications of such shifts in identity and language use.

Finally, Figure 3.4 also invites an integrated account of linguistic and social factors, such that the status of a linguistic form as more learner-like or more dialect-like affects its potential uptake for particular social uses. In a feedback loop between structure and social meaning, those forms still associated with less proficient speakers are less likely to be taken up for the indexing of new urban identities than those that have stabilized to a greater extent. This loop is likely to propel only a subset of features toward stable enregisterment (Agha 2003).

These empirical findings correspond in many ways to Mukherjee's (2007) three dimensions of variation in IndE. In his model, one dimension of variation involves L1 interference, a second involves independent innovations in IndE, and a third involves the more conservative force of conforming to a common core shared with, or deriving from, BrE and other native varieties.

Whereas Mukherjee (2007) concludes that these competing forces keep IndE at a "steady state equilibrium," caught between innovation and conservatism, the findings here show that ongoing change is possible within this system of opposing tendencies. Later chapters delve into these ongoing processes of partial focusing in educated urban IndE.

### 3.5.2. Why Are Some Features More Dialect-Like than Others?

What determines *which* grammatical innovations were more entrenched than others in Figures 3.2 and 3.3, outlasting stages of language acquisition and stabilizing across the entire bilingual continuum to become new dialect features?

The chapters that follow explore a number of competing proposals to answer this question. One major influence may be the degree of difference between English and the grammatical systems of local languages (e.g., Filppula 1999, 2004; Sharma 2009; Bao 2005, 2015). Another possibility is that universal tendencies arise across New Englishes regardless of the local languages in question (Chambers 2002; Mair 2003; Kortmann and Szmrecsanyi 2004), perhaps with both forces interacting (Sand 2004; Sharma 2005b; Filppula et al. 2009; Lange 2012). A third possibility that is explored is the amount of exposure a particular grammatical feature requires for acquisition, particularly given a particular L1-L2 contrast (Sorace and Filiaci 2006). I use two very different substrates and social ecologies—India and Singapore—to investigate these competing predictions.

When considering these larger motivating factors, it will prove important to distinguish between grammatical systems (e.g., the article system or the tense-aspect system) and individual constructions or forms (e.g., verb-particle constructions). The latter can exhibit more idiosyncratic patterns of usage, and I focus more on the former, namely, change in abstract grammatical subsystems.

In the chapters that follow, I explore a wide range of grammatical features on both the learner side and the dialect side of the IndE cline. We find little evidence that simple language universals drive change. Instead, the set of studies reveals an intricate interplay of transfer from local languages, innovative reanalysis by speakers (leading to "third grammars"), and amount of input needed to acquire specific grammatical features. The last of these is often overlooked in models of New Englishes but is argued in Chapter 9 to be an important element within a full account of dialect birth in multilingual, postcolonial settings.

# CHAPTER 4

# The Article System

Omission of the articles *the* and *a* emerged in Chapter 3 as very common in IndE. This might not be surprising, given that the article systems of English and of Indian languages are very different. But do Indian speakers simply graft their languages directly onto English? Or are they creating a system that differs from both Hindi and English—a "third grammar"? And how similar are IndE speakers in this novel usage?

Studying such questions in language contact can help clarify how bilinguals cope with and resolve conflicting language systems, in particular how much they depend on their other language(s) as opposed to more generalized inferential reasoning in negotiating a second language. Though not the focus here, such understandings can also be useful in pedagogy, indicating particular areas of difficulty and anticipating systematic types of reanalysis at different stages of learning.

Language transfer has frequently been invoked informally in relation to article use in New Englishes. Platt et al. (1984: 53–59) suggested early on that transfer from specificity marking in the first language (L1) is the primary factor in divergent article systems in new Englishes. They cite the two IndE examples in (1) to illustrate a direct transfer of L1 functions to two L2 forms—the use of *one* and omission of the article (Ø):

(1)  a.  I'm staying in <u>one</u> house with three other students. (*specific*)
     b.  I want to spend some time in Ø village, definitely if I get Ø chance. (*nonspecific*)

Isolated examples cannot establish whether the L1 grammar is fully transferred in this way in IndE speakers' usage. Instead, we adopt a combination

---

*From Deficit to Dialect.* Devyani Sharma, Oxford University Press. © Oxford University Press 2023.
DOI: 10.1093/oso/9780195307504.003.0004

of quantitative methods from second language acquisition (SLA) research and variationist sociolinguistics here. The chapter summarizes the findings of Sharma (2005b), to illustrate the interplay of L1 transfer and universals in shaping novel IndE usage. L1 transfer does play a role when the L1 has an overt form, but when no L1 forms exist as a clear model, speakers exploit universally available discourse knowledge to restructure the new L2 system. The closing discussion notes several studies that have since confirmed the original claims reported here.

The findings dovetail with Lange's (2012) overarching proposal of a shift to discourse prominence in IndE syntax, although a strict shift to the discourse-driven use of word order to mark old and new information in Hindi is not found.

## 4.1. DIFFERENCES BETWEEN HINDI AND ENGLISH

Articles in English perform two key functions: they help listeners identify entities in the world that speakers are referring to (specificity), and they help interlocutors keep track of entities that have been mentioned in their conversation (definiteness).

Specificity signals the existence of a unique real-world referent for a noun phrase (NP), or the speaker's "ability to identify the referent" (Fodor and Sag 1982). A nonspecific noun phrase could refer to any token of its type in the real world (*I'm looking for a book. Any book will do.*), while a specific NP has a unique referent in the real world (*I'm looking for a book. I think I left it here yesterday.*).

Definiteness, by contrast, is primarily rooted in discourse. Hawkins (1978) describes the definite article as an instruction for the hearer to "locate" the referent of that NP within a pragmatically defined set of objects that are part of the shared speaker–hearer knowledge. This can be referred to as the "givenness" of information that the speaker can treat as "recoverable either anaphorically or situationally" (Halliday 1967: 211). A definite NP has already been referred to by a speaker and can be assumed to be known (*I asked a girl for directions. The girl told me.*), while an indefinite NP has not been referred to by a speaker and cannot be assumed to be known (*I asked a girl for directions.*).

Many further semantic and pragmatic subtleties constrain the use of English articles, necessitating very rich input for learners. Furthermore, there is optionality and variation in native varieties, adding to the complexity of naturalistic input. This makes the system notoriously difficult to learn. It tends to be acquired late by native English-speaking children (Brown 1973), shows extensive variation among nonnative speakers, and differs among native varieties as well (Sand 2004).

[80]  *English in India*

To explore the reorganization of English article use in IndE, we need a basic understanding of how articles are used in Indian languages. As Hindi is the primary substrate for the IndE speakers analyzed here and is representative of typical article systems found across Indian languages, Hindi is used as the sample L1/substrate here.

The article systems of all Indo-Aryan and Dravidian languages spoken by the current sample of speakers mark a specific/nonspecific contrast, but not a definite/indefinite contrast. All of the languages optionally use their form for the numeral *one* to indicate specific indefinite meaning (Sridhar 1990; Cardona 1965; Schiffman 1999). And none of the languages have a definite article; instead, definiteness is marked by word order, case marking, and prosody.

The simplified diagrams in Figures 4.1 and 4.2 show that this system is the inverse of the English article system, which marks a definite/indefinite contrast but not a specific/nonspecific one.

In the absence of a definite article, word order plays an important role in signaling definiteness. In Indo-Aryan and Dravidian languages, as in many other unrelated language groups (e.g., Basque, Hungarian, Greek, Turkish), speakers iconically arrange information from older to newer in an utterance. Information familiar to the hearer is positioned clause-initially and new information clause-finally or sometimes preverbally. This pattern has been variably described as topic/focus, topic/comment, and theme/rheme (Dik 1978; Vallduví 1992; Lambrecht 1994; Birner and Ward 1998).

This system is exemplified in the Hindi examples in (2). Here, the definiteness interpretation of the NP *kitaab* varies according to its position in the clause rather than according to article choice, as is the case in the English translations.

| | Definite | Indefinite | |
|---|---|---|---|
| | *the* | *a* | Specific |
| | *the, a* (incl. generic) | *a* | Nonspecific |

Figure 4.1. English article system.

| | Definite | Indefinite | |
|---|---|---|---|
| | — | *ek* ('one') | Specific |
| | — (incl. generic) | — | Nonspecific |

Figure 4.2. Hindi article system.

THE ARTICLE SYSTEM [81]

(2)    a.    [kitaab]     [mez par]    [pari hai]
           book        table on     lying is
           'The book is lying on the table.'

       b.    [mez par]    [kitaab]     [pari hai]
           table on      book        lying is
           'A book is lying on the table.'

       c.    [mez par]    [pari hai]    [kitaab]
           table on      lying is      book
           'On the table is lying a/the book.' (disambiguated by prosody)

## 4.2. PREDICTED TYPES OF GRAMMATICAL CHANGE

We will consider four possible principles that might govern the omission of articles in conversational IndE speech.

Two of these predictions are based on transfer from Hindi: positional marking of discourse information (Hypothesis 1) and overt specificity marking (Hypothesis 2). The other two predictions are based on universal processes that are independent of the indigenous languages: universal semantic proto-types (Hypothesis 3) and discourse information (Hypothesis 4). The analysis will show that a new third grammar, integrating the predictions of Hypothesis 2 and 4, is found to prevail across speakers.

### 4.2.1. Hypothesis 1: Indo-Aryan Positional Marking of Discourse Familiarity

Given the use of word order rather than definite articles in Hindi, as seen in (2), Hindi speakers of English may choose to rely on clause position to mark topicality or discourse familiarity. Lange (2012) convincingly shows word order to be a major dimension of restructuring in IndE in relation to con-structions such as topicalization, left dislocation, cleft constructions, focus markers, and existential *there* constructions. The use of word order instead of articles to indicate the discourse familiarity of a referent could constitute a further instance of this type of restructuring.

The predictions for this sort of transfer from Indo-Aryan word order are outlined under Hypothesis 1:

**Hypothesis 1** (Transfer of L1 positional marking of discourse familiarity):

(i)  Old NPs in clause-initial position will favor zero articles. (unmarked position)
(ii)  New NPs in clause-final position will favor zero articles. (unmarked position)
(iii)  Old NPs in clause-final position will favor definite articles. (marked position)
(iv)  New NPs in clause-initial position will favor indefinite articles. (marked position)

These formulations are based on those in Young's (1996) study of English acquisition by speakers of Czech and Slovak, both also discourse-configurational languages. In this parallel situation, Young similarly predicts that NPs in unexpected (noncanonical) clausal positions would be overtly marked with articles, but that overt marking would be treated as redundant, and hence avoidable, elsewhere (p. 156). In other words, speakers are only predicted to use articles when an NP is not in its pragmatically determined (unmarked) clause position according to the Indo-Aryan system, that is, in situations (iii) and (iv).

### 4.2.2. Hypothesis 2: Indo-Aryan Specificity Marking

Hypothesis 1 is based on positional signaling of definiteness. An alternative type of transfer from Indian L1s would be a transfer of article meaning, rather than NP position. This type of transfer is more commonly proposed for article use in New Englishes.

Three distinct predictions for transfer of article meanings can be made based on Figures 4.1 and 4.2. First, the existence of a specific indefinite article in Hindi may lead speakers to restrict their use of the English indefinite article to specific NPs only, that is, to restrict *a* only to the region in the top right of Figure 4.1, on analogy with Figure 4.2. Second, they may favor the form *one* over *a*, on analogy with Indian languages. And third, speakers may avoid using articles with definite and generic NPs in English, since Indian languages have no such overt form. This can be summarized as follows:

**Hypothesis 2** (Transfer of L1 semantics):

(i)  a.  [+ specific, – definite] NPs will be marked overtly (possibly using *one*)
    b.  [– specific, – definite] NPs will have no article
(ii)  a.  [+ specific, + definite] NPs will have no article
    b.  [– specific, + definite] NPs will have no article

### 4.2.3. Hypothesis 3: Universal Prototypes

Transfer from first languages is not the only potential source of change. Bilinguals might cope with an unfamiliar L2 article system by appealing to universally more "natural" grammatical systems (Ionin et al. 2004).

Bickerton (1981) proposes a universally preferred triparite organization of the universal dimensions of specificity and definiteness, or [±specific reference] and [±hearer-known]: (i) [+SR, +HK], that is, referential definites, requiring an overt definite article; (ii) [+SR, −HK], that is, referential indefinites, requiring an overt indefinite article; and (iii) [−SR, −HK] or [−SR, +HK], that is, nonspecifics and generics, favoring zero marking. These universalist predictions for article use can be summarized as follows:

**Hypothesis 3** (Universal prototypes):

    (i)   [+SR, +HK] NPs will have a definite article
  (ii)   [+SR, −HK] NPs will have an indefinite article
 (iii)   [−SR, −HK] and [−SR, +HK] NPs will have no article

It is important to note that predictions (ii) and (iii) resemble the article systems of Indian languages. Hypothesis 3 thus overlaps significantly Hypothesis 2, making it difficult to draw a clear distinction between transfer and universals.

Some studies of article use in SLA and in new varieties of English that have identified elements of Bickerton's universal contrasts (Chaudron and Parker 1990; Huebner 1983; Mesthrie 1992) are similarly ambiguous between transfer and universalist explanations. For instance, Mesthrie (1992: 205) suggests that sporadic article use in South African Indian English is reminiscent of a prototypical Creole system, but the three examples he furnishes—*I bought one soda* [+SR, −HK]; *Food is lovely* [+SR, +HK]; *Because if they give us chance* [−SR, −HK]—lend equal if not more support to the transfer prediction of Hypothesis 2, since Hypothesis 3 predicts a distinct marker for each of the three types. We return to the difficulty of distinguishing between transfer and universals later.

### 4.2.4. Hypothesis 4: Discourse Status

Finally, a much simpler type of universal influence on L2 article use could come directly from the status of an NP in discourse, rather than prototypical pairings of form and meaning.

If we consider the newness of a referent in discourse as scalar rather than as a binary contrast of [±hearer-known] (J. Hawkins 1978; Prince 1981;

[84] *English in India*

Lambrecht 1994; Lyons 1999), then we might predict that the *relative* position of an NP along this scale will affect the *relative* need for articles to disambiguate reference.

Earlier studies have shown that topic continuity (Huebner 1983; Chaudron and Parker 1990; Jarvis 2002), discourse recoverability (Robertson 2000), and conversational genre (Tarone and Parrish 1988) appear to affect article use in learner speech. Here too we can consider the potential role of discourse status, as follows:

> **Hypothesis 4** (Discourse status): Speakers' rates of use of articles will vary according to the relative givenness or newness of the NP in question.

The analysis adopts Prince's (1981) model for degrees of givenness, presented in the next section. Hypothesis 4 deals with the relative newness of an NP in ongoing discourse, that is, at discourse level, whereas Hypothesis 1 dealt with the status of an NP as topic or comment in a single clause, that is, at clause level (cf. Jarvis 2002 for this distinction).

## 4.3. METHODOLOGY

The analysis uses one complete continuum of speakers, the California data set (see Chapter 1), to assess these competing predictions.[1] A secondary question examined is whether the same pattern holds across all individuals.

Studies of article use have used a range of methods, including controlled elicitation or judgment tasks (Agnihotri et al. 1984; Goto Butler 2002; Ionin et al. 2004; Y. Kachru 2003), semistructured elicitation (Trenkic and Pongpairoj 2013), and more naturalistic data (Huebner 1983; Jarvis 2002). To track naturalistic usage in an indigenizing variety of English, conversational speech is useful, as it avoids highly formal and standard registers that might elicit maximally standard usage or even distortions of natural usage due to linguistic insecurity. The long recordings in the present data set also generate rich layers of discourse reference, useful for Hypothesis 4.

The analysis here is limited to omission of *the* and *a* in contexts that would standardly require an overt article in English. There is of course variation within standard varieties, as in British and American dialectal variants of *in (the) hospital*. Such cases would have been omitted from the data set but none were encountered.

Contexts that standardly involve absence or optional use of articles were excluded from the coding, for example, indefinite mass nouns (e.g., *I need furniture*), indefinite plurals (e.g., *I teach children*), and generic and definite plurals (e.g., *[The] prices went up*). Following Huebner (1983), Tarone and Parrish (1988), and Young (1996), I excluded possessives, numerals, demonstratives, and quantifiers, mainly due to the lack of significant interaction between these determiners and *the* and *a*. Extraneous article insertion in contexts that standardly do not require an article (e.g., *We speak the Hindi*) are also excluded but discussed briefly later.

Two sets of tokens were therefore coded: the indefinite article *a* (presence/absence) and the definite article *the* (presence/absence).[2]

In the first set, the dependent variable was the absence of the indefinite article in contexts where standard varieties of English require the overt indefinite article *a*, as shown in (3). (All examples are from the present data set.)

(3)  a.  Overt indefinite article (standard):
         I told my employees, if I am talking to <u>a customer</u> don't talk to me in Punjabi.

     b.  Null indefinite article (nonstandard):
         Then he thought, what about getting <u>Ø girl</u> [to marry] from India?

In the second set, the dependent variable was the absence of the definite article in contexts where standard varieties of English require the overt definite article *the*, as in (4).

(4)  a.  Overt definite article (standard):
         Berkeley is just like a little India, because of <u>the cosmopolitan area</u> and <u>the students</u>.

     b.  Null definite article (nonstandard):
         Here I'm not working in <u>Ø kitchen</u>. Yeah, I'm in <u>Ø front desk</u>.

Six independent internal (linguistic) variables were coded for each token. Four of these relate to the four hypotheses outlined earlier, and two—grammatical function and modification—were included to cover as wide a range of potential factors as possible.

Standard examples of each independent variable, all taken from the data, are given in (5)–(10).

(5)  Grammatical Function
     a.  <u>The future</u> is safe if you get all the things.          [subject]
     b.  My wife owns <u>the store</u>.                               [VP object]
     c.  She's very involved in <u>the community</u> here.            [PP object]

Direct and indirect verbal objects were both coded under (5b). This factor is not discussed in detail later, as the analysis does not show it to be a strongly conditioning factor.

(6) Clausal Topicality
    a. If <u>the economic situation</u> would change I'm sure     [topic]
       lot of Indian will go back.
    b. This is <u>the major problem</u> I am facing here.     [transition]
    c. He had requested for <u>a Hindi teacher</u>.     [comment]

Following Young (1996), I coded three categories of clausal topicality: the topic of the clause, the comment on the topic, and a linking or transitional term if it occurred (Dik 1978; Lambrecht 1994; Birner and Ward 1998). The transition tends not to be picked up as a new theme, once introduced, but, rather, serves a narrowing or specifying function. Wider discourse familiarity, as opposed to clausal topicality, was coded separately and is discussed below in relation to (10).

(7) Clause Position
    a. <u>The other brother</u> was working in the factory.     [initial]
    b. So that's <u>the reason</u> so many Indian family are separated. [medial]
    c. So six months I was there in <u>the kitchen</u>.     [final]

Initial clause position included all NPs that occur at the left edge of the main clause. Final position, correspondingly, included NPs at the right edge of the clause, regardless of grammatical function. The category of medial position, also from Young (1996), covers various intermediate positions.

(8) Specificity
    a. There is <u>a association</u> that can help.     [specific]
    b. My Mom is <u>a teacher</u>.     [factive]
    c. The parents will look for <u>a girl</u>.     [nonspecific]
    d. And you spend more time waiting for <u>the bus</u>.     [generic]

Rather than using a binary or ternary distinction for specificity and genericity, I followed Sankoff and Mazzie (1991) in adopting the additional category of "factive" for predicative NP constructions as in (8b), which perform neither a strictly specific function nor an entirely nonspecific function but, rather, mark category membership. Sankoff and Mazzie treat factive as a variety of nonspecific. In the present data, factive NPs patterned almost identically to specific NPs in terms of null article use and were eventually grouped with specific NPs for the analysis. Most quantified NPs, such as *a couple of people* and *a lot of Indians*, were coded as nonspecific.

(9)   Modification
    a.   I worked as <u>a bartender</u>.                               [bare]
    b.   Bihar traditionally been <u>a poor state</u>.          [modified]
    c.   It's a problem for <u>a lot of families</u>.         [quantified]

The category of "quantified" in (9c) was very broadly interpreted and included ranking adjectives (e.g., *the first N, the last N, the best N, the whole N*), quantifying phrases (e.g., *a lot of N, a few of N*), and ordinal modifiers (e.g., *the eleventh N*). These categories are grouped because their modifier either uniquely isolates the referent or quantifies the referent set. By contrast, the category of "modified" included all other adjectivally modified NPs, in which the modifier simply restricts and specifies the potential real-world referents.

(10)   Discourse Givenness
    a.   We have <u>a Shiva temple</u>.              [brand-new, BN]
    b.   And it was <u>a policy of the restaurant</u> not to hire
       anybody with beard and long hair.
       [anchored-new, BN$^A$]
    c.   And then one day, <u>the American government</u>    [unused, U]
       was calling dentist, doctor, nurses over here.
    d.   They settle down over there so they have their    [inferable, I]
       own school. <u>The professors</u> were Indian and
       everything.
    e.   Because of <u>the nature of the work</u>, I'm always    [containing
       busy.                                  inferable, I$^C$]
    f.   Some have a mentality of joining a start-up      [evoked, E]
       company. . . . If <u>the company</u> goes to public, they
       become millionaires.

For the final independent variable, I relied on Prince's (1981) Scale of Assumed Familiarity to explore a finer gradient of discourse status. NPs were classified into six degrees of discourse familiarity, exemplified in (10a–10f), based on a scale of increasing discourse familiarity for the hearer. In (10a), the NP *a Shiva temple* is brand new in the discourse: it has not been mentioned previously, and the hearer cannot anticipate it based on prior knowledge. In (10b) the new NP is anchored to a known discourse entity (*the restaurant*) and so bears a slightly greater degree of familiarity to the hearer. In (10c) *the American government* is also new but can be assumed by the speaker to be known to all participants and is thus termed "unused" by Prince (1981). In (10d) *the professors* is inferable, as it has not been previously evoked but bears some prototypical relation to a familiar entity in the discourse and can therefore be anticipated by the hearer. The construction in (10e) contrasts with (10d) only

[88]   *English in India*

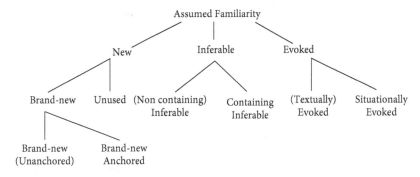

**Figure 4.3.** Taxonomy of assumed familiarity (Prince 1981).

in that the NP explicitly contains the evoked entity (*the work*) that provides the basis of the inference. Finally, in (10f), the second mention of *the company* is evoked: its referent has already been mentioned recently in the discourse and is familiar to all participants.

Based on an analysis of casual standard English speech, Prince argues that the subdivisions in Figure 4.3 form a Scale of Assumed Familiarity, shown in (11):

(11)  Scale of Assumed Familiarity (Prince 1981: 245):
      E, $E^S$ > U > I > $I^C$ > $BN^A$ > BN

Prince used this scale to account for discourse-driven choices of linguistic forms in standard English usage, such as articles, pronouns, subjects, or modifying phrases. For instance, if a discourse entity (e.g., *John*) is known to both speakers but is unused, then saying *John (U) bought a car* is felicitous, whereas *He (E) bought a car* and *A guy I know ($I^C$) bought a car* are not: *he* implies that the referent is accessible to the hearer, and *a guy I know* implies that the hearer does not know the individual in question.

Determining the givenness status of an NP is not always easy, particularly evoked, unused, or inferable NPs (Prince 1981: 244). The NP *my grandmother* could be considered inferable on the basis that individuals are known to have grandmothers, but it may also be considered unused information if the speaker and hearer both know the grandmother in question. To avoid variable coding, I only coded NPs as unused if they were culturally recognized entities such as *the yellow pages*, *the internet* or *the U.S. government*. The category of unused has relatively few tokens in the current analysis.

Another challenge is that of distance in time and discourse. The status of an NP as evoked fades as the discourse progresses, until it can become unclear as to whether the NP is still evoked. Ariel (1990) used a measure of distance to determine which parts of the discourse are still recent in the interlocutors' minds, and Lambrecht (1994) employed the notion of active (in the addressee's memory) and accessible (available but distant in discourse) discourse referents. In general, it was possible to determine from context whether an NP was active at a given time.

In order to remove other ambiguities from Prince's system, I was obliged to impose more explicit definitions on the categories of containing inferable and anchored new. I interpreted the category of containing inferable to include a number of NP structures: NPs with complementizer phrase (CP) complements (e.g., *the salesclerk that we hired*), NPs with following locatives (e.g., *the biggest market in this area*), and ellipsis NPs (e.g., *the first son was born last year and the second is . . .* ). The category of anchored new included NPs with an evoked locative (e.g., *a man in the market*), NP heads of relative clauses (e.g., *a man I know*), prepositionally modified NPs (e.g., *a problem with the suppliers*), and modified NPs relying on prior discourse knowledge (e.g., *a newer store*). Equative NP predicates, as in (9b), were classified as anchored too, since the identity of the referent is being indexed with a discourse-familiar subject; the only exceptions to this were when the construction was used with irrealis or negative meaning or when the NP was predicated of an expletive subject. In such cases, the NP was classified as brand new.

The lexical semantics of particular verbs occasionally presented coding challenges. For instance, if a speaker uses the verb *rent*, the likelihood of the following NP falling within the class of typically rented items such as real estate or vehicles is high. Nevertheless, the NP cannot be treated as strictly inferable if it is not a canonical or predictable extension of something already evoked (as is the case with *bus . . . driver*). Only NPs that were very strongly conditioned by the verb were coded as inferable; the rest were coded as new.

Finally, a wide range of NPs were excluded in both data sets based on criteria that I developed in the course of examining the data. As mentioned earlier, any contexts permitting optional article use in standard English were excluded. Proper names were excluded (e.g., *the United States, the Niagara Falls*). Articles within fixed constructions such as *most of the N, all of the N*, and *such a N*, and in adverbial uses such as *a little* and *a lot*, were also excluded, again due to the potential for these to function as fixed forms.

## 4.4. RESULTS FOR HYPOTHESES 1–3

The analysis first arranges the 12 individuals into three groups in order to keep track of linguistic behavior along different segments of the usage cline in Chapter 3. These are then grouped together for a final multivariate regression analysis of the two articles, *the* and *a*.

[90] *English in India*

Rather than dividing individuals evenly into three groups of four each, I follow the clustering of speakers according to formal and informal exposure and use that was presented in Table 3.3 in Chapter 3.

English has the lowest functional and educational level in the repertoire of three speakers: Kapil, Shalu, and Chandan (Group 1). It is used regularly as a second language among five speakers: Ronnie, Rahul, Kavita, Kishore, and Gopal (Group 2). And it is used nearly or entirely on an equal footing with other native languages for four speakers: Ram, Kumar, Sujit, and Nalin (Group 3).

### 4.4.1. Hypothesis 1: Transfer of L1 Positional Marking of Topicality

Hypothesis 1 predicted overt use of articles in unexpected or noncanonical contexts, that is, new information in initial position or old information in final position. This prediction is not confirmed.

The total $N$ values in Table 4.1 shows that IndE does follow the widespread (nearly universal, though see Mithun 1995) pattern of favoring new information in final position and old information in initial position, also in line with Lange's (2012) description of discourse prominence in IndE.[3] But crucially, there is no significant correspondence between these positions and article omission.

The only place in Table 4.1 where we see any indication of this pattern is where Group 1 has a significantly higher rate of article omission with clause-initial old information ($\chi^2$ (df = 1): 4.01, $p \leq 0.05$). However, even this isolated tendency does not support the predicted pattern of Hypothesis 1, as Group 1 does not correspondingly omit articles more with new NPs in final position, as would be expected.

***Table 4.1.*** ARTICLE OMISSION ACCORDING TO CLAUSE POSITION AND TOPICALITY OF NP

| Group | Initial/old | | Noninitial/old | | Final/new | | Nonfinal/new | |
|---|---|---|---|---|---|---|---|---|
| | $N$ | % omitted | $N$ | % omitted | $N$ | % omitted | $N$ | % omitted |
| 1 | 38 | 74% | 4 | 25% | 47 | 53% | 29 | 59% |
| 2 | 101 | 50% | 33 | 48% | 333 | 44% | 87 | 44% |
| 3 | 68 | 29% | 22 | 36% | 180 | 16% | 85 | 15% |
| Total | 207 | 47% | 59 | 42% | 560 | 36% | 201 | 34% |

*Note:* Omission with initial/noninitial old information, $\chi^2(1) = 0.46$, $p = 0.4976$; omission with final/nonfinal new information, $\chi^2(1) = 0.23$, $p = 0.6315$.

***Table 4.2.*** NULL ARTICLE USE WITH DEFINITE AND INDEFINITE NPS

| | Indefinite specific NPs | | Indefinite nonspecific NPs | | Definite NPs | |
|---|---|---|---|---|---|---|
| Group | $N$ | % omitted | $N$ | % omitted | $N$ | % omitted |
| 1 | 29 | 48% | 442 | 81% | 83 | 46% |
| 2 | 129 | 31% | 206 | 57% | 343 | 38% |
| 3 | 116 | 16% | 132 | 20% | 209 | 18% |
| Total | 274 | 27% | 380 | 47% | 635 | 33% |

*Note.* Omission with definite/indefinite NPs: $\chi^2$ (1) = 26.8, $p$ < .001.

### 4.4.2. Hypothesis 2: Transfer of L1 Form Contrasts

The first prediction of Hypothesis 2—that IndE will imitate Indian languages by only marking specific indefinites with an overt article—is supported by the data in Table 4.2. These data are illustrated separately for indefinite and definite articles in Figures 4.4 and 4.5, respectively.

Figure 4.4 shows that specific indefinite NPs, which would have an overt article in Indian languages, have significantly higher rates of overt article use than nonspecific indefinite NPs in IndE too. This distinction declines as proficiency increases but is consistent in all three groups.

Hypothesis 2 also speculated that the form *one* might be used in place of *a*. This was not supported. IndE speakers might use *one* with specific reference more than native English speakers might have, but very few instances are clearly nonstandard, as in (12).

(12)　a.　I went for a class. <u>One</u> Indian guy is there. Name is Anand. (RS)
　　　b.　Like, I had <u>one</u> big joke, you know, on that part . . . [narrative of funny experience follows] (RR)
　　　c.　There was <u>one</u> Britisher come over there. (KP)
　　　d.　First of all, the Indians have <u>one</u> distinct accent to begin with. (KK)

Platt, Weber, and Ho (1984: 56) listed this as an important transfer effect; their example was given earlier in (1). However, the far more robust quantitative pattern in the present data is the indirect transfer of function, not form, in Figure 4.4. The use of *one* may be salient and noticeable, but it is not the most robust of innovations within the system.[4]

The second part of Hypothesis 2 predicted high rates of absence of *the*, similar to high rates of absence of nonspecific *a*, due to a similar lack of an overt form in the L1s. However, Figure 4.5 (and Table 4.2) shows that omission rates for the definite article are more comparable to the lower rates of

[92]　*English in India*

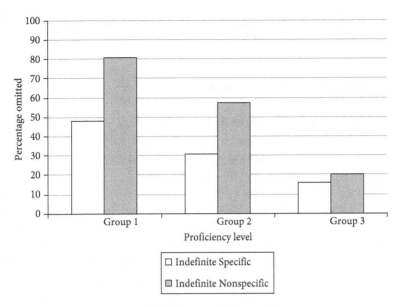

**Figure 4.4.** Percentage omission of indefinite articles by proficiency group.

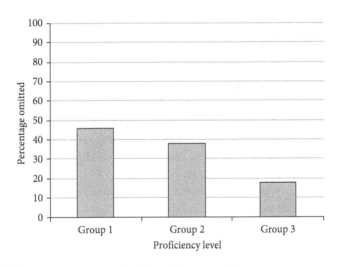

**Figure 4.5.** Percentage omission of definite articles by proficiency group.

omission of specific *a*. Neither exceeds the level of 50% absence for any proficiency group. The subprediction that the definite article will simply be absent based on Indian languages is therefore *not* supported.

This contrast between the two subpredictions is striking: Hypothesis 2 is confirmed only where the L1 has an *overt* form, namely, specific indefinites. Where a gap occurs—no definite article—we do not find a matching absence of use in IndE. The remaining hypotheses may offer an explanation for why and how English *the* is adopted and used despite absence in the L1.

### 4.4.3. Hypothesis 3: Universal Prototypes

Hypothesis 3 predicted a three-way set of universal distinctions: an overt form for [+HK, +SR], a different overt form for [−HK, +SR], and a zero form for [−HK, −SR]. Table 4.3 reports on these predicted uses, that is, overt use of two forms for the first two and null use for the third.

Groups 2 and 3 increasingly resemble the standard English system, but Group 1 does show a higher rate of omission with nonspecific and generics. However, this could be equally well accounted for by language transfer. As noted earlier, L1 transfer (Hypothesis 2) makes the same predictions for columns 2 and 3, and the standard English system makes the same predictions for columns 1 and 2, so it is very difficult to distinguish a universal prototypes prediction from substrate/superstrate outcomes. Overall, the results show little evidence of Bickerton's universal tripartite system.

In sum, none of the first three hypotheses are strongly confirmed aside from one part of Hypothesis 2: transfer of the specific/nonspecific distinction in Indian L1s to IndE use of the indefinite article *a*.

## 4.5. RESULTS FOR HYPOTHESIS 4

In this section, I consider Hypothesis 4, namely, whether universally available information about the status of referents in ongoing discourse influences IndE speakers' choices of articles. The analysis avoids the simplistic binary treatment of clausal discourse status used in Hypothesis 1 (see Chesterman 1991:39 for a critique) in favor of a more fine-grained model of relative familiarity of a referent as discourse unfolds.

***Table 4.3.*** ARTICLE USE ACCORDING TO PREDICTED UNIVERSAL TRIPARTITE SYSTEM

| Group | Overt *the* with definite NP | | Overt *a* with specific indefinite NPs | | Null article with nonspecific/generic NPs | |
|---|---|---|---|---|---|---|
| | *n* | % overt | *n* | % overt | *n* | % null |
| 1 | 72 | 56% | 29 | 52% | 53 | 75% |
| 2 | 248 | 60% | 129 | 69% | 301 | 50% |
| 3 | 193 | 81% | 116 | 84% | 148 | 19% |
| Total | 513 | 67% | 274 | 73% | 502 | 43% |

[94]   *English in India*

### 4.5.1. Modeling Givenness

As noted, definiteness is broadly concerned with the relative identifiability or givenness of a referent in discourse (Lambrecht 1994; Lyons 1999). Articles frequently begin their life as demonstratives or topic markers—highly discourse linked, deictic elements—which gradually grammaticalize toward more fixed grammatical usage (Greenberg 1978; Givón 1984; Lyons 1999). This can happen to different degrees; for instance, while English has not extended the definite article to proper nouns or plural generics, Greek uses it with the former, and French with the latter (Trenkic 2001: 109).

When we look at the use of the definite article in New Englishes, one possible source of variation is the resurfacing of these discursive origins, as nonnative speakers "undo" historically grammaticalized functions and favor a more transparent, discourse-linked association of form and meaning.

Hypothesis 4 explores whether the relative givenness of an entity in ongoing discourse, rather than more strictly conventionalized rules, governs article use in IndE. The models of particular interest are therefore those that treat identifiability as scalar and distinguish among several types or degrees of definiteness or givenness, such as Givón (1984), Hawkins (1978), and Prince (1981). The suitability of these more fine-grained taxonomies for the study of nonstandard article variation has been noted elsewhere too (Sankoff and Mazzie 1991; Y. Kachru 2003).

Prince's Scale of Assumed Familiarity, introduced earlier in Figure 4.3, has a number of advantages for the present analysis. It focuses on discourse entities (or NPs), and so it can be applied directly to the question of article use; it appeals to universal discourse principles and thus represents, in an L2 situation, an alternative potential universal influence to Bickerton's prototypes; and it makes implicational predictions for how discourse entities at different levels of the scale will relate to types of linguistic expressions.[5]

Standard examples of each type of discourse reference in Prince's model were given in (10). Examples of null article use for each type, also from the present IndE data set, are given in (13).

(13)  a.  Brand New        (BN)    We decided to rent Ø apartment.
      b.  Anchored New     (BN^A)  They speak Ø different kind of English.
      c.  Unused           (U)     You can browse through Ø internet.
      d.  Inferable        (I)     He has one son and Ø second is on the way.
      e.  Containing       (I^C)   From Ø first year of birth until . . .
          Inferable
      f.  Evoked           (E)     In tenth the medium was English. After that I took science. Ø Medium was English.

**Table 4.4.** NULL ARTICLE USE ACCORDING TO FAMILIARITY STATUS OF NP

| | BN | | BN$^A$ | | I$^C$ | | I | | E | |
|---|---|---|---|---|---|---|---|---|---|---|
| Group | N | % omitted | N | % omitted | N | % omitted | N | % omitted | N | % omitted |
| 1 | 11 | 36% | 15 | 53% | 13 | 46% | 50 | 40% | 11 | 73% |
| 2 | 29 | 7% | 87 | 34% | 62 | 35% | 126 | 37% | 57 | 60% |
| 3 | 42 | 5% | 73 | 22% | 74 | 8% | 81 | 17% | 23 | 43% |
| Total | 82 | 10% | 175 | 31% | 149 | 23% | 257 | 32% | 91 | 57% |

*Note.* Combined total $\chi^2(4) = 51.52$, $p < .001$.

Prince's scale underpins the Standard English article system to some extent: definite articles are associated with E, I$^C$, I, and U, and indefinite articles are mainly associated with BN$^A$ and BN.

In standard varieties of English, the scale relates to which article is used, not whether articles are omitted. Discourse-based article omission is not wholly absent in standard usage but tends to be very restricted to subjects in informal registers, typically definites (e.g., *Last film* I *watched was Star Wars* or *Guy* *didn't even blink*) or conventionalized indefinites (*Man* *walks into a bar*). The articles of NPs in object position are not omissible in standard English, whether definite (**I told** *man* *that the shop was closed*) or indefinite (*A lady wants* *gift* *for 3-year-old*).

The results in Table 4.4 show that IndE extends Prince's Scale of Assumed Familiarity to variable omission of articles. The analysis that follows will show that this is irrespective of the grammatical function of the NP.[6]

As Figure 4.6 shows, omission of articles *the* and *a* increases overall relative to the familiarity status of the NP. In all three proficiency groups, brand new NPs have the lowest rates of article omission, and evoked NPs have the highest rates of article omission. The intermediate categories of Prince's model—anchored new, inferable, and containing inferable—group together at equivalent, intermediate levels of article omission.

Overall, Figure 4.6 indicates that IndE may be using overt articles for purposes of discourse disambiguation, rather than as strictly grammaticalized forms. As before with the L1 specificity effect (Hypothesis 2i), the pattern holds across all three groups, indicating a degree of stability in IndE usage regardless of proficiency level.

The example in (14) illustrates this new, pragmatically motivated system. This single narrative was presented in Mishra (1982) as part of an entirely unrelated analysis of IndE prosody, making its conformity to the present proposal all the more striking.

[96]   *English in India*

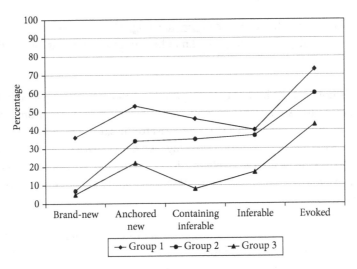

**Figure 4.6.** Omission of articles according to relative givenness.

(14) (from Mishra 1982: 58)

When I had completed the training, ten day training at the language school, and you know that what happened there, there was another week for the vacation. And during that vacation I contacted the union and union person contacted his representative at the school. And that representative contacted the headmaster and headmaster had contacted the authority. But before that instance in the morning, first day of the term, I had met him and told him that I'm worried.

| | |
|---|---|
| When I had completed <u>the training</u>, | I |
| <u>Ø ten day training</u> at the language school | E |
| | |
| and you know that what happened there there | I |
| was another week for <u>the vacation</u> | |
| and during <u>that vacation</u> | E |
| | |
| I contacted <u>the union</u> | I |
| and <u>Ø union person</u> | I$^C$ |
| | |
| contacted <u>his representative</u> at the school | I$^C$ |
| and <u>that representative</u> | E |
| | |
| contacted <u>the headmaster</u> | I |
| and <u>Ø headmaster</u> had contacted the authority | E |

THE ARTICLE SYSTEM [97]

but before that instance in <u>the morning</u>,      I

Ø <u>first day of the term</u>, I had met him and told him that I'm    E

worried.

What is noteworthy here is the exceptionless alternation between overt definite determiners *the* or *his* with inferables (I and I<sup>C</sup>), and either omission or *that* with subsequent evoked (E) references to the same entity.

The shorter examples in (15) from my own data show a similar alternation, such that a new or inferable referent includes the requisite article, following which an evoked or inferable (in the case of 15c and 15e) reference to the previous referent omits the article.

(15)    a.    I don't like <u>the climate</u>. Ø <u>Climate</u> too much cold.      [M1Lcal]

      b.    It was <u>a very small town</u> I used to live. So you had      [F2Lcal]
           to migrate to Ø <u>other town</u> for, like, after the
           seventh grade.

      c.    Somehow he thought ki [that] if I'm marrying <u>a</u>      [M5Hcal]
           <u>girl</u>, she should support him that I should continue
           enjoying my music. And then he thought, what
           about getting Ø <u>girl</u> from India?

      d.    So in tenth, <u>the medium</u> English. After that I took      [M7Hcal]
           science. Ø <u>Medium</u> is English.

      e.    They refer for <u>the credit history</u>. Where they don't      [M6Hcal]
           have Ø <u>credit history</u>, there I'm not getting <u>the credit</u>
           <u>card</u>. So now I have to go for Ø <u>secured credit card</u>.

These examples illustrate the importance of discourse status for article omission, but they also point to other potential factors such as the presence of modifiers (e.g., 15e) and subject position (e.g., 15a and 15d). In the final step of this analysis, multivariate analysis assesses the relative influence of these factors simultaneously.

### 4.5.2. Multivariate Analysis of Article Omission

This chapter has found an L1 transfer effect (specificity marking) as well as a more universal discourse identifiability effect on IndE article omission. But so far these have been reported independently. Multivariate analysis is needed to verify whether these are indeed the most influential of a range of factors.

As noted, the three proficiency groups showed parallel patterns (just different levels) for the specificity effect and the discourse effect and so are combined here. I separate regression analyses of definite and indefinite articles, as

[98]    *English in India*

there may be instances in which a factor is relevant for one but not the other. Table 4.5 presents results for omission of the definite article and Table 4.6 for omission of the indefinite article.

The statistical software package Goldvarb (Rousseau and Sankoff 1978) was used in the original analysis reported here.[7] Since the stepwise regression takes into account the relative effect of all the other factors, the best indicator of the strength of a factor in each table is the column containing factor weights. The relative magnitude of the weight relates to the relative strength of the effect of that factor on the dependent variable: a value below .5 indicates that the factor in question favors overt use of the article, and a value greater than .5 means that the given factor favors omission of the article. The independent factors in Table 4.5 and Table 4.6 are ordered according to their relative influence on the dependent variable. Values that were not found to be statistically significant are in brackets. The input value, or input probability, listed at the bottom of each table refers to the average probability that a rule will apply; thus, for instance, a weighting of more than .5 in Table 4.5 indicates that a null article will occur with a greater frequency than 0.275.

Both analyses confirm the importance of discourse givenness in the restructured article system. The predicted ordering of sublevels of this factor are perfectly replicated in both results, strongly confirming the effect of Prince's Scale of Familiarity.

Both tables also show the importance of one further factor—type of modification in the NP. In fact, this factor supports the wider givenness effect, as it similarly suggests that NPs with unambiguous discourse reference can drop their article more readily. As modifiers and quantifiers help the listener to identify a referent from a possible set, these should render the article even more redundant and therefore more omissible. This is precisely the pattern found.

Finally, the L1 transfer effect of specificity only arises for the indefinite article (Table 4.6), which is not surprising, as this is the article in which specificity distinctions arise. The added detail of high rates of article omission with generics in Table 4.6 may be related to a separate type of L1 transfer, namely, noun incorporation of generic objects in Indo-Aryan systems (cf. Mithun 1986; Wee and Ansaldo 2004).

## 4.6. DISCUSSION: PRAGMATIC REANALYSIS IN CONTACT SETTINGS

The analysis has revealed a very coherent system shared across the cline of IndE speakers. A reliance on isolated examples, as earlier in (2), wrongly suggests that IndE speakers simply recreate their L1 systems in English. The new

**Table 4.5.** MULTIVARIATE REGRESSION RESULTS FOR OMISSION OF DEFINITE ARTICLE

| Variable | Tokens (*n*) | Null (*n*) | Null (%) | Factor weight |
|---|---|---|---|---|
| Givenness: | | | | |
| Evoked | 102 | 58 | 57% | .779 |
| Unused | 54 | 18 | 33% | .589 |
| Inferable | 323 | 98 | 30% | .449 |
| Cont. inferable | 156 | 34 | 22% | .371 |
| Range | — | — | — | 408 |
| Modification: | | | | |
| Quantified | 100 | 51 | 51% | .774 |
| Modified | 127 | 58 | 46% | .654 |
| Bare | 408 | 99 | 24% | .378 |
| Range | — | — | — | 396 |
| Clause position: | | | | |
| Initial | 220 | 97 | 44% | .683 |
| Medial | 146 | 33 | 23% | .471 |
| Final | 269 | 78 | 29% | .362 |
| Range | — | — | — | 321 |
| Clausal topicality: | | | | |
| Rheme | 263 | 83 | 32% | .597 |
| Theme | 210 | 87 | 41% | .453 |
| Transition | 162 | 38 | 23% | .403 |
| Range | — | — | — | 194 |
| Grammatical function: | | | | |
| Subject | 203 | 89 | 44% | [.582] |
| Verbal object | 182 | 47 | 26% | [.466] |
| Prep. object | 250 | 72 | 29% | [.457] |
| Range | — | — | — | 125 |
| Specificity: | | | | |
| Generic | 122 | 41 | 34% | [.546] |
| Specific | 513 | 167 | 33% | [.489] |
| Range | — | — | — | 57 |

*Note.* Input value: .275; significance threshold: .05; values in brackets are nonsignificant.

system does arise due to a conflict between the speaker's language systems, but the resulting grammar goes beyond the contributing systems.

Where an overt form exists in the L1 (indefinite article), we do see direct L1 transfer restructuring the L2. However, where none exists (definite article), systematic pragmatic inferencing by speakers plays an important role in the

***Table 4.6.*** MULTIVARIATE REGRESSION RESULTS FOR OMISSION
OF INDEFINITE ARTICLE

| Variable | Tokens (*n*) | Null (*n*) | Null (%) | Factor weight |
|---|---|---|---|---|
| Modification: | | | | |
| Quantified | 122 | 84 | 69% | .818 |
| Modified | 228 | 80 | 35% | .489 |
| Bare | 304 | 86 | 28% | .361 |
| Range | — | — | — | 457 |
| Givenness: | | | | |
| Inferable | 68 | 46 | 68% | .804 |
| Anchored-new | 313 | 135 | 43% | .544 |
| Brand-new | 273 | 69 | 25% | .365 |
| Range | — | — | — | 439 |
| Specificity: | | | | |
| Generic | 14 | 13 | 93% | .971 |
| Nonspecific | 366 | 164 | 45% | .564 |
| Factive | 183 | 56 | 31% | .397 |
| Specific | 91 | 17 | 19% | .325 |
| Range | — | — | — | 646 |
| Clausal topicality: | | | | |
| Theme | 56 | 36 | 64% | .735 |
| Rheme | 498 | 185 | 37% | .502 |
| Transition | 100 | 29 | 29% | .354 |
| Range | — | — | — | 381 |
| Grammatical function: | | | | |
| Subject | 29 | 20 | 69% | [.633] |
| Verbal Object | 504 | 191 | 38% | [.506] |
| Prep. Object | 121 | 39 | 32% | [.443] |
| Range | — | — | — | 190 |
| Clause position: | | | | |
| Final | 400 | 156 | 39% | [.527] |
| Medial | 213 | 70 | 33% | [.472] |
| Initial | 41 | 24 | 59% | [.383] |
| Range | — | — | — | 144 |

*Note.* Input value: .345; significance threshold: .05; values in brackets are nonsignificant.

new, optimized usage. This represents an innovative third system—neither standard English nor Indo-Aryan—based on speaker inferences and universally available discourse solutions to L1-L2 structural clashes in the context of limited target input.

This analysis was originally presented in 2005, and a number of contemporaneous and subsequent studies have replicated and contextualized these findings. Here, I first discuss some closely related findings—five studies focused on IndE and several more on other Englishes—and then return to the overarching theme of pragmatic restructuring.

### 4.6.1. Corroboration across Studies

In a much earlier, pedagogically motivated study of IndE, Agnihotri, Khanna, and Mukherjee (1984) found that articles are more frequently omitted when adjectives are present and when an NP includes a superlative quantifier. No clear explanation was given in their discussion, but those results are accounted for by the present analysis.

Sedlatschek (2009: 203) investigated article omission in a subcorpus of written IndE in essays by schoolchildren—a corpus of intermediate proficiency comparable to the present Group 2—and found a rate of omission of definite articles of 38.9%, almost identical to the result in Figure 4.5.[8] The rate of omission of indefinite articles in the subcorpus was lower than in the present study, at 23.5%. But this figure may also correspond very closely to the present findings if specific and nonspecific indefinites were to be separated. Sedlatschek cites the role of NP familiarity and modification from Sharma (2005b) in reporting on his data, and his example in (16) is remarkably similar to the example given earlier in (14).

(16)     Man first lived in a part of land, that land became his home, his
         home made <u>a village</u>, <u>Ø village</u> made <u>a city</u> and <u>Ø city</u> made a country.
         (Sedlatschek 2009: 205)

Balasubramanian (2009: 165–177) also finds higher rates of omission with ordinal modifiers and quantifiers as opposed to unmodified NPs, a pattern accounted for by the present analysis.

George (2010) replicated Sharma (2005b) in evaluating a small corpus of IndE in an online discussion forum and found that Prince's category of evoked entities showed the highest rates of omission. He also found, as in the present study, that not all of Prince's categories were equally distinct.

Hundt (2014) also replicated part of Sharma (2005b) in examining the English of the Indo-Fijian diaspora and similarly confirmed both the higher rate of omission of nonspecific indefinite articles (L1 effect) and a clear effect of modification type (universal pragmatic restructuring).

Sand (2004) finds no significant substrate-driven under- or overuse of articles in eight varieties but does find more substrate-like use of articles in spontaneous conversation segments and lower use of definite and indefinite

[102]   *English in India*

articles among lower proficiency writers in the ICE-India corpus. (Pragmatic/ semantic categories are not separated in the study, which may mask some comparable patterns of article omission.)

Finally, a few studies of other New Englishes have also confirmed specifically that givenness in discourse can encourage omission of articles (e.g., Xhosa English, Siebers 2007; Malaysian English, Wahid 2009). Chapter 8 will extend these comparisons by showing parallels in SgE as well.

The capacity for discourse-familiar entities to shed their articles has been noted in a number of studies of SLA (e.g., Tarone and Parrish 1988; Young 1996; Robertson 2000; Jarvis 2002; Goad and White 2004; Trenkic 2007; Ionin et al. 2008; see also Trenkic and Pongpairoj 2013 for an interesting alternative account based on salience sensitivity). Jarvis (2002: 416) observes that

> [i]n the Finns' data, on the other hand, the use of Ø probably does not represent a simplified register as much as it represents the L1 Finnish convention of avoiding (what Finns perceive to be) redundant markers of definiteness and indefiniteness when these properties of an NP are already salient in a given discourse context.

He cites Givón's description of the relatively greater burden on processing of newer information, a factor that appears to be strongly reflected in the present data as well: "more continuous, predictable, nondisruptive topics will be marked by less marking material; while less continuous, unpredictable/surprising, or disruptive topics will be marked by more marking material" (Givón 1984: 126).

In relation to Spanish-English bilinguals, Klein (1980: 77) observed that "the actual choice between the more precise and the less precise alternatives . . . should be determined by pragmatic strategies based on relative need for precision." Klein and Perdue (1992: 311) also argued that individuals with different L1s have a basic variety at one stage of learning "which seems to represent a natural equilibrium between the various phrasal, semantic, and pragmatic constraints." This integral role of pragmatics also echoes Tarone and Parrish's (1988) finding that articles with referential definites were employed with greater native-like accuracy in narrative genres due to the greater communicative burden of precise and efficient reference.

Studies of Creoles have also found null marking with definites, contrary to Bickerton's universal bioprogram prediction that null marking will be associated with generics (Hypothesis 3 earlier). Bruyn (1995: 73) notes this for Sranan, and Sankoff and Mazzie (1991: 7) observe the pattern in Tok Pisin. They cite very early work by Corne (1977: 14) who, for Seychelles Creole, also noted that definite nouns may be unmarked "when no ambiguity is possible."[9]

Together, this body of work points to a robust system of discourse-based restructuring (and a narrow specificity effect from overt L1 morphology) in article use in IndE and in other learner and postcolonial varieties. In a separate body of work in SLA theory, work on the interface hypothesis has similarly suggested that bilinguals resort to discourse-based solutions to ease processing difficulties caused by featural conflict between their two languages. This is discussed in Chapter 9.

### 4.6.2. Implications: Contact Varieties and Discourse-Driven Restructuring

The first general implication of this is that, rather than acting as opposing forces or hypotheses, language transfer and universals can establish a complementary "feeding" relationship. In the present case, the existence of an overt specific article in individuals' L1s exerts a strong influence on the use of the English indefinite article, but discursively available pragmatic principles help to reorganize the subparts of the system that lack an explicit L1 model, for example, the use of English *the*.

These findings dovetail with the view that contact Englishes should "no longer [be] seen as 'slaves' of their mother tongues, passively and indiscriminately mapping structures from their first language onto a target language" (Lange 2012: 238), particularly where extensive multilingualism means that several substrate systems may co-occur in a single individual.

Lange (2012) identifies numerous distinct constructions that all point to a privileging of discourse prominence and topic continuity by Indian speakers, together giving rise to "a pan-Indian syntax of discourse organization" (p. 243). She argues that this does not derive from narrow substrate effects, even if elements of L1 and sprachbund influence can be identified in supporting this overall restructuring.

Sankoff (1983: 245) similarly cited the crucial role of agentive exploitation of linguistic contrast for discourse purposes by nonstandard users of a language:

> It has been proposed that creolization involves people generating linguistic rules for which they have no evidence in the input. I suggest that what people do is reanalyze "grammatical" input that is generated "discursively"—as the insertion of *pas* redundantly and emphatically in negative sentences in French was originally a discourse strategy that later became grammaticalized. The same sorts of strategies arise over and over in language, as people hit on the same solutions to their expressive problems, but rarely do these innovations become institutionalized—both first and second language learners must eventually conform to the preexisting norms of the languages they are learning. The genesis of both pidgins and creoles has taken place under conditions where the innovative

[104]  *English in India*

strategies do get more of a chance to survive, because they are not competing in the same way with existing rules.

New Englishes share with Creoles this widespread absence of native target norms, permitting a stabilization of discursive solutions.

This need not imply a pure discourse effect, such that the L1 languages are irrelevant. The shift to an economical, discourse-driven system is often triggered by the existence of L1-L2 differences (Jarvis 2002: 414), a lack of sufficient input to acquire a complex system, and the need to reduce processing difficulty.

The next chapter moves to another major grammatical domain—tense and aspect. Once again, we will see that L1-L2 differences and speaker inferencing give rise to a new third grammar in IndE.

# CHAPTER 5
# The Verbal System

Chapter 4 outlined clear evidence of language transfer in New Englishes but also showed that it cannot explain everything. Additional mechanisms, particularly pragmatic inferencing, intervene under specific conditions to give rise to new grammars that are distinctive in some ways from both input systems.

This chapter evaluates the same two sources of change—L1 transfer and speaker inferencing—in a different grammatical domain: the marking of verbal tense, modality, and aspect (TMA) in Indian English (IndE).

I first describe general properties of TMA systems in Indo-Aryan languages, once again with Hindi as the sample language, and then explore the extent to which this system arises in the English used by Indian bilinguals. I also consider competing universalist proposals such as the influence of inherent lexical aspect on the use of overt morphology. The chapter analyzes four dimensions of the TMA system of IndE: omission of past tense marking, use of progressive *-ing,* the perfect construction, and the use of modal verbs.

The chapter integrates earlier work (Sharma 2001, 2009; Sharma and Deo 2010) and new analysis to find, as in Chapter 4, substantial evidence of substrate influence but, again, not always with a complete replication of the substrate system. Instead, exactly as with article use in Chapter 4, we will see that mismatches between the L1 and L2 in certain parts of the system can lead to speakers *inferring* a typologically distinct and innovative grammar.

Chapter 3 showed that nonstandard TMA features arise across the usage cline of IndE. Omission of past tense was a learner-like trait, declining rapidly in use across the cline and only found among less proficient English speakers. By contrast, innovative uses of the progressive, the perfect, and modals were found to all be more stable dialect-like features shared across the entire cline.

---

*From Deficit to Dialect.* Devyani Sharma, Oxford University Press. © Oxford University Press 2023.
DOI: 10.1093/oso/9780195307504.003.0005

In this chapter I describe the novel tense-aspect system of IndE, and in Part II (Chapters 8 and 9), I use a comparison with SgE to account for why these features are distributed differently across the usage cline.

## 5.1. DIFFERENCES BETWEEN HINDI AND ENGLISH

In any language, a finite clause involves both an eventuality (a situation or event) with a specific location in time and a particular viewpoint on that eventuality adopted by the speaker. Tense morphology specifies the former kind of information, and aspectual morphology specifies the latter. Perfective aspect views situations as completed or temporally bounded, and imperfective aspect denotes the internal structure of situations rather than their boundedness (Comrie 1976).

Tense and aspect are both present in all languages, but languages differ in whether they mark these with overt verbal morphology. For example, clausal perfectivity can be conveyed simply by the inherent lexical aspect of a verb (i.e., telic verbs that contain an endpoint, such as *complete, build, dismantle*, and *drown*), by additional grammatical aspect markers (e.g., perfective morphology that imposes a bounded viewpoint on any predicate, such as Hindi *-(y)a*), or perfectivizing adverbials (e.g., *in two minutes*).

Verbal morphology in English focuses primarily on temporal location of events (tense), not on the perspective a speaker takes on those events (aspect). The main overt verbal morphology in English indicates past tense, and secondarily progressive aspect. Table 5.1 shows that English past tense marking is used consistently across both perfective and imperfective predicates. English has no morphological markers to distinguish perfective and imperfective aspect; it only has a narrow progressive marker, within aspect marking. (The English perfect construction *have washed* is distinct and discussed here and is addressed later.)

By contrast, Indo-Aryan languages are aspect oriented. They obligatorily mark perfective, imperfective, or progressive aspect with overt morphology in a clause, in addition to marking tense. Table 5.2 illustrates this system for Hindi, the primary Indo-Aryan substrate for IndE. It shows that, unlike the

***Table 5.1.*** MORPHOLOGICAL TENSE-ASPECT MARKERS
IN STANDARD ENGLISH

| | | Imperfective | |
|---|---|---|---|
| Tense | Perfective | Nonprogressive | Progressive |
| PRESENT | finish-*es* | wash-*es* | is wash-*ing* |
| PAST | wash-*ed* | wash-*ed* | was wash-*ing* |

**Table 5.2.** MORPHOLOGICAL TENSE-ASPECT MARKERS IN HINDI

| | | Imperfective | |
|---|---|---|---|
| Tense | Perfective | Nonprogressive | Progressive |
| PRESENT | — | dho-*t*-a hai | dho *raha* hai |
| PAST | dho-*ya* | dho-*t*-a thha | dho *raha* thha |

[*dho* 'wash,' *hai* 'is,' *thha* 'was']

English system in Table 5.1, Hindi verbal morphology aligns consistently with aspectual distinctions (columns) rather than tense (rows).

The three primary native languages of speakers in the current study (Hindi, Punjabi, Gujarati) are similar in terms of tense-aspect parameters relevant to this discussion: they all inflect obligatorily for imperfective or perfective using reflexes of the original Sanskrit participles, and they all mark progressive with an auxiliary verb comparable to Hindi *rahna* ('stay') (Masica 1991: 292–302).[1] I therefore again list only Hindi as a representative substrate system in the analysis.

The difference in tense orientation and aspect orientation in Tables 5.1 and 5.2 is substantial: in their use of TMA morphology, English speakers focus primarily on the temporal location of an eventuality, not its boundedness properties. So, a past tense English sentence such as *He washed the car* is neutral with respect to completion of the activity. This is not possible in Hindi, which requires the speaker to indicate completion (*dhoya*), progressivity (*dho raha thha*), or habituality/stativity (*dhota thha*). The one point of surface similarity in the two languages is the presence of a form for progressive aspect but, as will be shown, even this form is not equivalent.

IndE speakers are therefore a useful case study for contact effects in the domain of tense-aspect. Their L1 primes them to be sensitive to perfectivity distinctions, but these distinctions are absent in the verbal morphology of English. Do speakers adapt English forms to recreate their L1 perfectivity marking, or do they default to a natural, universally unmarked system in the face of this structural clash?

Before outlining hypotheses, I note two further differences in the TMA systems of the two languages: the perfect construction and modality.

The English perfect construction indicates anteriority relative to a specific point in time under consideration, a deictic zero point (Comrie 1976: 53; Binnick 1991: 161; Bybee et al. 1994: 55). The past perfect is generally used to refer to an event that occurred before a particular point in the past, but with relevance to that past point, and the present perfect refers to a past event with continuing relevance to the present. Comrie (1976: 53) thus suggests that the English perfect—whether in the past, present, or future—relates to two time

[108] *English in India*

points while simple tenses such as past or present refer to just one, with no implication that it bears a necessary relation to others. For this reason, the English perfect is often treated as a tense type (related to temporal order) and not an aspectual type (related to the composition of an eventuality).

Cross-linguistically, constructions like the English perfect often grammaticalize to convey simple past reference, losing the condition of continuing relevance, for example, in French *Elle a lu le livre* (Comrie 1976; Dahl 1985). Comrie (1976: 61) notes that such shifts in the function of the perfect construction, as seen in many Romance languages, result from the gradual relaxation of such requirements as degree of recentness and presence of adverbials.

Hindi has a perfect-like construction—formed with *be* rather than *have*—that shows evidence of this cross-linguistically common "relaxed" semantic range (Snell and Weightman 2003: 137; Katenina 1960, cited in Dahl 1985: 147). This Hindi past perfect can be used to indicate relative anteriority (as in English, see 1a below), but also simple anteriority relative to the present as well as remote past or completive (see 1b and 1c below).

(1)   a.   Past perfect meaning:
>       vah   vahan   do     din    pahle   gayii        thhi
>       she   there   two    days   earlier go.PAST-FEM  be.PAST-FEM
>       'She had gone there two days earlier.'

  b.   Present perfect meaning:
>       aaj    se     pehle  yah    kabhi      nahii  hua         thha
>       today  from   before this   sometime   never  happen.     be. PAST-
>                                                      PAST-MASC   MASC
>       'This has never happened before today.'

  c.   Remote past or completive meaning:
>       main  chhuttii  mein    Dehradun   gayii        thhi
>       i     holiday   during  Dehradun   go.PAST-FEM  be. PAST-FEM
>       'I went to Dehradun during my holidays.'

Some Dravidian languages also show an extension of the perfect construction to past meaning. These languages are not a major substrate for the present study, but the same implications of transfer to IndE are explicitly noted by Sridhar (1990: 229):

> [I]t is worth noting that the present perfect form is used in Kannada in some of those contexts where the simple past would be appropriate in some languages such as English. This leads to the very common use by Kannada speakers of English of sentences such as *I have bought the book yesterday* for *I bought the book yesterday*.

Finally, English modal verbs are markedly different from Indo-Aryan modal verbs. In Indo-Aryan languages, modal verbs typically show full grammatical agreement, unlike the defective paradigm of English modals, which do not behave like main verbs syntactically (Bhatt et al. 2011). The analysis in this chapter is limited to *will* and *would*, the semantics of which are discussed later. These forms have no parallel in Indo-Aryan systems, as most of the meanings relevant to these two modals (future, habitual, subjunctive, conditional) are marked by verbal inflections.

## 5.2. PREDICTED TYPES OF GRAMMATICAL CHANGE

The core hypotheses to be tested are those that predict direct transfer from Indo-Aryan systems for four TMA forms or constructions in English: past tense, progressive, perfect, and modals. These predictions are outlined below. Alternative universalist predictions are considered alongside these.

> **Hypothesis 1** (Transfer of L1 perfective meaning to English past tense morphology):
>
> IndE speakers will restrict the use of past tense marking to perfective contexts.

This prediction is based on the broad differences noted earlier between orientation to tense (English) and to aspect (Hindi). Indo-Aryan languages also indicate past tense, so they may acquire the form accurately, but the above hypothesis predicts that their additional obligatory marking of perfectivity may lead to a search for an equivalent to that form, and the past tense marker would be the only candidate for this function.

> **Hypothesis 2** (Transfer of L1 imperfective meanings to English progressive):
>
> a. IndE speakers will acquire the English progressive form accurately.
> b. IndE speakers will extend the progressive to other imperfective categories.

Since Hindi has a distinct progressive form, as does English, there may not be a significant L1-L2 mismatch. Instead, Hindi speakers might experience reinforcement, or positive transfer, matching the meaning of the Hindi progressive to the English progressive -*ing*, and acquiring the form accurately (Hypothesis 2a). However, they may have difficulty in finding a suitable equivalent for the additional, obligatory Hindi imperfective marker, as there is no parallel in English. This may lead to overgeneralization of the only available form, *-ing*, to all imperfective contexts (Hypothesis 2b).

An alternative to Hypotheses 1 and 2 is that universal or natural cognitive preferences for aspect marking will surface in contact situations. The most well-established proposal is that lexical aspect—the inherent aspect of a verb—will influence morphological choice in predictable ways regardless of the grammatical systems involved (Andersen and Shirai 1996). In particular, telic predicates (those with an intrinsic temporal endpoint) will be more likely to attract overt past tense morphology than atelic predicates (situations or states with no intrinsic endpoint). Under this view, progressive morphology is not predicted to be overextended to statives; it is expected to be naturally associated with activity verbs and incompatible with stativity. Details are provided later, in Section 5.3.3. These universalist hypotheses will be tested alongside the above transfer hypotheses.[2]

We can propose two further transfer predictions for the domain of TMA. With regard to the English past perfect construction, we predict a transfer of Indo-Aryan semantics, as outlined in Hypothesis 3.

> **Hypothesis 3** (Transfer of L1 extended perfect meanings to the English past perfect):
>
> IndE speakers will generalize the English past perfect construction to remote past and present perfect meanings.

Again, an alternative prediction here is that a universal semantic/pragmatic tendency to generalize will encourage a shift to a French-like system in contact settings. Indeed, shifts in the use of past perfect toward simple past meaning have been observed independently in other dialects of English with no substrate explanation (e.g., in African-American Vernacular English, Rickford and Rafal 1996). Once again, the analysis will consider the possibility that IndE usage may derive from universal semantic properties and reanalysis rather than substrate structures.

Finally, there is no specific transfer-based hypothesis for the modals *will* and *would* other than reduced usage, due to absence of a parallel in the L1. Non-transfer-based restructuring will also be explored.

> **Hypothesis 4** (Transfer of meanings for *will* and *would*):
>
> The modals *will* and *would* will be underused.

Hypotheses 1 and 4 involve a narrowing of usage of English forms, on analogy with L1 equivalents, while Hypotheses 2 and 3 involve a widening of English usage, based on L1 meanings that cover a wider range of constructions.

The analysis that follows integrates several earlier studies to present a unified description and explanation of IndE TMA use, with a focus on whether L1 transfer accounts for what we find.

## 5.3. METHODOLOGY

I briefly review here the use of data from the 24 speakers in the complete data set, along with details of data coding and analytic approach.

### 5.3.1. Data

Of the four features being studied, only omission of past marking occurs exclusively in the lower proficiency part of the IndE continuum (see Chapter 3). The data used in analyzing Hypothesis 1 are therefore only from the 12 less English-dominant individuals, those who exhibit some degree of omission of past tense marking. For the remaining three features, I consider the whole continuum of IndE speakers and highlight proficiency-linked differences where relevant.

Naturalistic sociolinguistic interviews are useful in studying TMA, as they allow for a wide range of past reference types, including remote past and habituality. In one case, for the past perfect construction, I rely on additional corpus data due to low numbers of tokens in the interview data set. The three parallel corpora used for this are the Kolhapur Corpus of Indian English, the Brown Corpus of present-day American English, and the Lancaster-Oslo/Bergen (LOB) Corpus of present-day British English (Sharma 2001).[3]

### 5.3.2. Analytic Approach for Four Hypotheses

To examine past tense use in IndE (Hypothesis 1), I first identify all instances of past time semantic reference in the data and then note whether past tense is overtly marked for each token. To determine whether the Hindi effect of sentential aspect (perfective or imperfective) or the universal effect of lexical aspect (verbal semantics) is stronger, I code for these two kinds of aspect. In a more detailed analysis (Sharma and Deo 2010), further factors were included. These are reported on briefly in Section 5.4.

To examine the progressive (Hypothesis 2), I similarly identify all instances of *-ing,* and then code these for the presence or absence of wider Hindi-like imperfective semantics. Because Hypothesis 2b predicts *over*generalization (unlike the *under*use predicted in Hypothesis 1 for past tense), it is necessary to use the reverse analytic method: instead of starting with a meaning and

[112]   *English in India*

checking for the choice of form, as in Hypothesis 1, I first identify all instances of overt progressive forms and then examine their aspectual meanings. This is also necessary because the progressive is optional in many contexts in standard English (e.g., *She's working there / She works there*), so it is impossible to identify all obligatory progressive reference contexts, as can be done for past tense use.

To examine the use of the perfect construction (Hypothesis 3), I similarly identify all past perfect constructions in the data and then code them for Hindi-like extended semantic meaning. As noted, this involved a very low total token count, and so the analysis is bolstered with corpus data.

Finally, to examine the use of modals *will/would* (Hypothesis 4), I again conduct a simple quantitative analysis of the frequency of these forms, along with their semantic and pragmatic associations across the cline of speakers.

It is worth noting that all four cases involve close analysis of divergent meanings, not just frequencies of forms. Shastri (1992: 274) suggests that unlike "transparent" features, where a new form is being used, more "opaque" syntactic, semantic, and pragmatic features may be very common in IndE, where "it is perhaps not the form that is at variance but the function." Corpus studies sometimes sidestep the close study of semantic change because of the difficulty of manual data processing of this sort, but many changes in New Englishes cannot be fully understood without this type of analysis.

### 5.3.3. Detailed Coding Criteria

In this section, I outline how sentential aspect, lexical aspect, semantics of past perfect forms, and the modals *will/would* were coded.

Each IndE clause analyzed for Hypothesis 1 and 2 was coded for sentential aspect (to test L1 transfer predictions) and lexical aspect (to test universal lexical semantic predictions).

Five categories of sentential aspect were coded: perfective and four types of imperfective (stative, progressive, delimited habitual, and nondelimited habitual). Each past or progressive token was classified as belonging to one of these five sentential aspectual classes based on lexical meaning, adverbs, narrative sequence, quantification, negation, and interviewer notes on intended meanings.[4]

The examples in (2) from the data illustrate these five categories. In (2a), the verb is inherently perfective—describing a temporally bounded event as a whole—and the adverbs *after* and *then* support this interpretation. (Adverbs can also override inherent verbal aspect to change the overall sentential aspect of the clause.) The other four examples in (2) illustrate imperfective categories. They all describe the internal properties of an event, not the event as a whole and so do not present a bounded view of these situations. A hallmark of imperfectives is homogeneity, or the subinterval property, namely, that the predicate applies to all subintervals or subsituations of the interval (Bennett and Partee 1978; Dowty 1979).

I chose to code two types of habitual categories (2d and 2e) due to a constraint on their use in standard native varieties of English. Habitual predicates describe a generalization over episodes rather than reporting a particular episode. Some temporal expressions, such as *(in) those days*, delimit the temporal extent of a situation and imply that the habit is temporary or temporally bound, as in (2d). Nondelimited habituals, by contrast, have no explicit or understood temporal bound on the habit described, as in (2e). Delimited habituals are licensed with *-ing* in standard English (*I'm cycling to work these days*), but nondelimited habituals are not (*\*I'm cycling to work*, with habitual meaning).

(2)   a.   Perfective: *After* he <u>finished</u> BCom degree, *then* he        [M3Lcal]
           said I want to do the ministry.
      b.   Stative: And father <u>was</u> the provider.        [F2Lcal]
      c.   Progressive: I <u>was</u> cracking up, I was like hahaha.        [M10Hcal]
      d.   Delimited habitual: *Those days* only social worker        [M7Hcal]
           <u>worked</u> in the Red Cross.
      e.   Nondelimited habitual: I <u>studied</u> with my aunt.        [F2Lcal]

Unlike sentential aspect, which is a viewpoint taken by a speaker on a given situation, lexical aspect is at a lower level in the clause and inherent to the verb or the event. The standard lexical aspectual classes are summarized in Table 5.3 (Vendler 1967; Dowty 1979). Stative and activity predicates are atelic; they denote situations that lack an intrinsic temporal endpoint and share the property of homogeneity or internal consistency. By contrast, accomplishment and achievement predicates are telic; they denote eventualities bounded by an intrinsic endpoint and lacking internal homogeneity.

I follow previous work (Kenny 1963; Mourelatos 1978; Bach 1986; De Swart 1998; Salaberry 1999) in adopting a three-way classification into states, activities, and events (which combines accomplishments and achievements). I also take lexical aspect labels to refer to the verb phrase (VP)—the verb together with its arguments—rather than atomic verbs (Verkuyl 1972; Housen 2002).

*Table 5.3.* LEXICAL ASPECT

|  | Homogeneity | Durativity | Dynamcity | Telicity | Example |
|---|---|---|---|---|---|
| State | + | + | − | − | *be, want, know* |
| Activity | + | + | + | − | *play, work, walk* |
| Accomplishment | − | + | + | + | *explain, write x* |
| Achievement | − | − | + | + | *realize, find* |

[114]   *English in India*

Lexical aspect was determined for past and progressive tokens using standard diagnostic tests (Dowty 1979; Robison 1990; Shirai 1991; Shirai and Kurono 1998). The examples in (3)–(6), repeated from Sharma and Deo (2010), illustrate some of the tests used.

(3)  State test: inability to take imperative form
    a.  * Be tall! (state)
    b.  Run! (activity)
    c.  Get organized! (accomplishment)
    d.  Win the race! (achievement)

(4)  Activity test: entailment from progressive to simple past
    a.  True: If Jim is walking then Jim walked. (activity)
    b.  False: If Jim is building a shed then Jim built a shed. (accomplishment)

(5)  Event test (accomplishments): acceptance with time span adverbials
    a.  Nina changed the tyre in ten minutes. (accomplishment)
    b.  ? Nina's foot slipped in ten minutes. (achievement)
    c.  ? Nina walked in ten minutes. (activity)

(6)  Event test (achievements): acceptance with punctual adverbials
    a.  Jim died at 8.25 pm. (achievement)
    b.  * Jim built a shed at 8:25 pm. (accomplishment)
    c.  * Jim was tall at 8.25 pm. (state)

For Hypothesis 3, clauses containing *had* + V-*ed* were coded for three possible meanings: past perfect (standard), simple past, and present perfect.[5] This was established through a close examination of the discourse context for reference to temporal points. In his discussion of time reference, Reichenbach (1947: 290) noted that, in order to distinguish among types of past and present tenses, one must make reference to three, not two, time points. In Figure 5.1, the past perfect, simple past, and present perfect are contrasted in terms of the time points R (reference point), E (event point), and S (speech point). The distinguishing feature of the past perfect in standard English is that R is distinct from both E and S. This R point may be signaled to varying degrees of explicitness in the immediate discourse context, opening up the potential for erosion of the narrower semantic interpretation of the construction.[6]

Finally, the coding for modal verbs (Hypothesis 4) was similar to that used for the study of the perfect construction. The modal verbs *will* and *would* were examined for frequency of standard and nonstandard semantic meanings across individuals.

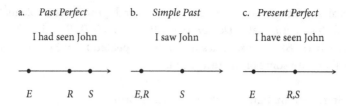

Figure 5.1. Tense and aspect time relations in English (adapted from Reichenbach 1947).

## 5.4. PAST TENSE (HYPOTHESIS 1)

Do IndE speakers graft Indo-Aryan perfectivity marking onto English past tense morphology by reserving their use of past tense marking for perfective situations (Hypothesis 1)?

IndE speakers' use of overt past tense marking across the five sentential aspect types is given in Table 5.4. Standard English requires overt past tense marking in all five categories when past reference is involved.

Table 5.4 shows that these 12 lower proficiency speakers—those who have variable past tense marking—clearly *do* favor overt English past morphology with perfective sentences. Perfective sentences have by far the highest rates of overt past marking, but even within imperfective types, degrees of overt past marking parallel degrees of boundedness: the highest rates of overt use are associated with delimited habituals (which include a temporal bound) and the lowest with nondelimited habituals (which are not temporally bound).

As with the analysis of article use in Chapter 4, multivariate regression can test whether an isolated pattern such as this masks any other influences. In particular, for the present discussion, we would like to know whether the universal factor of lexical aspect is a stronger effect than sentential aspect. In other words, is a universal account better than a substrate account?

As in Chapter 4, the multivariate regression result presented in Table 5.5 lists the total token number ($N$), the percentage of tokens that bear overt past tense marking, and finally, crucially, the relative weight of influence of that particular factor on overt past tense marking. Factor weights range from 0 to 1, with a weight above .5 favoring of overt past tense marking and a weight below 0.5 disfavoring it.

The multivariate analysis confirms sentential aspect as one of the strongest factors, certainly stronger than lexical aspect. Lexical aspect studies in SLA would predict that the strongest lexical aspect category in overt past tense marking would be event, followed by activities, and finally states (Andersen and Shirai 1996). This order is not found at all in the multivariate analysis. The effect of lexical aspect is neither strong, nor ordered as predicted. (See Sharma and Deo 2010 for a detailed critique of the lexical aspect model in

**Table 5.4.** PAST TENSE MARKING ACCORDING TO SENTENTIAL ASPECT

| Semantic type | N | % Overt past marking |
|---|---|---|
| PERFECTIVE | 346 | 76.6 |
| IMPERFECTIVE | | |
| Delimited habitual | 53 | 45.3 |
| Stative | 224 | 44.2 |
| Progressive | 3 | 33.3 |
| Nondelimited habitual | 76 | 18.4 |

$\chi^2$(df = 4): 119.2, $p \leq 0.0001$ (significant); $N = 702$

**Table 5.5.** MULTIVARIATE REGRESSION RESULTS FOR OVERT PAST TENSE MARKING

| Factor | Total N | Percentage | Factor weight |
|---|---|---|---|
| VERB | | | |
| 'say/tell' | 41 | 95.1% | .835 |
| 'be'-copula | 135 | 63.0% | .765 |
| 'go' | 44 | 77.3% | .657 |
| 'do' | 39 | 66.7% | .653 |
| 'be'-auxiliary | 52 | 46.2% | .517 |
| other lexical V | 282 | 52.1% | .355 |
| 'come' | 47 | 66.0% | .337 |
| 'have' | 32 | 15.6% | .283 |
| 'start' | 30 | 40.0% | .148 |
| | | | Range = 687 |
| SENTENTIAL ASPECT | | | |
| Perfective | 346 | 76.6% | .820 |
| Delimited habitual | 53 | 45.3% | .325 |
| Progressive | 3 | 33.3% | .234 |
| Stative | 224 | 44.2% | .176 |
| Nondelimited habitual | 76 | 18.4% | .141 |
| | | | Range = 679 |
| LEXICAL ASPECT | | | |
| Activity | 105 | 42.9% | .630 |
| State | 232 | 47.0% | .591 |
| Event | 365 | 68.2% | .404 |
| | | | Range = 226 |

INPUT: .426, LOG LIKELIHOOD: −374.135

NOT SELECTED AS SIGNIFICANT: stem type, phonetic factors (for regular forms)

SLA and why lexical aspect effects may be generally much weaker than the SLA literature proposes.) In short, the restriction of English past morphology to perfective aspect directly mimics the overt marking of perfectivity with -(y)a in Hindi. We can conclude that Hypothesis 1 is upheld, with evidence of direct substrate transfer, at least among less proficient users.

This new use of English past tense marking resembles the new use of the English indefinite article in Chapter 4. In both cases, a Hindi contrast is directly adopted into IndE. In both cases, a domain is *shared* by Hindi and English (past tense; indefiniteness) but also involves an *overt* morphological contrast within that domain in Hindi (perfectivity; specificity).

## 5.5. PROGRESSIVE (HYPOTHESIS 2)

For the progressive, Hypothesis 2 listed two different possible outcomes. Hypothesis 2a predicted that we should not find much divergence from British English (BrE) in IndE use of progressive -*ing*, since Hindi, like English, has a distinct progressive form.

It is well known that Hypothesis 2a is not supported: the overextension of the progressive in IndE is one of the best-known features of the variety, both in public awareness and in the research literature, reviewed shortly. This means that the universalist lexical aspect prediction is also not supported, as it predicted a lexically based restriction to activity verbs and no overextension to statives.

So why do IndE speakers not acquire the English progressive accurately, on analogy with their own progressive form?

Hypothesis 2b suggested that, despite the availability of a progressive form in both languages, the obligatory use of overt morphology across all imperfective sentences may cause Hindi speakers to extend -*ing* into those domains too.

In order to assess this, we need to examine the use of -*ing* in the five perfective and imperfective aspectual categories set out earlier. Table 5.6 reports the number of progressive -*ing* forms in the IndE data used with each aspectual type.

Standard varieties of English have no use of the progressive form in three of these categories. It is only standardly licensed in progressive (*I'm baking a cake*) and delimited habitual environments (*I'm riding my bike these days*). In these varieties, it is not grammatical with nondelimited habituals (*\*I'm eating meat*), statives (*\*I'm knowing the answer*), or perfectives (*\*I was moving to Miami in 1998*).[7]

In Table 5.6, 48.3% of IndE usage falls outside of standard usage, with extremely robust overextension to nondelimited habituals and statives, that is, the remaining imperfective categories.[8]

[118]  *English in India*

*Table 5.6.* FUNCTIONS OF PROGRESSIVE FORMS

|  | N | % Progressive forms |
|---|---|---|
| IMPERFECTIVE | | |
| Delimited habitual | 112 | 33.1 |
| Nondelimited habitual | 104 | 30.8 |
| Progressive | — | 18.4 |
| Stative | — | 14.8 |
| PERFECTIVE | — | 2.9 |

Examples of IndE use of *-ing* with nondelimited habitual reference are given in (7) and with stative reference in (8). The examples show that this usage is spread right across the cline of speakers described in Chapter 3.

(7) Overextension to nondelimited habituals
    a. I have got a driver. My son <u>driving</u> his own car.    [M11Ldel]
    b. Generally only dry-cleaning clothes <u>are coming</u>.    [M13Ldel]
    c. There's no Indian crowd [in Rochester] and it<u>'s snowing.</u>   [M3Lcal]
    d. Every week I<u>'m calling</u> [my parents].    [M3Lcal]

(8) Overextension to statives
    a. Some people <u>are thinking</u> it's a bad job.    [F3Ldel]
    b. For sociology they were asking me for 80% . . .
       But I <u>was</u> only <u>having</u> 70%.    [F5Hdel]
    c. Japanese patients . . . would not <u>be knowing</u> English
       at all.    [M17Hdel]
    d. Then what they'll feel is like, we <u>are knowing</u> each other.   [M3Lcal]

These data show robust support for Hypothesis 2b, namely, use of *-ing* for other imperfective categories on analogy with the other Hindi imperfective form, *-ta*.

Is this overextension a perfect replication of Hindi imperfectivity marking? Bickerton (1984: 155–156) suggests so: "Native speakers of Hindi frequently make mistakes such as *I am liking it* . . . Hindi speakers apparently commit [this error] because in Hindi imperfective marking can be used with statives." However, this characterization is slightly misleading. It suggests that Hindi has a single form used across all imperfectives. In fact, Hindi has a progressive form, *rahna*, that is prohibited with statives just as English *-ing* is, as shown in (9).

(9)   a. Mai chah<u>ti</u> huun ki vah aye. 'I want them to come.'
    b. * Mai chah <u>rahi</u> huun ki vah aye. 'I am wanting them to come.'

THE VERBAL SYSTEM   [119]

A separate nonprogressive imperfective form, *-ta*, must be used with statives. IndE usage is not the direct mapping of the functions of a Hindi form to *-ing*. It is a response to the absence in English of any other overt morphology for other imperfectives, which Hindi has.

The next section will show how the unusually wide scope of the English progressive encourages this overextension, and that the resulting grammar is a third grammar—neither English nor Hindi—as we saw for definite article use in Chapter 4. The next section offers a single analysis that unifies both IndE past and progressive use as a shift from a tense system to an aspect system.

Before turning to this fuller account, I briefly note recent quantitative investigations of the progressive in IndE, to highlight corroborating findings and further insights.

Balasubramanian (2009: 90) also found greater use of the progressive with stative verbs in IndE as compared with BrE and AmE and a generally higher use in spoken than in written registers. She comments on the lexical specificity of this usage, suggesting that it arises mainly with the verbs *have*, *hear*, *understand*, *see*, *find*, *think*, *know*, *feel*, and *hear*. The next section offers internal linguistic reasons for the emergence of these new uses.

In the ICE-India corpus, Paulasto (2014) confirms this lexical specificity in IndE, finding particularly frequent use with the statives *have* and *know* but somewhat less extension to habituals. Paulasto attributes this to more acrolectal or educated text samples and the availability of competing forms of habitual marking in English. She also suggests differing degrees of substrate influence relative to intensity of contact, a theme taken up later in Chapter 9.

A study that diverges slightly is that of Collins (2008), who finds data from ICE-India to be the *least* innovative out of nine varieties. However, Collins notes a number of factors to account for this, including, again, the more acrolectal nature of the corpus and relatively few tokens of "stative mental" verbs. He acknowledges higher rates of use in IndE with these underrepresented subcategories.

In general, these and many earlier studies concur with the finding that the progressive is extended to new contexts in IndE. The explanation that follows provides a basis for accounting for similar overextension in other varieties (Welsh English, Paulasto 2014; Black South African English, van Rooy 2006; various varieties, Kortmann and Szmrecsanyi 2004).

## 5.6. A UNIFIED ACCOUNT OF TENSE-TO-ASPECT SHIFT IN INDE

So far, Hypotheses 1 and 2b are confirmed, with IndE replicating the Indo-Aryan aspectual system closely. IndE speakers reassign English (past) tense and (progressive) aspect morphology to mark perfective and imperfective aspect, respectively. The former involves *underuse* relative to native standard

**Table 5.7.** VERBAL MORPHOLOGY IN HINDI, INDIAN ENGLISH, AND BRITISH ENGLISH

|  | Hindi | Indian English | British English |
|---|---|---|---|
| PAST |  |  |  |
| Perfective | dho-*ya* | wash-*ed* |  |
| Neutral |  |  | wash-*ed* |
| IMPERFECTIVE |  |  |  |
| Progressive | dho *raha* | wash-*ing* | wash-*ing* |
| Habitual | dho-*ta* | wash-*ing* | wash |
| Stative | jaan-*ta* | know-*ing* | know |

[*dho* 'wash,' *jaan* 'know']

varieties, and the latter involves *overuse*, a distinction that we return to in Chapter 9. Table 5.7 shows the emergent system alongside the input systems.

We could describe this ascription of substrate meanings to superstrate forms as a simple case of relexification (Lefebvre 1998). But this would gloss over the fact that the IndE imperfective system in Table 5.7 is distinct from both the Hindi and the English systems.

The examples in (10) and Table 5.8 show even more clearly that -*ing* in IndE covers progressive as well as other imperfectives, including possession, an imperfective category that is not marked by either of the Hindi imperfective forms. IndE -*ing* has thus become a fully generalized imperfective marker, unlike either of its input languages and more typologically similar to the French Imparfait.

| (10) |  | INDIAN ENGLISH | FRENCH IMPARFAIT (PAST) |
|---|---|---|---|
|  | Progressive | *She is running.* | *Elle courait.* |
|  | Habitual | *I am reading a lot.* | *À l'école, je lisais beaucoup.* |
|  | Stative | *I am knowing your friends.* | *Je connaissais vos amis.* |
|  | Possessive | *He is having some money.* | *Il avait de l'argent.* |

Why would a third grammar—neither the L1 nor the L2—arise? Why do we not see direct L1 transfer effect as we saw in the perfective?

First, we need to dispel the idea, supported by the simple data tables used so far, that Hindi and English have equivalent progressive forms.

The more detailed list in Table 5.9 shows that there is actually a significant mismatch between the Hindi and English progressive. The English progressive is much wider in its scope. This mismatch shows that Hypothesis 2a was not in fact well motivated, as the Hindi system does not mirror the English system.

Given the lack of any direct morphological parallel in Table 5.9, we can see that the Hindi speaker encounters a substantial challenge when faced

THE VERBAL SYSTEM  [121]

**Table 5.8.** MORPHOLOGY USED FOR IMPERFECTIVE SUBTYPES

|  | Hindi | Standard English | Indian English | French (past) |
|---|---|---|---|---|
| Progressive | rahna (*stay*) | -ing | -ing | IMPARFAIT |
| Stative | -ta | (-ing) | -ing | IMPARFAIT |
| Habitual | -ta | (-ing) | -ing | IMPARFAIT |
| Possession | case marking | have | -ing | IMPARFAIT |

**Table 5.9.** USE OF IMPERFECTIVE FORMS IN HINDI, BRITISH ENGLISH, AND INDIAN ENGLISH

| Type | Example | British English | Hindi | Indian English |
|---|---|---|---|---|
| Progressive | He is WRITING a letter. | **-ing** | **rahna** | *-ing* |
| Preliminary stage | He's ARRIVING now. | **-ing** | **rahna** | *-ing* |
| Future | She's LEAVING tomorrow. | **-ing** | **rahna** | *-ing* |
| Weather | It's RAINING. | **-ing** | **rahna** | *-ing* |
| Delimited habitual | She's DRIVING these days. | – / **-ing** | *-ta* / **rahna** | *-ing* |
| Adverb over time | FLYING all day, the bird got tired. | **-ing** | *-ta* | *-ing* |
| Adverb (simultaneity) | He walked towards me SMILING. | **-ing** | *-ta* | *-ing* |
| Persistent activity | The wind kept BLOWING. | **-ing** | *-ta* | *-ing* |
| State | You LOVE music. | – | *-ta* | *-ing* |
| Habitual | I DRIVE. | – | *-ta* | *-ing* |
| Dress | She is WEARING boots. | **-ing** | *-a* (perf) | *-ing* |
| Posture | He is STANDING outside. | **-ing** | *-a* (perf) | *-ing* |
| Location | A letter was LYING there. | **-ing** | *-a* (perf) | *-ing* |
| Temporary state | He is HOLDING the book. | **-ing** | *-a* (perf) | *-ing* |
| Possession | She HAS lots of friends. | – | (case) | *-ing* |
| Nonfinite | They like SWIMMING. | **-ing** | (infin) | *-ing* |

*Note:* Progressive forms are marked in bold, and other imperfective forms in italics.

with English: they are coming from a strict aspect-marking system, such that all finite clauses are obligatorily marked as either perfective or imperfective. To mark perfective, they find the English past tense form. But in the imperfective domain in English, they see just one form, *-ing*, with such an unusually wide distribution that Comrie (1976: 25) described it as "a kind of imperfective." Table 5.9 shows that it overlaps with the full range of *rahna* but also encroaches extensively on nonprogressive territory associated with *-ta* in Hindi, and even beyond. Its current expanding usage even in contemporary standard varieties reinforces this broad scope (Hundt and

[122] *English in India*

Vogel 2011). This makes it a rather good candidate for a generalized imperfective marker.

The substrate pressure to mark all imperfectivity overtly, and the presence of *-ing* in many of those imperfective contexts in English, leads Indo-Aryan L1 speakers to infer that *-ing* can be a general imperfective marker. While this is in part an instance of the substrate filtering through the lexicon of the superstrate (Bao 2015), the semantic value of *-ing* gets reset even beyond the L1. As noted, the resulting system bears a striking resemblance to imperfective systems such as French, quite distinct from both English and Hindi.

The comparison with Singapore English (SgE) in Chapter 8 will show that different substrates (with the same superstrate, English) lead to different outcomes, further supporting this analysis.

In sum, we see a global shift to a Hindi-like aspect-marking system, but not with exact replication of the substrate system. Past tense *-ed* use does show a direct substrate-based restriction to perfective meaning, but progressive *-ing* use produces a third grammar, distinct from both input languages.

This closely parallels the findings in Chapter 4, where we found that IndE article use did not always involve exact replication of the substrate system. Indefinite article use did, but definite article again involved a third grammar, distinct from both input languages.

One detail left unexplained is the discrepancy in distribution across the continuum: past tense omission is only found among less proficient IndE speakers, but the extended progressive occurs across the whole continuum. Chapter 9 will account for this difference as part of a more global analysis of dialect stabilization in India and Singapore.


## 5.7. THE PAST PERFECT (HYPOTHESIS 3)

Hypothesis 3 asks whether the wider range of Indo-Aryan meanings for the perfect construction is transferred to the English perfect, broadening its range of meanings.

A number of scholars have noted nonstandard uses of the past perfect construction in IndE. Leitner (1991) suggested informally that "past perfect might signal the notion of 'remote past' in Indian English" (Leitner, 1991: 228). Parasher (1983: 34) noted a related use of the present perfect for simple past meanings: "One of the major tendencies discovered in the corpus was the use of present perfect for simple past . . . [in] constructions such as *I have sent them two reminders last month* and *funds have been received last year*."

More recently, Balasubramanian (2009: 92) reports only slightly greater use of the past perfect without accompanying time adverbials in IndE as compared with BrE or AmE and concludes that IndE is not significantly divergent in this regard, contrary to Verma (1980) and other commentators. However, her analysis focuses on the presence of accompanying adverbials, a feature that varies within standard BrE and AmE too (Biber et al. 1999; Sharma 2001). The analysis here focuses specifically on the semantics of the construction based on time points, described earlier in Figure 5.1.

In the present IndE data set, 22 instances of *had* + V-*ed* were found, 16 conveying standard past perfect meanings and 6 (27%) conveying nonstandard (past or present perfect) meanings. Examples of each type are given in (11).

(11)   a.   Standard past perfect meaning:
         i.   First we came in as refugees because we had lost    [M8Hcal]
             all our property and everything.
        ii.   When I got married, I had done my graduation,    [F6Hdel]
             I knew English very well.

      b.   Simple past meaning:
         i.   Actually he's my younger brother. He's twenty-    [M7Hcal]
             four. He had come last year over here.
        ii.   My parents just visited. Last week they have,    [M7Hcal]
             means, we had seen them off. All of them have
             their visa, so they all are, like, coming and going.

      c.   Present perfect meaning:
         i.   My children are born here. They had been going    [M8Hcal]
             to India so they know little bit Hindi to speak
             but mostly English.
        ii.   And I have proved here my skill. Mean, I should    [M6Hcal]
             not boast about myself. Me as a Oracle DBA,
             okay. I had gone to the clients, I had success-
             fully installed the database. Mean, I was able to
             maintain the software.

The examples in (11a) indicate distinct E, R, and S time points (see Figure 5.1). In (11b), the R point is not distinct from the E point. And in (11c), the R point is not distinct from the S point, creating the effect of present relevance typical of the standard present perfect in English.

Together, the examples in (11a)–(11c) closely mimic the Indo-Aryan system presented earlier in (1a)–(1c). The usage appears to confirm the substrate transfer prediction of Hypothesis 3. Indeed, the close parallels to the examples in (1) may support a transfer analysis more than a general cross-linguistic tendency to shift to simple past meaning (as in French). But a general loosening of sequence of tense restrictions with the English perfect is very common and may also be at play here (Yao and Collins 2012).

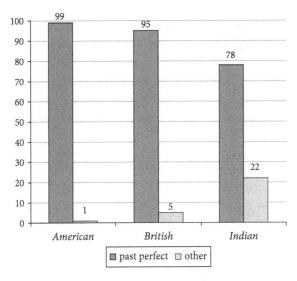

**Figure 5.2.** Meanings associated with *had* + V-*ed* by percentage.
$\chi^2$: IndE vs. AmE/BrE significant (p ≤ .001).
$\chi^2$: BrE vs. AmE not significant (p ≤ .1).

Given the relative scarcity of the construction in the present data set, I consolidate these observations with further evidence from the three corpora mentioned earlier: the Kolhapur, LOB, and Brown corpora.

For equivalent amounts of text in each corpus (88,000 words of press reportage data), the raw totals of *had* + V-*ed* were: AmE: 165, BrE: 230, and IndE: 266. Figure 5.2 shows the relative prevalence of standard and nonstandard meanings with *had* + V-*ed*—these were all coded according to E, R, and S time points evident in the discourse contexts. The relative proportion of nonstandardness in the IndE corpus data closely mirrors the proportion of nonstandardness in the present data set.

The corpus data—indicated with KC in the examples below—also confirm the extension of the past perfect construction to both simple past and present perfect, as predicted by Hypothesis 3. The 22% "Other" tokens for IndE in Figure 5.2 consist of 51 nonstandard uses—28 (12%) with present perfect meaning and 23 (10%) with preterite meaning. Examples of each are given in (12) and (13).

(12) Simple past meaning (nonstandard):
 a. REMOTE PAST. The event point (E) in these past perfect uses is located in the remote past. Many of these examples refer explicitly to a remote time point.
   i. In the past, there had been criticism in the J.P.P. Executive Committee over the issue . . .

THE VERBAL SYSTEM [125]

ii. The National Cooperative Development Corporation had contributed Rs.35.45 lakhs [100,000] during 1976–1977.

b. COVERT REPORTED SPEECH. These tokens occur without an explicitly quoted speaker but possibly with an inferable reporting voice to license past perfect (i.e., an implied discourse context of "X said that . . . ").
iii. The agitators . . . had also disrupted road traffic.
iv. Good care had been taken to use the leverage of canalisation to promote growth.
v. The capsule had been silent about the role of the early pioneers in the freedom struggle. . . . The document only mentions the names of. . . (KC A34 106)

(13) Present perfect meaning (nonstandard):
a. REMOTE OR SUSTAINED STATE OF AFFAIRS. Examples often include explicit extended time adverbials that are more commonly associated with present perfect. In all cases, the state of affairs is still in effect.
i. Similar concessions had been in force for years in the southern States . . .
ii. Politics in Bihar, for decades, had been caste-ridden . . .

b. REMOTE EVENT RELATIVE TO IMMEDIATELY PRIOR DESCRIPTION. A previously described event becomes the R point for a subsequent past perfect clause. Many examples include a reference to the prior description (e.g., "such an object").
iii. This is the second time that such an object had been sighted here.
iv. Rarely had a Ranji final taken such a course on the opening day itself.
v. New Friends Colony and Maharani Bagh area lie right in the way of the coming waters. Never before in the Capital's history these colonies had faced such a flood threat. The Okhla industrial complex in this sector is deserted. (KC A1 10)

It is worth noting the presence of slight variability within BrE and AmE in Figure 5.2. Along with substrate semantics, this sort of marginal instability within the superstrate itself can also be a contributing factor in change in contact systems.[9]

[126]  *English in India*

In general, there appears to be strong support for the transfer prediction in Hypothesis 3, with IndE expanding the perfect construction to match Indo-Aryan semantic categories.


## 5.8. MODALITY (HYPOTHESIS 4)

The discussion so far has focused on tense and aspect. The final hypothesis considers modality, specifically the behavior of *will* and *would* in IndE. In this case, we see the least availability of an overt form in Hindi to model usage on.

We will see that, under these circumstances, IndE use of these modals involves innovative usage that goes beyond the substrate system (as seen in the use of progressive morphology and indefinite articles). The findings suggest an intriguing additional interplay of social indexicality and grammatical restructuring.

I first review the standard English semantics of these forms and then explore their variable use in IndE.


### 5.8.1. The Semantics and Pragmatics of *Will* and *Would*

Although often described as a future tense form, *will* in English is not a marker of tense on a par with English past tense morphology. *Will* is not the only form that can indicate future, and future is not the only meaning associated with *will*. Other forms used for future meaning include present (*I leave tomorrow*), present progressive (*I'm leaving tomorrow*), and the progressive *go* construction (*I'm going to leave tomorrow*). *I will leave tomorrow* can be used as a "volition-colored" variant rather than a default future marker (Jespersen 1933: 272). Huddleston (1984: 133) and Sarkar (1998) note a number of further modal-like properties of *will*, including epistemic (*That will be the milkman*), dynamic (*John will get angry over nothing*), capability (*Nitric acid will dissolve zinc*), generic (*Accidents will happen*), and directive (*You will do as I say, at once*). Huddleston (1984: 172) also shows that modal *will* can be used in conditionals regardless of tense (e.g., past: *If she was there, he will have told her*).

Thus, while scholars differ on whether the future meaning of *will* derives from its modal meanings, they tend to agree that *will* behaves in many ways like a modal verb with additional tense functions, rather than as a pure tense marker (Jespersen 1933; Huddleston 1984; Kratzer 1991; Sarkar 1998; Jaszczolt 2009).

The first challenge from the point of view of a learner, then, is to correctly capture complex generalizations about this range of modal and tense associations of *will*.

Furthermore, a learner is faced with a second form, *would*, whose distribution bears a close resemblance to that of *will*. *Would* functions as the preterite of *will*—compare (14a) and (14b)—and also as its counterpart in irrealis contexts—compare (14c) and (14d). *Would* and *could* also have further extended uses, for example, past habitual action (*He would sit and wait outside for hours*).

(14)  a.  I think she will be back soon.
      b.  I thought she would be back soon.
      c.  If I can, I will be there at 11am sharp.
      d.  If I could, I would be there at 11am sharp.

For the present analysis, one of the most important exensions of *would* and *could* is that their irrealis functions feed into pragmatics and politeness. Irrealis, counterfactual, or subjunctive mood can mitigate the force of a request or statement by attenuating the speaker's assumptions regarding ability and volition (Brown and Levinson 1987), hence the greater politeness in English of *Could you hand me that pen?* as compared with *Can you hand me that pen?*

A second challenge for L2 speakers, then, is not only to acquire the precise distribution of uses of *will* across tense and modality, but also to distinguish the use of *will* and *would* (and similarly *can* and *could*).

### 5.8.2. *Will* and *Would* in IndE

Hypothesis 4 noted that no clear substrate transfer prediction can be made for these modal forms other than perhaps reduced usage.

The main nontransfer or universalist hypothesis comes from studies of the acquisitional trajectory of English modals. Reviewing the child acquisition literature, Shatz and Wilcox (1991) conclude that *can* and *will* are acquired earlier than *could* and *would*, and that their meanings are restricted at first and then expand to encompass the full range of meanings, with relatively little overgeneralization (Shatz and Wilcox 1991; Pinker 1984). Interestingly, *gonna* precedes *will* in children's marking of future meaning even though adult input uses more *will* than *gonna* (Stephany 1986). This may be related to the greater context dependence and pragmatic complexity of *will* (Klecha et al. 2008). As early acquisition of *can* and *will* cannot be tied to their frequency in child-directed speech, Shatz and Wilcox argue that their more basic semantic meanings of intention and ability account for the later acquisition of *could* and *would*, which have more derived functions.

Given the proficiency basis of the cline of IndE speakers in the present data set (see Chapter 3), we might expect this learning trajectory to be replicated across the IndE cline.

The results will show that this is not the case. Although *will* does appear "first," that is, in the speech of less proficient speakers, substantial overgeneralization occurs across all speakers, first of *will* and then of *would*.

[128]  *English in India*

Quantitative analysis of modals is difficult due to optionality in use. For example, *would* can be used to indicate habitual reference, but so can *used to* or the simple past tense. The frequency and choice of constructions can be sensitive to topic, register, and situation. For these reasons, I focus simply on the relative frequency of standard and nonstandard usage in the data.

A few examples of standard uses of *will* and *would* are given in (15). Examples of nonstandard uses of *will* and *would* are given in (16).

(15)　Standard uses
a.　Future *will*:
Within two months we will add steam-pressing.　[M13Ldel]

b.　Habitual/generic *would*:
My interest in English was so much that I would　[M16Hdel]
spare money from my pocket money and buy the
magazine and read it myself.

c.　Irrealis (subjunctive/conditional) *would*:
If I had gone to southern part of United States my　[M5Hcal]
thinking would have been different.

(16)　Nonstandard uses
a.　Future *would*:
(i)　So that's why I asked you yesterday, 'would you be　[M5Hcal]
on time?'
(ii)　So first we are trying to understand what all is　[M17Hdel]
required and then we would definitely be building
up a hospital.

b.　Habitual/generic *will*:
(i)　We used to sit and knit or embroider and do　[F6Hdel]
whatever is possible for us. And then once in
6 months we'll collect those things, put up a sale
by ourselves.
(ii)　She always asks me in Gujarati and I'll answer in　[F5Hdel]
Hindi.

c.　Irrealis (subjunctive/conditional) *will*:
(i)　(What about counting? Which language?) Maybe　[F6Hdel]
I will do it in Hindi.
(ii)　But I will never like to go there [America] with my　[M14Ldel]
son. If he wants to go, that's fine.

THE VERBAL SYSTEM　[129]

**Table 5.10.** USE OF *WILL*

| | Standard | Nonstandard | |
| --- | --- | --- | --- |
| | future | habitual | Irrealis |
| Less proficient | 126 | 26 | 4 |
| More proficient | 158 | 11 | 5 |

**Table 5.11.** USE OF *WOULD*

| | Nonstandard | Standard | |
| --- | --- | --- | --- |
| | future | habitual | Irrealis |
| Less proficient | 0 | 0 | 0 |
| More proficient | 5 | 9 | 47 |

Tables 5.10 and 5.11 summarize the rates of standard and nonstandard uses of *will* and *would*. The two tables show a reverse pattern of overgeneralization across the bilingual cline. Among less proficient users of IndE, *will* is acquired first with future meaning but, contra the predictions of child acquisition, is also overextended to habitual/generic and subjunctive/conditional (standardly *would*) contexts (19.2%); *would* is not used at all. Among more proficient speakers, the overextension of *will* continues at a reduced rate (9.1%), but use of the form *would* appears, with both standard meanings as well as overextended future meaning (standardly *will*).

### 5.8.3. Explaining *Will/Would* Variation in IndE

We can infer from the results that *will* is acquired first, and overgeneralized into *would* territory, following which *would* is acquired and overgeneralized. This does not resemble the child acquisition trajectory. How should we account for it?

As noted, there is no clear substrate counterpart in Indo-Aryan to account for the overall pattern, but isolated substrate effects may nevertheless play a role.

Balasubramanian (2009: 104) shows a high use of *will* with present tense habituals: 12.5% of all *will* forms in her corpus. This is similar to the proportion found in Table 5.10 (*I'll answer in Hindi* instead of *I answer in Hindi*). As Indic languages mark habituality with overt verbal inflections, speakers may feel uncomfortable using the bare verb form for anything other than default

[130] *English in India*

present tense. Recall that obligatory overt morphology has a similar effect on the restructured use of past and progressive forms in IndE.

IndE also favors the use of *will be* V-*ing* for future marking (*They'll be leaving tomorrow* instead of *They will leave tomorrow* or *They leave tomorrow*). Although less nonstandard, this too may indicate a substrate-driven preference for direct verbal inflection of tense.

In both cases, although the basic motivation for extended uses of *will* may come from the substrate, the usage we see is not a simple replication, in this case simply because of the lack of available morphology in English. Once again, we can think of this in terms of Bao's (2015) notion of the substrate being filtered through available superstrate morphology.

However, nonsubstrate explanations are also needed in a full account of the generalization of *will* and, among more proficient speakers, of *would*.

Why does *will* enter the IndE cline before *would*? Corpus data indicate that *will* is marginally less frequent than *would* in BrE and AmE (Leech 2003), so we can tentatively rule out frequency. A greater factor may be the more primary, prototypical, or context-independent meanings of intention that cause *will* to be acquired first, as in child acquisition (Shatz and Wilcox 1991; Klecha et al. 2008).

If this is the case, then why is *would* overgeneralized once it appears? Overgeneralization of modals is not common in L1 acquisition, yet overuse of *would* and *could* is extremely common across New Englishes.

In this case, the two most plausible reasons for IndE extension of *would* use are both related to properties of the superstrate, not the substrate: (i) the very close modal meanings of *will* and *would*, and (ii) the secondary politeness function of *would* and *could*, as opposed to their counterparts *will* and *can*.

An explanation based on (i) would simply be that the two closely related meanings get conflated, leading to interchangeable use (cf. Ziegeler 1996 on Singapore English, discussed in Chapter 8). The fact that the most proficient speakers of IndE lose overgeneralization of *will* but continue to overgeneralize *would* (and do the same for *could* and *can*) does not support this view.

An explanation based on (ii) is a more social one, namely, hypercorrection. Collins (2009) uses the term "extended *would*" for this phenomenon across New Englishes, describing it as "most likely motivated by the desire that speakers have to exploit the capacity of this form to convey a high level of polite and tactful unassuredness" (see also Deuber et al. 2012 for a full review).

As individuals acquire the forms *would* and *could*, they may notice its secondary politeness function in fixed constructions (*Would you please. . . ? May I ask if you could. . . ?*) before they are aware of its subtle, albeit primary, tense licensing conditions. Particularly in the Indian linguistic ecology, the high status of English means such politeness functions, however secondary to the semantics of the form, are highly salient. Furthermore, the lack of honorific marking in English causes many compensatory effects in IndE (Pandharipande 2007; Sridhar 1991; Y. Kachru 2006), and overuse of *would* is one option.

IndE speakers thus come to rank the [+polite, +formal] values of *would* and *could* as primary, demoting (or not fully acquiring) other semantic constraints such as [+irrealis] and [+past]. This leads to hypercorrections of the kind found in the email style used in examples (22).[10]

(22)  a.  I *would* be reaching the university around 9:30 AM. I completed my library work just now and would be free tomorrow.
      b.  I was told [the bus] takes about 10 minutes to reach M. C. Hence I *would* be little late.
      c.  I *would* be calling Mr. V. S. of M. Tours in a day or so to ascertain the sector New Delhi-Vienna's position. As already conveyed, the fare *would* be $1020.
      d.  V. *would* be coming to receive you on 15th and he *would* be bringing the ticket too. This is because Mr. J. *would* have gone to Delhi by then and we just want to ensure that the ticket is not misplaced. It goes without saying that he *would* be seeing you off too.

Three of these examples also happen to illustrate another IndE tendency noted earlier, namely, the preference for *will/would* + *be* + V-*ing* for future marking.

As has been seen for most grammatical features examined now, IndE modal use once again suggests a filtering of substrate semantics through superstrate morphology (Bao 2015), with a third grammar emerging that is distinct from both. But there is also a nonsubstrate effect of sociopragmatics in this case of grammatical change. The role of English as an elite, high-status code in post-colonial repertoires leads to a heightened salience of politeness and formality functions, which displace finer semantic distinctions over time.

### 5.9. DISCUSSION: AN INDIC PERFECTIVE-IMPERFECTIVE SYSTEM IN ENGLISH

Table 5.12 summarizes the diverse changes in the TMA system of IndE discussed in this chapter.

This summary of features leads to a number of interim generalizations about how the verbal domain is restructured in IndE:

(i)  When mismatches arise between L1 and L2 grammatical systems, overt morphology in the L1 exerts a strong influence on IndE speakers' choices, yet the L1 system is not always perfectly replicated in their new grammatical usage.

**Table 5.12.** INDE TMA FEATURES IN RELATION TO THE INDO-ARYAN AND ENGLISH SYSTEMS

| Form | New Indian English Meanings | Substrate semantics relevant? | Substrate system replicated? | Stable use across cline? |
|---|---|---|---|---|
| a. Past tense | perfective | yes | yes | no |
| b. Progressive -*ing* | imperfective | yes | no | yes |
| c. Past perfect | past; present perfect | yes | yes | yes |
| d. *will* | habitual, irrealis | yes | no | yes |
| e. *would* | future, polite | no | no | yes |

(ii) In two cases—past tense use and past perfect use—we do see substrate semantic contrasts being directly replicated in IndE.

(iii) However, in two other cases—progressive use and *will* use—substrate pressures and superstrate complexity lead speakers to infer a new third grammar, with substrate preferences filtered through English morphosyntax (Bao 2015).

(iv) In one case—*would* use—the lack of honorifics in English and its high register have led to a sociopragmatic reallocation of the form.

(v) There is little evidence for the emergence of pure universals, such as those arising out of lexical aspect or prototype semantics. Nevertheless, patterns that are unmarked typologically or in acquisition do arise in places, for example, in the acquisition of *will* before *would* and the alignment of past with perfective.

(vi) Surprisingly, the relative stability or persistence of a particular feature across the usage cline (final column in Table 5.12) cannot be accounted for straightforwardly by substrate influence.

In general, an Indo-Aryan-like system does emerge, with a strong emphasis on marking a perfective-imperfective distinction. However, there are equally important contributions from idiosyncrasies of the English system itself, such as the broad range of -*ing* (leading to its use as a general imperfective marker) and the subtle semantic distinction between *will* and *would* (leading to shifts based on prototypicality, salience, and politeness).

Features influenced by idiosyncrasies of English might be predicted to recur across varieties, as the same complexity of the English system must be tackled by any L2 speaker. By contrast, narrowly substrate-derived features are more likely to be limited to other varieties for which a similar substrate exists. These predictions are tested in Part II of this volume, in the comparison with Singapore.

One puzzle that remains is the final column of Table 5.12, which refers back to the implicational scaling of speakers in Chapter 3. Substrates underpin almost all the features listed and so cannot offer a ready explanation of why only one of these is not as stable as the others. Chapters 8 and 9 return to this puzzle of *which* features become entrenched over time and why.

Before that, Part I ends with a final chapter on the case of India: the social side of how dialects form and stabilize.

# CHAPTER 6
# Dialect Identity

The preceding chapters have examined the structural and cognitive dimensions of new dialect formation. The social correlates of this process have not yet been addressed: Is a new speech community, one that identifies with Indian English (IndE) as its own language, also emerging and stabilizing? If so, to what extent, and how can we tell?

In this chapter I turn to the birth of dialect identity. One measure of affiliation to a new dialect or style is how much a speaker adjusts their accent when they encounter a standard, native variety. Here, I look at how speakers of IndE respond to contact with American English (AmE). Quantitative analysis initially shows that, at least in relation to phonetic variation, IndE speakers show an emergent self-confidence in their dialect, *regardless* of their measurable level of proficiency in English. This shift from seeing themselves as L2 learners toward behaving like dialect speakers can be taken as evidence of burgeoning endonormative stabilization (Schneider 2007). The emergence of new grammatical and phonetic forms corresponds to new social indexicalities and personal affiliation with IndE. Qualitative analysis of expressed attitudes and wider language ideologies will show, however, that this shift to a new Indian dialect identity is only partial and fairly selective.

In Chapter 10 we will see differing degrees of alignment with New English dialect identities, in a comparison of English style repertoires and attitudes in India and in Singapore.

*From Deficit to Dialect.* Devyani Sharma, Oxford University Press. © Oxford University Press 2023.
DOI: 10.1093/oso/9780195307504.003.0006

## 6.1. BACKGROUND

### 6.1.1. Acceptance of Indian English

As noted in Chapter 2, it is difficult to describe IndE as moving in any one particular direction in terms of speech style and attitudes. IndE has been characterized as being pulled in two directions by "progressive forces and conservative forces" (Mukherjee 2007: 170), developing a vernacular voice but maintaining a conservatism about IndE "correctness."

A dramatic shift in attitudes has certainly taken place, with Indians now favoring IndE almost exclusively over British English (BrE) as a target norm, yet they tend to retain a conservative ambivalence and insecurity about indigenized English use and a narrower style range than speakers of established native varieties (discussed in detail in Chapter 10). In slight contrast to Mukherjee's (2007) conclusion that this interplay of forces gives rise to a "steady state," I follow Bao's (2003) view that these conservative forces slow down the degree and rate of ongoing change.

These conflicted stances toward indigenization among IndE speakers stand in contrast to the spectacular processes of indigenization and nativization underway in Singapore. In both varieties, ascriptions of stigma and prestige are still unresolved. But, as Chapter 10 will argue, vernacular SgE has developed more robust covert prestige despite the presence of strong countervailing institutional ideologies. By contrast, in IndE-speaking communities, one can still detect the long shadow of normative ideologies, insecurity with respect to standards, and a reluctance to claim ownership of the language, despite decades of gradual indigenization.

The present chapter examines just one piece of evidence of these evolving social identities, namely, the behavior of IndE speakers when in contact with native English speakers.

### 6.1.2. Predictions: Contact and Accommodation

Adult native speakers of a dialect may accommodate to a new dialect after migration but rarely adopt the new dialect in full. This is in stark contrast to foreign language learners, who often aim to approximate the local variety when immigration offers increased access to a native target variety (Andreasson 1994).

Furthermore, variability in how much a native dialect speaker accommodates to a new variety is very sensitive to their personal affiliation, or lack thereof, with the other group (Auer and Hinskens 2005). Trudgill (2004) has downplayed this role of identity in dialect contact, seeing the outcome of contact in "tabula rasa" situations as "purely a matter of who interacts most often

[136] *English in India*

with whom—a matter of density of communication" (Trudgill 2004: 149), but critics have asserted an inherent link between accommodation and social identification in native dialect contact settings (Coupland 2008; Holmes and Kerswill 2008).

Which behavior do we expect to find among IndE speakers who come into sustained contact with a native variety, in this case AmE? If we assume that IndE speakers affiliate with their own dialect the way a native speaker does, then we expect no major role for relative proficiency or use of English. IndE speakers will accommodate to AmE depending on their personal orientations, as native speakers do.

If, on the other hand, IndE speakers are more like second language learners in terms of social identity, we might anticipate that they will adopt or accommodate to the new AmE dialect to the extent that they can. We might see more adoption of AmE features among less proficient individuals, with the more proficient group being more strongly identified with IndE and less inclined to shift their dialect. Alternatively, we might see *less* adoption at the less proficient end due to less control over English variation. In either case, proficiency will correlate with the adoption of AmE features.

The California data set (see Chapter 1) was designed to examine such a situation of contact between IndE and a native variety and is the focus of analysis in this chapter.[1]

## 6.2. QUANTITATIVE PATTERNS IN GRAMMAR AND ACCENT

### 6.2.1. The Proficiency Cline: Grammar and Acquisition

The California data set is comprised of IndE speakers who grew up in India and migrated to the United States as adults (see Table 1.1 in Chapter 1). Chapter 3 (Tables 3.3 and 3.4) showed that the use of Indian grammatical variants by these individuals appears to correspond closely to their formal and informal exposure to English, in other words, their approximate levels of acquisition and proficiency. Figure 6.1 illustrates this close correspondence, particularly for the last three features, for the 12 individuals in the California data set.

The logistic regression (Goldvarb) results in Table 6.1 confirm the statistical significance of this pattern. The two strongest factors—daily use of English and education in English—show both statistical significance and the predicted gradient ordering within the factor.[2] (As in earlier regression tables, factor weights reflect the relative influence on the dependent variable in question: weights below .5 indicate that the factor in question favors standard use, while weights greater than .5 favor nonstandard use.)

The main point to note here is the lack of idiosyncratic or personalized patterns of use of these grammatical forms. Their use is driven to a large extent

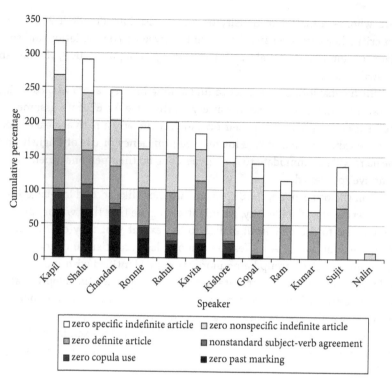

**Figure 6.1.** Cumulative percentage rates of use of IndE grammatical features by speaker (*N* values provided in Chapter 3).

*Table 6.1.* SIGNIFICANT PROFICIENCY FACTORS IN NONSTANDARD USE OF FOUR SYNTACTIC FEATURES

|  | Daily use of English ||||
| --- | --- | --- | --- | --- |
|  | With family and friends | With some friends | Frequently at work | Occasionally at work |
| Article omission | .250 | .548 | .658 | .728 |
| Lack of past tense marking | .074 | .412 | .953 | .993 |

|  | Education in English |||
| --- | --- | --- | --- |
|  | Mostly English education | English in higher education | No formal English education |
| Null copula | .186 | .652 | .909 |
| Lack of agreement | .243 | .642 | .730 |

Factors not selected or not gradient: age, time spent in the United States. $p < .001$

by formal and informal acquisition of English, suggesting individual identity considerations may exert less influence. Metalinguistic commentaries on "grammar" as opposed to "accent," discussed later, support this sense that IndE grammar is not extensively exploited for personal style choices.

### 6.2.2. Beyond Proficiency: Accent as Identity?

Does proficiency similarly determine these individuals' accents, in particular, how American or Indian they are after contact with AmE?

If so, the relative ordering of speakers will correspond to their proficiency as grammatical features did: less regular users of English (e.g., Kapil, Shalu, Chandan) will either be higher adopters of AmE due to lower dialect confidence, or lower adopters due to insufficient command of English. On the other hand, if proficiency is not related to accent choice, we should see no correspondence to the earlier proficiency-based ordering of speakers.

The three phonetic features examined are aspiration, l-velarization, and rhoticity, all of which are different in IndE and AmE. The two Dravidian language speakers are excluded, as South Indian English is quite distinct for these phonetic features.

In coding the three variables, only the least controversial, or most canonical, environments were considered, in other words, those contexts that almost categorically have aspiration, l-velarization, and rhoticity in most American dialects (certainly in California). Thus, for aspiration, only prevocalic, noncluster voiceless stops in primary stress syllables were included; for l-velarization, only coda and syllabic /l/ were included; and finally, for rhoticity, only /r/ in coda position was included. Selecting the least variable native contexts allowed a maximal contrast between the anticipated American realization and the alternative Indian realization of the phoneme. As noted in previous literature on IndE (see Agnihotri and Khanna 1994 and Sailaja 2009 for a summary), IndE generally has unaspirated stops, has no velarization of /l/, and is broadly nonrhotic. This is confirmed in the Delhi data set (though see Chand [2010] on increasing rhoticity among younger Delhi residents).

Full, partial, and no aspiration were coded separately in the analysis, but partial and full aspiration are merged in the results presented here. Similarly, full, light, and no velarization were coded separately, but full and light velarization are grouped here. The case of rhoticity is slightly more complex, as IndE varieties may either be nonrhotic or may have a partially devoiced, trilled /r/, and so IndE as a whole cannot be assumed to be nonrhotic (see also Chand [2010] and Cowie [2018] for recent changes in rhoticity). For this reason, absence of /r/, use of trilled /r/, and use of approximant /ɹ/ were coded separately, and in the present discussion I contrast the two Indian

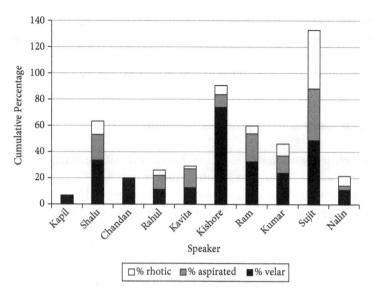

**Figure 6.2.** Cumulative percentage rates of use of AmE phonetic features by speaker (velarization $N$ = 590; aspiration $N$ = 1634; rhoticity $N$ = 1704).

variants against the variant more typically heard as American (approximant /r/).

Figure 6.2 shows cumulative rates of use of American variants by speaker. This figure retains the ordering of speakers from Figure 6.1 in order to assess whether the same proficiency-linked ordering of speakers arises for these phonetic features.

We can first observe that the overall use of American forms is low. Even when speakers have a relatively high degree of Americanization, the actual proportion relative to their overall use of Indian variants can be quite low, and they often use American features strategically in discourse-prominent and salient positions rather than consistently throughout their speech.[3]

For example, Sujit [M9Hcal] has the highest rate of rhoticity, but he is selective in his use. The extracts in (1a) and (1b) reflect his tendency to use approximant [ɹ] in word-final position and no /r/ word-internally. He always uses a rhotic pronunciation in the word *Masters* (as well as [æ] rather than [a]), possibly associating the term with the US topic—sensitivity of this sort may also underlie the shift to rhoticity in (1b).

(1)           ɹ    ɹ       ɹ
    a. Actually, I'm here for my higher studies. I'm trying to get admission
         ɹ       ɹ
      for my Masters.

　　　　　　　　　　　　　ø　　　　　　　　ø
b.　The way [an Indian] uses English, the terms and the words, is gonna

　　　ø　　　　　　　　　　　　　　　ɪ　　ɪ
　　be entirely different with the U.S., the people who're here uses it.

Similarly, Kishore [M5Hcal] has the highest rates of l-velarization but fluctuates in his use too. He consistently uses velar [ɫ] in the discourse marker *well*, as in (2a) and also employs dense clusters of American pronunciation in individual words, such as *girl* [gɹɫ] in (2b) or *call* [kʰɔɫ], while retaining Indian phonetic forms elsewhere in the utterance, as the combination in (2b) shows.

(2)　　　　　ɫ　　　　ɫ　　　　　　　　ɫ
　　a.　Well, I see myself as Indian . . . I have felt that I should not lose my
　　　　　　1　　　　　　1　1
　　　　basic moral values and cultural values . . .


　　　　　ɫ　　　ɫ　　　k　　　lk　　　k l　ø
　　b.　I always felt that I could still keep my culture and heritage if I marry a
　　　　　　ɹɫ
　　　　Indian girl.

Other Indian features such as monophthongization and retroflexion are widespread across individuals, indicating a limited degree of accommodation to AmE overall in the group.

Second, we can consider *relative* degrees of phonetic Americanization across different individuals. It is clear from the distribution in Figure 6.2 that speakers do not follow the same proficiency-linked ordering in their use of American accent features. The three speakers with the highest composite rates—Shalu, Kishore, and Sujit—are distributed right across the proficiency range. Similarly, the least proficient speaker (Kapil) and the most proficient speaker (Nalin) have comparably low composite rates of use of American style.

There is also much greater variability in rates of use per variable across speakers in Figure 6.2, as compared with the grammatical variables in Figure 6.1. Kishore leads in velarization, while Sujit leads in rhoticity and aspiration. This further corroborates the individualistic nature of variation in this set of features.

We can verify this with a regression analysis similar to that conducted in the previous section for grammatical features. In that case, the features showed a significant effect of daily use of English and amount of education

**Table 6.2.** SIGNIFICANT PROFICIENCY FACTORS IN USE OF
AMERICAN PHONETIC VARIANTS

| | Daily use of English | | | |
| --- | --- | --- | --- | --- |
| | With family and friends | With some friends | Frequently at work | Occasionally at work |
| Aspiration | .620 | .738 | .089 | .459 |
| Rhoticity | .878 | .558 | .027 | .351 |
| Velarization | .633 | .763 | .124 | .293 |

| | Education in English | | |
| --- | --- | --- | --- |
| | Mostly English education | English in higher education | No formal English education |
| Rhoticity | .499 | .728 | .267 |

| | Time spent in United States | | |
| --- | --- | --- | --- |
| | 0–5 years | 6–20 years | Over 20 years |
| Aspiration | .281 | .895 | .278 |
| Rhoticity | .463 | .901 | .189 |
| Velarization | .350 | .772 | .417 |

Not selected: age; $p < .01$.

in English. Table 6.2 shows a partial effect of these two social factors on phonetic variants too, but not as consistently as was found for syntactic variables in Table 6.1.

First, the *ordering* of internal distinctions for each factor in Table 6.2 does not correspond to the well-motivated ordering in Table 6.1. Second, "Time Spent in the United States" does appear to play some role here, where it was irrelevant for syntactic traits. Again, the ordering is not linear, but it is strikingly consistent in being high for intermediate periods of time in contact with AmE. Recent work on migrant groups in the United Kingdom has found a very similar pattern of accommodation to local phonetic variants three to five years after arrival and at the same life stage, possibly at a time of increased work-related and other extracommunity interaction (Sharma and Sankaran 2011; Drummond 2011).

The analysis so far reveals a curious split: syntactic variables do not show much individual stylistic variability and appear to be closely tied to proficiency, but phonetic features are quite delinked from proficiency. If proficiency is less central to phonetic variants, then what *does* motivate the differences we see in speakers' accent choices? In particular:

[142] *English in India*

(3)   a.   Why do certain individuals (Shalu, Kishore, Sujit) adopt more
           American accent traits?
      b.   Why is it their phonetic forms that are less tied to proficiency, not
           their grammar?

## 6.3. PERSONAL RESPONSES TO DIALECT CONTACT

Let us consider the first question in (3), why certain individuals are more Americanized. A native speaker's personal evaluation of a dialect contact situation can be a factor in greater or lesser adoption of new variants in dialect contact (Trudgill 1986; Barden and Grosskopf 1998). If we see a similar effect of personal orientation to American cultural contact here, we might conclude that Indians have come to behave more like native speakers than language learners in a contact situation.

In response to questions such as "Is there such a thing as Indian English?," "What do you think of Indians who move here and sound American?," or "Would you prefer to stay here or move to India?," clear differences in personal ideologies of cultural contact and speech style emerged.

For one set of individuals—Shalu, Kishore, and Sujit, the three highest users of American features—the rhetoric of dialect change revolves around ideas of flexibility and accommodation. In the examples in (4), Shalu talks about accents becoming "nicely Americanized," Kishore says it takes "efforts and guts to change," and Sujit contrasts flexibility in one's ability to change against having "a mental block" about remaining Indian.

(4)   a.   Indians really twist their tongue easily. Their accents be-
           come very Americanized easier. But other culture it's take
           little time . . . Indian peoples, their accents become very nice,
           Americanized.                                              [Shalu]
      b.   If the children were born in this country [and] they have adapted
           the American way of speaking, wonderful! People like myself
           who come to study here or went to school in India, you know,
           we come and pick up so fast and change . . . Gujarati families
           will stay here for hundred years, they will never change. Because
           they don't wanna change. It takes times and efforts and guts to
           change.                                                    [Kishore]
      c.   It depends on an individual's attitude. Some people are very flexible.
           So if they have this thing in mind that they can change to a partic-
           ular situation . . . within very short span of time. But some people
           are very rigid, and then they always have this mental block in them,
           you know. . . [But] if you're working in an American company, then
           you have to be like them. . . . You can't stand all alone.      [Sujit]

Other speakers are very different, citing loss of identity and superficiality when discussing accommodation. The examples in (5) are from two of the lower users of American variants. Kumar talks of being "proud" of his Indian accent and not having a "complex," while Nalin suggests that sounding American involves "insecurity." In addition, although Kavita does not express a view on dialect shift specifically, she expresses a strong critique of many aspects of American society and claims that she would leave if it were not for her children. This may also account for her low use of American markers despite 25 years in the country.

(5)  a.  Mine is an Indian English. I have not really went out of my way to pick up American slang and I have just kept it, my accent, the way it is and I feel very proud of it . . . I have no complex that way.                                          [Kumar]

     b.  (What if an Indian sounds very American after being here for a short time?) Oh, then I think he's just being facetious. [Or] he's got some kind of insecurity.                          [Nalin]

The remaining speakers express more ambivalent views on the issue of cultural contact and dialect shift, some shown in (6). Kapil and Chandan interpret my question as merely asking whether learning English is good, perhaps as they are early-stage speakers. Chandan and Kavita talk positively about the facility with which Indians integrate linguistically but also use very clear rhetorical devices, such as "those people" and additional descriptors, to distinguish themselves from such people. Rahul simply distinguishes between native-born and non-native-born individuals, and finally Ram exhibits an ambivalence that suggests he may still be negotiating a response to his new environment as he has only been in the United States for six months.

(6)  a.  It's necessary in America. You have to learn English before you have to come. . . . Otherwise you're too hard to convince any other people.                                        [Kapil]

     b.  If [people from India] want to live in this country, they should learn English. . . . They are educated people, right, those who come in this country? They have to live on their standard. They have to follow what the American does. . .        [Chandan]

     c.  Those who born and raised here, or kids, they usually speak, like, Americanized English. But those who are coming from India, they are always you know, different language, English language. They have their own accent.                            [Rahul]

[144]  *English in India*

d. Those people are coming from Bombay, Madras or somewhere, they speak fluently English and you don't feel even they are coming from India to here, you know. They blended in so fast, the kids. So those kids doesn't have problem. [Kavita]

e. If I don't like their culture so I'm not gonna adapt. . . . In every place, like America, you can pick a lot of good things, right? The truthness, explaining politely and truly. So these are some good things which I want to take. Rest all garbage. . . [Ram]

Metalinguistic commentaries and attitudes are not always a reliable indicator of actual use. Nevertheless, quantitative analysis shows that in this case the three attitudinal groups correspond surprisingly well to use of American markers in Figure 6.2.

Although qualitative factors as cultural allegiance are difficult to quantify, a simple ranking of speakers according to the kinds of views expressed in (4), (5), and (6)—views corroborated elsewhere in their interviews—allows us to divide the 12 individuals into three broad orientations. If this attitudinal factor of is added to the earlier regression analysis (Table 6.2), we find that a significant effect (in the predicted order, unlike the earlier proficiency factors) does surface for this factor (Table 6.3).

A more complete stylistic range for each speaker would of course be much more informative. The present results nevertheless give us a provisional answer to the question in (3i). Individuals did not accommodate to AmE either identically or predictably according to their proficiency level. Instead, they showed very individual attitudinal responses to the contact situation, some positive and some negative, with corresponding degrees of Americanized speech styles, as discussed earlier for native dialects in contact.

The findings support an interpretation of IndE as not simply generic or incomplete L2 acquisition but as a variety that speakers across the bilingual cline are increasingly confident of and identify with.

**Table 6.3.** SIGNIFICANT ATTITUDINAL FACTORS IN USE OF AMERICAN PHONOLOGICAL VARIANTS

|  | Attitude to American culture | | |
|---|---|---|---|
|  | Overall positive | Ambivalent | Overall negative |
| Aspiration | .657 | .488 | .383 |
| Rhoticity | .821 | .292 | .366 |
| Velarization | .764 | .507 | .216 |

Not selected: age; $p < .05$.

Proficiency cannot be discarded entirely. Although it does not appear to be the primary determinant of speech style, it may play a secondary, constraining role. A bilingual may develop a positive response to the American environment, but their limited ability in English may restrict the degree to which they can adopt new features, regardless of their orientation toward the culture. We might speculate that the upward trend across the "high Americanization" individuals in Figure 6.2 indicates that speakers' relative success in adopting AmE is affected by their facility with the language. Le Page and Tabouret-Keller's (1985: 182) notion of "acts of identity" describes such shifts as a projection of a speaker's personal experience and desire, but crucially one that is constrained by access and ability.

## 6.4. "GRAMMAR" VERSUS "ACCENT"

The second question in (3) asks: If IndE speakers have emergent confidence in their accent, why are they more comfortable using *phonetic*, not syntactic, forms to signal these allegiances?

One reason that syntax and phonology may behave differently for IndE speakers is that syntactic differences may simply be less salient, and if speakers are less aware of them, they may be less available for identity work. I use several types of data below as measures of relative awareness among speakers.

Alternatively, syntactic and phonetic forms may be equally available to conscious manipulation but may be being evaluated differently by individuals, with syntactic forms not as willingly employed in stylistic work. I use metalinguistic commentaries to assess this alternative explanation.

### 6.4.1. How Aware Are Participants of Their Syntax and Phonology?

Labov (1972) developed a well-known tripartite distinction among speech features based on their relative salience for users. Stereotypes are "overt topics of social comment and show both correction and hyper-correction," markers "are not at the same high level of awareness but, show consistent stylistic and social stratification," and indicators "are never commented on or even recognized by native speakers, but are differentiated only in their relative degrees of advancement among the initiating social groups" (Labov 1994:78). Indicators are rarely subject to style shifting or evaluative comment.

The difference found between how syntactic and phonetic variables behave for IndE speakers in contact with AmE could lie in differences of awareness. Trudgill (1986: 11) found such a mix of indicators, markers, and stereotypes among BrE speakers in contact with AmE, with consequences for patterns of use and accommodation. These distinctions have rarely been appealed to in

[146]   *English in India*

studies of postcolonial varieties but are important for understanding awareness and variation in New Englishes.

There is no clear prediction for greater awareness of one or another level of linguistic structure. Some scholars have proposed that morphosyntactic forms and abstract systems in general are less accessible for conscious monitoring (Labov 1993; Smith et al. 2007; Meyerhoff and Walker 2013; but see Levon and Buchstaller 2015) while others have suggested that lexical and grammatical forms are more accessible to metalinguistic awareness (Silverstein 2001; Preston 1996).

As markers are at an intermediate level of consciousness, evidence of this level of awareness is often indirect, for example, in moments such as self-correction.[4] In the present data, speakers corrected their utterances at several points in the interviews. Self-corrections occurred with phonetic as well as syntactic forms, suggesting no clear difference in awareness.

In (8), we see examples of phonetic self-correction. In (8a), Sujit first maintains the Americanized style he had been using but then reformulates with retroflexion, no aspiration, and falling intonation. In (8b), Kishore similarly repairs *forty* toward more IndE phonetic forms. The direction of style shifting is toward IndE in both cases, clearly influenced by features of my Standard Indian variety, which is nonrhotic and lightly aspirated.[5]

(8)   a.   Sujit:   Obviously you miss your own country, where you have spent like 23 years. You have that attachment. [ətʰætʃmənt] (rising intonation)

            D. S.:   Sorry?

            Sujit:   You have that attachment. [əʈætʃmənt] (falling intonation)

      b.   D. S.:   How long have you been here?

            Kishore:   About forty [fɔɹɾi] years.

            D. S.:   How many?

            Kishore:   Forty. [fɔʈi]

But self-repairs occur in syntax too, as in (9), suggesting that syntax is at no lower a level of awareness than phonetic forms.

(9)   a.   Everybody was saying that America is land of– a land of opportunity.   [Rahul]

      b.   No because they was– in India they studied in English.   [Kapil]

      c.   I mean, even if he go ba– goes backs to India, it's fine.   [Gopal]

The lack of a simple difference in awareness of syntax and phonology is also supported in participants' occasional stereotyping of IndE, which accessed linguistic features at all levels. For example, Kishore spontaneously volunteered an imitation of IndE when describing differences between IndE and AmE, shown in (10). He clearly targets phonological, syntactic, lexical, discourse, and intonational elements in his imitation, exhibiting awareness of Indian features at all levels.

(10) Indian English has little bit touch of British. And I have seen that the making sentencing is different. For instance, I'll give you example. For instance, 'I was there yesterday.' This is sentence: 'I was there yesterday.' American will say 'I was there yesterday.' The Indian will say 'I was there yesterday only.' (laughs) And then he would shake his head (shakes head and uses exaggerated intonation) 'I was there yesterday only and I tæll you what to do and you cannot– you can't understand what I am saying.' See this is the way [Indians speak]. American is simple and clear.

    a.   'can't': æ → a
    b.   'tell': ε → æ
    c.   greater retroflexion, no aspiration
    d.   discourse marker 'only'
    e.   attempt at stative progressive
    f.   exaggerated intonational contours

So far, the examples in (8)–(10) have shown no apparent difference in the awareness, that is, availability, of syntactic and phonetic forms for IndE speakers. But in fact, the examples do show a more subtle difference, namely, different *evaluation* of phonetic and syntactic forms: in (8) individuals repaired their phonology toward IndE, but in (9) they repaired their syntax *away* from IndE toward standard usage. I found no instances in the entire data set of syntactic self-corrections in which an initial standard American form was replaced with a nonstandard Indian form. This partly reflects accommodation to my speech, which has IndE phonetic variants but standard syntax. But speakers shift to their *own* IndE phonological variants, very different in some cases from mine. In addition, their stark differences in phonetic choices in Figure 6.2 cannot be explained by accommodation to my speech.

The final, and clearest, evidence of a difference in *evaluation*, not awareness, comes from metalinguistic commentaries.

### 6.4.2. Language Ideologies: Correct Grammar and Personal Accent

In interviews, I did not explicitly distinguish syntax and phonology when asking about attitudes. However, participants repeatedly drew a distinction

[148]   *English in India*

between the two. They talked about "grammar" in terms of prestige and correctness—indeed, given that all the speakers exhibited some degree of syntactic nonstandardness in their own speech, the number of voluntary references to the "correctness" of IndE grammar was remarkable.

(11)  a.  I've heard the people talking here [U.S.]. They use different kind of English. It's not actually English. Indian is more standardized. Standardized English is proper English. With grammar, adverbs, everything.                                                                  [Sujit]

   b.  [American English] is more slang and Indian English is more respectable. More words and they using proper grammars. But here nobody use the grammars.                                                       [Shalu]

   c.  Originally they learned from the Britishers, so our English is totally right English. They speak the slang language here.    [Kavita]

The descriptions in (11) valorize IndE as "more standardized," "respectable," "totally right English." These speakers are not consistently producing what they might consider proper or standard English syntax themselves, but they have a strong belief—dissociated from their own utterances—that the grammar of their variety is standard, particularly in relation to AmE.

Underlying this assertion of the relative "properness" of IndE is a perception of it as a more direct and legitimate heir of BrE than AmE is, a construction of IndE grammar as part of a superior linguistic lineage. This perceived direct lineage between BrE and IndE (which of course ideologically erases the similar lineage between BrE and AmE) could play some part in the stable maintenance of IndE features in the face of AmE.

The same speakers who identify with a grammatically correct and prestigious speech community use entirely different terms to discuss "accent" in (12). Sujit, who described IndE as "standardized" in (11), says that an Indian's accent is "up to you" and "just your accent." Kavita distinguishes "totally right English" in (11) from "accent problem." And Rahul observes that accent, not grammar, is what distinguishes Indians.

(12)  a.  Accent is different. It's fine, it's up to you. . . It doesn't matter, it doesn't, I mean, categorize you in some way. It's just your accent and the way you speak.                                                        [Sujit]

   b.  English is my second language. So I used to speak in India too. Still people don't understand because we have accent problem.
                                                                                                                       [Kavita]

   c.  (Would you say there's such a thing as Indian English, compared to American English?) Oh yeah, definitely, our accent, you know. Whoever is coming from India, their English accent is different.
                                                                                                                       [Rahul]

There is extensive evidence of this split ideology in IndE. Kachru (1986: 39) noted informally that syntax and phonology may be evaluated differently by second language speakers. Sahgal and Agnihotri (1985) found that IndE speakers gave the lowest acceptability ratings to syntactic nonstandardness (e.g., word order, complex sentence formation, or tag questions), concluding that "a common syntactic denominator acts as a bond among different English-speaking communities." Bhatia (1992) and Baker and Eggington (1999) similarly comment on "bilingual orthodoxy" in the written syntax of IndE. Chand (2009), discussed in more detail in Chapter 10, reports strikingly similar ideologies of IndE syntax to the present data. And the contrast has been noted in a recent study of the speech of Indians in London too: Hundt and Staicov (2018) found that syntactic variables—article omission and other features—did not correspond to an ethnic identity measure, but Zipp and Dellwo (2012) found that prosodic features did correlate with the ethnic identity measure for the same individuals.

IndE thus has selective dialectal conservatism. Syntax is seen as a more important domain of standard norm maintenance, in order to cultivate the status of a proficient and legitimate speaker. Phonology is seen in less prescriptive terms and may be recruited more readily for the construction of a local Indian identity.


## 6.5. DISCUSSION: LANGUAGE IDEOLOGIES IN INDIGENIZING GROUPS

Chapter 3 found a close correspondence between the use of grammatical features and a bilingual's proficiency and frequency of use of IndE. The present chapter has complicated this picture. Proficiency does not relate as closely to accent features. In terms of accent choice, IndE speakers behave more like native dialect speakers than foreign language speakers when in contact with native English speakers.

This is strong empirical support for Schneider's (2007) view that systematic shifts toward endogenous norms can occur quite independently of questions of fluency or nativeness. But IndE speakers do not show the same endonormative confidence with respect to *all* aspects of their linguistic system. Evidence from self-corrections and metalinguistic commentaries clearly indicated a view of nonstandard syntax as undesirable and nonstandard phonology as acceptable and potentially valuable.

A division of labor within the linguistic system appears to be one solution to resolving the competing social goals of being a "new speaker" (cf. O'Rourke and Pujolar 2013) of English. Morphosyntactic features can be used to signal education and proficiency and thus become more risky to use for stylistic purposes, while phonological variants can express allegiance and identity without posing the same threat to perceived legitimacy as an English speaker.

[150]    *English in India*

Stabilization of a dialect can thus be internally heterogeneous, with different degrees of endonormative stabilization in different parts of the language.

This is not to say that phonological features are never governed by proficiency, or that syntactic features never participate in style shifting, but these were less apparent in the data. A few phonetic forms, for example, variation in the use of /v/ and /w/, might be more linked to proficiency, and a few syntactic forms, for example, use of the focus marker *only* or rates of argument omission, may vary stylistically. There is no simple dichotomy in the behavior of syntax and phonology, and particularly in more informal situations in urban Indian contexts, the whole range of stylistic variability is likely to be observable (though see Chapter 10 for a discussion of limited style range in IndE). It may be the contact situation that heightens the risk of being misread by less familiar interlocutors and brings this differential ideology to the fore.

This dichotomous language ideology is widespread and can be found across New Englishes and other contact varieties. Eersel (1971: 320) notes that "A [Surinamese] student who speaks Dutch in perfectly formed sentences, choosing words from a well-stocked thesaurus, and without a Dutchman's pronunciation, is highly praised: a man without affectation!" Rickford and Rickford (2000) describe Standard African-American English as "a variety in which the speaker uses standard grammar but still sounds black" (2000: 224). They cite a study by Hoover (1978) that found a similar discrepancy in evaluative responses to the standard and vernacular, and Rahman (2002) offers further evidence of a division of labor between syntax and phonology in Standard African American English. A prescriptive preoccupation with syntactic conformity has also been documented for nonstandard varieties (e.g., Cameron 1995). Bourhis (1997: 312) even cites the French linguist Martinet's observation, in 1969, that accents and dialects of French should be respected as long as the speaker "uses impeccable syntax and vocabulary."

This conservatism with respect to syntax may derive from the "linguistic schizophrenia" (B. Kachru 1992), "schizoglossia" (Pakir 1994), or, more neutrally, "steady state" or "equilibrium" (Mukherjee 2007) of nonnative speakers' simultaneous resistance to indigenous forces at work in their varieties and to the imposition of external models. Forces may have conspired to make IndE a particularly conservative variety historically (see Chapter 2), so these effects may be heightened for IndE speakers. Later, Chapter 10 will investigate in detail whether SgE parallels IndE in this respect.

---

Part I of this volume has been devoted to the case of English in India: the historical conditions of its emergence as a cluster of speech practices, the origins of its new grammatical forms in the structures of Indian languages, and how grammatical and phonetic variation indicates nascent identity functions of the variety.

Next, in Part II, I broaden the lens. Adopting a comparative approach (Tagliamonte 2002; Szmrecsanyi 2009), this second part of the book will test hypotheses about the processes that underpin new dialect formation in postcolonial regions. Through a comparison of India and Singapore, I identify some of the most powerful historical, cognitive, and social mechanisms that shape New Englishes today.

# PART II
## *Comparing India and Singapore*

# CHAPTER 7
# Rates of Change

India and Singapore form an intriguing contrast. The regions have developed radically different varieties of English, despite somewhat comparable British colonial histories. Particularly striking is the fact that English has seen much more radical structural change and nativization in Singapore than in India, despite having been in the region for half the amount of time. This chapter compares the historical forces that shaped Indian English (IndE) and Singapore English (SgE), showing how key differences in the linguistic, ethnographic, and historical ecology led to distinct dialect formation dynamics in the two settings.

Mufwene (2001) describes language evolution as restructuring that involves competition and selection among a pool of linguistic traits that have been made available through ecological forces. Linguistic ecology in Mufwene's use may be external or internal to a language variety. Among external ecological forces, Mufwene includes ethnographic ecology (social relations among groups) and structural ecology (language forms in the contact setting); among ecological forces internal to a language variety, he includes such phenomena as heterogeneity of forms within one of the languages in contact, or congruence of features across multiple substrates. I compare the two regions across this range of social, historical, and structural forces.

In the discussion that follows, I first recap the ecology in which IndE developed, presented earlier in Chapter 2. I then compare this with the historical and ecological dynamics of SgE. The discussion reflects on which factors may or may not underlie the dramatic differences in how the two varieties have developed. Certain historical similarities appear to have been less influential than other markedly distinct ecological factors, which have driven divergent outcomes in the two regions. In closing I briefly show that, although the direction and rate of change has differed, the basic processes of linguistic change resemble those found in any contact situation.

*From Deficit to Dialect.* Devyani Sharma, Oxford University Press. © Oxford University Press 2023.
DOI: 10.1093/oso/9780195307504.003.0007

## 7.1. ENGLISH IN INDIA: A RECAP

Chapter 2 reviewed in detail a range of Englishes that emerged in India over a period of 400 years, noting social and linguistic hallmarks of these varieties over time. This historical ecology is briefly summarized below, before a comparison with the situation in Singapore.

(i) *Size of population and subcommunities*: IndE is unique among New Englishes in terms of the size and diversity of the region denoted by a single label. Both historically and currently, any discussion of English in India has to grapple with innumerable subcommunities within a larger national entity. Size alone has meant relatively slow and disjointed developments in IndE. As outlined in Chapter 2, while Babu English, elite British IndE, and varieties of Anglo-Indian English were developing through diverse types of contact with the British, the vast majority of India had little use of or contact with English. Processes of speech accommodation through face-to-face interaction (which can lead to focusing of dialect forms) were not widespread but, rather, concentrated in specific, smaller communities. Vast numbers of Indians still do not use English as a primary language, which places limits on the emergence of stable usage norms or a unified variety across the region.

(ii) *Language shift*: The relative stability of these large populations and the introduction of English via institutional channels have meant very little shift to English in any Indian community historically, with the exception of Anglo-Indian and other Christian communities and some bilingual urban speakers currently. The colonial incorporation of English into education did extend exposure to English, but low education rates meant no wholesale adoption of English. The three-language policy since independence also places limits on the extent of English-medium education. India is certainly witnessing a significant increase in English-medium enrollment (doubling between 2008 and 2009, and 2013 and 2014), but enrollment in such schools is still less than 10% of overall school enrolment (Nagarajan 2015). India maintains robust use of large-scale and influential indigenous languages at the state and local levels, and in many cases incursions into the vitality of local languages have been made by Hindi rather than English.

(iii) *Modes of acquisition:* Although India encompasses a range of contexts of English use, formal and informal, the primary mode of acquisition of English for Indians has been through education, either as a single subject or as the medium of instruction. Home acquisition and informal "street" acquisition occur too, but these are not major contexts for acquisition of English in India.

[156]   *Comparing India and Singapore*

(iv) *Founder effects*: As noted, a historical exception to the broad lack of language shift is the Anglo-Indian community, which showed an early shift to native English use. Chapter 2 suggested that this group may represent a founder effect in Indian English more generally, as Anglo-Indians, along with the wider Christian community, have historically been recruited into sectors such as teaching due their English ability (Maher 2007). Unlike native English-speaking countries, schools are a primary conduit for acquisition of English in India, and Chapter 2 noted a number of linguistic features that may have originated from this community. Further research may elucidate the intriguing question of whether their influence on Indian English arose primarily through their covert prestige in social networks within convent schools or their overt prestige as schoolteachers.

A more recent group that may "punch above its weight" in terms of influencing IndE more widely is the speech of native, bilingual IndE speakers in contemporary urban centers such as Delhi and Mumbai. These high-prestige varieties are spreading through social networks, media, and the education sector.

(v) *Migration*: Migration and population mixing can cause restructuring and rapid focusing in dialects (Kerswill and Williams 2000). Although India has seen massive population migration and replacements over its history, many of these tended to be in earlier periods. Also, partly due to the size of the region, IndE as a whole has not been affected by significant changes in population groups in recent centuries. Exceptions can be noted in specific instances, such the postpartition increase of Punjabi speakers in Delhi, which has certainly influenced the character of Delhi English.

(vi) *Typological class of contact languages*: Indo-Aryan and Dravidian languages are languages with rich morphology, much more so than English. As Chapters 4 and 5 have shown, there is strong pan-Indic substrate pressure to retain overt morphological marking of various grammatical categories in IndE. The lack of language shift to English in India reinforces this pressure, as continued bilingual dominance in Indic languages maintains this pressure at the individual level.

(vii) *Lingua francas*: India is well-known for stable, multiply embedded multilingualism. Most IndE speakers speak at least a local language and a wider state-level language. The latter may be Hindi, the primary language of wider communication in the North of India, or it may be a widely spoken regional language such as Tamil or Bengali. Although Hindi and Urdu have served as the major lingua francas in North India for centuries, this use has not led to radical simplification (except in specific cases, such as Hindi in Mumbai). There is therefore no influence of a structurally simplified substrate, nor was there any pressing need for English as a lingua franca, as these roles were already filled by indigenous regional languages of wider communication.

(viii) *Language policies*: As Chapter 2 noted, English infiltrated the Indian linguistic ecology most substantially through 19th-century colonial policies designed to displace indigenous models of education. It also spread through the civil services, again with the goal of creating an intermediary class of British-trained functionaries. These policies, combined with stable indigenous multilingualism, meant that the early stages of IndE were not associated with any rapid, organic, or informal spread of English. After independence, English was not adopted as the sole official language nor as the official medium of education. Since independence, English has seen some spread into informal domains but continues primarily in its limited high-prestige role in education, government, and media.

These factors have conspired to favor conservative rates and types of change in IndE. The grammatical features arising out of these historical and ecological conditions tend to be subtle: slight differences in grammatical structure (e.g., omission or overextension of selected forms) and differences in function despite surface similarity to native varieties (e.g., modal use or the past perfect construction).

This stands in dramatic contrast to the extent of change and the extent of dialect focusing—or emergence of new norms—in SgE, all within a shorter time frame.

## 7.2. SOCIAL HISTORIES OF ENGLISH IN SINGAPORE

What makes SgE remarkable, perhaps unique, among indigenized English dialects is its radical structural divergence from BrE within a relatively short space of time, entirely unlike the slow and diffuse accrual of change in the Indian subcontinent. Of this dramatic structural reorganization, Ansaldo asserts that "though considered a variety of English, [Colloquial Singapore English] is really typologically closer to languages of East and Southeast Asia" (2004: 139).

Particularly due to the striking features of its most vernacular variety, often termed Colloquial Singapore English, SgE is widely acknowledged to be much further along the path of dialect formation than India, despite the fact that English has been used in India for twice as long. Schneider (2007: 153) describes SgE as being "far advanced" at Phase 4 (endonormative stabilization), with an expectation that elements of Phase 5 (differentiation) may follow soon. More recently, scholars have noted that language shift and

[158] *Comparing India and Singapore*

ongoing localization may well place SgE at Phase 5 (Tan 2012; Wee 2014). As discussed in Chapter 2, Schneider (2007: 161) and others place IndE at an earlier stage of indigenization: Phase 3 (nativization), with indications of Phase 4.

Here, I briefly review the history of English in Singapore and then examine a parallel list of ecological features to those described for IndE in the previous section. The comparison will show that the majority of factors differ markedly between IndE and SgE, in particular differences in policies, informal use, language shift, population sizes, and contact languages. The few similarities are outweighed by these differences, leading to radical change in one variety (SgE) and conservatism in the other (IndE).

Lim (2007, 2010a) identifies the first age of Singaporean linguistic history as the "age of the original immigrant substrates." The incorporation of Singapore into the British East India Company as a trading post in 1819 led to rapid migration to the area from Southern China, Malaysia, Indonesia, and South Asia, and a population increase from a few hundred in 1819 to half a million by 1931. The Malay group was initially dominant but were numerically outnumbered by the Chinese within a few decades in the 19th century. Among the Chinese subcommunities, Hokkien (mutually intelligible with Teochew) was associated with the more economically powerful group and became the primary lingua franca among Chinese groups (Lim 2010a).

In addition to these groups was an indigenous Straits-born Chinese group, the Babas or Peranakan Chinese, a group of mixed ethnic heritage (often Chinese men and local Malay or Indonesian women) that settled on English and Baba Malay, a Malay-lexified Hokkien substrate Creole, as their languages (Lim 2010b). As discussed later in this section, this group bears some resemblances to the Anglo-Indian population discussed in Chapter 2 with respect to early native English use, aspects of social status, and founder effects. In addition to the presence of languages associated with various other small groups—South Asians, Eurasians—Lim (2010a) notes crucially that Bazaar Malay, a restructured contact variety of Malay distinct from Baba Malay, was used as a lingua franca across ethnic groups in the region for centuries.

During this first age, English was introduced into this context very much as in India: In 1834 the first English-medium schools were founded via colonial educational ordinances, with a steady increase in English-medium teaching. Gupta (1994) notes that English-medium schools in the early stages of this policy did not always use English exclusively, and a lot of Malay was present as well. Nevertheless, despite some countervailing pressure for Chinese schools to be maintained, enrollment in English schools increased steadily. Approximately 32% of students were enrolled in English-medium schools by 1947; this figure was up to 43% by 1952 and close to 80% by the 1980s (Tickoo 1996; Lim and Foley 2004).

RATES OF CHANGE [159]

Despite some similarities to India in terms of colonial policy during the first age, the surrounding social and linguistic ecology was very different. Singapore's small population and role as a trading center involved extraordinary internal diversity, frequent shifts in demographics, and constant interaction across ethnic boundaries (despite the maintenance of ethnically defined enclaves), forming restructured lingua francas long before the arrival of English. This meant that English in Singapore during the 19th and early 20th centuries had, as its linguistic ecology, high levels of contact with Bazaar Malay, Hokkien, and Baba Malay, and additionally Teochew, Malay, Cantonese, Mandarin, Hakka, and Indian languages. Informal English use as a trade lingua franca was part of these diverse early contacts.

What Lim terms the "second age" begins with Singapore being granted self-rule in 1957, and becoming independent from the Federation of Malaysia in 1965. This period is considered the early incubation of what we now know as SgE, a time that Schneider (2007: 155) describes as the start of Phase 4. Differences from India's sociolinguistic history increase further during this postcolonial period.

At the time of Singaporean independence, English was expanding rapidly through the school system but had not yet gained a foothold as a primary language. The substrates of Hokkien and Bazaar Malay dominated demographically (Lim 2007; Ng 2008), as indicated by home language statistics for 1957: Hokkien 30% > Teochew 17.0% > Cantonese 15.1% > Malay 13.2% > Mandarin 0.1% (Ng 2008). The Singaporean variety of Bazaar Malay, the major lingua franca, was itself structurally influenced by Hokkien (Ho and Platt 1993: 9; Lim 2007: 453), reinforcing the influence of convergent structures among these varieties.

While scholars agree that intense multilingual contact was at play throughout, there is some debate over which of these languages have exerted a more formative influence on SgE, due to significant shifts in the balance of different inputs during the 20th century. English and Mandarin received intensive institutional promotion in later decades, and Bao (2005) takes Mandarin as a dominant input for later stages of the establishment of SgE, due to its promotion in education since 1970.

However, as SgE began to form much earlier than independence in 1965, Baba Malay, Bazaar Malay, Hokkien, Teochew, and Cantonese are widely seen as constituting the most important formative inputs (Ho and Platt 1993: 27; Gupta 1994: 41; Ansaldo 2004; Lim 2007: 452; Yip and Matthews 2007: 236). Some grant a greater role to Baba Malay and Bazaar Malay (Gupta 1998; Low and Brown 2005; Ng 2011), while others favor a greater role for Chinese languages (Alsagoff et al. 1998; Bao 2005; Hiramoto and Sato 2012).

Gupta (1994: 41) and Lim (2007: 454) warn against pure demographic inferences, noting that although Hokkien speakers may have dominated numerically in the mid-20th century, they may not have been the major Chinese input to early SgE, as the Cantonese adopted English more readily and may have played a central role in the resulting variety.

Independent Singapore has been characterized by a shift from this plurality of indigenous languages to a dominance of a small set of official languages—English, Mandarin, Malay, and Tamil (Gupta 2001; Lim 2007). Mandarin in particular has experienced a dramatic surge in use due to various forms of institutional promotion, such as the Speak Mandarin Campaign, promoted from the 1970s onward in education and media. This increase has seen a steady replacement of other Chinese languages as the primary home language. In 1980, 59.5% of Singaporeans reported "Chinese dialects" as their primary home language, but this dropped to 14.3% in 2010 and 8.7% in 2020. Mandarin replaced these other Chinese languages, expanding from 10.2% in 1980 to 35.6% in 2010. In 2020 this figure dropped to 29.9% in 2020, reflecting some shift from Mandarin to English as the primary home language. Census figures show a slower decline for Malay (13.9% in 1980 to 9.2% in 2020) and Tamil (3.1% in 1980 to 2.5% in 2020) over the same period (Singapore Census of Population 2020; Leimgruber 2013: 7). This change has undoubtedly made Mandarin a more relevant substrate language for SgE in recent decades. As will be shown in Chapter 8, it is important to bear in mind that this substrate is itself a contact variety, affected by other languages in Singapore.

Contemporary Singapore has experienced a significant language shift to English. English was declared the main language of education in 1987 and much earlier had become the new lingua franca, being used as the main language of business, government, and schooling (Lim 2007). Lim and Foley (2004: 6) report that in both the 1990 and 2000 censuses, the reporting of English as the dominant language was higher among those aged 5–14 than among older groups, indicating a language shift. They quote Newbrook (1987: 12) as already describing Singapore as "well on the way towards becoming a largely English-speaking country" nearly 30 years ago and suggest that "for many young people, English is the only language spoken confidently" (Lim and Foley 2004: 4). In the 2020 census, 48.3% of Singaporeans reported English as their main home language, up from 12% in 1980.

I do not comment in detail on Lim's (2010a) "third age" (late 1980s onward) and "fourth age" (2000 onward) here, except to note that they involve a continuing dominance of Mandarin and English, established since the 1970s, with the added influences of recent high-status Cantonese-speaking migrants from Hong Kong and the repackaging of Singapore for a multiethnic mix of English-speaking professionals, who additionally maintain various community languages (Jain and Wee 2015).

With this history in mind, we can now compare Singapore and India directly according to the list of sociohistorical factors outlined for India in Section 7.1.

(i) *Size of population and subcommunities*: The difference in size between the two countries, and its consequences for processes of language change, cannot be overstated. Singapore's small size and rapid population growth (a few hundred in 1819; half a million in 1931; 5 million in 2012) has meant intensive contact among most of its speakers and clear potential for focusing and founder effects. By contrast, India's massive population has meant very diffuse processes of accommodation and focusing only in pockets of regular users, with vast swathes of stable indigenous multilingualism and gradual change. These population differences impact upon many of the factors that follow.

(ii) *Language shift*: The difference in population sizes has direct consequences for the implementation of policies and rates of social change. Because of the small scale of Singapore, English-medium education was thoroughly instituted over the course of 150 years, with all children now completing content education in English. Contrast this with the earlier cited English-medium education figures of less than 10% in India. The majority of Singaporeans are bilingual with English as a dominant or equal language, and with constant contact between grammars, whereas English use is extremely limited among the vast majority of India's population. In short, Singapore is experiencing large-scale language shift to English, while India is not.

(iii) *Modes of acquisition*: Acquisition via the educational system is widely noted for Singapore, as for India, and emphasized in early work as an important factor (Ho and Platt 1993). However, this focus on education at the expense of other contextual factors has been critiqued (Deterding 2007: 87). Leimgruber (2013) and Bao (2001, 2015) also question the exclusive importance of education as a mode of acquisition in Singapore historically, noting the relatively late establishment of instruction in English. Crucially, Lim and Foley (2004: 3) and Bao (2001) highlight the presence of informal modes of English use and exchange via trade in the period before English education was well established. Bao (2001: 285) asserts that "it is certain that a pidginized form of English, either local or foreign in origin, preceded the present-day Singapore English" and that, at the time, "most people, if they knew English, acquired it without the benefit of formal instruction."

This points to a pincer-like development for SgE: distinct basilectal and acrolectal starting points, with a broader continuum of use emerging later. The historic development of a pidgin or basilect is very much at odds with the more conservative history of IndE, where the vast scale of early East India Company operations meant far more interaction via local intermediaries. Creolization and radical or rapid contact-based restructuring was very limited in the Indian context.

[162] *Comparing India and Singapore*

(iv) *Founder effects*: There are some interesting parallels in Singapore to the founder effects mentioned earlier for India. Lim (2009: 233, 2010b: 283) describes an early, nativized variety of English spoken by a local elite in the 19th century in Singapore, the Peranakan Chinese (descendants of Chinese migrants and Malay/Indonesian women), and suggests that it may represent a founder population for SgE. Although their status seems to have been less conflicted than that of Anglo-Indians, this group bears a number of striking similarities to the Anglo-Indian community in sociolinguistic terms: they favored English-medium education, attended convent schools, developed a role as intermediaries between the British administrators and local populations, exhibited greater political allegiance to the British than other groups, aligned with English as a community language, and retained a number of distinctive BrE influences, for instance in more British, rather than SgE, articulation of certain stops and fricatives (Lim 2010b: 339). As with the Anglo-Indian community, this group may have had a founder effect on wider SgE due to their high educational levels, particularly in English, their greater interaction with BrE speakers as intermediaries, and their prominent role socioeconomically (Lim 2011: 283). Needless to say, this interesting parallel in founder groups does not imply any resemblance in the specific linguistic structures that arose in IndE and SgE.

There may have even been a direct link between the two groups historically: Parviainen (2012), citing Hogue (2001: 169), Platt et al. (1983: 8), Rai (2007: 178), and Gupta (2001: 49), notes a number of sources of direct influence of IndE on SgE, including British adoption (and pan-Asian colonial use) of Anglo-Indian lexicon, British exportation of Anglo-Indian teachers during British rule, a continued presence of Indian teachers in Singapore, and the continuing immigration of educated Indian English speakers in Singapore. These influences are intriguing, but ultimately unlikely to significantly outrank other influences such as substrate typologies and wider population dynamics.

(v) *Migration*: Unlike the relatively stable influences of Hindi and other majority language populations on IndE, Singapore has seen dramatic changes, described earlier, in demographic proportions during the last two centuries. This regular turnover in substrate proportions within a small population may have meant, in theory, regular *re*-restructuring; for example, a Hokkien and Bazaar Malay-driven variety inherited by more recently Mandarin-dominant speakers would be restructured again, increasing the opportunity for even more leveling and other contact processes.

(vi) *Typological class of contact languages*: Unlike the inflectional (e.g., Indo-Aryan) and agglutinating (e.g., Dravidian) languages of India, the Sinitic languages that English has had contact with within Singapore are highly analytic. Malay, an Austronesian language, is agglutinative, but both Bazaar Malay and Baba Malay underwent simplification processes leading to an analytic structure (Lim and Foley 2004: 3). The history of intensive trade contact and multilayered interethnic communication patterns described above constantly reinforced this analytic model in the structural ecology of SgE. IndE arose much more out of stable bilingual use of English alongside inflectional or agglutinative languages. This difference has important structural consequences for grammatical subsystems in the two varieties, compared in the next chapter.

(vii) *Lingua francas*: As noted above, most of the languages of Singapore have experienced grammatical restructuring through use as a lingua franca or through acquisition by nonnative speakers. Bazaar Malay and Baba Malay were simplified vernaculars used as lingua francas in the context of trade and intermarriage. Hokkien served as a lingua franca for diverse subgroups, adapting in structure to a heterogeneous speech community. Even Singaporean Mandarin experienced leveling of a number of morphological and semantic contrasts through rapid acquisition by speakers of other Chinese languages after it was instituted as an official language (Sharma 2009; see also Chapter 8). Furthermore, as noted in (iii) above, English was used as a trade lingua franca in the early stages of contact, with basilectal uses developing to a much greater extent than in India. These layered contact varieties in Singapore represent a major source of restructuring, much less so in the Indian context.

(viii) *Language policies*: Colonial English policies in Singapore were similar to those in India, with an official, institutional presence after 1835, just as in India, and selection as a co-official language at independence. But subsequent to independence, Singapore pursued a markedly different policy than India, granting official status to four languages and promoting English and Mandarin institutionally at the cost of other languages. As described above, this has had a dramatic impact both on language ideologies and on the use of English, which has seen substantial shift to native use.

Before pulling these observations together to assess which forces best account for the different linguistic outcomes in India and Singapore, let us briefly consider the linguistic structures of SgE that have resulted from this sociohistory, as we did for IndE in Chapter 2.

## 7.3. COMMON FEATURES OF SINGAPORE ENGLISH

As with IndE, the preponderance of SgE traits derive directly or indirectly from contact with local substrates, while a few features derive from the original

British English input and some others from general cognitive processes of regularization and change. The main difference from IndE is in the form and degree of change in grammatical structures.

In this section I list a few illustrative examples of the same three sources of change outlined for IndE in Chapter 2—British-derived retentions, substrate structures, and independent innovations. It is beyond the scope of this chapter to provide a comprehensive overview of grammatical features of SgE. Numerous excellent studies and collections exist for further reference (e.g., Deterding et al. 2003; Deterding et al. 2005; Lim 2004; Deterding 2007). Chapter 8 takes a closer look at a selection of grammatical structures.

### 7.3.1. British-Derived Retentions

The phonetic characteristics of IndE that derived from BrE hold for SgE as well. Two are listed in (1):

(1)  a.   nonrhoticity in acrolectal varieties
     b.   split in pronunciation of words in TRAP/BATH lexical sets

Archaic retentions from BrE are not as commonly cited for SgE as for IndE, but, as noted earlier, Lim (2010b) has observed that Peranakan English—an old, educated variety of English in Singapore that may have played a role in the early stages of SgE—does retain some colonial usage and a penchant for somewhat outdated British English idioms, many of which are common in IndE too. A few of the many examples listed by Lim (2010b: 342–343) are provided in (2).

(2)   *hopes . . . are soon dashed; a jolly time; dressed in his Sunday best; still life in the old grey mare; kith and kin*

As with IndE, much more substantial than British retentions in SgE are indigenizations based on contact with local languages.

### 7.3.2. Substrate Structures

As noted, the numerous substrate inputs for SgE are typologically very distinct from those of IndE, and the proportion of these input systems has varied dramatically in the past century. As a result, a range of influences from Sinitic and Austronesian languages can be seen in what is termed colloquial SgE.

RATES OF CHANGE  [165]

As in most standard-dialect continua, many phonetic features in SgE are only attenuated in more standard registers, whereas many morphosyntactic features are absent altogether. Here I list just a few features of colloquial SgE—phonetic and morphosyntactic—to illustrate the types of traits that derive from substrate structures, and to highlight their divergence from IndE.

Examples of substrate-derived phonetic features are listed in (3) (see Deterding 2007 for details).

(3) a. inventory substitutions (e.g., substitution of /θ/ and /ð/ with [f] word-finally or [t] and [d] word-medially and word-initially)
   b. phonemic differences (e.g., lack of vowel length contrast)
   c. phonotactic differences (e.g., coda cluster simplification)
   d. addition or loss of allophonic rules (e.g., word-final devoicing)
   e. prosodic differences (e.g., syllable-timing, lexical tone)

The very different substrate phonologies for IndE mean the varieties share only a few of these features, such as syllable timing. Bao (1998) suggests that the syllable-timed stress system of colloquial SgE arises from the substrates being tone languages, noting that Bantu substrates of African Englishes share this property. Certainly tone in SgE is one of the most distinctive features of the variety and may interact in complex ways with stress (see Ng 2011; Chong and German 2017). Syllable timing in South Asian Englishes derives directly from substrate rhythm, not tone (Fuchs 2016); this may play a part in SgE rhythm too.

In the domain of syntax, SgE is striking for its radical distance from standard native varieties of English. The examples in (4) show how the co-occurrence of several syntactic features—noun phrase omission, use of *one*, use of *got* (Lee et al. 2009; Hiramoto and Sato 2012), relative clause structure (Alsagoff and Lick 1998)—can produce highly distinctive syntactic structures. The IndE examples in Chapter 2 showed that IndE does not exhibit anywhere near this degree of systematic restructuring in syntax.

(4) a. Why so slow one? Wait, got no more, then you know.
      ("Why are you taking so much time? If you delay any further, nothing will be left, and then you'll learn a lesson.")

   b. That boy pinch my sister one very naughty.
      "That boy who pinched my sister is very naughty."

      (Alsagoff and Ho 1998)

[166] *Comparing India and Singapore*

Chapter 8 explores several grammatical features of SgE in more detail, comparing the system with that of IndE.

SgE is well known for extensive use of discourse particles borrowed from substrates (Wee 2003; Wong 2004; Lim 2007; Wee 2010). Again, this is markedly different from the much more limited use of pragmatic markers in IndE, such as focus *only*, invariant tags, and a few borrowed tags (e.g., *na*). Interestingly, this distinctive and established component of SgE grammar appears to creatively generate new variants that go beyond substrate languages, such as *know* (Wee 2003) and *right* (Tan 2010).

Lexical indigenization in SgE parallels comparable processes in IndE and other New Englishes, such as direct loans, as in (5a), and calques, as in (5b), both deriving from the substrate.

(5)   a.   Ali is a very *kiasu* person ('worried about losing out'). The boss likes him because he knows how to *angkat* ('curry favour').
      b.   Don't sit here and shake legs—get to work!

(Alsagoff and Ho 1998)

Some constructions in SgE combine lexical and syntactic innovations, such as the *kena* passive, in (6), which includes a Malay loan word accompanied by further specific syntactic structure such as use of the infinitival or past participle verb form, an optional *by*-phrase, and adverse effects implied for the subject (Bao and Wee 1999; Fong 2004).

(6)   He also kena play out lor
      "He was played out."                    (Fong 2004: 98)

In IndE we saw some similar innovations, as in the use of the Hindi imperative inflection as a verbal template for novel code-switched forms. SgE shows much greater use of systematic grammatical innovations of this type.

### 7.3.3. Independent Innovations

As in all contact settings, some innovations are simply internally driven changes particular to that speech community, not necessarily related to contact with substrates. The example in (7) shows lexical shifts specific to SgE.

(7)   There's Nina with that <u>batch</u> of girls. She's a nice <u>fellow</u>. (Alsagoff and Ho 1998)

Some semantic shifts may be based on universal cognitive, semantic, or other structural principles, resurfacing in unrelated postcolonial varieties. Two examples that are also found in IndE are given in (8).

(8)  Semantic shift
    a.  My uncle staying [= 'living'] there.        (Leimbgruber 2011: 51)
    b.  I'm going to keep [= 'put'] these photos in that drawer.
                                  (Bautista and Gonzalez 2006: 134)

It is conceivable that these uses of *stay* and *keep* arise in both varieties because of natural extensions in semantic space. However, both Hindi and Mandarin also use *stay* and *keep* with these meanings, so distinguishing substrate from noncontact effects is a challenge. Wee (1998) offers the intriguing suggestion that semantic broadening is more common than narrowing in SgE because of the use of the variety by heterogeneous subgroups, each of which may add innovative meanings or uses to the full range of a lexical form. This may hold true more generally for indigenized Englishes, as most function as languages of wider communication or as an auxiliary language.

Other processes observed in IndE, such as "un-fixing" of idioms and the loss of mass/count distinctions, are also observable in SgE and other New Englishes, similarly pointing to general processes of regularization and increased structural transparency.

SgE thus shares a few features with IndE that derive from British sources or from cognitively natural processes of regularization or shift. It diverges from IndE most markedly in the domain of substrate transfer, for typological reasons, and also in terms of the extent of grammatical change and dialect formation, for sociodemographic reasons.

## 7.4. MECHANISMS OF CHANGE: ECOLOGY AND POLICY

We are now in a position to evaluate the broad linguistic outcomes of English in Singapore and India—structure and use—in terms of various historical, social, and language ecology factors. These are summarized in Table 7.1.

Let us first compare the current status, or outcomes, of English structure and use. As indicated in the last section in Table 7.1, linguistic outcomes are extremely different in the two settings despite a few similarities, such as BrE retentions and a few universal cognitive or semantic shifts. As Chapter 8 will show in more detail, SgE exhibits much more radical restructuring in all parts of the language. Chapter 10 will also show that style range in the *use* of SgE is also extremely wide—wider than in most native varieties of English and certainly wider than IndE, which tends to have a narrow style range and more

[168]   *Comparing India and Singapore*

**Table 7.1.** FACTORS AND OUTCOMES IN INDIAN AND SINGAPORE ENGLISH

|  | India | Singapore |
| --- | --- | --- |
| *Similarities* | | |
| Colonial language policy | via L2 education | via L2 education |
| Existing lingua franca(s) | yes | yes |
| *Differences* | | |
| Length of contact | 400 years (since 1600) | 200 years (since 1819) |
| Primary substrate type | inflectional | analytic |
| Prior lingua franca(s) | Farsi, Urdu, Hindi | Bazaar Malay, Baba Malay |
| Historic informal channels of use (e.g., trade) | limited | substantial |
| Population | 1.25 billion | 5.5 million |
| Demographics | coexistence of massive, stable groups | immigration and intensive contact in a small space |
| Postcolonial English policy | official, not compulsory | official, compulsory |
| *Outcomes* | | |
| Language change | conservative | radical |
| Shift to English | slow | rapid |
| Speech style range | narrow | broad |

direct influence from the speaker's L1 and proficiency level. Furthermore, Chapter 10 will show stable dialect focusing in SgE at *both* ends of this style continuum, basilectal and acrolectal. This contrasts with IndE, which was shown in Chapter 3 to exhibit L2-type variation at one end.

In short, language shift, linguistic restructuring, endonormative stabilization, and internal dialect differentiation (as evidenced in extensive diglossia) are underway in Singapore to a degree not witnessed at all in India.

What explains these differences in extent of change and nativization?

The first three factors in Table 7.1 do not offer answers. Colonial language policies were similar, and both regions had existing lingua francas in the ecology. Moreover, more radical change has occurred in the variety that has had *less*, not more, time to change, so length of contact also fails to offer a simple explanation.

It is the remaining factors listed under Differences in Table 7.1 that together offer an explanation.

First, we have seen that the typological class of substrates, including lingua francas, is dramatically different for these two varieties.

Second, the historical use of a pidginized version of English as an informal language of trade—a use broadly absent in the Indian context—was likely to have played a key role in the development of a stable basilectal variety of SgE, but not IndE.

RATES OF CHANGE [169]

Third, demographic dynamics in Singapore—population migrations and intensive interethnic communication—caused multiple cycles of grammatical leveling, simplification, and restructuring, again broadly absent in India. The small population size allowed such changes to diffuse more completely than in the Indian subcontinent.

Finally, language ideologies and policies pursued in the two regions have been markedly different after independence, with direct consequences for the use of English and attitudes toward it. Policies and wider ideologies have constructed English as the vehicle of global orientation, technology, and economic activity in Singapore, with other languages coming to be carriers of compartmentalized and more personal ethnic identities (Wee 2006). This has driven changes in language use in Singapore in a direction broadly absent in India, which has tended to favor ideologies that interleave home, state, and national languages, valorizing English as a prestige code, but not solely so; Hindi, English, Tamil, and other major regional languages also play this role. Other factors such as stable multilingualism, limited availability of English-medium schooling, large community size, and a long-standing history of language activism supporting vernacular languages all act as further countervailing forces.

A perhaps ironic outcome of the concerted institutional pressure since the 1970s to promote English in Singapore is that the faster rate of language shift that resulted was very likely also a contributor to faster vernacularization and stabilization of the basilectal variety. Prescriptivists in Singapore have favored native acquisition of English by Singaporeans while reviling its more vernacular forms (see Rubdy 2001); such ideologies fail to recognize that creating native speakers almost by definition creates vernacular speakers. I return to these issues in more detail in Chapter 10.

These different outcomes in India and Singapore complicate Schneider's (2007: 122) privileging of identity, and in particular its link to an identifiable Event X (e.g., independence), around which endonormative orientations develop. None of the factors described here—typology, trade use, demographics, and educational policy—constitute individual identity, yet they offer a solid basis for broad differences in outcome in the two settings. Evans (2014) similarly questions independence as a strict trigger for Phase 4, using archival material to show that in the case of Hong Kong, it is language policy, rather than changing identities among settlers and indigenous groups, that corresponds to increased indigenized usage.

The next chapter asks the same question—why are IndE and SgE so different?—but from a microlinguistic, not macrosocial, level. With a detailed comparison of grammatical structures in the two varieties, I assess the contribution of substrates or universal forces in shaping the new grammars.

[170]  *Comparing India and Singapore*

# CHAPTER 8
# Grammatical Universals?

The previous chapter reviewed large-scale historical differences between English in India and Singapore, in particular rate and degree of language change and language shift. Here, we turn to microlevel grammatical differences and similarities between Indian English (IndE) and Singapore English (SgE) that have arisen under these conditions. This chapter and the next assess competing possible accounts of why these specific combinations of features developed in the two varieties.

There has been considerable recent interest in grammatical traits that seem to recur across unrelated varieties of English, raising the possibility of emergent universals across Englishes around the world. These claims have been countered by robust evidence of transfer from indigenous languages, leaving open the question of which forces predominate in New Englishes.

This chapter assesses these two sources of change by comparing several grammatical features in IndE and SgE. The analysis finds no evidence for broad universals. Instead, it confirms two mechanisms of change proposed in Part I, both related to substrate structures. First, it confirms that *direct* substrate transfer is particularly strong where the substrate (or L1) involves overt and obligatory morphology and English offers no direct counterpart. Second, the comparative analysis also confirms a more *indirect* role of the substrate in change, whereby speakers make systematic inferences regarding mismatches between L1 and L2 systems and reorganize the grammar to generate novel "third grammar" systems.

*From Deficit to Dialect.* Devyani Sharma, Oxford University Press. © Oxford University Press 2023.
DOI: 10.1093/oso/9780195307504.003.0008

## 8.1. METHODOLOGICAL PRELIMINARIES

### 8.1.1. Data: Comparing Like with Like

A major challenge in comparative dialect analysis is matching data. Speech samples must come from reasonably similar segments of the two speech communities, bearing in mind, of course, that no two speech communities can ever be identical.

In order to compare the syntactic properties of the present IndE data to SgE, I use two types of data: (i) directly comparable published analyses of SgE, and (ii) original analysis of the International Corpus of English (ICE)-Singapore corpus.

For past tense use and copula use in particular, prior studies of SgE offer closely parallel analyses, and these can be compared with the primary data from IndE. These data tend to be from John Platt's early studies and involve a lower proportion of native SgE speakers. They are therefore compared with the 12 less-proficient IndE speakers identified in Chapter 3. This is also because these two grammatical features are only observable in the speech of less regular users of IndE.

Features that do not have parallel published analyses for SgE are examined through a comparison with the ICE-Singapore corpus. ICE corpora do not provide speaker information, so it is impossible to construct a continuum of speakers as was done for IndE, but an aggregated comparison of linguistic features is feasible. In order to facilitate a direct comparison with the IndE sociolinguistic interviews, a subset of 10 spoken data files totaling 20,000 words [S1A-018, 020, 022, 023, 025, 027, 044, 051, 085, 086] was selected from ICE-Singapore based on three key criteria: (i) the presence of some variation in the grammar for most of the features of interest—this reduced the size of the sub-sample, as many speakers in ICE-Singapore have relatively standard syntax, (ii) presence of a relatively casual and naturalistic style that is comparable to the casual sociolinguistic interviews conducted for IndE, and (iii) a sufficient quantity of speech per speaker. These conversational data exhibit a high level of native-like fluency and a well-represented mesolectal and acrolectal range. This group is therefore most appropriately compared with the 12 speakers in the present IndE data sets who formed the more proficient end of the IndE continuum in Chapter 3.

For all of the comparisons that follow, careful consideration was also given to the potential role of different SgE substrates. This is particularly important to consider for older SgE studies that predate substantial language shift. The analysis therefore also consults published descriptions of Hokkien, Teochew, Cantonese, and Malay and draws on elicited judgments and consultation with eight native speakers of these languages in order to identify precise substrate structures. This includes the Singaporean variety of Mandarin, which, as we

[172] *Comparing India and Singapore*

will see, has itself undergone change through contact with other Singaporean languages.

## 8.1.2. Hypotheses: Universals of New Englishes?

The five features listed in (1) were analyzed for IndE in Part I of the book. The analysis in this chapter compares that IndE usage with SgE usage of the same features.

(1)  a.  Irregular use of articles
     b.  Zero past tense forms of regular verbs
     c.  Wider range of uses of the progressive
     d.  Deletion of *be*
     e.  Variable use of modals

Together, these five forms allow several tests of grammatical change in New Englishes. Some of the forms involve similar substrate systems in the regional languages of India and Singapore, while others do not.

This allows us to ask whether substrates or wider universals drive the two new dialect systems: Do the dialects diverge at exactly the points of discrepancy between substrates (supporting a strong substrate view), or do they converge in spite of discrepancies between their substrates (supporting a strong universalist view)?

All the forms in (1) have been described as widespread across New Englishes, raising the possibility of some very general or universal processes. Kortmann and Szmrecsanyi (2004) list the first four as shared across a number of regions, including Asian Englishes, and suggest exploring these as candidates for universals of new Englishes. (See Kortmann 2013 for a more detailed discussion.) They list irregular use of articles as one of the "Top 12–15" features shared among varieties of English (p. 1155), and this feature is cited extensively as a shared trait in the World Englishes literature. Kortmann and Szmrecsanyi list zero past tense as a feature typical of Caribbean, American, Pacific, and Asian varieties (2004: 1189; see also Jenkins 2003: 26). Extension of the progressive to stative verbs is listed as typical of Asian, American, and African varieties (2004: 1189; see also Platt et al. 1984: 72–73; Williams 1987: 172–173; Jenkins 2003: 26; Melchers and Shaw 2003: 22, 158; Trudgill and Hannah 2008: 107, 130, 137). Deletion of *be* is listed as typical of Caribbean, Pacific, and Asian varieties (Kortmann and Szmrecsanyi 2004: 1193); Chambers (2004: 129) lists this as one of his top four candidates for English vernacular universals as well. Finally, innovative use of modals is absent from Kortmann and Szmrecsanyi's typology but is similarly mentioned as a common area of divergence in World Englishes (Jenkins 2003: 45; Mesthrie and Bhatt 2008: 64).

Thus, all five features are tantalizingly widespread and might indicate the operation of universal processes in New English grammars. Indeed, the examples in (2) and (3) do appear to show parallel usage in IndE and SgE for all five features.

(2)     Examples from IndE:
   a. I'm not working in Ø kitchen, I'm in Ø front desk.
   b. Before marriage I <u>enjoy</u> myself.
   c. I was only <u>having</u> 70% [in exam results].
   d. Because of competition customers Ø divided.
   e. V. <u>would</u> be coming to receive you on 15th and he <u>would</u> be bringing the ticket too.

(3) Examples from SgE:
   a. Cannot even promote Ø holiday in front of him muh.
      [ICE-SIN:S1A-023#215]
   b. I <u>watch</u> one or two episode.         [ICE-SIN:S1A-086#134]
   c. Maybe that's why I'<u>m having</u> a crush on him.
      [ICE-SIN: w1b-010.txt:342]
   d. I mean LK Ø very long-winded.         [ICE-SIN:S1A-023#243]
   e. The framework of analysis [in this paper] <u>would</u> be geared to look at the policy context.         [ICE-SIN:W1A-007#31]

As will be shown, very broad universals, for example, unmarked features of Universal Grammar, are not found to underpin these surface similarities. This is not to deny the potential for genuine universals. These have certainly been shown to govern cross-linguistic variation in the present grammatical forms, for example, in article use (Ionin et al. 2004), tense-aspect systems (Bybee et al. 1994) and copula systems (Stassen 1994). Some of these wider universals overlap with the substrate systems under examination here and so may indeed be reinforcing factors. However, across the present data we see no unambiguous instances of pure typological universals restructuring a new variety, independently of the structures of the L1 and L2.

A proposal that will be shown to be more relevant to IndE and SgE is the notion of "varioversals," namely, "features recurrent in language varieties with a similar sociohistory, historical depth, and mode of acquisition," such as L2 varieties of English (Szmrecsanyi and Kortmann 2009: 33). These acquisitional universals or Angloversals "may be the result of learning strategies of nonnative speakers, in other words properties typical of L2 varieties"

[174]   *Comparing India and Singapore*

(Kortmann and Szmrecsanyi 2004: 1192). These might include universal processes of simplification in L2 speech, or other natural orders of acquisition for English "irrespective of the languages involved" (Sand 2004: 281, see also Mesthrie 1992; Hilbert 2008; Davydova 2011). Some limited support for acquisitional processes is found in the present analysis, both generically shared by L2 learners (this chapter) and effects of quantity of input to the learner (Chapter 9).

Against this line of research into universals stands the view that careful analysis can show indigenous languages in a given region to be a primary source for restructuring in the local varieties of English (e.g., Filppula 2004; van Rooy 2006; Bao 2005, 2015). New grammatical usage in New Englishes may primarily arise from direct or indirect transfer of substrate language systems and contrasts. Such transfer features can often masquerade as universals, as they may be typologically very common. Close, comparative analysis of grammatical systems is therefore crucial in order to trace subtle distinctions in substrate predictions. The present analysis finds strong evidence of such effects.

Filppula et al. (2009) attempt to reconcile universalist and substratist perspectives, proposing a continuum between universal and contact sources of change and suggesting that some innovative structures may fall at the boundary between the two accounts.

### 8.1.3. Methods for Comparing Englishes: Frequencies, Constraints, and Sources

A common approach to the study of shared traits is to track their prevalence across varieties. Szmrecsanyi and Kortmann (2009), for example, define "as *pervasive* any feature that is attested in at least 75% of the varieties" (p. 1647). This raises two immediate questions for methodology. What do we mean by a "feature," and how do we interpret "pervasiveness"?

A "feature" can refer simply to a surface form or construction, as in (2) and (3). However, mere presence of a surface structure in two grammars cannot be taken to imply genuine similarity unless its grammatical conditioning is comparable (Tagliamonte 2002; Rickford 2006; Sharma 2009; Davydova 2011). If a surface form behaves differently in two grammars, it may not be accurate to describe it as the same feature. Kortmann and Szmrecsanyi readily acknowledge that a "bird's-eye view approach necessarily abstracts from many details and (partly necessary) qualifications in individual varieties" (2004: 1143).

Similarly, "pervasiveness" of a feature may be quite unrelated to universality. High regional prevalence of some features is certainly very intriguing, and the panvarietal overview of the *World Atlas of Variation in English* (Kortmann and Lunkenheimer 2013) gives us a unique snapshot of global resemblances. But what does pervasiveness represent? If a majority of Asian varieties exhibit zero past marking but also have aspect-oriented substrates with limited use of past morphology, then the prevalence of the feature simply points to regional or genetic similarities in substrates. Similarly, if three out of four Asian varieties exhibit a substantial deletion of articles, but in different grammatical contexts, based on different substrate semantics, surface prevalence again does not reflect any sort of universality.

We must therefore be careful not to aggregate surface similarities and obscure subtle but important differences between varieties at an early stage of analysis. This chapter (see also Sharma 2009, 2012) suggests that a more reliable method for establishing the extent of universality in New English traits should start with two basic steps: (i) ascertaining genuine similarity through quantitative examination of grammatical conditioning, and (ii) eliminating substrate transfer explanations before making any appeals to universality.

In the sections that follow, I apply this approach to evaluate the role of universals and substrate influence in the development of these two New Englishes.

## 8.2. ARTICLE USE

Many studies of New Englishes have noted a high degree of variability in article use. Substrate transfer was suggested in early work, based on qualitative examples (Platt et al. 1984; Williams 1987). However, a straightforward L1 effect was not clearly confirmed in Sand's (2004) ICE corpus comparison of article use, in which robust underuse of articles was not found in varieties whose substrates lacked articles. Sand did find greater substrate influence in spoken than in written genres and, by ruling out substrate explanations elsewhere, argued convincingly that a number of semantic extensions in definite article use across varieties can be accounted for by "a common tendency to expand the rules of English article use in a certain way" based on universal semantic properties (2004: 295).[1]

This tension between competing forces in New Englishes was seen for IndE article use in Chapter 4, where we saw a substrate-driven omission of specific indefinite *a*, but also a more universally discourse-driven omission of articles based on discourse familiarity.

Do these two effects—L1 influence on indefinite articles and a general discourse pragmatic effect on definite articles—arise in SgE as well?

Figure 8.1 shows that Mandarin resembles Hindi in only marking specificity in the article system, with the numeral *one* (Li and Thompson 1981; Robertson 2000; the same system holds for Malay, another Singaporean

[176]  *Comparing India and Singapore*

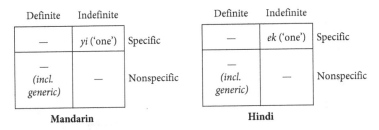

Figure 8.1. Mandarin and Hindi article systems.

substrate, Wong and Quek 2007: 215). This predicts a parallel to IndE usage, namely greater use of English *a* with specific indefinites.

Omission of articles has been widely noted for SgE. Wee and Ansaldo (2004: 58, 61) attribute article omission with indefinite and definite generic noun phrases (NPs) in the examples in (4) to the presence of noun incorporation, or the formation of verb-object compounds, in Sinitic substrates.

(4) a. Ok, you want to go to watch movie . . .
    b. Please open window.

The substrate transfer prediction in Figure 8.1 focuses on slightly different elements of the substrate but predicts some of the same outcomes as Wee and Ansaldo (2004). Genericity—the context for noun incorporation in Sinitic and Indo-Aryan substrates—was found to be a highly significant factor in IndE indefinite article omission (Table 4.6) and a less strong conditioning factor on definite article omission (Table 4.5).

Figure 8.2 compares the 12 proficient or regular IndE users from the present data set with the comparable subset of 10 ICE-Singapore transcripts of mesolectal SgE speakers described in Section 8.1.1. The distributions in Figure 8.2 show strong quantitative support for the predictions in Figure 8.1. The indefinite article *a* is omitted significantly more often in both varieties when the NP has nonspecific reference. The overt morphology for specific indefinites in the respective substrates (Figure 8.1) appears to clearly govern this pattern.

Remember from Chapter 4 that this pattern may not be a direct transfer from the substrate but, rather, an effect exerted by a universal preference to mark specificity overtly, as opposed to nonspecificity/genericity (Bickerton 1981). These different interpretations are extremely difficult to tease apart; the present data cannot disentangle the two, as both the Indo-Aryan and Sinitic substrates share the "unmarked" system of overtly marking specificity. Nevertheless, the fact that IndE and SgE diverge where their substrates diverge—to be shown shortly for other grammatical features—points to a role for substrates here.

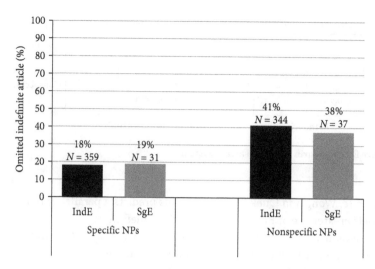

**Figure 8.2.** Omission of indefinite article in IndE and SgE according to specificity. $\chi^2 (3) = 48.2, p < .001$.

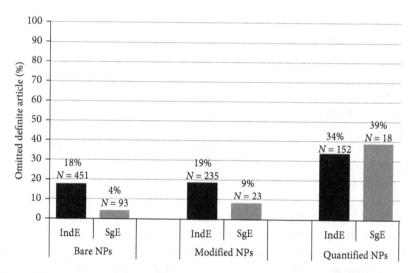

**Figure 8.3.** Omission of definite article in IndE and SgE according to modification. $\chi^2 (5) = 41.1, p < .001$.

Recall that IndE article omission was not entirely accounted for by L1 transfer, particularly the selective use of definite articles. A set of related universal semantic and pragmatic factors was shown to give rise to an economical redundancy effect, whereby the more discourse-familiar an NP, the more likely it was to appear without an article (Chapter 4).

Figure 8.3 shows that the same distribution arises for SgE. In both varieties, bare NPs omit articles the least, modified NPs marginally more,

[178] *Comparing India and Singapore*

and quantified NPs by far the most. This distribution was explained in Chapter 4 in terms of increasing discourse identifiability of the NP, an economical system that optimizes article use by minimizing redundancy. The parallel examples in (5)—from ICE-SIN and the present IndE data set—illustrate this system.

(5)  a.  Overt article with bare NP:
    i.  IndE: I worked as a bartender.
    ii.  SgE: And her husband is a policeman.  [ICE-SIN:S1A-023#276]

  b.  Omitted article with modified, identifiable NP:
    i.  IndE: From Ø first year of birth till . . .
    ii.  SgE: I'm not going to stay back for Ø next trip.
                      [ICE-SIN:S1A-023#48]

The analysis of IndE suggested that this universal pragmatic inferencing and optimization intervenes due to the prevalence of the form *the* in the input but the absence of any native basis for modeling its use. (We will further refine the theoretical characterization of this process in Chapter 9.)

Wee and Ansaldo (2004: 61) do not make a strong claim regarding overall systematicity in article omission and suggest, with Gil (1995), that "as with our earlier discussion of indefinite articles, we think it is worth taking seriously the more modest possibility that the use of definite articles in CSE is not yet conventionalized." The quantitative analysis here in fact shows a consistent basis in discourse for article use in both two varieties.

A study of Chinese learners of English (Robertson 2000) found striking parallels to this pattern. In a quantitative analysis of the conversational English of Mandarin L1 postgraduate students in the United Kingdom, Robertson found the following three factors to be most influential:

(6)  a.  a syntactic principle of "determiner drop," whereby an NP with definite or indefinite reference need not be overtly marked for [± definiteness] if it is included in the scope of the determiner of a preceding NP;
  b.  a "recoverability" principle, whereby an NP need not be marked for [± definiteness] if the information encoded in this feature is recoverable from the context; and
  c.  a "lexical transfer principle," whereby some of these learners are using demonstratives (particularly *this*) and the numeral *one* as markers of definiteness and indefiniteness respectively.
                      (Robertson 2000: 135)

All three factors parallel the findings here: (6a) and (6b) relate to universal discourse-identifiability and (6c) to substrate transfer.

As discussed in Chapter 4, these findings have also been confirmed in a number of other quantitative L2 studies. Sharma (2005b) originally reported the IndE findings for article use, and later studies replicated these results with distinct data sets (Sedlatschek 2009; George 2010; Hundt 2014). Similar results have been reported for Malaysian English (Wahid 2009), as well as for Turkish L2 speakers (Goad and White 2004) and Serbian L2 speakers (Trenkic 2007).

These rather striking correspondences across many data sets genuinely suggest a shared semantic-pragmatic effect in L2 speech (Trenkic 2009), one that is relatively substrate independent.[2] This is in line with Lange's (2012) argument of a "syntax of discourse organization," perhaps not just in IndE but in New Englishes more generally. English articles present particularly subtle semantics for acquisition, and this common solution may point to an Angloversal of sorts.

However, one major difference between IndE and SgE article use should be noted. Colloquial or basilectal SgE has been described as almost entirely omitting the definite article (Gil 1998), with mesolectal SgE in the Grammar of Spoken Singapore English corpus (GSSEC) (which is now part of the ICE-SIN corpus; see Section 1.7) showing more intermediate rates of omission with indefinite and definite articles (Wee and Ansaldo 2004: 58, 61). This contrasts with the present IndE data, in which even the least proficient group showed only 46% omission of the definite article.

This greater *degree* of omission in Colloquial SgE distinguishes it from IndE and may either be caused by the generally less inflectional nature of Chinese substrates or by the more rapid and less instructed channels of early dialect formation in SgE (Chapter 7). Given this, it is also very interesting to see *less* omission in SgE than in IndE in Figure 8.3, which represents mesolectal SgE, pointing to the much more dramatic colloquial-standard diglossic range of SgE as compared with IndE (discussed in detail in Chapter 10).

## 8.3. PAST TENSE

To compare past tense use in SgE and IndE, I rely on Ho and Platt (1993; henceforth H&P), who examined similar semantic subclasses for a large data set of SgE. H&P's speakers date from the 1970s–1980s and are less likely to be native speakers of SgE or of Mandarin (Ansaldo 2004; Lim 2007). This makes them slightly more comparable to the lower proficiency range of the present IndE data set. Their data consist of conversational interviews (also a close parallel to the type of data gathered for the present IndE data set) with 100 ethnically Chinese speakers of SgE, stratified into five educational levels. All participants had completed some level of English-medium education, which is only the case for some of the IndE participants in my database. Given that past tense omission was

[180] *Comparing India and Singapore*

limited to the less proficient half of the IndE data set (Chapter 3), it is these speakers who are compared with the basilectal end of H&P's data here.[3]

### 8.3.1. Substrate Grammars for IndE and SgE

For the two tense-aspect features examined in this section and the next, we again need to first consider the tense-aspect systems of the substrates. These are presented in Table 8.1—the Hindi system is repeated from Chapter 5, along with Mandarin and English.

Recall from Table 5.1 earlier that English is a tense-oriented language. Hindi and Mandarin, by contrast, are aspect-oriented languages. Both Hindi and Mandarin indicate an aspectual distinction between the perfective and imperfective in their verbal morphology, while English only marks tense. (Perfective morphology denotes completed or temporally bounded situations, while imperfective sentences denote unbounded, ongoing situations; Comrie 1976, see Chapter 5).

Within past tense reference, the two substrates are similar. An overt verbal marker is used to indicate perfective or completive aspect (in contrast to past imperfective) in both Hindi and Mandarin. This differs from the tense-prominent English system, in which morphological marking on the verb indicates past tense, regardless of aspect. (In Hindi, the auxiliary *be* can additionally mark tense independently, a difference from Mandarin.)

Within imperfective morphology, however, the two substrate systems diverge. In the lower half of Table 8.1, the only apparent similarity across all three imperfective systems is overt marking of progressive aspect. The substrates differ for other imperfective contexts: Hindi requires overt marking of imperfectivity in all clauses, whereas Mandarin has semantically restricted use of the imperfective marker *-zhe*, which is also sometimes optional. In fact, Yip and Rimmington (2004: 107) suggest that the treatment of *-zhe* as an

*Table 8.1.* TENSE MARKING IN HINDI, MANDARIN, AND ENGLISH

|  |  | Hindi | Mandarin | English |
|---|---|---|---|---|
| PAST | i. Perfective | -(y)a | le | -ed |
|  | ii. Imperfective | — | — | -ed |
| IMPERFECTIVE | a. Progressive | rahna | zai | -ing |
|  | b. Stative | -ta | (-zhe) | — |
|  | c. Habitual | -ta | — | — |

GRAMMATICAL UNIVERSALS? [181]

**Table 8.2.** TENSE-ASPECT MARKING IN SINGAPOREAN LANGUAGES

| | | Singapore Mandarin | Cantonese | Teochew | Hokkien | Malay |
|---|---|---|---|---|---|---|
| PAST | i. Perfective | le | tso | lio | liau | sudah, telah |
| | ii. Imperfective | — | — | — | — | — |
| IMPERFECTIVE | a. Progressive | zai | gan | do | tja | sedang |
| | b. Stative | (-zhe) | (zyu) | (do) | — | — |
| | c. Habitual | — | (hoi) | — | — | — |

aspectual marker at all is erroneous, and that it is more precisely a "manner indicator." The form is reserved for temporary result states (Sun 2006), and its use is also affected by prosodic factors (Yip and Rimmington 2004: 127).

Published grammars of Mandarin typically describe the mainland Chinese variety. Table 8.2 instead outlines the tense-aspect systems particular to the contact variety of Singapore Mandarin and other substrates Cantonese, Teochew, Hokkien, and Malay (Prentice 1990; H&P 1993; Matthews and Yip 1994; and input from consultants).[4] It shows that the perfective pattern is consistent across Chinese languages and Malay. By contrast, the limited use of imperfective marking in Mandarin is even further reduced in other systems, including in Singapore Mandarin (see the Appendix for a full profile of these reduced systems).[5]

We can conclude from Tables 8.1 and 8.2 that, although Indo-Aryan and Chinese languages are all typologically similar in terms of being perfectivity-marking systems, they are typologically distinct in the domain of the imperfective.

This makes them a very useful comparative case study. If substrate languages are driving the emergent systems, we should expect to see the patterns in (7):

(7) a. Shared feature (-ed use): IndE and SgE will both transfer perfective meaning to past tense morphology.
　　b. Divergent feature (-ing use): IndE and SgE will differ in the imperfective.
　　　i. IndE will exhibit greater use of -ing as a general marker of imperfectivity, due to obligatory overt imperfective morphology in Indian substrates.
　　　ii. SgE will exhibit less use of -ing as a general marker of imperfectivity, due to the limited scope and use of overt imperfective morphology in Singaporean substrates.

[182] *Comparing India and Singapore*

The next subsection evaluates (7a), and the section that follows evaluates (7b).

## 8.3.2. Past Tense Omission in IndE and SgE

The IndE data for past tense marking (Chapter 5) is reorganized in Table 8.3 according to the aspectual divisions used by H&P for their SgE data. This permits a direct comparison with their results.

A close examination of H&P's (1993: 81–83, 151) coding methodology reveals that, as in the analysis in Chapter 5, their analysis goes beyond lexical aspect and incorporates most core elements of clausal aspect. They follow Bickerton (1981) in using the term "punctual" "in a very broad sense" to include predicates bearing the features [+completive] and [+telic]; this corresponds to the standard term "perfective." Similarly, their category "stative non-punctual" includes predicates bearing the feature [+stative], and their category "non-stative non-punctuals" includes predicates bearing the features [+duration], [+activity], and [+habitual]; these correspond to standard categories of "imperfective." Their results, presented in Table 8.4, are therefore directly comparable to the IndE data.

Figure 8.4 shows how strikingly similar the omission of past tense morphology in SgE and IndE are, with past tense being used significantly more with perfective predicates than with imperfective predicates.[6]

*Table 8.3.* PAST TENSE MARKING ACCORDING TO SENTENTIAL ASPECT IN INDE ($N$ = 702)

| | | % OVERT PAST | $N$ |
|---|---|---|---|
| | Habitual, progressive | 29.5 | 132 |
| IMPERFECTIVE | Lexical stative | 44.2 | 224 |
| | PERFECTIVE | 76.6 | 346 |

$\chi^2(2) = 109.96, p \leq 0.001$

*Table 8.4.* PAST TENSE MARKING ACCORDING TO SENTENTIAL ASPECT IN SGE ($N$ = 8725)

| | | % OVERT PAST |
|---|---|---|
| | Habitual, progressive | 14.7 |
| IMPERFECTIVE | Lexical stative | 36.9 |
| | PERFECTIVE | 56.2 |

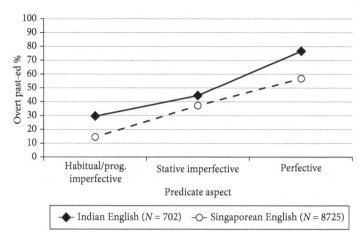

**Figure 8.4.** Past tense use according to clausal aspect in IndE and SgE.

Although her study did not use the same set of semantic categories, Gut (2009: 269) also found higher omission of overt past marking in SgE in habitual contexts, alongside phonological and morphological effects.

As predicted in (7a), we see a direct replication in both IndE and SgE of perfectivity marking in the substrate systems. The IndE and SgE patterns of use can be described as a straightforward instance of direct transfer (Lefebvre 1998; Bao 2005), as in (8), whereby the semantic component of a form–meaning pairing in the L1 is reattached to an L2 form.

(8) i. Hindi: [PERF -a] → IndE: [PERF -ed]
    ii. Chinese: [PERF le] → SgE: [PERF -ed]

It is worth noting, however, that Figure 8.4 also shows a secondary similarity that may go beyond the substrate effect, namely, the relative ordering of the two imperfective categories. This might be based in universal properties of aspectual semantics and how prototypical their association with punctual reference is (Andersen and Shirai 1996), though it could also be due to the presence of a distinct progressive form in the substrates. Only a comparison with English varieties with typologically different substrates can verify the extent to which semantic prototypes are relevant at all.

The primary substrate account has support elsewhere in the SgE system too. *Already* has been grammaticalized as an additional perfective marker (Bao 2005), on formal analogy with analytic Chinese and Malay forms *le* and *sudah/telah*. Hindi does not have isolated forms of this kind, and consequently IndE has not grammaticalized adverbs for aspectual functions.

An interesting suggestion, discussed in Gut (2009, drawing on Alsagoff 2001; Ho 2003; Deterding 2003), is the possibility that a first use of overt past tense in discourse sets up a discourse frame for continued reference such that omission actually constitutes extended uses of the present tense form. However, Gut cites Fong's (2004) counterargument that past adverbials and absence of agreement may suggest otherwise. The IndE data do not conform consistently to this extended historical present reading, and so I maintain a semantic transfer interpretation here, although both may occur for some speakers.

Gut (2009) and Deterding (2007: 41) also note phonological effects on past tense omission in SgE, through consonant cluster simplification, which renders a purely semantic analysis of -ed in SgE problematic. Bao (1998) describes this as a phonological change leading to a morphological change, which can allow semantic conditioning to intervene. I return to the question of phonological effects in Chapter 9. For the present, I simply note the striking correspondence in semantic conditioning according to predictable aspectual properties in the substrate, and a secondary role for universal prototypes as well.

## 8.4. PROGRESSIVE

The predictions in (7b) anticipated divergence rather than similarity between IndE and SgE in the domain of imperfectivity, due to a clear difference between imperfective marking being obligatory in Hindi but very limited in Chinese and Malay.

The imperfective categories examined for IndE (Chapter 5) were: progressive, stative, delimited habituals, and nondelimited habituals. Delimited habituals assert or presuppose a time-bound on the habit described, whereas nondelimited habituals do not. Since the form -ing in standard English primarily imposes a dynamic, in-progress reading, the form can be used with delimited habituals due to their time-bound property, for example, *I'm eating meat these days*, but not with nondelimited habituals, which are not tied to a particular time span, for example, *\*I'm eating meat*.

Thus, of the four imperfective categories, only two—progressive and delimited habitual—can occur with -ing in standard native varieties. The progressive is not standardly licensed with nondelimited habituals, statives, and perfectives, for example, *\*I'm eating meat, \*I'm knowing the answer, \*I was moving to Miami in 1998*. Its apparent use with states, for example, *I'm wanting to move back*, tends to be licensed by implicit time-bounds, for example, a change in degree or temporary state.

**Table 8.5.** FUNCTIONS OF PROGRESSIVE FORMS ($N$ = 339)

|  | % OVERT PAST | $N$ |
| --- | --- | --- |
|  | IMPERFECTIVE |  |
| Delimited habitual | 33.1 | 112 |
| Nondelimited habitual | 30.8 | 104 |
| Progressive | 18.4 | 63 |
| Stative | 14.8 | 50 |
| PERFECTIVE | 2.9 | 10 |

Table 8.5 repeats the main result for IndE progressives reported in Chapter 5, namely, robust overextension to nondelimited habituals and statives, that is, to the remaining imperfective categories.

(7b)   predicts that this would not occur in SgE. So, what do we find?

Unfortunately, H&P do not provide quantitative data on semantic contexts of -*ing* use for SgE. However, some indication of SgE usage can be gleaned from qualitative comments in the literature and from the ICE corpora. These commentaries and data suggest slight variation in SgE, but not on the scale of IndE.

Bao (2005: 249–250) takes a strong line on SgE standardness in the use of the progressive. He cites the substrate contrast between *zai/zhe* as a basis for acquisition:

> The imperfective aspect in Singapore English is unremarkable. It is formally identical to the English progressive, with the optional use of a copula . . . I was not able to collect any data from ICE-SIN which would show statives (*love, believe, know*) being used in the V-*ing* form. . . . The stative imperfective is not found in Singapore English.

Note that this reasoning implies that the *rahna/-ta* contrast in Hindi should also lead to acquisition of the standard system in IndE. It does not, for reasons discussed in Chapter 5 and expanded on in this chapter.

H&P (1993: 64–66) differ slightly from Bao and find a number of instances of overextension of the progressive to habitual and lexically stative contexts in their data, some of which are listed in (9).[7] However, they to emphasize that

[186]   *Comparing India and Singapore*

"in general, the state-process distinction holds for Singaporean Chinese learners of English" (1993: 189).

(9)  Like sometime dey <u>having</u> dinner.
     You <u>having</u> excess (cash) in your box.
     I <u>living</u> here.
     Most of de time I <u>speaking</u> English down there.
     I use(d) to go in and <u>flying</u> in and out.
     Den he <u>carrying</u> an umbrella.

Corpus data corroborate their view. An examination of the entire ICE-Singapore corpus reveals that some slight overextension of -*ing* does occur, but in quantitative terms it is negligible compared with the corresponding IndE uses of -*ing* in the parallel corpus, ICE-India.

As a brief illustration, I present all BE + V uses of *having* and *knowing* in ICE-Singapore and ICE-India, building on Balasubramanian's (2009) and Paulasto's (2014) observations of these two verbs as particularly common for IndE.

Table 8.6 shows a dramatic difference. The extremely high rates of use of progressive with statives by IndE speakers is not matched in SgE.[8] SgE use of -*ing* with statives is negligible, but it is still noteworthy that two of the four uses of *having* in SgE are stative, indicating very slight divergence from standard native varieties. Low rates of use of the progressive in SgE are confirmed in other studies (Bao 2005; Hundt and Vogel 2011). Hundt and Vogel also furnish evidence of sporadic nonstandard uses in SgE, despite low usage, exactly as observed here.

Standard and nonstandard examples of *having* from each corpus are given in (10) and (11), respectively. As noted, SgE shows no evidence of recasting -*ing* as a general imperfective marker as IndE does, but (11a) and (11b) indicate slight variation in use.

*Table 8.6.* USE OF MAIN VERBS *HAVING* AND *KNOWING* IN ICE-INDIA AND ICE-SINGAPORE

|  | ICE-India | | ICE-Singapore | |
|---|---|---|---|---|
|  | standard | nonstandard | standard | nonstandard |
| BE + HAVING | 47 | 141 | 4 | 2 |
| BE + KNOWING | 0 | 24 | 0 | 0 |

(10)    Standard examples of *having*:
   a.   *Experiential:* <u>Having</u> my hols now and <u>am having</u> a great time.
                                                  [ICE-SIN: w1b-010:545]
   b.   *Experiential:* I'<u>m having</u> a real tough time categorizing the sex you know.
                                                  [ICE-IND: S1a-048:1131]
   c.   *Future:* This afternoon we <u>are having</u> high tea with the Rustomjees.
                                                  [ICE-IND: W2f-016:238]
   d.   *Habitual:* So each and every party <u>is</u> uh <u>having</u> a bandh [strike] everyday.
                                                  [ICE-IND: S1a-057:174]


(11)   Nonstandard examples of *having*:
   a.   Maybe that's why I'<u>m having</u> a crush on him.
                                                  [ICE-SIN: w1b-010.txt:342]
   b.   I'<u>m having</u> a talk [speech] next week.
                                                  [ICE-SIN: w1b-010.txt:342]
   c.   We <u>are having</u> different beaches.
                                                  [ICE-IND: S1a-065:670]
   d.   He therefore uh doesn't say that the deceased <u>was</u> also <u>having</u> O group.
                                                  [ICE-IND: S2a-067:514]


Thus, unlike perfectivity marking with *-ed*, which was very similar in IndE and SgE, imperfectivity marking with *-ing* is very different in the two varieties. In both we find some variation with respect to the semantic range of *-ing*, but only in IndE does this lead to a systemic shift to marking all imperfective categories with *-ing*.

In Chapter 5 we noted a puzzle for IndE: Hindi and English both have a progressive marker, so why do IndE speakers dramatically extend this form as a general imperfective marker? The answer lay in the obligatory overt marking of all types of imperfectivity in Hindi (*a substrate effect*) and the idiosyncratically broad range of *-ing* use in English (*a superstrate effect*), allowing it to be interpreted as a general imperfective marker.

Chinese and Malay languages similarly have a progressive marker, like English, yet we see a slight tendency to overextend *-ing* in SgE. In their case, there is no obligatory imperfective marking, so why does the variability arise at all? Once again, this can be accounted for by the fact that the Chinese and Malay progressives, as in Hindi, have a much narrower semantic scope than *-ing* in English (see Appendix). This quirk of the superstrate gives rise to the slight variability that we see in SgE. H&P (1993: 189) similarly cite the "extended use of *-ing* constructions in the established varieties of English" as an influence on overextension of *-ing* in SgE.

[188]   *Comparing India and Singapore*

Crucially, it is a major difference in the Indian and Singapore substrates that determines the final outcome: the lack of an obligatory imperfective marker in Chinese means that there is ultimately no significant and sustained pressure to find an overt marker of imperfectivity. Thus, we see mild overextension due to differences in the use of the progressive, but no fundamental shift in SgE grammar.

The relative standardness of this domain of grammar in SgE as compared with IndE, despite the overall greater scale of innovation in SgE, is a powerful piece of evidence for the specific role of substrates in New Englishes. It limits the extent to which we can say that SgE has undergone a generalized, Creole-like loss of all grammatical morphemes.

Indeed, progressive markers are known to regularly grammaticalize into general imperfective markers cross-linguistically (Bybee et al. 1994: 140), yet the substrates of SgE appear to block this process.

This substrate–superstrate interaction can be schematized as in Figure 8.5. The first two rows for each variety show the conflict between an unusually wide domain for use of the English progressive and the more typologically common narrow progressives in both regions. But the third row for each dialect indicates the key substrate difference: the robust, obligatory imperfective marker -ta in Hindi (not just an abstract contrast of perfective/imperfective) gives rise to an expanded -ing system in IndE. The limited, optional Chinese and Malay result state markers, in contrast, exert no such lasting effect on the SgE system.

The typologically unusual and idiosyncratic nature of the standard English progressives makes it potentially an "Angloversal" that conflicts with many other languages, triggering change (as was the case for the English article system). And indeed we see widespread nonstandardness in this domain in New Englishes (van Rooy 2006; Sharma 2009; Gut and Fuchs 2013; Paulasto

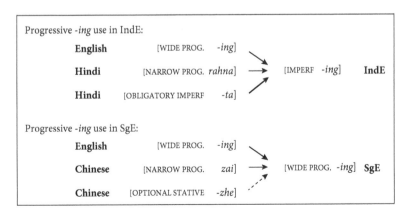

**Figure 8.5.** Past tense use according to clausal aspect in IndE and SgE.

2014; Rautionaho 2014; van Rooy and Piotrowska 2015). The present discussion shows, however, that the contact situation nevertheless drives outcomes in either accelerating or constraining such shifts.

One remaining mystery is why underuse of the progressive does not occur in SgE, to match the restricted domain of *zai*. Table 8.6 indicates some quantitative underuse, but the sources cited suggest acquisition of broadly standard meanings. Chapter 9 accounts for this detail by appealing to the additional factor of learner input and the Subset Principle.

## 8.5. COPULA ABSENCE

Copula absence, like past tense omission, was found to occur only among less proficient IndE users in Chapter 3.

Here I briefly compare IndE copula omission with that found in SgE. The discussion relies on details from a larger study of copula omission in L2 varieties of English, African-American Vernacular English, and Creoles (Sharma and Rickford 2009). Following previous studies of *be* deletion, I use the term "copula" here to include strictly copular *be* (with nonverbal predicates, e.g., nominal: *She is my sister*; adjectival: *She is funny*; locative: *She is in the hall*) and auxiliary *be* (with verbal predicates, e.g., V + *ing*: *She is hiding*; future *gonna*: *She is gonna pay*).

The copula systems of SgE and IndE substrates vary considerably. In this section, I rely on a wider set of secondary sources to compare the two varieties. The IndE data comprise only the less proficient IndE speakers in the present data set, as they were the only ones who exhibited this feature.

Table 8.7 provides a simplified summary of four different substrate systems for these varieties, Malay and Chinese (Platt 1979: 5–9) for SgE; Hindi (Masica 1991: 336) but also Tamil (Pillai 1992: 15; Schiffman 1999: 141) for IndE. Parentheses indicate the presence of semantic restrictions on use—for example, favoring, disfavoring, or optionality in such contexts as contrast, emphasis, assertion—as determined through consultation of sources cited above and native speakers.

*Table 8.7.* COPULA SYSTEMS IN SUBSTRATE LANGUAGES

|  | NOM | LOC | ADJ | VERB |
| --- | --- | --- | --- | --- |
| Malay | no | no | no | no |
| Cantonese/Mandarin | (✓) | ✓ | no | no |
| Tamil | no | ✓ | (✓) | no |
| Hindi | ✓ | ✓ | ✓ | ✓ |

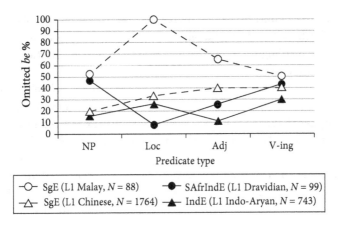

**Figure 8.6.** Copula absence by predicate type.

Figure 8.6 draws together rates of copula absence according to each predicate type for four sets of data, one for each of the four Indian and Chinese substrates in Table 8.7.[9]

The L1 Malay and L1 Chinese speakers of SgE are from Platt (1979) and the basilectal data in H&P (1993: 48). The Indo-Aryan speakers of IndE are from the present data set, and the Tamil speakers of South African IndE are from Mesthrie (1992: 158).

Although each of the four data sets exhibits some degree of copula absence, the underlying system differs substantially. To a great extent, the substrate system in each case can account for relative frequencies of copula absence.

SgE (Malay L1) has the highest absolute rates out of the four bilingual varieties in Figure 8.6, and Table 8.7 shows that Malay does not require a copula in any of the predicate contexts.

SgE (Chinese L1) has lower rates of copula absence than SgE (Malay L1) but higher than IndE, and, as Table 8.7 indicates, the relevant substrates have an intermediate system of copula use as well. The two highest contexts for omission in SgE (Chinese L1) are the two contexts in which Chinese systems omit the copula.

Basilectal South African IndE (Dravidian L1) shows yet another distribution, again paralleling the two highest contexts for copula absence in Tamil in Table 8.7.

IndE (Indo-Aryan L1) shows the lowest rates overall of copula absence, and indeed, as Table 8.7 shows, the substrate languages involved have an obligatory copula with all predicate types. Copula absence is not robust in IndE: Recall from Chapter 3 that more balanced English-Hindi bilinguals do not have copula omission at all. Also, each individual IndE speaker in the composite data in Figure 8.6 was found to have a different ordering of contexts, suggesting no strong underlying system.

GRAMMATICAL UNIVERSALS? [191]

As with past omission and progressive overextension, copula omission occurs in both IndE and SgE, but again quantitative analysis reveals a distinct patterning according to grammatical context in the two varieties, driven by substrate differences.

The comparison here is based on limited data, and it is likely that direct L1 effects in the individual are now weaker for SgE than the IndE. Ansaldo (2004) argues that copula absence across SgE substrates has had a "ganging-up" effect on copula absence in the emergent variety. H&P's data are relatively old, and it is possible that SgE subvarieties have now focused toward a new, more unified omission pattern. Indeed, Schröter (2010) does not find a Chinese substrate effect of overt *be* forms in negated contexts in informal SgE, pointing to possible limits on how finely substrate distinctions are maintained in New Englishes over time, particularly those that are nativizing quickly.

## 8.6. MODALITY

Of all the grammatical features examined here, English modals have the least resemblance to substrate systems in both regions. Chinese languages have a class of verbs that are in some ways parallel to English modals, though with differences in their ability to denote epistemic and deontic meanings (Bao 2010; Siemund 2013), and lacking the interaction with tense that is found for English *will* and *would*.

This typological distance means that modals exhibit some of the clearest nonsubstrate outcomes in IndE and SgE. This could be seen as support for Bao's (2005) view that, for transfer to take place, the lexical filter of the L2 must include a suitable target form for the L1 category; it should "transfer to somewhere" (Andersen 1983). In the absence of such a match, we see an interesting combination of acquisitional and social forces leading to some parallels in IndE and SgE, as well as other New Englishes, in the use of *will* and *would*.

The analysis of IndE use of *will* and *would* in Chapter 5 found a dual pattern, whereby *will* is overextended (into the domain of habituality that standardly requires *would*) by less proficient IndE users, and *would* is overextended (into the domain of *will*) among the more balanced bilinguals. *Will* was argued to be acquired for future meaning early, as in child acquisition, for reasons of prototypicality. And it was argued to be extended to habitual uses due to the existence of an overt habitual morphology in Hindi. The extension of *would* was attributed to a heightened awareness of the politeness index associated with *would* (cf. Collins 2009).

Extended uses of *will* are found with habituals in SgE too. Deterding (2007: 49) reports this and speculates an influence from Hokkien and Mandarin auxiliary verbs. Thus, in this case, a parallel substrate influence of overt habitual marking can be identified for the two varieties. This substrate account is somewhat complicated by Deuber et al.'s (2012) finding that habitual uses of *will* occur in all 10 varieties they look at. They attribute this in part to a relaxation of sequence of tense rules, which also occurs in IndE (Sharma 2001). So, a nonsubstrate factor is plausible too. They also find higher levels of use of *will* than *going to* in IndE, which may relate to historical conservatism and low vernacularity, again a possible nonsubstrate factor.

In terms of extended uses of *would* in future contexts, my earlier interpretation of IndE related to heightened formality, following Collins' (2009) suggestion that "[t]he development of extended *would* in the New Englishes is most likely motivated by the desire that speakers have to exploit the capacity of this form to convey a high level of polite and tactful unassuredness." Collins finds such uses in both IndE and SgE. Other studies have also noted this use of *would* in future *will* contexts for SgE (Gupta 1986; Ziegeler 1996; Deterding 2007: 51), often citing the same reason, namely, that the more polite form is being seen as the more correct one.[10] H&P (1993: 6) intriguingly suggest this usage may even be traced to direct influence from Indian teachers in Singapore.

Ziegeler (1996: 310) cites earlier politeness accounts for SgE as well:

> The explanation for the alternation between *will* and *would* was attributed to a hypercorrection rule: *would* is commonly applied to contexts where *will* would standardly be used (e.g. *this office would be closed next Saturday*) and is reported to be considered a polite form and therefore more "correct." (Newbrook and Chinniah 1987: 255)

However, hers is one of the few studies that questions this politeness interpretation. Examining the use of *would* and *will* in SgE hypothetical complement clauses, for example, *I wish there will/would be peace in the world* in place of *I wish there was peace in the world*, she argues against a hypercorrection interpretation and instead suggests a link to overgeneralization deriving from the lack of specification of past tense in statives and nonpunctuals:

> If past stative verb forms are not categorically perceived as conveying implicatures of present counterfactuality amongst Singaporean speakers of English, then it is hardly likely that the differences of irrealis meaning between *will* and *would*, as stative verbs, will have a great deal of significance either. (p. 325; see also Ziegeler 2015)

This proposal is intriguing for SgE, linking a change in one domain (past marking) to a change in another (modal). The analysis does not apply well to IndE: past tense omission in IndE was limited to lower-proficiency IndE users, whereas extended *would* is found among the more proficient IndE users, who have no past tense omission.

Given this, and evidence of widespread emergence of this trait independently in many New Englishes (Mesthrie and Bhatt 2008: 65; Deuber et al. 2012), I leave this as a striking example of a non-substrate-based New Englishes feature, a grammatical change that repeatedly arises in the status-sensitive context of postcolonial Englishes, out of the universal association of polite speech with correctness.

## 8.7. MECHANISMS OF CHANGE: SUBSTRATE TYPOLOGY

The comparison of five different grammatical features in IndE and SgE has allowed us to evaluate the role of context-specific factors such as the local languages as well as context-neutral factors, such as universal semantic, syntactic, or discourse-pragmatic tendencies.

Table 8.8 pulls together the linguistic features examined in this chapter, ordered from most direct substrate influence to least. Even in cases where an innovative third grammar has arisen (all cases with ×), these new systems have been triggered by an initial L1-L2 clash. Similarly, when the substrate system is replicated, this does not always mean divergence from the original lexifier, BrE. In cases such as IndE copula use or SgE progressive use, the substrate facilitates acquisition of the standard BrE system, even if the variety involved is one with radically reduced morphology, as in SgE. The findings thus support robust and specific influence from substrate systems, whether in encouraging similar or divergent usage practices in the two varieties.

A cline of degrees of direct substrate influence thus emerges (Filppula et al. 2009), but with a stronger substrate element, as even the lower end

*Table 8.8.* INDE AND SGE FEATURES IN RELATION TO SUBSTRATES

| Form | Indian English usage | Substrate pattern? | Singaporean English usage | Substrate pattern? |
|---|---|---|---|---|
| past -*ed* morphology | perfective | ✓ | perfective | ✓ |
| nonspec indefinite article | omitted | ✓ | omitted | ✓ |
| copula/auxiliary *be* | overt [=standard] | ✓ | null | ✓ |
| progressive -*ing* | imperfective | (×) | progressive [= standard] | (×) |
| definite article | redundancy/givenness | × | redundancy/ givenness | × |
| modals | polite, nonirrealis | × | polite, nonirrealis | × |

[194] *Comparing India and Singapore*

of the cline implicates an initial L1-L2 difference. Unlike Creoles, these varieties show little evidence of pure universals. The discussion did find that some typologically unmarked traits emerge, for example, the association of perfectivity with past tense morphology or of specificity with overt marking. But these are mostly reinforced by the substrate systems and so are difficult to interpret as pure emergence of the unmarked (unlike clearer cases of emergence of the unmarked in Indian English phonologies; Wiltshire 2014). The case of the progressive also militates against a universal reading: we know that typologically progressive markers regularly grammaticalize into general imperfective markers (Bybee et al. 1994: 140), and yet SgE did not show the same robust overextension of *-ing* as IndE, for substrate reasons.

However, the analysis has shown the mechanism of substrate influence in New Englishes to be complex, involving a number of components:

- *Degree of divergence* from the superstrate language: This directly influences acquisition or nonacquisition of the target system.
- *Presence of overt morphology* in the substrate: For example, both Indo-Aryan and Sinitic languages make a perfective–imperfective distinction, but only the former has overt morphology across all subcategories of the paradigm. It appears to be overt morphology, not just abstract contrast, that gets reconstituted in the offspring system.
- *Presence of a target form* in the superstrate: Substrate systems appear most likely to be recapitulated in the offspring variety when a reasonable candidate exists in the superstrate morphology. This supports Bao's (2005, 2015) conceptualization of substrate transfer being filtered through the lexicon of the lexifier or superstrate language.
- Inferences that can lead to *third grammars*: We see this in the novel imperfective-marking system of IndE, whereby an Indic "parameter" is applied to a single English morpheme, and in novel discourse-based usage of definite articles.
- *A conspiracy of substrates:* Substrates can play a reinforcing role in regions where areal convergence and genetic relatedness are extensive (Ansaldo 2009: 134).

Similarly, nonsubstrate or universal factors, though secondary, also appear to operate in several ways:

- *Angloversals* (e.g., unusual scope of English *-ing*) and *varioversals* (e.g., politeness effects of modals) are more attested in the data than pure universals.
- *Discourse-pragmatic solutions* to gaps between the L1 and L2 are common, supporting Lange's (2012) notion of a "syntax of discourse" in New Englishes (albeit with a substrate trigger in each case).

- *Prototypes*: In a few selected cases we see a familiar acquisitional order, for example, early acquisition of *will*.
- *Typological unmarkedness* also emerges in the data, though again as a secondary effect of substrate typologies.
- Even *social factors* of prestige and status can filter into the grammar given a sufficiently discourse-sensitive form (English modals) and lack of a substrate architecture for their use.

Certainly wider universals in syntax and processing are powerful forces and are not ruled out here. However, this chapter has shown that, in the search for such universals, we cannot simply treat bilingual varieties that exhibit presence of a particular trait as parallel. Surface similarities across new Englishes can be skin deep, diverging significantly upon closer examination. If we wish to identify potential universals, then it is inadequate to define a feature in very broad terms. The degree and distribution of a given feature must be understood in relation to the substrate before any universal claims can be made.

The next chapter encounters a surprising complication to this story. There is a major gap in the account provided so far: we have focused on structural transfer but paid little attention to the extent to which these features have become entrenched and stabilized across speakers. Chapter 3 showed that some features are only found among less proficient or regular users of IndE, while others are spread across the usage cline and are more established. This chapter has shown that, in SgE, a different set of features has indigenized across the usage cline and become established.

Can transfer from substrates also account for whether or not a feature has become an established new dialect feature? In the next chapter, I show that transfer in fact overpredicts change and cannot fully account for the selective stabilization of dialect features. To address this puzzle, I turn to an additional consideration: the role of input and cognitive factors affecting the trajectory of language acquisition in the individual. With this added insight from second language acquisition theory, we can approach a more complete account of incremental change over time.

# CHAPTER 9
# The Role of Input

We might conclude based on the findings of Chapter 8 that regional languages are clearly the strongest source of change in postcolonial New Englishes. This picture emerged through the common practice of conducting a side-by-side comparison of the two grammars in contact, focusing on structural differences.

However, McMahon (1994: 248), following Weinreich et al. (1968: 102), frames the real actuation problem in historical linguistics as asking not just how innovations arise but "why some of these innovations die out and others catch on, spreading through the community, or why certain instances of variation become changes and others don't." We have not yet considered this question fully for Indian English (IndE) and Singapore English (SgE).

In this final chapter on the grammars of New Englishes, I turn to this less commonly asked question. Are all the novel syntactic traits examined so far equally well established in the two dialects? If not (as Chapter 3 has already indicated), why not? The substrate-based analysis is powerful when we analyze individual features, as in previous chapters. However, when we look across the whole dialect and ask why only a subset of these forms has become entrenched over time, we find that a simple substrate model seems *too* powerful: it overpredicts change.

In this chapter, I propose that a full account of new dialect formation out of bilingualism must factor in the role of input in individual learning alongside pure structural contrasts between languages.

*From Deficit to Dialect.* Devyani Sharma, Oxford University Press. © Oxford University Press 2023.
DOI: 10.1093/oso/9780195307504.003.0009

## 9.1. VARIATION VERSUS STABILIZATION

Chapter 3 showed that some syntactic forms in IndE are limited to less regular and proficient users of IndE, while others are shared across most or all speakers. Of the substrate-linked features analyzed in Chapter 3, only three are stable across the usage cline of IndE:[1]

(1) a.  Less proficient IndE users: copula omission, past tense omission
    b.  Full spectrum of IndE users: article omission, extended progressive, modal use

The latter set of features appears in educated IndE, and it is these that are typically listed in published descriptions as typical of IndE (e.g., Kachru 1983; Platt et al. 1984; Agnihotri et al. 1984; Williams 1987; Jenkins 2003; Melchers and Shaw 2003; Lange 2007; Schneider 2007; Trudgill and Hannah 2008; Sailaja 2009; Sedlatschek 2009; Balasubramanian 2009). They also appear commonly in stylizations and parodies of the dialect.

By contrast, although past tense omission and copula omission show some presence in the current data set, they were not used by the more balanced bilinguals, are not mentioned as typical of IndE in the above works, and do not appear as often in performances of the variety.

An account of the birth of IndE must distinguish between these types of outcomes. Chapter 8 only provided an explanation of variable use, not degree of stabilization over time.

To add to the challenge, a *different* subset of features has stabilized over time for SgE. The literature on SgE suggests that all of the features listed in (1) except for extension of *-ing* can be considered typical of the variety (Wee 2004; Deterding 2007).

We can see quantitative support for these intervarietal differences in a simple comparison of frequency of nonstandard usage among proficient, native, or balanced bilingual IndE and SgE speakers. Such speakers use a subset of the features used by nonproficient speakers, and so this set of forms represents the ones that are more established across the whole speech community.

Figure 9.1 presents frequencies of nonstandard use of five grammatical forms in IndE and SgE. The speakers here are the subsample of 12 more proficient IndE speakers and the subsample of similarly standard or educated SgE speakers from the International Corpus of English (ICE)-Singapore conversational recordings described in Chapter 8. (Modals are less frequent and so are not quantified here.)

Figure 9.1 shows clearly the different stabilization patterns proposed for these two varieties. On the right of the figure, we can see a very similar pattern of omission of articles in the two varieties. By contrast, the left half of the

[198]   *Comparing India and Singapore*

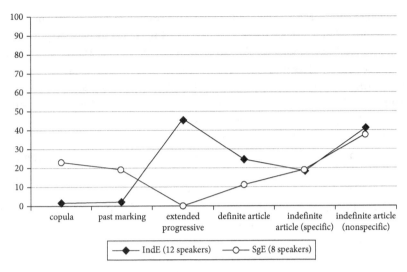

**Figure 9.1.** Rates of nonstandardness among more proficient speakers of IndE and SgE (SgE N values: 111, 129, 135, 31, 37; IndE N values: 1437, 758, 339, 602, 536).

figure shows three features that differ for the two varieties: educated or proficient IndE speakers do not omit copula/auxiliary *be* or past tense marking, but they do use the extended progressive robustly. Educated or proficient SgE speakers do omit copula/auxiliary *be* and past tense marking but do not exhibit extended progressive use.

Are substrates still a viable explanation for why these different subsets of forms diverge more substantially from standard native English varieties? In the case of copula omission in IndE and progressive use in SgE, the similarity of the L1 to English might indeed account for the lack of stabilization in each variety. But the nonstandard use of past marking with perfective meaning was found in both IndE and SgE, due to a shared L1-L2 difference, so why has it only stabilized robustly in SgE? Chapter 8 showed a substrate basis for almost all syntactic divergence, and we now find that substrates predict more divergent outcomes than we actually find.

In this chapter I add a missing piece of the puzzle by considering specific theories of learner input, a dimension that is not always explicitly addressed but that it is implicit in all models of language contact.

## 9.2. SHIFTING THE FOCUS FROM PRODUCT TO PROCESS

Scholars of New Englishes have often suggested going beyond the linguistic systems involved and taking account of acquisitional processes too (e.g., Sridhar 1985; Sridhar and Sridhar 1991, 1992; Mesthrie 1992; Hilbert 2008;

Davydova 2011; Meriläinen and Paulasto 2014). However, as in the study of Creoles, there has also been a long-standing resistance to acquisitional accounts of New Englishes, due to a desire to recognize these varieties as "full-fledged varieties with the potential to develop endonormative and local standards and norms" (Mukherjee and Hundt 2011: 1–2). As Meriläinen and Paulasto (2014: 2) observe, "[d]rawing parallels to learner English has therefore not been of primary interest to most researchers."

The analysis in Chapter 8 followed the classic structuralist tradition of studying language contact by setting the two abstract grammatical systems in contact side by side and predicting outcomes. Innumerable studies of language contact, Creoles, and bilingualism have taken this approach, and it offers a solid methodology for studying broad processes of grammatical transfer or universal tendencies, in line with the methods of language typology and formal linguistics.

By comparison, in second language acquisition (SLA) research, a static comparison of the two language systems is rarely the sole focus of analysis, as the incremental process of acquisition and exposure to input is a central concern. In this chapter, this perspective is added to the analysis given in Chapter 8.

Two models of input sensitivity in learner grammars are explored: the Subset Principle and the Interface Hypothesis. The goal is not to assess which better accounts for the data but, rather, to show that models such as these highlight the important role of what I call *input demand*—the amount of rich input a feature needs to be acquired—in New Englishes.

Looking at New Englishes as the outcome of dynamic, input-sensitive phases of L2 development, rather than as static semiotic systems, helps to factor in the sociohistorical hallmark of World Englishes: declining input from the original target variety over time. SLA models make precise predictions for specific syntactic forms that should or should not be easily acquired, allowing for a fine-grained account of New English grammars.

New Englishes may in turn prove an interesting new diachronic testing group for such SLA theories. In fact, while the chapter will propose a very important role for input, it will also suggest that some key data indicate that the boundaries of the L1 grammatical system are an even stronger constraint on full acquisition.

The two models described next both relate fundamentally to how much input is needed by a learner. In the case of new postcolonial varieties, this input shifts from native speakers of BrE in the colonial period to indigenous, often nonnative or bilingual diffusion within the postcolonial region. Input is therefore very likely a crucial dimension of acquisition that is implicated in long-term postcolonial dialect outcomes.

A few studies have expanded the exploration of contact to include general learning processes but have tended to focus on the inherent or absolute difficulty or orders of acquisition of forms in English. For example, Davydova

[200] *Comparing India and Singapore*

(2011: 108) uses a continuum of relative complexity and difficulty of acquisition of selected English forms adapted from Housen (2002) to argue that L2-easy and L2-difficult features behave differently in New Englishes, irrespective of the L1. In a large-scale comparison of English varieties, Szmrecsanyi and Kortmann (2009) examined contrasts in morphosyntactic complexity and analyticity across variety types, invoking a general acquisitional basis for simplification. The present analysis similarly investigates relative difficulty of acquisition and the need for rich input, but it predicts the level of input demand from the specific nature of each L1-L2 contrast in question.

## 9.3. THE SUBSET PRINCIPLE

Let us first address the puzzle of why IndE past tense omission has not stabilized, unlike other substrate-derived features in IndE and unlike the greater establishment of past tense omission in SgE. To do this, I adopt an early proposal in SLA, the Subset Principle. I show that the proposal offers a key insight into differential outcomes in learning, but also that it cannot fully account for dialect outcomes. In Section 9.4, I broaden the analysis to accommodate further factors relating to input demand and then assess the overall role of input.

The Subset Principle (Berwick 1985; Wexler and Manzini 1987; Pinker 1984, 1989; White 1989; Fodor and Sakas 2005) was proposed as a model of how learners navigate toward a target grammar. The model has been critiqued as too strong to offer a global account of first language acquisition. Nevertheless, the fundamental contrast it describes is very likely to play some part in selected acquisitional differences, perhaps even more concretely in SLA, where a clear contrast arises between two grammars (White 1989; Ayoun 1996).

Figure 9.2 illustrates two possible relationships between an L2 speaker's hypothesized grammar for the target language and its actual grammar. If a learner is starting from a grammar that generates a subset of the grammatical constructions of the target grammar, then they can expand straightforwardly to the target based on positive evidence that they naturally encounter in the input. However, if their initial hypothesized grammar generates a superset of the constructions allowed by the target grammar, then it already generates all standard uses and would require explicit negative evidence to eliminate ungrammatical outputs.

The difference between Scenario A and Scenario B is significant for a learner, particularly in the context of naturalistic, rather than classroom, acquisition. In Scenario A, the learner only needs to encounter a few naturally occurring tokens of a type not yet covered by their L2 grammar in order to notice the discrepancy and update their L2 grammar. By contrast, in Scenario B, no amount of natural input will inform the learner explicitly of the ungrammaticality of

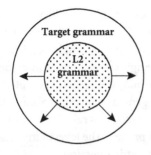 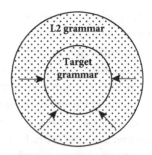

A: Subset scenario (easy): Set of constructions generated by L2 grammar is a subset of those of target grammar, so counterevidence encountered naturally will help expand toward target grammar

B: Superset scenario (difficult): Set of constructions generated by L2 grammar already generates target grammar so explicit negative feedback needed in order to contract L2 grammar appropriately

Figure 9.2. Subset and superset grammars in acquisition.

some of their utterances. The only way out of a superset L2 grammar is either from explicit negative feedback (i.e., being told that certain sentences are not grammatical in the target grammar) or by resorting to complex stochastic matching of one's own output with the forms encountered in the input. In either case, a good deal more complexity is involved than in Scenario A.

An example of the Subset Principle affecting SLA can be seen in Larrañaga et al.'s (2012) study of English and French learners. In English, manner verbs such as *run* can occur with or without the crossing of a boundary (*He runs toward the house. / He runs into the house.*). In French, manner verbs cannot occur with a boundary crossing (*Il court vers la maison. / *Il court dans la maison.*).[2] This means that the set of sentences generated by French manner verbs is a subset of those generated by English. The Subset Principle would predict that English learners of French would have more difficulty in acquiring the French system, as their grammar already generates all grammatical French sentences; by contrast, French learners of English should have less difficulty, as their grammar is a subset, and so they would encounter positive evidence in natural speech (i.e., *He runs into the house* as a grammatical sentence in English) to amend their hypothesis. Larrañaga et al. (2012) found that this prediction was upheld, and that indeed English learners were less accurate with manner verbs in French than their matched French counterparts' accuracy with English manner verbs.

In child L1 acquisition, children were hypothesized to start with the most restricted grammar and expand incrementally, in order to avoid the trap of overgeneralization. However, in L2 acquisition, as the previous example shows, the starting point is often the L1 system, which can immediately set up a subset or superset relation.

Let us return to IndE and consider whether the four types of tense, modality, and aspect (TMA) in IndE examined in Chapter 5 are subsets or supersets of standard BrE.[3]

The restriction of past tense marking primarily to perfective clauses in IndE generated a *subset* of standard English use of the past tense. Learners would therefore be predicted to very quickly encounter explicit counterevidence (in the form of past imperfective clauses in English, e.g., *I knew him well* or *I was cooking*). This should allow them to eventually move past this particular L1 effect.

By contrast, imperfectivity-driven use of *-ing* in IndE involved overextension to habitual and stative contexts, thus generating a *superset* of standard English uses. This means that IndE speakers already produce the entire set of standard English constructions (and more) and so would need explicit evidence to notice that the additional constructions are not standard. The remaining two features—past perfect use and modal use—both also involve generalization beyond standard English grammatical constraints and are therefore also *superset* grammars, which already generate standard usage and cannot rely on naturally occurring counterevidence.

Notice that even though past tense use and past perfect use were quite similar, both arising out of substrate transfer of perfective meaning, they are very different in terms of the Subset Principle: IndE past tense use involves narrowing to perfective meaning, whereas IndE past perfect use involves broadening to new contexts. As a result, we should see IndE past perfect use being more deeply entrenched, as it requires explicit correction to move toward native standard varieties. This is exactly what we find.

Table 9.1 outlines the four IndE TMA features in terms of whether they are subset or superset grammars in relation to native standard varieties. It gives us a possible answer to the puzzle of why past tense omission is the only IndE TMA feature in this set that is not found among more proficient speakers of IndE. Past tense omission is the only feature with a simple subset relation to the target variety—historically British English (BrE), now standard IndE—and so is the easiest feature to amend toward a more standard target.

*Table 9.1.* SUBSET PRINCIPLE PREDICTIONS FOR INDE TMA

| Form | Indian English usage | Subset or superset of target use? | Predicted to persist? | Found to persist? |
|------|------|------|------|------|
| Past tense | perfective | subset | no | no |
| Progressive *-ing* | imperfective | superset | yes | yes |
| Past perfect | remote or sustained past | superset | yes | yes |
| *will/would* | inversion of uses | superset | yes | yes |

Let us briefly extend this analysis to SgE as well. In Chapter 8, we saw that Singaporean substrates do not generate a robust base of superset uses for English -*ing*. As a result, L2 or bilingual speakers of SgE do not experience this initial dramatic expansion to all imperfectives (a superset in quality and quantity). They might initially restrict their use to narrow progressive meanings in their L1s (see Appendix) but can easily expand this subset grammar to converge toward the broader scope of standard English -*ing*. Thus, different outcomes for a single English form, progressive -*ing*, obtain in the two varieties. The establishment of past tense omission in SgE despite the predictions of the Subset Hypothesis may support the view that a separate factor (phonology) has driven that change; this is discussed further in Section 9.6.

The contrast between SgE and IndE outcomes for the progressive in relation to the Subset Hypothesis highlights how central the relationship of learner grammars to target grammars (i.e., the L1-L2 pairing) is in this model, as opposed to asserting inherent difficulty of a given English form (cf. Housen 2002; Davydova 2011). If we focus solely on an inherent ordering of difficulty of English forms, we should expect to see the same forms diverging over time in IndE and SgE, which is not the case.

Of course, the same L1-L2 differences can arise repeatedly. The quirky nature of the English progressive, with its wide range of constructions, may pose a challenge for speakers of many languages with non-English-like TMA systems. Thus, speakers of German and French, like IndE speakers, converge on standard English past tense marking easily but retain L1 effects in their use of the progressive and often need explicit negative evidence to change it.

A difficulty with this proposal is that, although it appears very well suited to the TMA data, it does not work as well for article use. In Chapter 8 we saw that both SgE and IndE *under*use articles, as both sets of substrates initially generate a subset of the constructions used in standard native varieties. This should make it relatively straightforward to expand their grammar through natural exposure, yet this feature has stabilized as a trait in these and many other New Englishes.

We can see intuitively what is wrong with a narrow Subset Principle analysis of articles: the English article system involves notoriously complex semantic and pragmatic constraints. Thus, even a learner who starts with a subset grammar will require extremely rich input before they can begin to approach native-like use. Complex systems cannot always be reduced to a simple subset or superset relation. The Subset Principle has been useful in drawing our attention to one example of asymmetric *input demand*—how much input a speaker of a particular L1 needs in order to acquire the use of a given L2 grammatical feature—but a superset grammar is not the only type of situation that demands rich input.

Next, I review a more recent input-related model from SLA and show how it too can bear on the present data. I then group these examples in terms of input demand more broadly defined and assess its overall role in language contact and change.


## 9.4. THE INTERFACE HYPOTHESIS

### 9.4.1. The Interface Hypothesis in SLA and Language Contact

A large body of recent work in SLA has argued that syntactic properties that involve an interface with another cognitive domain, particularly the syntax–pragmatics interface, may be more difficult to acquire fully (Sorace and Filiaci 2006; Sorace and Serratrice 2009; see also Müller and Hulk [2001] for bilingual L1 acquisition). The model does not aim to account for all processes in acquisition but, rather, "patterns of non-convergence and residual optionality found at very advanced stages of adult second language (L2) acquisition" (Sorace 2011: 1). This description fits our present focus on entrenched or more stable features of New Englishes found among proficient, balanced bilingual speakers.

In line with this chapter's critique of an exclusive reliance on the L1 grammar as a source for change, Sorace and Serratrice (2009: 202) too observe that "it is becoming apparent that cross-linguistic influence at the level of grammatical representations cannot be the only explanation for extended optionality in bilinguals." The Interface Hypothesis proposes an additional layer of difficulty for bilinguals, namely, that differences between the L1 and the L2 at the syntax–pragmatics interface cause greater difficulty due to the nature of input needed for acquisition and related processing loads. The approach suggests that "narrow syntactic properties are completely acquirable in a second language, even though they may exhibit significant developmental delays, whereas interface properties involving syntax and another cognitive domain may not be fully acquirable" (Sorace and Filiaci 2006).

For the present analysis, a relevant detail is that, in situations of interface difficulty, the Interface Hypothesis proposes that learners may resort to general discourse solutions. For example, L1-L2 differences in the topic sensitivity of subject drop can lead to an erosion of featural requirements such as [+topic] or [+subject] in one or both languages. This in turn leads to underspecification and ambiguity, which are often resolved in favor of universal discourse pragmatic licensing to optimize processing.

Sorace (2012) has acknowledged a number of critiques of the Interface Hypothesis, and the present analysis does not argue specifically in favor of the Interface Hypothesis over other SLA models; rather, it makes general use of the model to highlight another domain of high input demand for the acquisition of certain grammatical features.

Research has explored the syntax–pragmatics interface in a range of contexts. In bilingual child data, for example, acquisition of topic/nontopic object drop rules has been shown to be slower than that of root infinitives (narrow syntax) in Germanic/Romance contact (Müller and Hulk 2000). In individual L1 attrition, English-like overt forms have been found to be used for null subjects in diaspora Catalan, Italian, Greek, and Spanish (Carminati 2005; Tsimpli et al. 2004; Montrul 2004).

A number of studies have adopted this principle in the study of more naturalistic long-term language change. In heritage language use in diaspora communities, gender agreement in pronominal reference (at the external syntax–discourse interface) has been found to be more problematic for heritage speakers than adjectival predication (at the internal morpho–syntax interface), with sensitivity to the quantity and quality of input (van Osch et al. 2014). Changes of this kind at the individual level for first-generation speakers are also found to be more pronounced and widespread in the next generation, sparking more large-scale change in contact communities (Lapidus and Otheguy 2005; Montrul 2004; Toribio 2004).

In even longer-term historical change, akin to the cases in this book, Ingham (2017) argues that interface effects account for more change at the syntax–semantics interface than in narrow syntax in long-term contact outcomes for Anglo-Norman French. And Yao (2016) has proposed that the Interface Hypothesis may similarly account for the use of cleft construction in Hong Kong English.

### 9.4.2. Applying the Model to Long-Term Outcomes in IndE and SgE

Recall that the Subset Principle corresponded to TMA usage in IndE, but not to article use, one of the most vulnerable domains for variability and change in New Englishes.

Let us revisit the puzzle of IndE and SgE article omission through the lens of the Interface Hypothesis—why are these divergent uses so established, even though the set of constructions generated is a subset of the target system and so could in principle expand easily toward the target?

English articles, particularly definite articles, involve conditioned optionality with a host of subtle semantic and pragmatic constraints. They undoubtedly operate at the syntax–pragmatics interface and, given the subtlety of those constraints, have very high input demand. The status of article omission as a subset grammar is counterbalanced by these other considerable acquisitional challenges.

Chapter 8 showed that, in both IndE and SgE, overt article use settled on a discourse pragmatic principle, rather than strict L1 transfer. This outcome

[206]   *Comparing India and Singapore*

bears a striking resemblance to the types of outcomes found in Interface Hypothesis studies.

Serratrice, Sorace, and Paoli (2004) studied bilingual English-Italian children, for whom objects are obligatorily overt in both languages and not sensitive to discourse (and therefore acquired from the earliest stages), whereas topic drop rules for subjects differ in the two languages and create an obstacle. They find that children resort to an optimized discourse strategy in this situation: "both in English and in Italian, null subjects . . . were constrained by discourse pragmatics: null arguments were significantly more likely to be associated with uninformative than informative features" (p. 199).

This is exactly what was found for IndE and SgE articles in Chapters 4 and 8: they were significantly more likely to be omitted with uninformative (redundant) noun phrases (NPs). The fine-grained conformity across IndE speakers to a pattern of article omission when the NP is uninformative in discourse was given earlier in Figure 4.6. As noted in the discussion, this pattern is now well established for article use in many L2 English varieties, some replicating Sharma (2005b) for IndE (Sedlatschek 2009; George 2010; Hundt 2014) and others for different L2 speakers (Robertson 2000; Goad and White 2004; Trenkic 2007; Wahid 2009). This phenomenon may represent a true Angloversal (Szmrecsanyi and Kortmann 2009). A combination of high input demand and processing pressure (for a complex, idiosyncratic syntax–pragmatics interface feature in English), insufficient input, and a lack of definite articles in many L1s repeatedly conspire to give rise to the same economical, discourse-based solution.

In classroom SLA such strategies may not find a permanent footing, due to targeted, explicit input. The sociohistorical context of New Englishes means that these processes can stabilize much more.

## 9.5. INPUT AS A CORE FACTOR

The role of input has been reasserted in recent SLA debates, with the proposal of new analytic approaches (Polinsky and Scontras 2019; Hicks and Dominguez 2019), alongside more critical responses that calibrate its relative importance (DeKeyser 2020). In this section I suggest that input demand is important in long-term contact outcomes, but Section 9.6 also contextualizes this in relation to the powerful constraints of the substrate.

To start with, the above discussion forces us to acknowledge that abstract differences between substrate and superstrate grammatical systems, though extremely powerful, cannot solely account for long-term outcomes. Considering the additional role of input demand—how much input a speaker of a particular L1 needs in order to acquire the use of a given L2

**Table 9.2.** INDE GRAMMATICAL FEATURES AND INPUT DEMAND

| Grammatical feature | Rich input needed? | Predicted to persist? | Widespread across IndE? |
|---|---|---|---|
| Past -*ed* omission | no | no | no |
| Zero subj.–verb agreement | no | no | no |
| Copula *be* omission | no | no | no |
| Extended progressive -*ing* | yes | yes | yes |
| *will/would* | yes | yes | yes |
| Extended past perfect | yes | yes | yes |
| Indefinite article omission | yes | yes | yes |
| Definite article omission | yes | yes | yes |

grammatical feature—has helped solve a number of puzzles regarding long-term outcomes. The Subset Principle and the Interface Hypothesis are two of many ways in which we might recognize the role of high input demand in the acquisition of a given grammatical feature by a speaker of a particular language.

As noted, most acquisitional studies have defined the challenge of acquisition in New Englishes in terms of the inherent difficulty or complexity of a given English form, with a use of global "difficulty" metrics. The comparison of IndE and SgE here has shown that in some cases the same English forms stabilize differently over time in different linguistic ecologies. The definition of input demand in terms of the specific nature of the L1–L2 conflict allows for such differences to emerge.

Table 9.2 lists the grammatical features that were differentially distributed across the bilingual cline of IndE in Chapter 3 and relates their distribution to input demand. Although the correspondence to input demand is clear, many of these features are also well accounted for by substrate syntax, for example, the lack of a substrate difference driving copula omission. The role of input demand is particularly clear for certain features. The established change in *will/would* use may be mainly input demand, due to complex syntax-pragmatic constraints, and not the substrate system, leading to the prestige-based reallocation described in Chapter 5. Input demand may also contribute to the discourse-driven reorganization of the article system. And low input demand may account for the nonpersistence of past tense omission.

However, it is difficult to set aside the role of substrates in any of these completely. Input demand itself arises in part out of L1–L2 distance, so the substrate/L1 is always implicated. And there are further underlying subtleties in substrates that could affect uptake (Hicks and Dominguez 2019) in contact. For instance, if a [+ tense] feature exists in the substrate, even if it is subject

[208] *Comparing India and Singapore*

**Table 9.3.** SgE GRAMMATICAL FEATURES AND INPUT DEMAND

| Grammatical feature | Rich input needed? | Predicted to persist? | Widespread in SgE? |
|---|---|---|---|
| Past -ed omission | no | no | yes |
| Copula be omission | no | no | yes |
| Extended prog -ing | no | no | no |
| will/would | yes | yes | yes |
| Indefinite article omission | yes | yes | yes |
| Definite article omission | yes | yes | yes |

to completely different rules of use, this may have very different implications for contact outcomes than if [+ tense] is simply absent in the L1 grammar. I return to this in Section 9.6.

But first, does input demand also correspond to the different set of stable features of SgE? SgE was briefly reviewed in relation to the two SLA approaches above. Table 9.3 draws together the grammatical features examined so far for SgE in relation to input demand.

Tables 9.2 and 9.3 attest to a degree of conformity of input demand to which variable usage becomes long-term dialect outcomes but also highlights a few challenges, which we turn to next.

## 9.6. INPUT IS NOT THE ONLY FACTOR

The two immediate contradictions to an input demand account of SgE in Table 9.3 are the stability of past tense omission and copula omission over time. Both have low input demand—in terms of both the Subset Principle and the Interface Hypothesis—and so should not be predicted to diverge substantially.

Past tense omission in SgE has been argued to be a morphosyntactic constraint that originally derives from a phonological process of consonant cluster reduction (Bao 1998; Deterding 2007; Deterding and Poedjosoedarmo 1998). This appears to be confirmed in Gut's (2009) finding that irregular forms are more frequently realized for past tense. Further confirmation comes from the fact that past tense does appear to be more established in varieties with consonant cluster simplification, for example, African American English, Singapore English, and many Creole languages (eWAVE atlas, Kortmann and Lunkenheimer 2013). So, in this case, it is not the TMA system of the substrate at all that leads to the entrenchment of this feature; it is a *domino effect* from a completely separate part of the linguistic system, the phonology. In the absence of this phonological source, we would predict that SgE would show limited presence of past tense omission, as IndE does.

THE ROLE OF INPUT **[209]**

A phonological argument does not extend as easily to copula omission. Although a case has been made that African American Vernacular English copula omission arises out of phonetically reduced forms (Wolfram 1969; Labov 1969, 1972; Wolfram and Thomas 2002), this is not a likely account for SgE copula deletion, which is specifically associated with unreduced contexts that convey emphasis and intensification, based on substrate semantics (e.g., *This coffee house very cheap*; Wong 2014). Intriguingly, a different sort of domino effect could be a source, namely, the absence of verbal tense marking in SgE reinforcing other forms of omission, including that of past tense and copula/auxiliary *be* (in addition to changes in modal use, Ziegleler 1996).

These details remind us not to fall into the trap of asking *whether* substrate transfer or input accounts for changes but, rather, to ask what their relative contribution is to long-term change. (Winford [2009: 226] similarly laments the "unfortunate tendency to treat universals and substrate influence as if they were opposing factors in the genesis of contact languages.")

A typological analysis of grammatical change in New Englishes is underway to investigate this question more fully but is beyond the scope of this book. However, the typology has identified some key disambiguating cases that involve low input demand yet nevertheless show systematic divergence due to a deep absence of a core grammatical feature in the substrate.

The most striking of these is errors in the use of *he* and *she* by advanced L2 English speakers: this is a very low input demand feature yet shows non-native-like usage by otherwise near-native English speakers of L1s such as Mandarin or Hungarian. It appears to reveal hard limits on learnability, regardless of input, for speakers of language with no grammatical gender feature (Sharma 2017).

This suggests that input is certainly not the exclusive factor in accounting for whole dialect outcomes. To quote DeKeyser (2020: 79), "input is not a panacea." The example of simple pronominal gender errors shows how powerful hard L1 constraints can be on the learnability of some domains of L2 grammar, in particular the total absence of a core grammatical feature in the L1.

These observations show how New Englishes can contribute directly to mainstream theoretical debates. On the one hand, this chapter has offered some support for SLA models such as the Subset Principle and the Interface Hypothesis. On the other, despite this extensive evidence that input affects long-term dialect outcomes, the closing example casts some doubt on whether adequate input renders an L2 fully learnable by adults, as proposed by models such as Full Transfer/Full Access (Schwartz and Sprouse 1994). The indication of some hard limits placed by L1 systems may in fact support models that do not predict full acquisition of all features, for example, Failed Features Hypothesis (Hawkins and Chan 1997; Smith and Tsimpli 1995), Feature Reassembly and the Bottleneck Hypothesis (e.g., Lardiere 2009; Slabakova 2008), and the Interpretability Hypothesis (Tsimpli and Dimitrakopoulou 2007).

[210]    *Comparing India and Singapore*

## 9.7. MECHANISMS OF CHANGE: THE DYNAMIC LEARNER

This chapter has introduced a new dimension to the story of long-term change in postcolonial contact dialects: dynamic development in the individual language learner's grammar as the basis of large-scale historical change. In a version of ontogeny recapitulating phylogeny, the incremental development of an individual's L2 grammar is argued to be reflected, in part, in the long-term dialect outcomes we see in postcolonial regions, with different degrees of learning difficulty represented in the degree of divergent outcomes. SLA theory has shown that quality and quantity of input play a central role in these developmental phases, with certain features being acquired faster than others.

Previous studies have similarly explored such acquisitional effects in New Englishes, but with a focus on absolute difficulty of forms (e.g., Szmrecsanyi and Kortmann 2009; Davydova 2011). That approach makes more universalist predictions for shared outcomes across New Englishes, which are indeed observable. The acquisitional models explored here encourage us to also consider the difficulty in terms of the relationship between corresponding forms in the L1 and L2.[4]

This wider definition of input demand—as the amount of input a speaker of a particular L1 needs in order to acquire a given L2 grammatical feature—has a number of advantages for understanding dialect outcomes in New Englishes. It links structural complexity in the target language to the degree and type of L1-L2 difference. It creates systematic predictions for different long-term outcomes in New Englishes relative to their linguistic ecologies, not just broad Angloversals. It shows how the sociohistorical context of declining (historical) target variety input affects language outcomes through individual cognition. And it accounts for the emergence of possibly universal information-structural solutions (cf. Lange 2012) at very specific places in the syntax–pragmatics interface. The closing discussion intriguingly suggested that, in some cases, the total absence of a feature in the substrate may outrank input demand; a wider typology will help to further establish their relative role.

For now, the present exploration of input demand in two varieties with different substrates has moved us toward a more precise understanding of how two of the most powerful cognitive forces at play in contact-based language change—substrates and input demand—interact to generate the new dialects we see around the world.

# CHAPTER 10
# Style Range and Attitudinal Change

Indian is more standardized [than American English]. Standardized English is proper English. With grammar, adverbs, everything.

—Indian English speaker in California, 2001

Singlish is broken, ungrammatical English sprinkled with words and phrases from local dialects and Malay which English speakers outside Singapore have difficulties in understanding.

—Prime Minister Goh Chok Tong, Singapore, 1999

The two statements above invoke ideologically loaded notions of "properness" and "brokenness" of English in India and Singapore, respectively, one rooted in an idea of genealogical descent from an idealized historical superstrate, Standard British English, and the other rooted in an equally abstracted ideology that frames highly vernacular speech as problematic.

Both views convey an anxiety that is deeply invested in the prestige of standard languages. But the opposing direction of these distortions derives from some genuine differences between the two dialects. Scholars too have described Singapore English (SgE) as "hyper-colloquial" in opposition to "bookish" Indian English (IndE) (Mesthrie 1992; Mesthrie and Bhatt 2008: 162). IndE was shown in earlier chapters to be a conservative, slow-changing dialect. This lack of rapid language shift permits prescriptivists even within India to discount all nonstandard usage as learner errors, even if they represent stable innovations. SgE, by contrast, includes a radically divergent colloquial variety, Singlish, and much greater nativization, leading to a much more acute moral panic than in India.

This final chapter explores stark differences in style ranges between the two varieties, and the attitudes associated with them, as a final piece of

*From Deficit to Dialect.* Devyani Sharma, Oxford University Press. © Oxford University Press 2023.
DOI: 10.1093/oso/9780195307504.003.0010

the picture of incipient dialect birth in both regions. I first illustrate the different style ranges found in the two regions through a discussion of registers, style shifting, degrees of focusing toward new norms, language attitudes, and language dominance in individuals in each speech community. I frame these differences in terms of a continuum of types of style range in varieties of English, such that narrower and more expanded ranges correspond to Schneider's (2007) Phase 4 (endonormative stabilization) and Phase 5 (differentiation), respectively, with Singapore much further along in the process.[1]

## 10.1. STYLE RANGE IN INDIA

As shown in Chapter 3, English in India forms a cline of bilingualism (Kachru 1965). At one end is a tiny minority of upper- and middle-class, urban, balanced bilinguals who now share a largely endonormative variety of English (Chand 2010; Punnoose 2017; Domange 2020). At the other end is the vast majority of L2 users of English, with late and limited acquisition and use of English, for whom English "serves its classic role in an ESL country, that of an interethnically neutral link language" (Schneider 2007: 167). On a scale of contact variety types (Clements 2003), the majority of IndE speakers are closer to naturalistic L2 learners than to nativized speakers. Irish English is an example of a variety at the other end of the scale, in which all or nearly all individuals have undergone complete language shift and exhibit native-like variation quite distinct from L2 speech.

SgE has not nativized completely but is dramatically further along than IndE and nativizing rapidly. In 2020, 48.3% of Singaporeans reported English as their primary home language (Singapore Census of Population 2020; up from 23% in 2001 and 12% in 1980, Lim and Foley 2004). By contrast, fewer than .02%—200,000 people—reported English as a mother tongue in India in 2001 (informal accounts report higher levels of use, e.g., 10 million native speakers [Pathak 2013], but still a tiny fraction of the population). The speech of the majority of nondominant IndE users continues to resemble SLA in several ways. It has not yet stabilized toward an endogenous norm. It does not yet involve bidirectional patterns of style shifting or bidialectalism across established formal and informal registers, in contrast to Creoles, African American Vernacular English, and SgE. And it varies more relative to each speaker's other languages than SgE does (Sailaja 2009; Wiltshire and Harnsberger 2006). The implicational scaling in Chapter 3 outlined this asymmetry in variation found at the proficient and nonproficient ends of the Indian bilingual continuum. In this section I describe some of the characteristic social features of IndE today.

### 10.1.1. Conservatism in IndE

As noted in Chapter 2, a small proportion of highly educated, fluent Indian users of English have been a recognizable group in India for possibly over two centuries. On hearing a speech by the politician V. K. Krishna Menon in the 1930s, H. G. Wells reported, with a note of irony:

> A very eloquent man! I can't speak as well as he does, I am a mere Kentish man; once a haberdasher's assistant; learnt to speak and write English the hard way. But you fellows speak very clearly, and for all to hear. We mumble, bumble, grumble. (Skinner 1998: 33)

These forms of IndE are notable for their relative conservatism and formality, until recently even archaic, style. Sanyal's (2007) objection to "clumsy Victorian English [that] hangs like a dead albatross around each educated Indian's neck" may seem strongly worded, but this conservatism is to some extent confirmed in corpus studies that find IndE to rate highest among New Englishes for grammatical markers of "informative elaborate discourse" and lowest for markers of "interactive casual discourse" (Xiao 2009). The heavily bureaucratic and wordy style of Babu English was discussed in Chapter 2, and Xiao (2009) attributes this conservative, "nouny" style to the influence of the Raj and the East India Company as well as discourse styles in Indian languages.

Quantitative support for an elaborated and relatively formal norm in IndE is provided in Tables 10.1 and 10.2, using the parallel LOB, Brown, and Kohlapur corpora for British, American, and Indian English, respectively. Table 10.1 shows that IndE is significantly more resistant to the use of all contracted forms in press registers as compared with AmE and BrE. Similarly, Table 10.2 shows that sentence length is longer for IndE than either AmE or BrE in every written genre. (Notice also that AmE exceptionlessly conforms to its stereotypical characterization as more direct and informal than BrE for both measures.)

This sort of conservatism in style may not be a strictly Indian phenomenon but, rather, a characteristic of regions in which English was initially and

*Table 10.1.* CONTRACTED FORMS IN THE PRESS REGISTERS
OF THREE CORPORA

| Contracted form | American English | British English | Indian English |
|---|---|---|---|
| will → 'll | 5.4% | 2.5% | 0% |
| have → 've | 4.0% | 1.9% | 0.1% |
| not → n't | 28.7% | 18.2% | 0% |

[214] *Comparing India and Singapore*

**Table 10.2.** AVERAGE SENTENCE LENGTH (WORDS PER SENTENCE)
IN THREE CORPORA

| Register | American English | British English | Indian English |
|---|---|---|---|
| Press (reportage) | 7.9 | 8.7 | 10.6 |
| Press (editorial) | 8.1 | 9.2 | 10.8 |
| Skills, trades, hobbies | 8.3 | 9.9 | 11.1 |
| Scholarly/scientific writing | 8.3 | 9.8 | 10.3 |
| Detective fiction | 8.8 | 10.1 | 11.5 |
| Humor | 8.7 | 10.3 | 11.2 |

primarily introduced through colonial institutions, and where it may have acquired qualities of the indigenous verbal cultures for formal registers. Greater formality has also been claimed, for instance, for East African varieties of English (van Rooy et al. 2010).

As Chapter 7 described, colonial institutions were not the only conduit for the infiltration of English into Singapore, and the consequences of this different history for style variation and range are discussed later.

A second type of support for a fairly conservative norm for IndE comes from Sahgal and Agnihotri's (1985) survey of acceptability judgments among IndE speakers. Examining IndE speakers' relative assessments of acceptability of a number of syntactic and lexical "deviations," they found that the greatest acceptability was associated with the lexical level (e.g., collocational restrictions) whereas the least acceptable tokens were those involving syntax (e.g., word order). Again, this contrast is likely to hold for many varieties, but incomplete endonormative stabilization and limited vernacular English use in India supports this continued orientation to an idealized, "correct" use of English.

### 10.1.2. Ongoing Supraregionalization and Vernacularization of IndE Styles

IndE is described by Schneider (2007: 162–172) as spanning Phase 3 (nativization) or Phase 4 (endonormative stabilization) of his dynamic model for the development of New Englishes. This is because indigenous sociolinguistic norms have not stabilized fully; for instance, there is little, if any, codification of Standard Indian English, and pedagogical norms tend to be exonormatively oriented (except in the domain of pronunciation). Mukherjee (2007) favors a broad classification of the variety as Phase 4 as well, with some traits of Phase 3. In a wide-ranging analysis of register variation, Balasubramanian (2009: 232) suggests that, at least for regular English users, IndE may be moving from Schneider's Phase 4 into Phase 5, the final stage characterized by internal differentiation among subdialects.

As discussed in detail in Chapter 2, the complexity of the social context of India means that different subcommunities currently participate in all three phases. Proficient and regular users of IndE are elaborating the formal and vernacular ends of the range, a Phase 5 activity, while less regular users are still transitioning from Phase 3. The speech and writing styles we see emerging out of this elaboration reflect seemingly contradictory (yet cross-linguistically common; Hickey 2004) processes of *supraregionalization* and *vernacularization* simultaneously.

Supraregionalization is the "replacement of salient features of a variety by more standard ones, frequently from an extranational norm. The motivation for this move is to render a variety less locally bound, more acceptable to a wider community" (Hickey 2004: 72). To what extent to do we find IndE style variation shifting toward less local norms? And are these extranational?

Certainly focusing toward a less local, emerging standard of high proficiency IndE (Sedlatschek 2009: 4) is an ongoing process in the cities of India. Sedlatschek shows stabilization of several lexical and grammatical features of IndE over time, illustrating pan-Indian use of originally Hindi forms (e.g., the term *lathi-charge*) and even pan-South-Asian use of originally Indian terms (e.g., *eve-teasing*). Balasubramanian confirms many of these consistent usage patterns for educated IndE, and Maxwell et al. (2018) show convergence in prosody across educated IndE speakers with different L1 speakers.

Using variationist sociolinguistic methods, Chand (2010) clearly shows that nonrhoticity is a panurban prestige variant, preferred by female interviewees and Delhi residents, and accommodated to by incoming migrants to the city. Domange (2020) similarly documents recent phonetic change in New Delhi that resembles vowel shifts in native dialects.

All of these examples, at different levels of language structure, indicate the establishment of broadly nonregional, yet specifically Indian, norms. Today, highly proficient and educated bilinguals in the upper middle classes in major Northern cities cannot be easily distinguished regionally based on their accents but can most certainly be identified as Indian, rather than British. South Indian speech from these upper social strata may bear slightly clearer Southern regional markers (discussed in Chapter 2) but can also converge fairly closely toward what may be described as an emerging supraregional variety. Many of the best-known Indian writers in English represent this variety, which, like other native varieties, has a distinctive phonetic norm but relatively few grammatical divergences from British English (e.g., invariant tags, focus *only*).

However, this supraregionalization does not orient substantially to extranational norms. In general, IndE has moved steadily away from, not toward, a British norm. IndE speakers in urban centers are becoming more similar to

[216] *Comparing India and Singapore*

one another (i.e., less regional), but simultaneously recognizably Indian (i.e., less extranational).

Recent studies have documented some elements of infiltration of AmE traits into proficient IndE, in both phonology (Cowie 2007, 2018; Chand 2010; Sailaja 2009; Domange 2020) and lexicon. For example, Sedlatschek (2009) shows an increased lexical choice of AmE forms *sidewalk* and *workday*; these are particularly favored by journalists with explicit ties to the United States, implying a social-network conduit for new forms (p. 136). This might suggest an element of recent AmE influence, but Meyerhoff and Niedzielski's (2003) insight that imported features are typically localized in use and indexical in meaning applies here. These instances of extranational diffusion need not involve direct mimicry of AmE, particularly when embedded in an otherwise Indian style.

In contrast to these leveling processes across Indian urban centers, we also find signs of the reverse process of ongoing indigenization and vernacularization (Hickey 2004) in speech style.

One source of indigenization is the constant influx of L2 speakers into the core group of IndE users, reinforcing bilingual sources of divergence. For example, the continued influx of nondominant English speakers continues to expand the presence of indigenized forms in formal written registers. Despite their stigmatization at the time, most of the innovations described in Sahgal and Agnihotri's (1985) study are widespread enough now to appear in mainstream newspaper writing. All the grammatical and lexical traits described in Chapter 2 are prevalent in the Kolhapur corpus of written IndE (created in 1971; see Shastri 1996), existing comfortably alongside British archaisms and highly standard style in formal written registers.

Sharma (2005b) showed that these regular IndE forms are more frequent in regional than national press, and more frequent in bureaucratic than in press texts, but also that they are present across these categories. Examples of the use of IndE syntactic forms in print media are given in (1).

(1) a. On <u>the</u> economic affairs, the party now has virtually endorsed the 1991 reforms but clarifies that it remains committed to Ø mixed economy. (*The Tribune*, September 4, 1998)

 b. The Foreign Secretary-level talks <u>had</u> bogged down after the third round. (*Hindustan Times*, September 4, 1998)

 c. We believe they <u>would</u> be taking instructions from their leader. (*The Tribune*, September 4, 1998)

Lexical indigenization is even more extensive and less subject to prescriptive pressure. The newspaper extract in (2) illustrates unmarked use of local forms.

(2) A dais was erected, from which, the safai netas using hailers, did their best to incite the safai karamcharis to keep up their dharna. (*Times of India*, April 1, 2003)

[*safai* 'cleaning,' *netas* 'leaders,' *karamcharis* 'workers,' *dharna* 'strike']

This balance between convention and change is also apparent in Indian literature in English. While some early Indian prose and poetry mimicked the British canon, from the very beginning Indian writers have experimented with Indian verbal imagery and meanings. Some writers have specifically employed vernacular style in their English (e.g., Mulk Raj Anand, R. K. Narayan, Raja Rao), and almost all rely on indigenous cultural knowledge and postcolonial experience in their linguistic choices, narrative styles, and actors' voices (e.g., Salman Rushdie, Vikram Seth, Amitav Ghosh).

Sedlatschek (2009) distinguishes between more formal, high-register cultural loans and informal loans that voice the urban Hinglish style of speech. He also presents instances of retentions of earlier BrE forms (e.g., *upliftment*, p. 86) and adoption of new AmE trends (e.g., *price hike*, p. 153), complicating claims that IndE lexical choices are consistently more conservative.

Much contemporary vernacularization also derives from natural, colloquial use of IndE as a default code by young, urban, middle-class people who readily identify with this vernacular. This group is also strongly associated with the related urban speech style of Hinglish.

Hinglish—a default register of Hindi-English code-mixing—is increasingly the main casual spoken register of many young, urban Indians and may be one of the main conduits of vernacularization of IndE:

> Hinglish commands national and international recognition, is used across a range of genres and mediums, e.g., informal discourse, popular handbooks, fiction novels, advertising, TV shows and films, and demonstrates nascent codification efforts. Ideologically, it indexes a middle ground between upper and lower classes, values and broader dispositions, as a modern but locally grounded way of presenting oneself, while this positive value is challenged by purists. Some urban elite youth, canonical Bilinguals per census reports, even consider Hinglish their mother tongue and claim only limited Monolingual Hindi competence. (Parshad et al. 2016: 378; citations removed)

Parshad et al. refer here to Hinglish speakers as an established category, based on census reports. The variety is clearly enregistered—that is, subject to explicit social awareness and commentary (Agha 2003)—with books (Kothari and Snell 2011), mainstream news stories (*BBC News*, November 27, 2012;

British Council *Voices Magazine*, October 30, 2015), and Bollywood films (*Jab We Met*, 2007) devoted to the phenomenon.

It is worth noting that Hinglish does not always entail an empowering sub-version of linguistic hierarchies, as is often suggested. It can bring into sharp relief a class divide that derives from whether the base code used is Hindi or English. Roy (2013) observes correctly that "while ushering in linguistic demo-craticization, Hinglish has not been able to bridge social difference" (2013: 21).

Nevertheless, all of these varieties of Hinglish play an important part in the vernacularization of IndE, integrating English into the historically more well-established vernacular styles of Hindi. The quote in (3), from an inter-view with Ram [M7Hcal], illustrates this well-established, casual style:

(3)  *Pata hai kya hai?* The culture *wahan pe* has so much deteriorated, means, I can't explain it. Because I've been into that place. *Maine dekha hai. To maine jo* feel *kara hai* it's not worser actually, it has gone. The culture has gone out of Indian Air Force. *Wakai mein. Pata hai*, you won't believe, like, *jo maine dekha hai*. Now just to tell you *kya*, like I have seen, *jo mujhe sabse ganda laga hai*, I'm just telling you frankly as a friend, *ki jis vajay mai ne chhori hai* is due to the total deterioration of the culture, Indian culture.[2]

Code-switching is known to accelerate syntactic convergence across languages (Toribio 2004) and Hinglish is no exception. The example in (4) is from a fic-tional Hinglish dialogue (Chaudhary 2001: 27). The first sentence employs Hindi syntax with English lexicon and a Hindi discourse marker; the second sentence employs English syntax with an inserted Hindi adverb ('at once; totally'). The example shows the potential for convergence and blending be-tween the most common structures of Hindi and English, and even the poten-tial for a new fused language (Auer 1999).

(4)  What senti letter, *rey*! Shah is *ek dum* touched.

Code-switching can also assign or maintain particular roles for the languages involved, which can also have an impact on their functional or stylistic range of use. Krishnaswamy (2009) notes that in Tamil-English mixing, light or hu-morous registers tend to be associated with English while serious registers are reserved for Tamil, suggesting the potential for an incipient diglossia that inverts the traditional, colonial high status of English.

In sum, many speakers are caught between the twin forces of progression and conservatism (Mukherjee 2007), with both supraregionalization and ver-nacularization occurring simultaneously around them, for different linguistic features and in different settings.

### 10.1.3. Limited Style Range

Despite some expansion in vernacularization, one of the most important characteristics of the IndE continuum, not often noted in comparative studies of New Englishes, is the relatively limited style shifting and style range of its speakers, as compared with native varieties and particularly SgE. Native-like style ranges are now observable in English-dominant Indians but are still uncommon.

In the original corpus of 24 sociolinguistic interviews, for example, speakers show very little style range between typically casual and formal phases of the interview, unlike the classic style range captured by sociolinguistic interviews with native speakers (Labov 1972).

A possible exception is shown in the example in (5). Here, a shop owner, Kumar [M8Hcal], was being interviewed in California when an Indian customer entered the store. The Indian customer has a much higher proportion of nonstandard features in his English than Kumar. As Kumar carries out a quick transaction, he accommodates noticeably to his interlocutor and then shifts back to a more standard register with the interviewer:

(5)  Kumar:       At one time in my life I thought it was- I'm a PhD and I'm
                        a- academic and a professor, Ø will be beneath my thing to
                        come and sell merchandise in a small store like this. Cause
                        I'm much more qualified. Today I come here and I sweep
                        all the sidewalks and everything and I enjoy it. So that's an
                        adjustment. So I'm saying it's all in the mind. That's a life,
                        that's a growth, that's understanding about who we are,
                        what life is all about.
        DS:            These are all, kind of, identity issues-
        Kumar:       Can you excuse me, I have-
        DS:            Yeah.
        Kumar:       Can I -? Sorry.
                        (calls to customer) <u>You want some help?</u> (leaves to help
                        customer, then returns with customer and starts calcu-
                        lating tax on purchase) That's good, I think it's very nice to
                        have your own business. Oh! When one doesn't use one's
                        mind, then one makes Ø mistake. So how long have you
                        been here?
        Customer:   Ten year.
        Kumar:       Ten years? Okay. And - in California or-?
        Customer:   Yeah, California.
        Kumar:       So you know these people? <u>This</u> R–– and J––, these people?
        Customer:   J––. Yeah.

[220]   *Comparing India and Singapore*

| | |
|---|---|
| Kumar: | J––. He used to work with R–– as Ø waiter and he started his own restaurant. <u>Doing very well.</u> Were you working with these people too? |
| Customer: | No, San Jose. |
| Kumar: | San Jose? S––? |
| Customer: | Yeah. |
| Kumar: | <u>You worked with S––?</u> |
| Customer: | Yeah. |
| Kumar: | Are you still working with them? |
| Customer: | Yeah. |
| Kumar: | All right. He has done very well. And taxes two, nine. So when are you planning to go there? <u>Leaving today?</u> |
| Customer: | Yes. |
| Kumar: | Oh. What made you decide to go to Atlanta? Let me get this quick. <u>Your card is okay,</u> right? |
| Customer: | Yeah, card is okay. |
| Kumar: | <u>Card is okay</u> [laughing]. <u>Trust you. Otherwise go to J––. Eh?</u> [smiling] <u>But you already leaving today to Atlanta?</u> |
| Customer: | Oh, no, come back later. |
| Kumar: | All right, this is yours and mine. There you go. |
| Customer: | Thank you. |
| Kumar: | Best of luck. Best of luck to you. <u>Eh- you have a family?</u> |
| Customer: | Yeah, family. |
| Kumar: | Heh. <u>Children, how many?</u> |
| Customer: | Two. |
| Kumar: | You'll be fine. I think in this country you'll have more respect, have your own business. |
| Customer: | Okay, thank you. |
| Kumar: | Take care. No negotiations. Keep one price, whatever in life. [referring to earlier exchange about bargaining] |
| DS: | He's starting a restaurant or something? |
| Kumar: | He was working, seemed like, with S–– and J––, who himself was a waiter. See how enterprising people are here? And- [customer returns] oh you left your [laughing, gives something]. Good luck to you! And er- I know because I've been here Ø long time and the guy R––, who opened this restaurant, he's the first one to open restaurants here. So his waiter J–– learned from him. These people come from, you know, very poor families. No education. And then he started and opened his own restaurant. And he is doing amazingly well. |

STYLE RANGE AND ATTITUDINAL CHANGE  [221]

At the start of the extract in (5), during his first turn, Kumar employs predominantly standard grammar, including in his use of articles, the verb *be*, and wider sentence structure. When the client with limited English competence enters, we see a clear shift in style on the part of Kumar, including greater omission of articles, lack of inversion, omission of subjects, and omission of auxiliary *be*. His rates of nonstandardness in his interview placed him among the "more proficient" group on the cline of bilingualism in Chapter 3, but here he displays an ability to manipulate his morphosyntactic usage considerably in relation to his addressee.

However, unlike the repertoire of many SgE speakers, he would not claim the style that he shifts into as his own vernacular. It is very clear that the customer is not an English-dominant speaker, and his speech—which in linguistic terms patterns with the learner-like speakers in Chapter 3—is not an enregistered vernacular variety as Colloquial Singapore English is. Kumar's shift resembles a shift outside his normal range, a type of "foreigner talk" (Ferguson 1971), rather than a shift to Kumar's personal vernacular. Sailaja (2009: 114) offers a similar example of shifting to simplified syntax, rather than a focused vernacular, in such intercultural exchanges.

As we will see in the next section, SgE is very different in this regard. It shows extensive intraspeaker code-switching between a speaker's own Standard and Colloquial SgE. The examples will show situational shifting, but also metaphorical (within situation) code-switching between the two styles in a single episode, which is also very rare in IndE. The exception is switching between IndE and Hinglish, which is more widespread.

Some scholars now treat IndE as a regular nonstandard dialect but, as will be shown in the comparison with SgE next, heavily indigenized IndE speech is still closer to a heterogeneous L2 learner spectrum than Colloquial SgE. IndE has moved robustly toward indigenization, but given the size of the country, its diverse multilingualism (that often excludes English), and its robust indigenous lingua francas, it has not yet focused toward a unified dialect continuum comparable to native or diglossic systems. Despite incipient vernacularization among young urban IndE speakers, English remains something of an awkward newcomer in India's rich inventory of indigenous vernaculars.


## 10.2. STYLE RANGE IN SINGAPORE

### 10.2.1. Continuum and Diglossia Models of SgE Lectal Range

Although Singapore is also home to a range of types of bilinguals, its lectal range in English is dramatically different from that of India. Individual SgE speakers have much wider style ranges than IndE speakers, and, because it has been used natively by a higher proportion of the population, SgE is much more focused at the level of the speech community, that is, speakers share norms of usage for both standard and colloquial registers.

The range of SgE is so broad that much of the literature on SgE has debated whether it exceeds what is typically described as a stylistic or lectal continuum. Earlier studies adopted the view that SgE is a dialect continuum (e.g., Pakir 1991; Platt 1977), while others argued that the regular alternation within individual speakers implies a diglossic situation, with Standard Singaporean English as the H(igh) variety and Colloquial Singaporean English as the L(ow) variety (Gupta 1994, 2001; Bao and Hong 2006).[3]

The diglossic approach arose out of the view that speakers natively acquire L and H codes for English in Singapore and are aware of the clear complementarity in their functional roles:

> There is a High variety of English, which I call Standard English, which is much like Standard Englishes in the rest of the English-speaking world. . . . This H-variety is the norm in formal circumstances, in education, and in all writing except some representations of dialogue.
>
> However, the Low variety of English in Singapore is sharply different from Standard English, especially in syntax and morphology . . . SCE (Singapore Colloquial English) is the main kind of English used in the home and in casual situations. It is the normal variety to be used to small children, outside a pedagogical situation. Nearly all those children who have learnt English from birth will have SCE, rather than Standard English, as their native language. (Gupta 1994: 7–9)

Examining the use of *already* and *also* as grammatical markers in four types of corpus data—private dialogue, public dialogue, monologue, and writing— Bao and Hong (2006) find novel SgE meanings used systematically in private dialogue, but much more standard meanings in the other registers. They conclude that these distributions strongly support a diglossic model, with "CSE [Colloquial Singapore English] as the vernacular L variant associated with informal occasions and SSE as the local standard H" (p. 112).

Others have attempted to reconcile these positions. For example, Platt (1977) uses the term "polyglossia" to move beyond binary variation across a continuum. This can also accommodate multiple origins of different subvarieties during different phases of the formation of SgE. Gupta (2006: 22) treats Singapore as a case of "leaky" diglossia, and Leimgruber (2013: 45) goes further, concluding that SgE is better described in terms of indexicality than as a "clear-cut example of Fergusonian diglossia." Alsagoff's (2010) cultural orientation model similarly avoids casting varieties as wholesale alternations but, rather, styles as suited to specific hearer orientations.

As discussed in Chapter 7, a number of ecological factors contributed to this more established standard-vernacular system in Singapore. In Schneider's dynamic model, SgE occupies a more advanced position than IndE overall, well within in the range of Stages 4–5.

### 10.2.2. Colloquial SgE

Colloquial SgE is much more radically divergent in phonology and syntax than equivalent colloquial or learner varieties of IndE and is more focused as a variety with clear semantics and grammaticality conditions for use. The densely vernacular example in (6), from Alsagoff and Ho (1998: 129), can be contrasted to the simplified syntax in the earlier IndE example in (5):

(6)  Eh, better do properly lah. Anyhow do, wait kena scolding. And then, you always ask her for favour, and still don't want to do properly. Must lah. Like that do cannot. Do again. Come, I help you.

('You had better do this properly. If you don't, you may get told off. And since you are always asking her for favours, you should at least do this properly for her. You should! You cannot do it like this. Do it again. Come, let me help you.')

Colloquial SgE is subject to covert, and often overt, prestige, despite originally severe government resistance to the variety, discussed later in this chapter. The variety is highly enregistered, with films, books, and websites devoted to it. The example in (7) is from the website Talking Cock (a slang term for speaking Colloquial SgE):

(7)  Tolkien for bengs:[4]
*The Fellowship of the Ring:*
Last time got this short-short person with si-beh hairy legs called Bilbo, lor. He, hor, got this ring that last time belong to some monster. But then, hor, one day suay-suay the monster want it back, and send his kah kiah to Bilbo's house to settle, lah. But the ring, hor, acherly can make people very powderful. But then, hor, if you wear too long will also kena sai. Si beh hiong one, so better faster go and destroy it, lor. So Bilbo's nephew Frodo . . . Aiyah, dun ask me why their name all so funny, can or not? You ask me, I ask who? Anyway, Frodo and some peng yew kena arrow to go and destroy the ring. But donno why also, they must do it in the monster's home, which is at the end of New Zealand there. So they walk and walk and walk across New Zealand, lah. And then along the way, got monster chase them, got people want to hoot them, some of them dieded, all sorts of thing, lah. At the end, Frodo and Sam, his pooi-pooi friend who I think so is a bit ah quah, got separated from the rest.

*The Two Towers:*
Frodo and Sam meet up with this thing called Gollum, who look like he take too much Slim 10 like that. At the same time, hor, the other friends get into some powderful hooting session, where, wah lau eh, even the trees can do gongfu one. They all fight over what, I also donno, but quite kan cheong, lah.

*The Return of the King:*
In the end, Frodo and his peng yew all win leow, lah. Arbuthen?

The very existence of a popular slang term for the variety, as well as its use to playfully subvert a classic text from the English literary canon, are both further signs of enregisterment (Agha 2003) and vernacular confidence.

### 10.2.3. Intraspeaker and Intrasituational Code-Switching

A major difference from IndE is that a single speaker of SgE may frequently and consciously code-shift between colloquial and standard styles across and within situations.

Leimgruber (2008a) examined intraspeaker variation in the use of two types of forms—SgE discourse particles and existential *got*—by 36 Singaporean college students of three different ethnic backgrounds. The use of discourse particles showed clearly that the students shift consistently between two discrete (perhaps diglossic) levels of use of discourse particles, rather than making smooth, incremental adjustments along a continuum in different situations.

In addition to situational code-switching, SgE speakers also routinely engage in metaphorical, or *intra*situational, code-switching (Blom and Gumperz 1972). This phenomenon can be seen clearly in the two extracts from ICE-SIN in (8).[5]

(8)  a.  D: These fellas cannot close. <u>Everyday must open</u>. Without fail until five o'clock <u>like that</u> you know.
　　　　E: You mean <u>one day also cannot close</u>?
　　　　. . .
　　　　E: You seem to be enjoying your beef kway teow so much
　　　　D: <u>Shiok what</u>
　　　　. . .
　　　　D: Hinduism never stipulated that you cannot eat beef
　　　　E: It did.
　　　　D: Where?
　　　　E: I don't know <u>lah</u>. Just shut up <u>lah</u>.

D: You see it's a cultural concept. Wait. It's not fair. You see ah beef was probably not to be eaten in the Indian culture because cow gives milk and milk is also given by the mother. And therefore cows were compared as sacred to mothers. And that's why they say you shouldn't eat cows. It's got no religious connotations.

E: Yah it is associated with Siva <u>what</u>.

D: No, Siva himself is just a construct because humans were not able to focus on a particular point. They cannot pray to the formless so humans created for themselves forms, alright. Therefore Siva is just a fictitious thing from the mind.

b. B: Excuse me <u>cannot</u> even promote ∅ holiday in front of him <u>muh.</u> Got to sweat you know. <u>Group pressure</u> he cannot survive.

C: <u>Wah lau.</u>

A: <u>Afterwards tell him want pressure lah.</u>

. . .

B: <u>Got time we can.</u>

A: <u>Can lah</u> so we'll meet uh two to four. After ∅ fourth service. I mean LK ∅ very long-winded. <u>The only way end</u> four thirty-five <u>lucky.</u>

. . . *[topic shift to teasing B about a female friend]*

B: Excuse me. She's forty-five. She has two kids and she's the one who has been trying to match-make me.

C: We have a new generation woman uh

B: Ya. And her husband is a policeman.

A: Short of saying he's a bouncer, right?

B: And he is not as (unintelligible) as a bouncer uh near his son is bad enough. He's about twice my size. But he's not fat, you see. He's just big.

In (8a), both interlocutors use various typically colloquial SgE constructions in the earlier segment of their conversation. When the topic shifts to beef, the initial code continues to be colloquial, but there is a sudden and complete shift to Standard SgE when D adopts the new goal of persuading E of his view of whether and why beef is not eaten by Hindus. Notice that it is D who shifts more dramatically to Standard SgE, as he is the one who has adopted a new persuasive and academic stance; E continues to use markers of colloquial style.

[226] *Comparing India and Singapore*

Similarly, in (8b), we see the three interlocutors using a range of colloquial SgE constructions at first. When A starts to tease him about a female acquaintance, however, he shifts to a Standard SgE voice in which he enumerates factual rebuttals to the insinuation. B's shift is not unlike D's shift in (8a), as both involve a shift to structured argumentation and heightened (though playful) conflict.

The strong dialect identity evident in this active use of two registers of SgE by its speakers stands in stark contrast to the struggle in public discourse over attitudes to the dialect, particularly the colloquial variety, discussed later.

## 10.3. COMPARING STYLE RANGES ACROSS NEW ENGLISHES

### 10.3.1. Style Ranges in English

Table 10.3 briefly summarizes the major differences in lectal ranges in the IndE and SgE speech communities.

As reviewed in detail in Chapter 7, the acrolectal end of the range in both countries derives historically from a similar structured imposition of English via colonial institutions (schools, universities, colonial employment). Both varieties thus have an educated register that looks to historic prestige (older, conservative varieties of British English) as a reference norm, at least in the domain of grammar.

The basilectal end is very different in the two countries. In Singapore, a history of informal use in trade may well underpin Colloquial SgE, now a native language for many of its users. In IndE, these varieties simply reflect very limited access to English among a vast array of nondominant L2 users.

The examples of individual usage patterns in the preceding sections illustrated the very different style range outcomes of these macroecological differences. Figure 10.1 compares types of style ranges that might be found across dialects that have experienced distinct sociohistorical conditions of emergence. The visualization is a simplified version of Platt's (1977) and Ho and Platt's (1993) model for SgE and BrE, and it is extended to IndE.

*Table 10.3.* AVAILABLE CODES IN INDE AND SGE

| Continuum | Indian English | Singapore English |
|---|---|---|
| Acrolectal end | conservative style: declining conservatism | conservative style: less conservative than IndE acrolect |
| Basilectal end | second-language variation: nonnative; not used by acrolectal speakers | vernacular style: some native; used by acrolectal and mesolectal speakers |

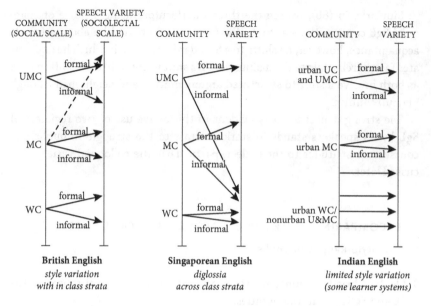

**Figure 10.1.** Sociolinguistic variation in three English varieties (adapted from Ho and Platt 1993, Fig. 1.3, p. 5).

Ho and Platt related socioeconomic status (the left-hand scale in each column in Figure 10.1) to sociolects or registers observed in the community (the right-hand scale in each column). The column for British English shows class-stratified style ranges, as Ho and Platt represented them, but with the addition of the potential for middle-class crossover, or hypercorrection (Labov 1972). In Ho and Platt's characterization, the lowest sociolects in SgE have a narrower stylistic range than the equivalent in British English, but the highest sociolects in SgE have a wider range than their equivalent in British English due to their diglossic control of two functionally separated varieties.[6] The group with a narrower style in this community is working-class speakers, who may still be dominant in other languages and have limited use of, and access to, English. But Ho and Platt highlight the access that many Singaporeans have, regardless of class, to Colloquial SgE.

Adding IndE to this comparison, we see a negligible degree of style range among Indians who use English the least in their multilingual repertoires. And the style repertoires of middle- and upper-class speakers are more restricted than those of native varieties such as British English, much less the diglossic complexity of SgE. As discussed in earlier sections, this narrow style range in IndE is starting to change among young urban speakers with gradual vernacularization underway. Nevertheless, a shift to nonstandard grammar still risks being heard as nonnative rather than colloquial.

The correspondence to class for IndE in Figure 10.1 is complicated by the urban/rural divide in India. Class is more closely tied to English use and style range in urban contexts; in rural contexts it plays a less direct role, and both upper- and lower-class rural individuals can be at the lower end of the column in Figure 10.1.

One of the most telltale differences in style variation between SgE and IndE speakers is that in their vernacular styles, SgE speakers share *the same* dialect traits, to some extent independent of the traits of their other languages, if they speak others. A Tamil-speaking SgE speaker will have features of Chinese and Malay in their SgE even if they do not speak these languages, simply because Colloquial SgE has converged on a core dialect grammar that is acquired by most users. This *can* be the case for a Tamil speaker who acquires IndE in Delhi—they too may have Hindi-influenced IndE traits even if they don't speak Hindi—but it is still very much the case that a nondominant IndE speaker's L1 exerts a direct influence on their English. In other words, non-English-dominant IndE speakers are like individual language learners, and differ from one another accordingly, whereas speakers of basilectal or very colloquial SgE are part of a speech community that shares that variety.

### 10.3.2. Style Range across a Speaker's Languages

Particularly for IndE, the individual ranges in Figure 10.1 are only one part of *multilingual* repertoires, unlike the BrE monolingual style ranges. The reduced stylistic variation in IndE naturally does not reflect an absence of further styles, only an absence of *English use* in those styles. If we were to overlay native languages on Figure 10.1, additional style lines would appear, for example, formal and informal styles in Hindi. As noted earlier, Tamil-English bilinguals tend to allocate Tamil to some functions (serious, traditional) and English to others (light, humorous) (Krishnaswamy 2009). A narrow IndE style range does not mean a narrow style range overall.

Style range in any given language, in a multilingual, should be interpreted relative to their overall cross-linguistic repertoire. For example, we saw in Chapter 6 that many IndE speakers freely adopt AmE upon contact with such varieties. This may be in part because they are more concerned about language shift than accent shift, as shown in (9) and (10).

(9) Quotes from Sujit [M9Hcal]:
    a. You have to keep your mother tongue. That's your identity, that's the way you are. That's your regional thing. So you have to stick onto the mother tongue, definitely.
    b. [Your English accent] doesn't matter. It doesn't, I mean, categorize you in some way, it's just your accent and the way you speak.

STYLE RANGE AND ATTITUDINAL CHANGE [229]

c. If you're working in a company or a store full of Indian customers, then you are gonna be, like, more towards India. Their style. But if you're working in a multinational company, which is an American company, then you have to be like them. If you have to sustain there, you have to be like them. You can't stand all alone.

One might say that, to Sujit, what one speaks is more important than the way one speaks. As long as one's language is maintained, functionally motivated dialect shift need not be negatively evaluated. Shalu similarly adopts a pragmatic, functional stance toward adopting AmE.

(10) Quotes from Shalu [F1Lcal]:
a. Lot of people change when they come here. They change theirself and they become Americanize. But we are still- we keep our children and culture. And tell them our customs. They speak very good Punjabi. Mostly, people when they come here, after one year, they forget how they talk. They always talk in English and I don't like that. Don't forget your mother tongue. That's my mother tongue. So I always- in my home we talk Punjabi.
b. Most of the womans come from the village, from the small city, they don't speak English. So they should, when they come, the first thing I always say: learn English, get the driving license. Very important, and then you can start your job.
c. Accents is little different, but Indian is much better than Chinese and Spanish. They really twist their tongue easily. Their accents become very Americanized easier. But other culture it's take little time . . . Indian peoples, their accents become very nice, Americanized.

Here again, Indian identity is primarily maintained through native language use, not maintenance of IndE. Dialect fluidity appears to be less stigmatized for these individuals than for monolingual English speakers; indeed it is observable in uptake of AmE forms even within India (Cowie and Pande 2017). For IndE speakers such shifts may not be linked to "becoming" American as much as signaling temporary, instrumental affiliations. (It is interesting to consider whether SgE, which is rapidly nativizing, is more like IndE or native varieties in this regard.)

## 10.4. IDEOLOGIES OF NEW ENGLISHES

The orientation of a speech community or region toward exogenous or endogenous norms (exo- and endonormativity) is of course a form of ideology

[230] *Comparing India and Singapore*

about language. Schneider's (2007) phases of development of New Englishes are therefore by definition rooted in ideology.

Do the range of speaking styles described so far for English users in Singapore and India correspond to how they are characterized in each region's dominant discourses and attitudes? Do ideologies systematically evolve along with the distinct stages of dialect formation, in the same way that style ranges have been argued to above?

Schneider (2007) showed that changes in ideology often do accompany changes in dialect over time, but causality can be very difficult to establish. An ideology or identity that favors political independence may promote dialect divergence, but the inverse story is also plausible, that innovative dialect forms develop first, and self-identification with those forms arises in response to those changes. Through meticulous processing of historical data on the emergence of Hong Kong English, Evans (2014) found robust support for a demographic basis for phases of change, but little reliable evidence of an origin in identity or ideology, contrary to Schneider's predictions.

The assumption here is therefore not that attitudes and ideologies are necessarily the reason for SgE and IndE to have diverged, but that they nevertheless can be indicators of a stage of dialect development.

As we found with style range, metapragmatic commentary also reveals a difference between the two varieties, namely, a more positive self-identification with their dialect among SgE speakers along with lower exonormative orientation, consonant with the higher degree of nativization in the region. As we will see, this takes the form of a more realistic recognition of syntactic divergence among SgE users, as opposed to an erasure of syntactic divergence, and an imagined ideal of IndE as the most correct of Englishes, among IndE users.

However, despite a softening of institutional opposition to Colloquial SgE, discussed shortly, we also see a lasting element of insecurity and marginal exonormative self-consciousness in both regions, perhaps a shared hallmark of the legacy of colonial otherness that takes many generations to dissipate.

### 10.4.1. IndE: "Correctness" and Incipient Dialect Confidence

Chapter 6 showed that some Indians in an AmE environment will not accommodate to the new variety as learners might but instead comfortably retain their IndE accents. Others prefer to adopt an American style, behaving more like a foreign language learner might in terms of identification with one's own accent. In the area of grammar, however, there was a conspicuous absence of affiliating with IndE syntactic divergences.

An important recent study (Nayak et al. 2016) used perception experiments to examine the implicit grammatical knowledge of IndE speakers of a widespread IndE grammatical form—the use of *only* with focus meaning—as well as participants' self-reports on usage and attitudes. They found a shared understanding of the indigenized meaning, but a range of exonormative/prescriptive and endonormative/affiliative stances taken by Indians toward their emerging variety.

The extracts in (11) are broadly ordered from exo- to endonormative and illustrate these conflicting orientations (Nayak et al. 2016: 279–280):

(11) a. *Do you use IndE-only yourself?* Sometimes I do use it, but I usually notice the ungrammaticality and correct myself

    b. *Do Indians speak English differently from other English speaking groups?* Yes, but mostly when talking to other Indians. Most of the perceptible differences stem from wrong usage

    b. *Are there "correct" and "incorrect" sentences within Indian English?* Some common differences feel less wrong than others

    c. *Should Indian English be considered a separate dialect?* A lot of people don't really think in English, and just have a running translation going, which is probably why Indian English has perceptible differences

    e. *Do you use IndE with non-Indians?* I'm only able to speak or think in this dialect if certain criteria are met, like where I am and who I'm speaking to

    f. *When asked about acceptability of IndE* only use

        i. People do say it, but it's wrong English, obviously

        ii. [IndE-*only*] is grammatically wrong. I would cringe if I saw it written, but I'm fine with hearing it. It would be weird for me to see it written in formal print . . . I'm just more used to hearing it . . . I do get it if it's in a casual atmosphere, but it's grammatically wrong because my frame of reference is British English—due to high school . . . I think grammatical correctness has to do with the written form of a language.

        iii. I know it's wrong, but I do understand it, and sometimes say it too—I'm not sure why.

        iv. If you're speaking, it's okay, but when you're writing it's weird.

        v. It makes sense, it's just a way of being more emotionally expressive and emphatic

Chapter 6 also pointed to a preoccupation with grammatical correctness. In those extracts, repeated in (12) below, we saw a studied sidestepping of the reality of IndE syntax. This would seem to contradict the focus on errors in the quotes above, but the concern with correctness is parallel; the difference is simply that below the speakers choose to focus on an imagined ideal rather

[232] *Comparing India and Singapore*

than real language use. (Recall that the same speakers expressed much more accepting views of accent, as opposed to grammatical, divergence.)

(12)  a.  Indian is more standardized. Standardized English is proper English. With grammar, adverbs, everything.

[M9Hcal]

b.  [American English] is more slang and Indian English is more respectable. More words and they using proper grammars. But here nobody use the grammars.

[F1Lcal]

c.  Originally they learned from the Britishers, so our English is totally right English. They speak the slang language here.

[F2Lcal]

It is worth noting in passing that the same ideology of historically derived correctness in IndE can even be found among British Asians (Sharma 2014), as illustrated in (13), from two different individuals.

(13)  a.  Their [Indians'] command of the English language is far better than the command of the English language in this country [the United Kingdom]. Far better. But obviously they have an accent and they have a dialect, you know, which they use.

b.  Because they [in India] know proper English, like from the book yeah?

And Chand (2009: 410) finds almost identical articulations of a bookish correctness in her data gathered in New Delhi, shown in (14).

(14)  I think India by far has the best command of the language, the people who have, who are educated. Even better than English people. I can't say what will happen ten years from now because, in India, English language was taught with more emphasis on the grammar. Then on the spoken English, in the initial years. That is why, you will find that the spoken English in India is grammatically more correct than anywhere else in the world.

Like Nayak et al.'s (2016) commentaries, Chand also finds layers of ideology and insecurity, torn between an ideal and a very different reality:

(15)  At college . . . we're considered snobs because we speak supposedly good English, which I don't agree with, because I find myself mispronouncing so many words. (p. 411)

Mukherjee (2007: 182), who describes IndE as a "semiautonomous variety" with indigenized norms, similarly describes IndE speakers' stances as resembling "ESL speakers' self-critical attitude and . . . orientation toward international intelligibility." (The question of international intelligibility surfaces later in SgE attitudes too.)

Chand (citing John 2007 and Vaid 1977) notes the profusion of Indian exonormative publications for the improvement of English, a $100 million English teaching industry in India invested in prescriptive norms, and observes that "Indian media offer no local value for [IndE], and they do not dialogically respond to individual attributions of local authority and authenticity through [IndE] practices" (p. 406).

This final claim is perhaps no longer true—considerable change is now underway in terms of ideological contestation of IndE norms. Writers, entertainers, and public figures are increasingly rejecting exonormativity and asserting indigenous dialect style in Indian media, advertising, television, and even political discourse (Orsini 2015). This has mainly involved a rise in the popular prestige of Hinglish specifically, but as Hinglish involves the incorporation of English into Hindi structures and vice versa, it brings along with it similar changes to the status of vernacular IndE.

Very early uses of a self-conscious vernacular Hinglish style appeared in the 1970s in light entertainment such as gossip columns (Shobhaa De's "Neeta's Natter" in *Stardust* and Devi's "Frankly Speaking" in *Star and Style*, both hugely popular film and gossip magazines), and more recently in the speech of presenters on popular culture television shows. Hinglish then moved into mainstream advertising—Pepsi, Virgin Mobile, Coca-Cola, Snickers—and has continued to move from the periphery to the center, becoming increasingly associated with mobility, urbanness, and being cool (Orsini 2015; Vohra 2015; Desai 2015). Even in call centers, Cowie (2007) notes the presence of stances that are resistant to the expectation of "accent neutralization."

Needless to say, these moves have fostered moral panics around the loss of Hindi in the face of Hinglish, and the spread of ungrammatical English. But these shifts also attest to increasing vernacularization of use as well as attitudes to IndE in India.

Table 10.4 shows a steady shift in attitudinal alignment with IndE, starting with a survey by Kachru in 1976 (700 graduate students across Indian universities), to a parallel survey by Sahgal in 1991 (45 middle- and upper-class residents of Delhi), and finally an informal replication of their questions with the India-based component in my own study (12 residents of Delhi across all classes). Note the low level of explicit alignment with AmE despite recent uptake of AmE-like forms such as rhoticity among some Indians in recent years.

Schneider's (2007: 172) observation that "an 'idealized linguistic norm' of British English is still upheld in educational institutions" is questionable, and

[234]   *Comparing India and Singapore*

**Table 10.4.** PREFERRED MODELS OF ENGLISH AMONG INDIANS
ACROSS THREE DECADES

| | 1976 (Kachru 1976) | 1991 (Sahgal 1991) | 2005 (present study) |
|---|---|---|---|
| British English | 66% | 24% | 8% |
| Indian English | 27% | 74% | 92% |
| American English | 3% | 2% | 0% |

Table 10.4 suggests a robust continuation of the shift in alignment toward Indians' own dialect noted by Sahgal (1991), subtler prescriptive attitudes about grammar notwithstanding.

Two other recent surveys of attitudes to IndE represent an intriguing contrast to Table 10.4. Hohenthal (2003) surveyed a much broader sample across the country, asking which variety would serve as the best model for Indian English. She found that only 17% of respondents preferred the Indian variety of English. Seventy percent felt that British Received Pronunciation would serve as the best model, and 10% favored General American English. She quotes very similar ideologies of historical British influence as well as emerging IndE affiliation.

Bernaisch and Koch (2016) similarly surveyed a broad national sample, with a focus on much subtler semantic scales to establish finer ideological associations. Like Hohenthal, they found British English to be evaluated the highest on almost all scales, but that IndE was rated the highest for the attributes "humble" and "friendly"—classic indexes of solidarity rather than status.

The difference between Hohenthal and Bernaisch and Koch's surveys on the one hand, and Sahgal's and Sharma's on the other, may primarily be due to very different samples, with the latter two focused on Delhi. It could also be that the identity of the researcher or the mode of data collection might have had an effect, as Sahgal and Sharma elicited their attitudinal questions at the end of a casual, face-to-face conversation whereas Hohenthal and Bernaisch and Koch's surveys were collected online.

Together the surveys give us a multidimensional picture of heterogeneous and fragile dialect self-perception. In their attitudes, as in their usage, Indians have historically been conservative about English use, with an ideological commitment to highly idealized, hypercorrect British origins. However, as always with language change, vernacularization in usage and attitudes has marched on simultaneously, with burgeoning associations of solidarity, if not yet status.

How do these metalinguistic commentaries, attitudinal surveys, and institutional stances compare with what is found in Singapore?

STYLE RANGE AND ATTITUDINAL CHANGE [235]

### 10.4.2. SgE: Robust Dialect Confidence and Vestigial Insecurity

We saw in Section 10.2 that speakers of Standard SgE routinely make marked shifts toward vernacular forms for a range of reasons, including indexing social stances in conversation. This is itself a sign of strong positive alignment with Colloquial SgE, a process that is much less observable in IndE.

These forms tend to be seen by Singaporeans as colloquial rather than consistently as errors, although the latter characterization can certainly be found. In situations of contact with native variety speakers too, then, SgE speakers might be predicted to be less likely to abandon their variety and shift wholesale to an American style, as a few IndE speakers were inclined to do in the data in Chapter 6.

As in India, attitudes and ideologies have changed markedly in recent years in Singapore. In this section I first outline the very explicit history of exonormative prescriptivism in Singapore (see Wee 2018 for a full history of this movement) and then describe simultaneous shifts that have occurred toward positive valuations of SgE.

As in perhaps all postcolonial, multilingual settings, dominant ideologies of local English in Singapore were deficit based at first. Lim and Foley (2004: 5) cite a 1986 meeting to address the "falling standards of written English in the Civil Service" as a landmark in the prescriptive approach to English use in Singapore. Error-based accounts persisted long after evidence (e.g., Tongue 1979) that, by the 1960s and 1970s, Singapore had already entered the phase of endonormative stabilization, Schneider's Phase 4.

Not surprisingly, given this rapid nativization and deeply vernacular range, but also due to its particular political ideology, Singapore became the site of heated and well-documented ideological battles in the public sphere during the 1990s, particularly between the government and public figures and academics.

Bao (2003: 26) summarizes this tension: "Despite its status as a native language for a sizable segment of the population, and as a language of solidarity and intimacy among speakers, [Colloquial Singapore English] is stigmatized and actively discouraged by the government, the media, and the English-medium school system." Some early expressions of prescriptivism are provided in (16), from the website of the Speak Good English Movement, launched by the government in 2000 and extensively critiqued by linguists and public commentators (see e.g., Wee 2005; Lim et al. 2010; Wee 2018).

(16)  a.  "I think it's important that you know the English language because it is the international language, and you speak it in the standard form. Do not speak Singlish! If you do, you are the loser. Only foreign academics like to write about it."
(Lee Kuan Yew, speech to National University of Singapore students, July 29, 1994)

b. "Do not popularise Singlish. Do not use Singlish in our television sitcoms, except for humorous bits, and in a way that makes people want to speak standard English. We will see a difference in another one generation. The people who will benefit most are those who can only master one kind of English. Singlish is a handicap we must not wish on Singaporeans."

(Senior Minister Lee Kuan Yew, National Day celebrations, August 22, 1999)

c. "For them to master just one version of English is already quite a challenge. If they get into the habit of speaking Singlish, then later they will either have to unlearn these habits, or learn proper English on top of Singlish. Many pupils will find this too difficult. They may end up unable to speak any language properly, which would be a tragedy . . ."

(Singaporean Prime Minister Goh Chok Tong, 1999)

d. "Teachers complain that their students are picking up catch-phrases like: 'Don't pray pray' and using them even in the classroom. The students may think that it is acceptable and even fashionable to speak like Phua Chu Kang [TV personality]. He is on national television and a likeable, ordinary person. The only character who tries to speak proper English is Phua Chu Kang's sister-in-law Margaret, and she is a snob. Nobody wants to be a snob. So in trying to imitate life, Phua Chu Kang has made the teaching of proper English more difficult."

(Prime Minister Goh Chok Tong, *The Straits Times*, 1999)

These statements have direct counterparts in moral panics in public discourse around varieties such as African American English and Multicultural London English. The local variety is not ideologically linked to correctness through the perceived prestige of its origins as IndE often is. By this point SgE was clearly becoming a native and radically restructured vernacular, and the ideological response is much more alarmed and negative than in the Indian context. (16c) is a response to "additive" proposals that young people could simply acquire a register range. And (16d) acknowledges a popular, cool quality of SgE, an association that is only nascent in the case of India.

One resemblance to IndE, however, is an acceptance of phonetic divergence but not syntactic divergence. This is evident in the rhetoric of the Speak Good English Movement:[7]

(17) a. "We don't have to speak English with British, American, or Australian accents. Most of us speak with a Singaporean accent. We are so used to hearing it that we probably don't notice it. But we should speak a form of English that is understood by the British, Americans, Australians, and people around the world . . . "

b. "On this subject of education, let me state clearly the disadvantages of Singlish. There are as many varieties of English as there are communities that speak English. In spite of differences in accent and pronunciation, people in Britain, America, Canada, Australia and New Zealand understand each other easily because they are speaking the same language, using the same words with the same grammar and sentence structures. Singaporeans add Chinese and Malay words into Singlish, and give different meanings to English words like 'blur' to mean 'blank.' Worse, Singlish uses Chinese sentence structure. In fact we are creating a different new language . . . "

(Lee Kuan Yew, 2004)

The Speak Good English Movement was countered by grassroots responses such as the Save Our Singlish Campaign and the Speak Good Singlish Campaign (see Rubdy 2001; Wee 2018). These movements defended the unique and rich cultural life of Colloquial SgE, promoted the acquisition of a register range, and supported long-standing SgE solidarity among the public. An early example is given in (18), from Kachru (2005: 241).

(18) "It is about time the arbiters of our Singapore life style realise that while good writing requires a certain amount of formality and literary convention, the charm and vitality of colloquial speech depends completely on spontaneity and a total lack of self-consciousness. What a pompous, boring and insufferable society we will be if all Singaporeans were to speak as though they were writing a prize winning essay."

(Letter to the editor, *The Straits Times*, 1982)

Ho (2006) suggests that normative Singaporean language ideologies have not only secured a dominant status for Mandarin and English in particular, but also, less visibly, fostered widespread linguistic insecurity that leads to uncertain ideological positioning and cultural behavior. She suggests that

> Singlish mirrors a people experiencing identity flux, not really knowing who they are and what cohesive set of values and beliefs to attach themselves to as a community . . . this flux may be traced back to two contributing factors in

[238]  *Comparing India and Singapore*

Singapore's linguistic history: (a) the rejection of standard British English, and therefore Western imperialist culture; (b) the substantial loss of the vernacular tongues, particularly among the Chinese ethnic groups, which made up some 70% of the total population in Singapore in the late 1970s and early 1980s. (2006: 18–19)

Her broad description, rather than a celebratory image of a speech community that has transitioned easily to endonormativity, is of a group rejecting exogenous culture but increasingly removed from endogenous familial or heritage cultures as well. We might see the rapid emergence of SgE and its associated vernacular culture as partly a response to this process of cultural reprogramming and loss.

Institutional language ideologies and disputes in Singapore are reviewed extensively elsewhere (see e.g., Lim et al. 2010; Wee et al. 2013; Wee 2018). For the present discussion, this brief overview simply highlights a very different level of institutional intervention to that found in India, in part a response to the more advanced degree of vernacularization, and constraining the full stabilization of the variety (Bao 2003).

Recent work has indicated resistance to institutional intervention through growing dialect confidence (Wee 2014, 2018; Wong 2014; Lee 2021).[8] In an attitudes study, Tan and Tan (2008) found strong solidarity ratings for Colloquial SgE, as was found by Bernaisch and Koch (2016) for IndE. These affiliations are much stronger for SgE, given its status as a native code for many of its users. Cavallaro and Ng (2009) found comparable solidarity ratings for Standard and Colloquial SgE. And Hum (2015) designed a more fine-tuned study, a modified matched-guise technique study that factored in context, that is, what sort of interlocutor is involved (British, Indian, or Singaporean), and in what setting. He found that the majority of SgE speakers were endonormatively oriented and confident in their ratings regardless of interlocutor. He also found that the small subset of Singaporeans who admitted feeling self-conscious when speaking to foreigners downgraded their ratings of SgE when a British interlocutor was involved. This finer approach helps to identify both a shift from covert or overt prestige for the variety, but also residual insecurity in terms of global acceptability (see Starr 2019 for evidence of this dual status in expatriate and local children's variable acquisition of -t/d deletion in Singapore).

## 10.5. MECHANISMS OF CHANGE: STYLE, IDEOLOGY, AND LANGUAGE CHANGE

English in India and Singapore differs in many social dimensions: style range, personal attitudes, institutional ideologies, and moral panics. SgE speakers often have a remarkably broad, diglossic-like style range, whereas IndE speakers typically have a narrower style range than speakers of native varieties. SgE speakers are also much more homogeneous across their speech repertoires—standard and colloquial—as their dialect has focused toward endogenous norms at both ends. IndE speakers show greater direct L1 influence overall, once again linked to less advanced dialect stabilization, a process proceeding faster in Indian cities.

It is tempting to see this as indicating different stages of Schneider's (2007) model of indigenization and differentiation. However, the two cases may be better characterized as simply two different stories of how linguistic and social change progress, political climate, and linguistic ecology. SgE is the target of both greater prohibitive intervention by the government and greater positive affiliation by speakers than IndE. IndE is associated with prestige and a lack of vernacularity. There is no reason to expect that IndE will later experience the level of moral panic or diglossia seen in Singapore, nor that SgE used to have the conservative flavor of IndE and then lost it.

As noted, a causal relationship between beliefs about language and language practices is notoriously difficult to establish: style ranges may be the result of attitudes and institutional ideologies, but, equally, ideologies may impinge on usage and affect lectal ranges. Or the two can be bidirectional in their influence, or indeed both be driven by an independent factor such as demographic change.

Nevertheless, the greater vernacularization in style and popular ideology of SgE does mirror its distinctive ecological and historical context (Chapter 7) and its degree of structural change (Chapter 8). Regardless of causality, these parallels suggest a close correspondence of the microstructural, the microsocial, and the macrosocial in dialect birth. The final chapter pulls together these many levels of analysis that have been explored and considers how feedback loops among them might drive forward postcolonial dialect formation.

[240]  *Comparing India and Singapore*

CHAPTER 11

# Summary and Implications

India and Singapore share a colonial linguistic past—the early introduction of English in both regions, the transition to independence and self-rule, and high-register associations of English in a multilingual ecology. Does this mean that the two regions are following the same path of dialect formation, perhaps just at different stages of the process (Schneider 2007)?

The preceding chapters have shown this to be true in a general sense, for example, in an incremental process of vernacularization and in conflicted ideologies in the present day, torn between external and internal norms.

However, an overly linear historical model would obscure the most important explanations for the actual shape of these two new dialects. For example, Schneider suggests that a salient rupture from the colonial power, Event X, might mark the onset of endonormative stabilization. This would suggest earlier and possibly more advanced vernacularization in India than in Singapore, given India's earlier and much more explicit separation of political identity when gaining independence from Britain. Yet Singapore English is the variety that is far more radically restructured and nativized, within half the timescale and with less explicit political dissociation.

The present study has instead triangulated three perspectives—historical, cognitive, and social—to identify a specific set of mechanisms that together drive dialect formation. The basic mechanisms are the same across the two regions, but their specific settings or inputs differ substantially. It is these settings, not general progression through the phases of Schneider's model, that account for specific dialect outcomes—the linguistic and sociolinguistic character of postcolonial varieties. India and Singapore are two separate stories, whose similarities and differences help us to identify some of the strongest mechanisms of change.

*From Deficit to Dialect.* Devyani Sharma, Oxford University Press. © Oxford University Press 2023.
DOI: 10.1093/oso/9780195307504.003.0011

In this final chapter I pull together the many processes through which English has taken shape in India and in Singapore. I reflect on how these micro- and macrodynamics interact with one another, and I explore wider implications for method and theory in the study of new dialect formation.

## 11.1. SUMMARY

Part I of this book focused on a single case study—Indian English—exploring its social history (Chapter 2), language structure (Chapters 3–5), and social identity (Chapter 6). Part II considered the same three forces in a second region, comparing the cases of India and Singapore. These cases were chosen to investigate the following questions:

1. Describing New Englishes
   a. Can we distinguish between learner errors and innovations, either structurally or socially? Do both exist in the cline of IndE speakers?
   b. How similar are New Englishes in terms of grammatical structures, linguistic history, and social practices?
2. Explaining New Englishes
   a. Do universal forces give rise to similar processes and outcomes across regions?
   b. Or do local languages and histories determine the shape of English in each region?
   c. Why have some linguistic innovations stabilized more than others in each variety?

Part I offered a detailed response to Question 1a. The usage cline for IndE speakers in Chapter 3 showed clear differences between learner-like variation for some language traits and stable use of others, with the latter shared across all users. This finding defuses the tension between "deficit" and "dialect" depictions of these varieties, showing clear elements of incomplete learner stages as well as robust dialect-like developments, depending on where in the cline of speakers we look.

The addition of Singapore English in Part II allowed us to offer a more global description of New Englishes, in response to Question 1b. In all three domains—social history, language structure, and social identity—difference, rather than similarity, was the primary focus. First, despite some similarities in colonial policy and institutions, English was inserted into very different sociohistorical conditions in India and Singapore. The analysis in Chapter 7 showed that English grew out of multiple "rhizomatic" histories, developing very differently in diverse subcommunities of users, complicating linear models of postcolonial dialect formation. Second, Chapters 4, 5, and 8 used

[242] *Comparing India and Singapore*

comparisons of grammatical features to illustrate robust and distinct innovation in the two varieties. And finally, Chapters 6 and 10 showed a steady shift toward endonormative orientation in both regions, but to different degrees. Prescriptivism, linguistic insecurity, style range, and focusing were all found but with distinct qualities and specifics.

The comparison in Part II also enabled questions of explanation posed in Question 2. In terms of social history, the factors of demographics, type of contact, and postindependence policy were found to underpin very different degrees of language change, dialect focusing, and nativization in India and Singapore (Chapter 7). In terms of language structure, substrate systems were found to be by far the strongest influence on new dialect formation, through either direct transfer or indirect transfer leading to inferred "third grammars." Language universals, by contrast, played a very limited part in any emergent language structures (Chapter 8). And finally, the greater stability or entrenchment of certain features over time required us to go beyond substrates and additionally factor in input demand and individual language learning (Chapter 9).

In this closing chapter, I review the numerous mechanisms observed and reflect on how these cogs might interlock and drive one another to generate regular, contact-driven change.

## 11.2. MECHANISMS OF CHANGE IN BILINGUAL SETTINGS

Nativization through communal language shift is both a process of cognitive change in individuals and a societal transformation. Many of the differences between IndE and SgE, particularly in how stable new language forms are and how they are used and evaluated, come down to differences in how nativized English is in the two regions. Differences in the actual shape of these forms can to a large part be traced to a different primary source, namely, differences in the substrate languages that English has been in contact with in the two regions.

We have also seen certain similarities between the two Englishes, linguistically and socially. Linguistically, we saw a number of shared discourse-driven grammatical tendencies (e.g., in article use), argued to derive from the shared experience of historically limited access to BrE in grammatical domains that require high levels of input, in part because the regional languages are very different from English (e.g., aspect rather than tense in verbal morphology; specificity rather than definiteness in nominal morphology).

Social similarities between the two varieties included conflicted dialect identity and a preoccupation with grammatical (as opposed to phonetic) correctness. These could be traced to concerns about prestige, authenticity, and ownership of the changing language, concerns that prevail across postcolonial, multilingual regions.

Figure 11.1 draws together these multiple factors in postcolonial dialect formation. The two key domains involved are individual cognition and wider social history.

At the level of individual cognition—for generations of individual language learners, sometimes over centuries—the two processes identified as the most instrumental in determining dialect structures were substrate language systems and, relatedly, input demand. Generic language universals and generic learner strategies such as simplification were not as evident.

The top left corner of Figure 11.1 shows the central role of substrate languages. These might directly restructure new English usage (e.g., copula omission in SgE), or they might lead to novel third grammar outcomes, where the speaker draws on their L1 to infer a novel interpretation of the semantic or syntactic properties of an L2 form (e.g., IndE imperfective use of -ing). The more shared influence of limited input for the individual is shown in the top right corner of Figure 11.1. This leads to parallel discourse-driven solutions in both varieties when input demand is high. Even input demand is defined in terms of L1-L2 structural distance and so is linked to substrates. The emergence of several major syntactic features across the two varieties were accounted for by the interaction of these two features of individual learner cognition.

The lower half of Figure 11.1 illustrates how individual cognition feeds into the particular sociohistorical ecology of each region, driving the degree to which these new forms become embedded in each society. While individual cognition determines the set of linguistic forms and their likelihood to become established, the sociohistorical context determines the bilingual cline of speakers, extent of nativeness, rates of change, self-confidence in contact

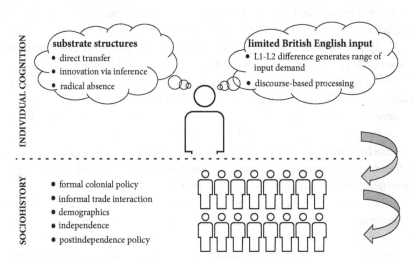

Figure 11.1. Dynamics of new dialect formation in postcolonial settings.

[244] *Comparing India and Singapore*

with native speakers, and style range and ideologies. The sociohistorical context included factors such as formal and informal channels of introduction of English historically, demographics, consequences of independence (e.g., removal of the target variety), and postcolonial policy.

All of these differ dramatically in Singapore and India, and we see correspondingly large differences in nativeness and language use. The factor of identity, central in Schneider's (2007) model, is not listed as on a par with these more material effects, but it is certainly not irrelevant. Identity and attitudes so closely track the more material conduits for change listed in Figure 11.1 that they are better seen as emergent rather than causal, as coconstituted through these historical dynamics.

Finally, the arrows in the lower right-hand corner of Figure 11.1 remind us that rates of change, diffusion, and most importantly *focusing*—stabilization of dialect norms—depend heavily on intergenerational transmission of the language as either a primary or an auxiliary language, another big difference between the two regions.

## 11.3. FEEDBACK LOOPS BETWEEN THE LINGUISTIC AND THE SOCIAL

How exactly do the layered processes in Figure 11.1 interact? It is easy to see that the structural feeds into the social, but does the social feed into the structural too?

There are many potential feedback relations across the processes in Figure 11.1. Below I list a sequence of example feeding relations between these mechanisms over time, to illustrate how the structural and social can interlock and feed one another in many ways.

- *L1/L2 difference → new grammars:* First, in the mind of a bilingual or nonnative user of English in a postcolonial setting, acquisitional processes driven by substrate structures and input demand start to generate new individual grammars.
- *Networks → spread of grammars:* These grammars are the raw material that may diffuse through social networks and be transmitted across generations, converging at different rates on new focused dialects.
- *Sociohistory → networks:* The social networks that carry these innovations— both personal and institutional—are in turn determined by wider sociohistorical conditions.
- *Attitudes, politics → sociohistory:* Sociohistorical conditions are ultimately generated by the personal political stances and attitudes of the actors involved, for example colonial and postcolonial education policy.
- *Attitudes → grammars:* Finally, it is again the microsocial world of personal stances and attitudes that sets up a feedback loop *back into language*

*structure.* Wider social conditions may drive individuals to ideologically prefer certain variants over others in a given situation, out of a wide feature pool of language forms. This selectivity inhibits or accelerates usage and grammatical change.

In some cases, feedback loops can lead to a pair of factors mutually opposing one another, creating an equilibrium. Bao (2003: 40), for example, describes a feedback relationship between grammatical and social stabilization for Colloquial SgE:

Its unstable grammatical features and its light functional load are locked in a vicious circle: Nonautonomous grammatical features [in this case, those that require reference to standard native varieties] are not easily codifiable, and lack of codification hinders the development of functional capabilities of the language, which in turn retards the growth of sophisticated and codifiable grammatical resources.

Similarly—indeed to a much greater extent than in Singapore—the high volume of learner grammars among less regular users of English in India likely sustains Indians' greater idealization of "correct" English and reluctance to acknowledge stable grammatical innovations. Here too, a bidirectional feedback loop results in insecurity in language use, slowing down language shift and dialect identity (cf. Mukherjee 2007).

However, some factors can also tip such equilibria over, accelerating or arresting change. For example, the institutional promotion of English over all other languages, as occurred in Singapore but not India, creates a sudden shift from adult L2 acquisition to childhood English acquisition. This in turn sets up a qualitative different environment for individual learner cognition (see Figure 11.1). The cognitive principles of child language acquisition mean that the new native speaker generation will quickly develop a much more focused dialect norm, with less heterogeneous individual L2 influence, *regardless* of ambient ideologies or codification. This is why varieties such as American English, Australian English, and perhaps most relevantly, due to its bilingual origins, Irish English, did not remain stuck in a cycle of low prestige and lack of codification.

## 11.4. IMPLICATIONS FOR METHOD

In recent years, the study of World Englishes has increasingly favored a comparative dialectological approach, which greatly enhances our ability to make more general claims about processes of language change. In practical terms, this requires close comparability of data sets, and some solutions to this challenge have been explored here. Direct comparison of social processes— ideology, attitudes, style range, accommodation to other varieties—is much more difficult methodologically and is thus necessarily speculative in the present study. As the comparison of different attitudinal studies in India in Chapter 10 showed, differences in method can lead to limited comparability of results.

A number of other methods were adopted here to assess the relative strength of one explanation over another. Grammatical conditioning of traits, not just presence and frequency, proved crucial in establishing the relative extent of similarity in the two varieties of English. Substrates were examined very closely, and when parallel systems were found in substrates, claims of universal effects were necessarily deferred, though not precluded.

One methodological route not often taken was the focus on how stable or established features are across a community and over time, taking the study beyond a focus on the mere presence of variation. It was this specific focus that helped bring to light a role for input demand in long-term outcomes.

Relatedly, the decision to develop an overarching *whole dialect* account—examining not isolated features or a single variety but, rather, the overall grammars of the two varieties, spanning the full cline of speakers—forced the question of how sets of features, and sets of speakers, cluster. For example, the whole-dialect approach identified three distinct elements of SgE grammar along the way that may all be underpinned by the lack of a [+tense] feature (past tense marking, copula omission, and modal use). It also identified overarching changes in tense-aspect or in discourse-based restructuring across multiple features, along with implication patterns across features and speakers.

Finally, mixed methods were also necessary and useful when looking at social factors. Data included naturalistic speech production, metapragmatic commentaries, style range, and institutional stances. Although not directly comparable across regions, these elements permitted some reflection on correspondences across social scales as well as feedback cycles between the structural and the social.

Despite the daunting level of variability found across multilingual speech communities, a triangulation of quantitative and qualitative analyses helped to start disentangling the puzzle of language change.

## 11.5. IMPLICATIONS FOR THEORY

The study of new dialect formation, in both bilingual and monolingual settings, is relevant to many core theoretical debates, including structural change, societal change, and how style variation relates to language change. I briefly reflect, in closing, on these three theoretical discussions.

In terms of sources of new dialect *structures*, the study confirmed the strong role of substrates in long-term bilingual contact, but the degree to which we saw direct transfer of L1 patterns (Matras and Sakel 2007) was mediated by the nature of the lexifier system (English) and the richness of input required. These three elements were unified in a single model that focused on L1-L2 difference and implications for input demand. Thus, even where speakers of different varieties resorted to the same optimized discourse processing due to insufficient input, this was not a pure universal but, rather, a result of the particular L1 and L2 involved. This helps to unify existing models that emphasize the role of L1-L2 contrast (Bao 2015) and discourse (Lange 2012) in bilingual dialect formation.

The study also offered novel analyses of dialect formation using models of input sensitivity from second language acquisition. The present study has shown that second language acquisition theory may offer fine-grained explanations for diverse New English dialect structures, but also that New Englishes may be a major new testing ground for the predictions of those theories. For example, support was found for both a subset effect and a syntax–pragmatics interface effect, even with the predicted discourse-based optimization, but at a higher level there was evidence that input alone cannot override certain types of constraints imposed by the L1 on full L2 learning.

In terms of *macrosocietal* change, Schneider's (2007) dynamic model of new dialect formation was assessed and found to be useful for a general description of India's and Singapore's advanced, yet different, positions along a path to new dialect formation. However, a number of fundamental challenges were encountered too. A megavariety such as IndE occupies many positions along the continuum simultaneously, with distinct subcommunities moving differently along it (recall Anglo Indian English and Babu English). Secondly, identity did not emerge as a clear basis for change. Ideology and attitudes certainly correspond to usage, but other more powerful contextual factors were found to be operative. For example, subcommunities of stable IndE speakers arose long before independence, partial exonormativity persisted after, and SgE changed more radically even though it was India that rejected colonial identification earlier and more resolutely. The analysis of sociohistorical factors favors demographic and usage factors over identity (cf. Evans 2014). Finally, the model is limited to the broad historical level and so does not offer an account for the specific grammatical outcomes and stylistic specifics of each region.

The combination of proximate linguistic causes (substrates, input) and distal sociohistorical causes (demographics, policy) in the present analysis brings us to another long-standing theoretical debate in contact linguistics, namely, whether sociohistorical or linguistic factors are stronger in determining linguistic outcomes. Thomason and Kaufman (1988: 35) suggest that "it is the sociolinguistic history of the speakers, and not the structure of their language, that is the primary determinant of the linguistic outcome of language contact." Treffers-Daller (1999: 1) investigated this claim in relation to French–German contact in Brussels and Strasbourg and concluded

[248] *Comparing India and Singapore*

that, on the contrary, "the structure of the languages plays a more prominent role in the outcome of language contact than the sociolinguistic history of the speakers."

The same tensions hold for the present situations of change. We might make a case for linguistic factors: the relative structural conservatism of IndE being primarily due to the morphological complexity of Indian languages, and the radical form of SgE due to the analytic nature of the regional languages in Singapore. But many English-lexifier pidgins and Creoles developed radically analytic grammars despite highly inflectional African substrate languages. And a simplified pidgin-like variety of IndE (Butler English) developed in an environment of morphologically rich Indian languages. The key difference appears to be the social conditions of language exposure and use, with substrate languages only providing the structural "map" or "direction" of the offspring language. Critics of Treffer-Daller's study (Poplack and Meechan, Sebba, Singh, and Winford in the same issue) reiterated Thomason and Kaufman's position, and this study too has suggested that sociohistorical factors are at least as important as substrate languages in defining the degree, but perhaps not direction, of change. The direction of change was closely linked to substrates and input demand, as in Treffers-Daller's study.

Do studies of bilingual dialect formation have implications for the study of monolingual dialect birth? We do see very similar processes of focusing, simplification, reallocation, and analogy. But in contact varieties these processes are often triggered or accelerated (Silva-Corvalan 1994) via external actuation, the grammar of another language. We also see similarities in terms of varying social identification with a new way of speaking over generations (cf. Trudgill 2004). However, there is again a difference: Chapter 10 showed that the availability of other languages for identity work can permit more variability in English and a lack of focusing (due to a lack of primary identification with the code), and so slower language shift. The present discussion might also offer a new perspective for monolingual dialect formation, namely, the factor of relative input demand of different features.

Finally, some of the social life of IndE and SgE observed here relates to models of *style variation* recently developed in sociolinguistics, primarily in relation to monolingual speakers. Recent treatments of style variation look at how fine linguistic detail constructs interactional stances, projects personas, affiliates with interlocutors, and ultimately performs identity (Bell 1984; Schilling-Estes 1998; Bucholtz and Hall 2004; Coupland 2007; Eckert 2012). At the heart of these models are the idea that language indexes identity, and the idea that any linguistic material can potentially do this work.

These forces are certainly at play in SgE and IndE. We saw this in style shifting, ideologies, and (non)accomodation to other varieties. However, the observations in Chapter 10 also pose a challenge to two assumptions mentioned above.

First, the surprisingly versatile choices made by IndE speakers with respect to adding new styles of speech to their repertoire (perhaps more so than SgE speakers) relates to the continued availability, even primacy, of *other* languages for identity work, leaving variation within their L2 less tied to identity and more available for instrumental purposes. This has direct consequences for variability, focusing, social meaning, and change, and it suggests that analysts should take care with the assumption that multilinguals' linguistic variation will index identity in exactly the same way as monolinguals' usage.

Second, ideologies in both IndE and SgE showed a rather stark and conscious division of labor between phonetic and syntactic forms, with the former available for identity work and quickly accepted by new speakers of these varieties, but the latter often subject to deeply prescriptive, exogenous norms. This asymmetry may be particularly acute among bilingual or recently nativized speakers who wish to minimize the risk of being seen as nonnative, and so the behavior of these two domains of language variation—phonetic and syntactic—may be quite different in such speakers.

## 11.6. IMPLICATIONS FOR PUBLIC UNDERSTANDING

Pedagogical and other applied questions have not been the focus of this study. However, the study of World Englishes started in applied linguistics, and hopefully this empirical overview of how dialects emerge in postcolonial sociolinguistic ecologies will help to support realist and evidence-based understandings of language learning, language use, and dialect identities in complex multilingual environments.

Punnoose (2017: 209–210) describes English in India as being at a crossroads, poised for potentially massive expansion:

> The increase in the number of English speakers horizontally and vertically in the class structure of postliberalisation India, together with the effects of increased globalisation and the internet boom on the relationship between schooling, class and the English language in urban India all point towards the start of a new phase of growth and development for IndE.

As this large community expands, the forms of speech described in the current volume will circulate more widely and continue to change. And reactions to them will play a role in the life experiences of their users.

This book was written in the context of active public debates in both regions, and of course globally, over grammatical correctness and the status of colloquial speech. Some such arguments are to do with taste—a preference for

[250]   *Comparing India and Singapore*

tradition or an appeal of the new—and so will never change, always feeding a primal opposition between conservative and liberal affiliations.

But assertions of correct and incorrect language also always directly affect the allocation of material resources (degrees, jobs, income, status) as well as simple speaking rights to people who already face social marginalization. When these assertions are founded on conjecture, misunderstanding, or social bias rather than fact, a great deal of social damage can be done.

So, a final hope is for public discourse about English dialects to rely not solely on opinion and taste, but also on an empirical understanding of how the human mind works, why vernacular culture exists in all societies, and why new speech communities are always forming.

# Appendix: Use of Imperfective Forms in English and Chinese Languages

| Example | Standard English (and SgE) | Singapore Mandarin | Hokkien | Teochew | Cantonese |
|---|---|---|---|---|---|
| He is WRITING a letter. | **-ing** | **zai** | **tja** | **do** | **gan** |
| He's ARRIVING now. | **-ing** | — | — | — | — |
| She's LEAVING tomorrow. | **-ing** | — | — | — | — |
| It's RAINING. | **-ing** | — | — | — | (gan) |
| She's DRIVING these days. | —/ **-ing** | — | — | — | — |
| He walked towards me SMILING. | **-ing** | (-zhe) | — | (do) | (zyu) |
| The wind kept BLOWING. | **-ing** | — | — | — | — |
| You LOVE music. | — | (-zhe) | — | — | — |
| I DRIVE. | — | — | — | — | — |
| The car is in the garage. | — | (-zhe) | — | (do) | zyu |
| She is WEARING boots. | **-ing** | — | — | — | zyu |
| He is STANDING outside. | **-ing** | (-zhe) | — | (do) | (gan) |
| A letter was LYING there. | **-ing** | (-zhe) | — | (do) | (gan) |
| He is HOLDING the book. | **-ing** | (-zhe) | — | (do) | zyu |
| They like SWIMMING. | **-ing** | — | — | — | — |

Appendix Use of Imperfective Forms
(a) English and Chinese Languages

# NOTES

**CHAPTER 1**

1. In the 2010 release, Google adopted intriguing editorial differences for the dialects on their website. The Indian English page used simpler syntax, and the American English page used more colloquial lexicon such as 'any size' and 'like':

   *English (U.S.)* Reliable, secure web-based office tools for any size business—Powerful, intuitive applications like Gmail, Google Calendar and Google Docs can help reduce your IT costs and help employees collaborate more effectively—all for just $50 per user per year.

   *English (U.K.)* Reliable, secure web-based office tools for your organisation—Powerful, intuitive applications: Gmail, Google Calendar, Google Docs, and more can help reduce your IT costs and help employees collaborate more effectively—all for just £33 per user per year.

   *English (India)* Reliable, secure online applications wherever you work—Google Apps reduces IT costs and empowers today's employees. Gmail, Google Docs, Google Sites and more—USD $50 per user per year.

2. A note on terminology: In this book, I follow many scholars in using the term *New English(es)* to refer specifically to indigenized postcolonial Englishes. As many have noted, the term is not unproblematic, given that a "new" English such as IndE predates varieties such as Australian English (Schneider 2007: 3; Lange 2012: 15). *New* here denotes the more recent acceptance of these varieties, in research and in wider public discourse. In some places in the book I emphasize the difference between language dominance in a bilingual, with the terms *L1/L2*. In other places I use the terms *superstrate/substrate*, to emphasize the original community language and the overlaid (English) language. I occasionally use other terms, such as *contact variety* or *indigenized variety*, to highlight other salient processes. Needless to say, each term comes with its own set of advantages and complications.

**CHAPTER 2**

1. This strand of British Orientalists even revived ancient Indic language debates over which vernacular to promote. At Calcutta's College of Fort William, founded in 1800, John Gilchrist favored Hindustani and Persian and produced Roman transliterations of classic Indic texts for a British audience. By contrast, his colleague William Carey vociferously promoted a refinement of Bengali, enriched from Sanskrit and vernacular languages (Paolucci 1984: 225). Carey's goal as a missionary was to convert Hindus to Christianity, but unlike later Evangelists he

chose to translate the Bible into Bengali to achieve this purpose rather than displace Bengali with English.

2. Source: http://sourapplemartini.blogspot.co.uk/2005/12/you-know-youre-ban dra-boy-when.html (accessed December 23, 2016).

3. The British author aims to ridicule Indian names with "Baboo Jabberjee" but inadvertently satirizes the British themselves, as Bengali names such as Chatterjee and Banerjee were vernacular simplifications of Sanskrit equivalents (Chattopadhyaya and Bandhopadhyaya in this case) that the British could not, or would not, pronounce.

4. I am indebted to Shazia Sadaf for drawing my attention to many details of this variety through her doctoral research (Sadaf 2007).

5. Sources All India School Educational Surveys (AISES; https://ncert.nic.in/all-india-school-education-survey.php) and National Institute of Educational Planning and Administration (NIEPA; http://www.niepa.ac.in/).

6. I use Wells' (1982) keywords to refer to standard lexical sets for vowels throughout this book.

7. Some IndE lexicon that appears to come directly from Indian languages in fact passed through the pre-British Portuguese colonial presence in India: *palanquin* (Skt. *palyanka* > H. *palaki* > Pg. *palanquim* 'bed, litter'), *sepoy* (U. *sipahi* > Pg. *sipae* 'Indian soldier or horseman under European command'). Portuguese contact was relatively local and functional and, aside from a few instances of this type, did not have any lasting impact on general IndE.

8. Despite substantial contact with Irish English in convents, Irish influence is not extensive in IndE (e.g., the IndE TRAP/BATH split resembles that of Southern BrE, not Irish English).

9. Jenny Cheshire (pers. comm.) has also observed instances of clause-final *still* with Indic-like transferred function of "nevertheless" in her data from second-generation British Asian teenagers.

## CHAPTER 3

1. Singh's (1994, 2012) reasoning might suggest that all 24 individuals in the present data set actually recognize the IndE grammar used by the proficient end of the continuum as the target grammar, i.e., that they share the same norms for use (and are therefore all native users of the variety), but half are unable to produce those grammars. Informal discussions of language forms with the less proficient half of the continuum indicated no such radical divergence between extremely finely tuned native-like intuitions and wholly non-native-like production. These are genuinely second language speakers of English, with all the attendant variability in both production and judgments; L2 learners usually do have greater target accuracy in judgments than production, but not such that their judgments are convergent with native speakers of the target variety.

## CHAPTER 4

1. The detailed study here is limited to one data set, as this was the basis of the original analysis (Sharma 2005b), but Chapter 3 showed that the two data sets are very similar, including in their article systems (Tables 3.2 and 3.3).

2. All coding was done by the author. In order to check for reliability, a random selection of 100 NPs were coded independently by a trained researcher. Before

discussion between coders, the average interrater reliability was 97.9% for standardness judgments on articles and 93.25% for the six internal factors coded for each article token.

3. The total number of tokens in Tables 4.2 and 4.3 is 1,289. This total is slightly lower in Tables 4.1 and 4.4. This is because in Table 4.1 the category of "transition" is omitted (only "topic" and "comment" are examined), and in Table 4.4 only specific NPs are counted and the category of "unused" is omitted due to low $N$ values.

4. Nonstandard *one* is marginally more common among the South Indian speakers in the data, possibly due to subtle substrate differences (nonstandard uses of *one* are also more common in Sri Lankan English; Herat 2006). In fact, the South Indian languages Kannada and Tamil both allow demonstrative and quantifier forms to be used as indefinite articles, and the two speakers of these languages frequently used *some* and *this* as specific indefinite articles, and *that* as a definite article.

5. Hawkins' (1978) taxonomy in some respects allows more detail than Prince's (1981) model. For instance, his distinctions among associative anaphoric use (*a book... the author*), larger situation use (*in a village... the church*), and explanatory modifier use (*I remember the beginning of the war very well . . .*) are all subsumed under Prince's category of inferables. However, his taxonomy does not order the various types that he identifies with respect to one another, a feature of particular interest to the present study.

6. In order to temporarily factor out the L1 effect driving omission with nonspecific NPs, Table 4.4 excludes nonspecific NPs; all data are included in the final multivariate analysis. Also, the category of unused was highly variable, sometimes patterning like a new category and at other times resembling the rates for inferable NP types; as the number of unused NP tokens was very low, this was also excluded from Table 4.4.

7. Goldvarb was used widely in sociolinguistics and related studies in SLA (e.g., Bayley and Preston 1996; Young 1996); mixed effects modeling is now preferred (Johnson 2009).

8. Sedlatschek also found regular insertion of *the* in standardly null contexts (p. 203). This occurred in the present data as well (details in Sharma 2003), though article omission was the more robust pattern.

9. Sankoff and Mazzie (1991) also employed Prince's model to access the role of discourse status distinctions in article choice in Tok Pisin. However, their study is not directly comparable to the present one, as their focus is on the specialization of different *forms* (e.g., *dispela, ia, wanpela*) for different functions, mirroring a pattern shared by the Austronesian substrate languages. Sankoff and Mazzie (1991) critique both Bickerton and Givón—both of whom have in the past argued for the Creole prototype in Hypothesis 3—on methodological grounds. They argue that both scholars found instances of null-marked definites in their own data but chose to exclude them. Givón discounted such instances as referring to characters peripheral to the main story, and Bickerton, using somewhat circular reasoning, chose to discard such cases because they did not fit his definition: "A total of 260 zero articles are found in the texts under consideration. 24 of these—almost one-tenth—may immediately be discarded, since they refer to things which have definite reference" (Bickerton 1977: 235).

*Notes* [257]

# CHAPTER 5

1. In Gujarati, the progressive alternates with the imperfective form for events in progress. Gujarati also forms the present imperfective with the reflex of a different Sanskrit paradigm (Masica 1991: 302). Dravidian languages are similar to Indo-Aryan systems in having overt aspect morphology but diverge in that the use of these forms is optional (Schiffman 1999: 82). These languages are spoken by only 3 of the 24 individuals in the data set, so they are not analyzed separately.

2. See Sharma and Deo (2010) for details of the lexical aspect approach and for a summary of the extensive literature on the Aspect Hypothesis in SLA.

3. The texts in these corpora are from 1978, 1961, and 1961, respectively. All corpora were obtained from the International Computer Archive of Medieval and Modern English (ICAME) and were specifically selected because they are comparable in terms of design, text selection from various registers, and size. They are all million-word corpora, containing 500 texts of approximately 2,000 words each, distributed across 15 text categories.

4. To check reliability, 10% of both data sets were independently recoded by a colleague. Interrater reliability was 85.2% (postdiscussion: 96.3%).

5. Other uses of the form *had* were excluded, including obligative (*I had to be at the airport on time*), possessive/stative (*They had two seconds remaining on the clock*), causative (*She had the offending item removed*), and counterfactual/subjunctive (*If I had known, I would have left sooner*) uses. Of these, only counterfactuals may potentially relate to the use of the past perfect. For instance, in AmE, the general reduction in the use of the past perfect construction, as observed in Elsness (1997: 229), may be accompanied by an increase in use of the simple past form in the protasis of counterfactuals (*If I knew, I would have left sooner*). The rates of occurrence of counterfactuals in the three corpora were low and not notably different, so they were not included.

6. In order to control for subjective bias in coding of meanings, a subset of the data was independently recoded following the same criteria by a second coder; the two sets of results matched with 94% accuracy (Sharma 2001).

7. Apparent stative uses of the progressive in standard varieties (e.g., with temporary states *I'm wanting to move back*) are not usually stative but, rather, involve a dynamic or change-of-state interpretation (Comrie 1976). Nevertheless, an interesting possibility is that native speakers of BrE may be shifting this boundary of "pseudo-stative" uses to be more permissive (Hundt and Vogel 2011), possibly even through contact with speakers of New Englishes.

8. The few perfective verbs that occur with the progressive are *come*, *start*, and *begin*. Although telic, these verbs are also associated with null marking of past tense in this data set. This might suggest that inchoatives and ingressives (denoting the start of a state or an action) present a semantic clash with perfective interpretations for these speakers.

9. The American corpus has the lowest use, confirming earlier studies (Elsness 1997; Harris 1984; Dušková 1976). The different directions of change in AmE and IndE relative to BrE are discussed in Sharma (2001), as is the behavior of further factors such as time adverbials, tense in surrounding clauses, register, and region.

10. Newbrook and Chinniah (1987: 255) suggest a similar hypercorrection origin for Singapore English use of *will* in place of *would*. This brings us back to secondary, nonmodal uses of *will* noted earlier (Huddleston 1984; Sarkar 1998), which tend to be associated with educated speech and formal register. These uses may be

absent in the present data due to the conversational register of the interviews but are certainly found in formal IndE.

## CHAPTER 6

1. Many of the findings reported here first appeared in Sharma (2005a).
2. Note that the amount of time spent in the United States does not have a significant effect on these features. This may relate to limited language plasticity in adulthood or to the fact that many immigrants establish Indian social networks after emigrating, so time in the United States is not a good indicator of exposure to AmE (cf. de Leeuw et al. 2010).
3. Although not the focus of the present analysis, there may be further factors at play governing the slightly greater use of aspiration and velarization. Both of these are shared to some extent with Standard BrE, which tends to have high prestige for IndE speakers and so may be favored over rhoticity, which is not. Another factor is that aspiration and velarization can be adjusted incrementally in phonetic terms, whereas rhoticity requires a phonological change.
4. Another indication of marker-like status is in style shifting, which was also evident in some interviews when speakers switched away from speaking to me and entered conversations with customers, colleagues, or family members. Like self-corrections, these instances of shifts also indicate a degree of awareness of linguistic features at every level of the language: phonological, lexical, and morphosyntactic. One such example of style shifting is given later in Chapter 10 in the discussion of IndE style range.
5. It is worth noting that this goes against claims that clarification requests result in a stylistic shift toward the global standard or prestige form, because of an increase in attention to speech (Labov 1972). In these instances of heightened attention to speech, Kishore and Sujit accommodate to me as an Indian interlocutor.

## CHAPTER 8

1. Sand suggests that shared overuse of *the* in a number of varieties, notably Irish English, Singapore English, Jamaican English, and East African English may also derive from universal rather than L1 forces. However, Filppula et al. (2009) counter that if a universal or logical extension of *the* is at work, then the absence of overextended uses of *the* in other varieties is left unexplained. This type of critique of generalist accounts is taken up in Chapter 9.
2. Though this may still not be entirely independent of a triggering L1-L2 clash, as most of the L1s studied here have similar systems to those in Figure 8.1.
3. H&P have been critiqued for their reliance on a lectal continuum rather than diglossic model and, relatedly, the lack of distinction between uneducated English speech and informal, educated SgE (Lim and Foley 2004; Foley et al. 1998).
4. I am grateful to these native speaker consultants in Singapore for their generous assistance: Huang Zhipeng, Amanda Cheung, Youping Han, Jiang Dan, Lim Chey Cheng, Huifong Chen, and Dorothy Tan.
5. Published grammars claim that -*zhe* is required with stative verbs such as *ai* ('love') and with verbs of posture and activity verbs signaling states, but Singapore Mandarin consultants reported optionality in all contexts in the Appendix. In Standard Malay, *sedang* is not used for future reference or simultaneity and is "much less frequent than English progressive" (Svalberg and Fatimah 1998: 39). Bazaar Malay is missing from the Appendix due to lack of access to native speakers, but the column would be comparable to Hokkien and Malay, which lack stativity

*Notes* [259]

markers. Teochew also has only one primarily progressive marker *do*, which shows some uses in *zhe* contexts, such as with posture and location (this slight difference in the dynamic/stative boundary is also true for the use of Cantonese *gan*). Thus, all of these systems further reduce any substrate pressure to mark imperfectivity in SgE.

6. A chi-square test of significance could not be presented for the SgE data in Table 8.4 as the original study only provides a composite $N$ value.

7. One clear difference between IndE and SgE in (9) is the absence of *be* in the SgE sentences. H&P (1993: 65) observe that this is based on a direct analogy with the lack of *be* in Chinese systems. Indo-Aryan languages require a *be* auxiliary with imperfective markers, and so this difference too can be ascribed to substrates. This feature is discussed in Section 8.5.

8. Eleven of the 24 uses of *knowing* by IndE users included modals (e.g., *You must be knowing this all history, don't you?*; *As you may be knowing . . .*). These were coded as nonstandard based on eight native BrE consultants' grammaticality ratings, all of which were lower than ratings given for the nonprogressive equivalents. Variation did occur in the degree of ungrammaticality for these BrE consultants, indicating increasing permissiveness with stative progressives in standard native varieties (Hundt and Vogel 2011).

9. The high Loc values in SgE (Malay) in Figure 8.6 are based on a low total $N$ value of 5. As individual speaker rates cannot be extracted for some of the data sets in Figure 8.2, standard deviation measures could not be included. All of these data sets are discussed more extensively, and with further statistical testing, in Sharma and Rickford (2009).

10. Deuber et al. (2012) find limited use of the form *would* in the ICE-Singapore corpus in general. They observe that "[a]s in the Indian data, it tends to be mainly restricted to pragmatically specialized uses, though not quite to the same extent" (p. 96), which may again indicate a greater concern with prestige and politeness markers in the more conservative and less vernacular of the two varieties, IndE.

**CHAPTER 9**

1. Numerous other features fall in the category of (1b) but cannot be examined in detail here. Some, like focus *only*, were noted in Chapter 3 (see Parviainen [2012]; Nayak et al. [2016] for evidence of the established nature of these forms).

2. The latter French sentence is ungrammatical for the meaning "He runs into the house."

3. Naturally, standard BrE is no longer the local target variety, but the goal remains to account for certain features becoming more divergent from an initial target over time, and we can assume a variety of BrE formed the original target. Furthermore, acrolectal IndE speakers have continued access through networks to standard British-like grammars, so their nonacquisition of certain grammatical traits but not others needs explanation.

4. Even Hilbert (2008), a study that clearly identifies an attested order of acquisition for English questions in New English data, deals with varieties whose substrates all involve in situ wh-forms, and so even here there is an underlying substrate trigger for the apparently universal acquisitional effect observed.

**CHAPTER 10**

1. An additional type of evidence of greater dialectal stability in SgE would be speaker behavior in situations of contact with native varieties, as examined for

IndE in Chapter 6. Unfortunately, no such study exists for SgE. The prediction would be less variability in a contact situation among SgE speakers as compared with IndE speakers (e.g., less wholesale adoption of American English upon migration), given greater nativization in the former group; informal observation appears to support this.

2. *Pata hai kya hai?* 'you know what?'; *wahan pe* 'there'; *maine dekha hai* 'I've seen (it)'; *to maine jo feel kara hai* 'so what I've felt'; *wakai mein* 'really'; *pata hai* 'you know'; *jo maine dekha hai* 'what I've seen'; *kya* 'what'; *jo mujhe sabse ganda laga hai* 'what seemed worst to me'; *ki jis vajay mai ne chhori hai* 'what my reason for leaving is.'

3. Unlike the lay term "Hinglish," which refers to the mixing of Hindi and English rather than a variety of IndE, popular uses of "Singlish" tend to refer to the colloquial variety of SgE, whether or not it features code-switching and loan words from indigenous languages.

4. http://www.talkingcock.com/html/article.php?sid=1275. Accessed September 12, 2016.

5. Source for (7a): ICE-SIN corpus text S1A-23, spoken conversation, lines 324–328, 335–336, 356–375. Source for (7b): ICE-SIN corpus text S1A-86, spoken conversation; lines 215–220, 239–244, 271–282.

6. Diglossia does not reflect a particular phase of development in Schneider's (2007) temporally oriented model. It arises under particular conditions that involve very distinct subgroups in a speech community, as discussed in Chapter 7 for Singaporean English, and can be very stable.

7. (17a) is from an online discussion: https://issuu.com/themockfrock/docs/sing lishlah (Retrieved November 20, 2019)

8. There are also signs of the government taking a slightly less strident and more pragmatic stance (Lee 2021: 17).

# REFERENCES

Agha, Asif. 2003. The social life of a cultural value. *Language and Communication 23*: 231–73.

Agnihotri, R. K., and A. L. Khanna, eds. 1994. *Second language acquisition: Sociocultural and linguistic aspects of English in India*. New Delhi: Sage.

Agnihotri, Rama Kant, A. L. Khanna, and Aditi Mukherjee. 1984. The use of articles in Indian English: Errors and pedagogical implications. *International Review of Applied Linguistics in Language Teaching 22* (2): 115–143.

Agnihotri, R. K., and Rajendra Singh, eds. 2011. *Indian English: Towards a new paradigm*. New Delhi: Orient BlackSwan.

Allen, Charles. 1975. *Plain tales from the Raj*. London: Deutsch.

Alleyne, Mervyn. 1980. *Comparative Afro-American: An historical-comparative study of English-based Afro-American dialects of the New World*. Ann Arbor, MI: Karoma.

Alsagoff, Lubna. 2001. Tense and aspect in Singapore English. In V. Ooi (ed.), *Evolving identities: The English language in Singapore and Malaysia*. Singapore: Times Academic Press, pp. 79–88.

Alsagoff, Lubna. 2010. English in Singapore: Culture, capital and identity in linguistic variation. *World Englishes 29* (3): 336–348.

Alsagoff, Lubna, Zhiming Bao, and Lionel Wee. 1998. Why you talk like that?: The pragmatics of a *why* construction in Singapore English. *English World-Wide 19* (2): 247–260.

Alsagoff, Lubna, and Ho Chee Lick. 1998. The relative clause in colloquial Singapore English. *World Englishes 17* (2): 127–138.

Andersen, Roger. 1978. An implicational model for second language research. *Language Learning 28*: 221–282.

Andersen, Roger. 1983. Transfer to somewhere. In S. Gass and L. Selinker (eds.), *Language transfer in language learning*. Rowley, MA: Newbury House, pp. 177–201.

Andersen, Roger, and Yasuhiro Shirai. 1996. The primacy of aspect in first and second language acquisition: The pidgin-creole connection. In W. C. Ritchie and T. Bhatia (eds.), *Handbook of second language acquisition*. London: Academic Press, pp. 527–70.

Andreasson, Anne-Marie. 1994. Norm as a pedagogical paradigm. *World Englishes 13*: 395–409.

Ansaldo, Umberto. 2004. The evolution of Singapore English: Finding the matrix. In L. Lim (ed.), *Singapore English: A grammatical description. Varieties of English around the world G33*. Amsterdam: John Benjamins, pp. 127–49.

Ansaldo, Umberto. 2009. The Asian typology of English: Theoretical and methodological considerations. *English World-Wide 30*(2): 133–148.

Anstey, Frank. 1897. *Baboo Hurry Bungsho Jabberjee, B.A.* New York: D. Appleton and Company.

Ariel, Mira. 1990. *Accessing NP antecedents.* London: Routledge.

Auer, Peter. 1999. From codeswitching via language mixing to fused lects: Towards a dynamic typology of bilingual speech. *International Journal of Bilingualism 3*(4): 309–332.

Auer, Peter, and Frans Hinskens. 2005. The role of interpersonal accommodation in a theory of language change. In P. Auer, F. Hinskens, and P. Kerswill (eds.), *Dialect change: Convergence and divergence in European languages.* Cambridge: Cambridge University Press, pp. 335–357.

Ayoun, Dalila. 1996. The subset principle in second language acquisition. *Applied Psycholinguistics 17* (2): 185–213.

Bach, Emmon. 1986. The algebra of events. *Linguistics and Philosophy 9*: 5–16.

Baker, Philip. 1998. Investigating the origin and diffusion of shared features among the Atlantic English creoles. In P. Baker and A. Bruyn (eds.), *St. Kitts and the Atlantic Creoles.* London: University of Westminster Press, pp. 315–364.

Baker, Wendy, and William Eggington. 1999. Bilingual creativity, multidimensional analysis, and world Englishes. *World Englishes 18*: 343–357.

Bailey, Charles James Nice. 1973. *Variation and linguistic theory.* Washington, DC: Centre for Applied Linguistics.

Balasubramanian, Chandrika. 2009. *Register variation in Indian English.* Amsterdam: John Benjamins Publishing Company.

Bamgbose, Ayo. 1998. Torn between the norms: Innovations in world Englishes. *World Englishes 17*(1): 1–14.

Bansal, R. K. 1990. The pronunciation of English in India. In S. Ramsaran (ed.), *Studies in the pronunciation of English.* London: Routledge, pp. 219–33.

Bao, Zhiming. 1998. Theories of language genesis. In J. Foley et al. (eds.), *English in new cultural contexts: Reflections from Singapore.* Singapore: Oxford University Press, pp. 41–72.

Bao, Zhiming. 2001. The origins of empty categories in Singapore English. *Journal of Pidgin and Creole Languages 16* (2): 275–319.

Bao, Zhiming. 2003. Social stigma and grammatical autonomy in nonnative varieties of English. *Language in Society 32*: 23–46.

Bao, Zhiming. 2005. The aspectual system of Singapore English and the systemic substratist explanation. *Journal of Linguistics 41*: 237–67.

Bao, Zhiming. 2010. *Must* in Singapore English. *Lingua 120*: 1727–1737.

Bao, Zhiming. 2015. *The making of vernacular Singapore English: System, transfer and filter.* Cambridge: Cambridge University Press.

Bao, Zhiming, and Hong Huaqing. 2006. Diglossia and register variation in Singapore English. *World Englishes 25* (1): 105–114.

Bao, Zhiming, and Lionel Wee. 1999. The passive in Singapore English. *World Englishes 18* (1): 1–11.

Barden, Birgit, and Beate Großkopf. 1998. *Sprachliche Akkommodation und soziale Integration.* Tübingen: Niemeyer.

Bautista, Maria Lourdes, and Andrew Gonzalez. 2006. Southeast Asian English. In B. B. Kachru, Y. Kachru, and C. L. Nelson (eds.), *The handbook of World Englishes.* Oxford: Blackwell, pp. 130–144.

Bayley, Robert. 1994. Interlanguage variation and the quantitative paradigm: Past tense marking in Chinese-English. In E. Tarone, S. Gass, and A. Cohen (eds.), *Research methodology in second language acquisition*. Hillsdale, NJ: Erlbaum, pp. 157–181.

Bayley, Robert. 1999. The primacy of aspect hypothesis revisited: Evidence from language shift. *Southwest Journal of Linguistics 18* (2): 1–22.

Bayley, Robert, and Dennis Preston, eds. 1996. *Second language acquisition and linguistic Variation*. Amsterdam: John Benjamins.

Bell, Allan. 1984. Language style as audience design. *Language in Society 13*(2):145–204.

Bennett, Michael, and Barbara Hall Partee. 1978. *Toward the logic of tense and aspect in English*. Bloomington: Indiana University Linguistics Club.

Berdan, Robert. 1996. Disentangling language acquisition from language variation. In Robert Bayley and Dennis R. Preston (eds.), *Second language acquisition and linguistic variation*. Amsterdam: John Benjamins, pp. 203–244.

Bernaisch, Tobias, and Christopher Koch. 2016. Attitudes towards Englishes in India. *World Englishes 35* (1): 118–132.

Berwick, R. C. 1985. *The acquisition of syntactic knowledge*. Cambridge, MA: MIT Press.

Bhatia, V. K. 1992. The bilingual's orthodoxy in professional genres. *World Englishes 11*: 225–34.

Bhatt, Rakesh M. 2000. Optimal expressions in Indian English. *English Language and Linguistics 4*: 69–95.

Bhatt, Rakesh. 2008. In other words: Language mixing, identity representations, and "third space." *Journal of Sociolinguistics 12* (2): 177–200.

Bhatt, Rajesh, Tina Bögel, Miriam Butt, Annette Hautli, and Sebastian Sulger. 2011. *Urdu/Hindi modals*. In M. Butt and T. King (eds.), *Proceedings of LFG 11*. Stanford, CA: CSLI publications, pp. 47–67.

Bhatt, R. M. and A. Mehboob. 2008. Minority languages and their status. In B. B. Kachru, S. N. Sridhar, and Y. Kachru (eds.), *Language in South Asia*. Cambridge: Cambridge University Press, pp. 130–150.

Biber, Douglas, Stig Johansson, Geoffrey Leech, Susan Conrad, and Edward Finegan. 1999. *The Longman Grammar of Spoken and Written English*. London: Longman.

Bickerton, Derek. 1971. Inherent variability and variable rules. *Foundations of Language 7*: 457–492.

Bickerton, Derek. 1977. Pidginization and creolization: Language acquisition and language universals. In A. Valdman (ed.), *Pidgin and creole linguistics*. Bloomington: Indiana University Press, pp. 49–69.

Bickerton, Derek. 1981. *Roots of language*. Ann Arbor, MI: Karoma.

Bickerton, Derek. 1984. The language bioprogram hypothesis. *The Behavioral and Brain Sciences 7*: 173–221.

Bickerton, Derek. 1986. Beyond roots: The five year test. *Journal of Pidgin and Creole Languages 1*: 225–32.

Binnick, Robert. 1991. *Time and the verb*. Oxford: Oxford University Press.

Birner, Betty, and Gregory Ward. 1998. *Information status and noncanonical word order in English*. Amsterdam: John Benjamins.

Blom, Jan-Petter, and Gumperz, John J. 1972. Social meaning in linguistic structure: Code-switching in Norway. In J. J. Gumperz and D. Hymes (eds.), *Directions in sociolinguistics*. Oxford: Basil Blackwell, pp. 407–434.

Bourhis, Richard. 1997. Language policies and language attitudes: Le monde de la Francophonie. In Nikolas Coupland and Adam Jaworski (eds.), *Sociolinguistics: A reader*. New York: St. Martin's Press, pp. 306–323.

Brown, Roger. 1973. *A first language: The early stages*. Cambridge, MA: Harvard University Press.

Brown, Penelope, and Stephen Levinson. 1987. *Politeness: Some universals in language usage*. Cambridge: Cambridge University Press.

Bruyn, Adrienne. 1995. *Grammaticalization in creoles: The development of determiners and relative clauses in Sranan*. Amsterdam: IFOTT.

Bucholtz, Mary, and Kira Hall. 2004. Theorizing identity in language and sexuality research. *Language in Society 33*: 469–515.

Butler, Yuko Goto. 2002. Second language learners' theories on the use of English articles. *Studies in Second Language Acquisition 24*: 451–480.

Bybee, Joan, R. Perkins, and W. Pagliuca, eds. 1994. *The evolution of grammar: Tense, aspect, and modality in the languages of the world*. Chicago: University of Chicago Press.

Cameron, Deborah. 1995. *Verbal Hygiene*. London: Routledge.

Canagarajah, Suresh. 1999. *Resisting linguistic imperialism in English language teaching*. Oxford: Oxford University Press.

Cannadine, David. 2001. *Ornamentalism: How the British saw their empire*. New York: Oxford University Press.

Cardona, George. 1965. *A Gujarati reference grammar*. Philadelphia: University of Pennsylvania Press.

Carminati, M. N. 2005. Processing reflexes of the feature hierarchy (Person > Number > Gender) and implications for linguistic theory. *Lingua 115*: 259–85.

Cavallaro, Francesco, and Bee Chin Ng. 2009. Between status and solidarity in Singapore. *World Englishes 28*(2): 143–159.

Chambers, Jack. 2002. Dynamics of dialect convergence. *Sociolinguistics 6*: 117–130.

Chambers, Jack. 2004. Dynamic typology and vernacular universals. In B. Kortmann (ed.), *Dialectology meets typology*. Berlin: Mouton de Gruyter, pp. 127–145.

Chand, Vineeta. 2009. [v]at is going on? Local and global ideologies about Indian English. *Language in Society 38*(4): 393–419.

Chand, Vineeta. 2010. Post-vocalic (r) in urban Indian English. *English World-Wide 31*(1):1–39.

Chand, Vineeta, Devin Kapper, Sumona Mondal, Shantanu Sur, and Rana D. Parshad. 2017. Indian English evolution and focusing visible through power laws. *Languages 2* (4): 26.

Chaudenson, Robert. 2001. *Creolization of language and culture*. London: Routledge.

Chaudhary, Rakesh. 2001. Usage 2: 'Aati kyaa New York?'—a Nampally monologue. *English Today 17*(1): 27–38.

Chaudron, Craig, and Kate Parker. 1990. Discourse markedness and structural markedness: The acquisition of English noun phrases. *Studies in Second Language Acquisition 12*: 43–63.

Chesterman, Andrew. 1991. *On definiteness: A study with special reference to English and Finnish*. New York: Cambridge University Press.

Chong, Adam J., and James S. German. 2017. The accentual phrase in Singapore English. *Phonetica 17*(2): 63–80.

Clements, J. Clancy. 2003. The tense-aspect system in pidgins and naturalistically learned L2. *Studies in Second Language Acquisition 25*: 245–281.

Coelho, Gail. 1997. Anglo-Indian English: A nativized variety of Indian English. *Language in Society 26* (4): 561–589.

Collins, Peter. 2008. The progressive aspect in World Englishes: A corpus-based study. *Australian Journal of Linguistics 28*(2): 225–249.

Collins, Peter. 2009. Extended uses of *would* in some Asian Englishes. *Asian Englishes* 12 (2): 34–46.

Comrie, Bernard. 1976. *Aspect*. Cambridge: Cambridge University Press.

Corder, S. P. 1967. The significance of learners' errors. *International Review of Applied Linguistics 5*: 160–170.

Corne, Chris. 1977. *Seychelles Creole grammar: Elements for Indian Ocean Proto-Creole reconstruction*. Tübingen: TBL-Verlag Narr.

Coupland, Nikolas. 2007. *Style: Language variation and identity*. Cambridge: Cambridge University Press.

Coupland, Nikolas. 2008. The delicate constitution of identity in face-to-face accommodation: A response to Trudgill. *Language in Society 37*(2): 267–270.

Cowie, Claire. 2007. The accents of outsourcing: The meanings of "neutral" in the Indian call center industry. *World Englishes 26* (3): 316–330.

Cowie, Claire. 2018. "Accounting for BATH fronting in Indian English." Paper presented at Interspeech Satellite Workshop, English in India and Indian Englishes: New Horizons in the Study of Phonetics and Phonology, Hyderabad, India, September 7.

Cowie, Claire, and Anna Pande. 2017. Phonetic convergence towards American English variants by Indian agents in international service encounters. *English World-Wide 38* (3): 244–274.

Croft, William. 2000. *Explaining language change: An evolutionary approach*. London: Longman.

Cutts, Elmer, H. 1953. The background of Macaulay's Minute. *The American Historical Review 58* (4): 824–853.

Dahl, Östen. 1985. *Tense and aspect systems*. Oxford: Blackwell Press.

Dasgupta, Probal. 1993. *The otherness of English: India's auntie tongue syndrome*. New Delhi: Sage Publications.

Davies, Alan. 2003. *The native speaker: Myth and reality*. Clevedon: Multilingual Matters.

Davydova, Julia. 2011. *The present perfect in non-native Englishes: A corpus-based study*. Berlin: Mouton de Gruyter.

DeCamp, David. 1971 [1968]. Toward a generative analysis of a post-creole speech continuum. In D. Hymes (ed.). *Pidginization and creolization of languages*. Cambridge: Cambridge University Press, pp. 349–370.

DeKeyser, Robert. 2020. Input is not a panacea. *International Journal of Bilingualism* 24(1): 79–81.

de Leeuw, Esther, Monika Schmid, and Ineke Mennen. 2010. The effects of contact on native language pronunciation in an L2 migrant context. *Bilingualism: Language and Cognition 13*: 33–40.

Deleuze, Gilles, and Félix Guattari. 1980. *A thousand plateaus*. New York: Continuum.

Desai, Santosh. 2015. "One whisky and one masala dosa: The many meanings of Hinglish in advertising." Paper presented at Workshop, Hinglish: Social and Cultural Dimensions of Hindi-English Bilingualism in Contemporary India, School of Oriental and African Studies, London, May 28, 2015.

de Swart, Henriette. 1998. Aspect shift and coercion. *Natural Language and Linguistic Theory 16*: 347–385.

Deterding, David. 2003. An instrumental study of the monophthong vowels of Singapore English. *English World-Wide 24*: 1–16.

Deterding, David. 2007. *Singapore English*. Edinburgh University Press.

Deterding, David, A. Brown, and E. L. Low. 2005 *English in Singapore: Phonetic research on a corpus*. Singapore: McGraw-Hill.

Deterding, D., E. L. Low, and A. Brown, eds. 2003. *English in Singapore: Research on grammar*. Singapore: McGraw-Hill.

Deterding, David, and G. Poedjosoedarmo. 1998. *The sounds of English: Phonetics and phonology for English teachers in Southeast Asia*. Singapore: Prentice Hall.

Deuber, Dagmar, Carolin Biewer, Stephanie Hackert, and Michaela Hilbert. 2012. *Will* and *would* in selected New Englishes: General and variety-specific tendencies. In M. Hundt and U. Gut (eds.), *Mapping unity and diversity world-wide. Corpus-based studies of New Englishes*. Amsterdam: Benjamins, pp. 77–102.

Dik, Simon. 1978. *Functional grammar*. Amsterdam: North-Holland Press.

Dixon, R. M. W. 1991. *A new approach to English grammar on semantic principles*. Oxford: Clarendon Press.

Domange, Raphael. 2015. A language contact perspective on Indian English phonology. *World Englishes 34*: 533–556.

Domange, Raphael. 2020. Variation and change in the short vowels of Delhi English. *Language Variation and Change 32*(1): 49–76.

Dowty, David. 1979. *Word meaning and Montague grammar*. Dordrecht, the Netherlands: Kluwer.

Drummond, Rob. 2011. Glottal variation in /t/ in non-native English speech: Patterns of acquisition. *English World-Wide 32* (3): 280–308.

D'Souza, Jean. 2001. Contextualising range and depth in Indian English. *World Englishes 20*: 145–159.

Dulay, Heidi C., and Marina K. Burt. 1974. Errors and strategies in child second language acquisition. *TESOL Quarterly 8*: 129–136.

Dušková, Libuše. 1976. On some differences in the use of the perfect and preterite between British and American English. *Prague Studies in Mathematical Linguistics 5*: 53– 68.

Eckert, Penelope. 2012. Three waves of variation study: The emergence of meaning in the study of sociolinguistic variation. *Annual Review of Anthropology 41*: 87–100.

Eersel, Christian. 1971. Varieties of creole in Suriname: Prestige in choice of language and linguistic form. In Dell Hymes (ed.), *Pidginization and creolization of languages*. Cambridge: Cambridge University Press, pp. 310–322.

Elsness, Johan. 1997. *The perfect and the preterite in contemporary and earlier English*. Berlin: Mouton de Guyter.

Emeneau, Murray. 1956. India as a linguistic area. *Language 32* (1): 3–16.

Evans, Stephen. 2014. The evolutionary dynamics of postcolonial Englishes: A Hong Kong case study. *Journal of Sociolinguistics 18* (5): 571–603.

Fasold, Ralph W., William Labov, Fay Boy Vaughn-Cooke, Guy Bailey, Walt Wolfram, Arthur K. Spears, and John R. Rickford. 1987. Are black and white vernacular diverging? *American Speech 62* (1): 3–80.

Ferguson, Charles A. 1971. Absence of copula and the notion of simplicity: A study of normal speech, baby talk, foreigner talk, and pidgins. In Dell Hymes (ed.), *Pidginization and creolization of languages*. Cambridge: Cambridge University Press, pp. 141–150.

Ferguson, Charles. 1983. Language planning and language change. In H. Cobarrubias and J. Fishman (eds.), *Progress in language planning*. Berlin: Mouton, pp. 29–40.

Filppula, Markku. 1999. *The grammar of Irish English: Language in Hibernian style*. London: Routledge.

Filppula, Markku. 2004. Irish English: Morphology and syntax. In B. Kortmann and E. Schneider, in collaboration with K. Burridge, R. Mesthrie, and C. Upton (eds.), *A handbook of varieties of English*. Berlin: Mouton de Gruyter, pp. 73–101.

Filppula, Markku, Juhani Klemola, and Heli Paulasto. 2009. Digging for roots: Universals and contacts in regional varieties of English. In Markku Filppula, Juhani Klemola, and Heli Paulasto (eds.), *Vernacular universals and language contacts: Evidence from Varieties of English and beyond*. London: Routledge, pp. 231–261.

Fishman, Joshua. 1967. Bilingualism with and without diglossia; diglossia with and without bilingualism. *Journal of Social Issues 23*: 29–38.

Fodor, Janet D., and Ivan Sag. 1982. Referential and quantificational indefinites. *Linguistics and Philosophy 5*: 355–398.

Fodor, Janet D., and William G. Sakas. 2005. The Subset Principle in syntax: Costs of compliance. *Journal of Linguistics 41*: 513–569.

Foley, J. A., Thiru Kandiah, Bao Zhiming, Anthea F. Gupta, Lubna Alsagoff, Chee Lick Ho, Lionel Wee, Ismail S. Talib, and Wendy Bockhorst-Heng. 1998. *English in new cultural contexts: Reflections from Singapore*. Oxford: Oxford University Press.

Fong, Vivienne. 2004. The verbal cluster. In Lisa Lim (ed.), *Singapore English: A grammatical description*. Amsterdam: John Benjamins, pp. 75–104.

Foucault, Michel. 1969. *The archaeology of knowledge*. London and New York: Routledge.

Fuchs, Robert. 2022. Colonial lag or feature retention in postcolonial varieties of English: The negative scalar conjunction 'and that too' in South Asian Englishes and beyond. In P. Rautionaho, H. Parviainen, M. Kaunisto, and A. Nurmi (eds.), *Social and regional variation in world Englishes: Local and global perspectives*. London: Routledge, pp. 123–148.

Fuchs, Robert. 2016. *Speech rhythm in varieties of English: Evidence from educated Indian English and British English*. Singapore: Springer.

Gal, Susan. 1978. Peasant men can't get wives: Language change and sex roles in a bilingual community. *Language in Society 7*: 1–16.

Gargesh, Ravinder. 2006. South Asian Englishes. In B. Kachru and Y. Kachru (eds.), *Handbook of world Englishes*. Oxford: Wiley-Blackwell, pp. 90–108.

George, Stephen. 2010. "Article omission in Indian English and discourse universals: A study of online discussion forums." Presentation at the Seventeenth Annual UTASCILT Conference, Arlington, Texas, 19 February 2010.

Gil, David. 1995. Multiple (in)definiteness marking in Hebrew, Mandarin, Tagalog, Indonesian and Singlish. In F. Plank (ed.), *Overdetermination, EUROTYP Working Papers*, Series 7 (24). Berlin: EUROTYP Programme, pp. 189–227.

Gil, David. 1998. Patterns of macrofunctionality in Singlish noun phrases: A questionnaire survey. In S. L. Chelliah and W. J. de Reuse (eds.), *Papers from the Fifth Annual Meeting of the Southeast Asian Linguistics Society*. Tempe: Arizona State University, pp. 147–182.

Givón, Talmy. 1984. The pragmatics of referentiality. In D. Schiffrin (ed.), *Georgetown University round table on language and linguistics*. Washington, DC: Georgetown University Press, pp. 120–138.

Goad, Heather, and Lydia White. 2004. Ultimate attainment of L2 inflections: Effects of L1 prosodic structure. In S. H. Foster-Cohen, M. Sharwood Smith, A. Sorace, and M. Ota (eds.), *EUROSLA Yearbook*, Vol. 4. Amsterdam: Benjamins, pp. 119–145.

Greenberg, Joseph. 1978. *Universals of human language*. Stanford, CA: Stanford University Press.

Gumperz, John J., and Robert Wilson. 1971. Convergence and creolization: A case from the Indo-Aryan/Dravidian border in India. In D. Hymes (ed.), *Pidginization and creolization of languages*. Cambridge: Cambridge University Press, pp. 151–167.

Gupta, Anthea Fraser. 1986. A standard for written Singapore English? *English World-Wide* 7 (1): 75–99.

Gupta, Anthea Fraser. 1994. *The step-tongue: Children's English in Singapore*. Cleveland, UK: Multilingual Matters.

Gupta, Anthea Fraser. 1998. The situation of English in Singapore. In J. A. Foley et al. (eds.), *English in new cultural contexts: Reflections from Singapore*. Singapore: Oxford University Press, pp. 106–126.

Gupta, Anthea Fraser. 2001. Realism and imagination in the teaching of English. *World Englishes* 20 (3): 365–381.

Gupta, Anthea Fraser. 2006. Singlish on the web. In A. Hashim and N. Hassan (eds.), *Varieties of English in Southeast Asia and beyond*. Kuala Lumpur: University of Malaya Press, pp. 19–37.

Gupta, R. S. 2001. English in post-colonial India: An appraisal. In B. Moore (ed.), *Who's centric now? The present state of post-colonial Englishes*. Melbourne: Oxford University Press, pp. 148–164.

Gut, Ulrike. 2009. Past tense marking in Singapore English verbs. *English World-Wide* 30 (3): 262–277.

Gut, Ulrike, and Robert Fuchs. 2013. Progressive aspect in Nigerian English. *Journal of English Linguistics* 41(3): 243–267.

Hackert, Stefanie. 2009. A discourse historical approach to the English native speaker. In T. Hoffmann and L. Siebers (eds.), *World Englishes - problems, properties and prospects*. Amsterdam: John Benjamins, pp. 385–406.

Hackert, Stephanie. 2012. *The emergence of the English native speaker: A chapter in nineteenth-century linguistic thought*. Berlin: de Gruyter.

Hall, Robert A. 1966. *Outline of stratificational grammar*. Washington, DC: Georgetown University.

Halliday, Michael, A. K. 1967. Notes on transitivity and theme in English. *Journal of Linguistics* 3: 199–244.

Hartford, Beverly. 1996. The relationship of new Englishes and linguistic theory: A cognitive-based grammar of Nepali English. In R. J. Baumgardner (ed.), *South Asian English: Structure, use, and users*. Urbana: University of Illinois Press, pp. 88–103.

Hawkins, John. 1978. *Definiteness and indefiniteness: A study in reference and grammaticality prediction*. London: Croom Helm.

Hawkins, Roger. 2001. *Second language syntax: A generative perspective*. Oxford: Blackwell Publishers.

Hawkins, Roger, and Chan, Cecilia. 1997. The partial availability of Universal Grammar in second language acquisition: The "failed functional features hypothesis." *Second Language Research* 13: 187–226.

Herat, Manel. 2006. Substitute one in Sri Lankan English. *Leeds Working Papers in Linguistics* 11, University of Leeds, UK. Available at: https://www.latl.leeds.ac.uk/lwplp/.

Hickey, Raymond, ed. 2004. *Legacies of colonial English*. Cambridge: Cambridge University Press.

Hickey, Raymond. 2007. *Irish English: History and present-day forms*. Cambridge: Cambridge University Press.

Hicks, Glyn, and Laura Domínguez. 2019. A model for L1 grammatical attrition. *Second Language Research* 36(2): 213–217.

Hilbert, Michaela. 2008. Interrogative inversion in non-standard varieties of English. In Peter Siemund and Noemi Kintana (eds.), *Language contact and contact languages*. Amsterdam: Benjamins, pp. 261–289.

Hiramoto, Mie, and Yosuke Sato. 2012. *Got*-interrogatives and answers in Colloquial Singapore English. *World Englishes 31* (2): 198–207.

Hirson, A., and Sohail, N. 2007. Variability of rhotics in Punjabi-English bilinguals. In J. Trouvain and W. Barry (eds.), *Proceedings of the International Congress of the Phonetic Sciences 16*, pp. 1501–1504. Available at: http://www.icphs2007.de/.

Ho, Debbie G. E. 2006. I'm not west. I'm not east. So how leh? *English Today 22* (3): 17–24.

Ho, Mian Lian. 2003. Past tense marking in Singapore English. In D. Deterding, E. L. Low, and A. Brown (eds.), *English in Singapore: research on grammar*. Singapore: McGraw-Hill, pp. 39–47.

Ho, Mian Lian, and John Platt. 1993. *Dynamics of a contact continuum: Singaporean English*. Oxford: Oxford University Press.

Hoffmann, Sebastian, Marianne Hundt, and Joybrato Mukherjee. 2011. Indian English - an emerging epicentre? A pilot study on light verbs in web-derived corpora of South Asian Englishes. *Anglia 129* (3–4): 258–280.

Hoffman, Thomas, and Lucia Siebers, eds. 2009. *World Englishes - Problems, properties, and prospects*. Amsterdam: Benjamins.

Hogue, Cavan. 2001. The spread of Anglo-Indian words into South-East Asia. In B. Moore (ed.), *Who's centric now? The present state of post-colonial Englishes*. Melbourne: Oxford University Press, pp. 165–197.

Hohenthal, Annika. 2003. English in India: Loyalty and attitudes. *Language in India 3* (5). http://www.languageinindia.com/may2003/annika.html.

Holmes, Janet, and Paul Kerswill. 2008. Contact is not enough: A response to Trudgill. *Language in Society 37*(2): 273–277.

Hoover, Mary. 1978. Community attitudes toward Black English. *Language and Society 7*: 65–87.

Hosali, Priya. 2005. Butler English: An account of a highly distinctive variety of English in India. *English Today 21*(1): 34–39.

Housen, Alex. 2002. The development of tense-aspect in English as a second language and the variable influence of inherent aspect. In R. Salaberry and Y. Shirai (eds.), *The L2 acquisition of tense-aspect morphology*. Amsterdam: John Benjamins, pp. 155–197.

Huddleston, Rodney. 1984. *Introduction to the grammar of English*. Cambridge: Cambridge University Press.

Hudson, Thomas. 1993. Nothing does not equal zero: Problems with applying developmental sequence findings to assessment and pedagogy. *Studies in Second Language Acquisition 15*: 461–493.

Huebner, Thomas. 1983. *A longitudinal analysis of the acquisition of English*. Ann Arbor, MI: Karoma.

Hum Chong Kai, Darren. 2015. *Effect of interlocutor accent on attitudes to Singapore English: A modified matched-guise study*. MA dissertation, Queen Mary University of London.

Hundt, Marianne. 2009. Colonial lag, colonial innovation, or simply language change? In Günther Rohdenburg and Julia Schlüter (eds.), *One language, two grammars?: Morphosyntactic differences between British and American English*. Cambridge: Cambridge University Press, pp. 13–37.

Hundt, Marianne. 2014. Zero articles in Indian English: A comparison of primary and secondary diaspora situations. In M. Hundt and D. Sharma (eds.), *English in the Indian diaspora*. Amsterdam: Benjamins, pp. 131–170.

Hundt, Marianne, and Devyani Sharma, eds. 2014. *English in the Indian diaspora*. Amsterdam: Benjamins.

*References* [271]

Hundt, Marianne, and Adina Staicov. 2018. Identity in the London Indian diaspora: Towards the quantification of qualitative data. *World Englishes 37*: 166–184.

Hundt, Marianne, and Katrin Vogel. 2011. Overuse of the progressive in ESL and learner Englishes—fact or fiction? In J. Mukherjee and M. Hundt (eds.), *Second-language varieties and learner Englishes*. Amsterdam: Benjamins, pp. 145–166.

Ingham, Richard. 2017. Maintenance and change in language contact: The case of Anglo-Norman. *Zeitschrift für Dialektologie und Linguistik 84* (2–3): 383–402.

Ionin, Tania, Heejeong Ko, and Ken Wexler. 2004. Article semantics in L2-acquisition: The role of specificity. *Language Acquisition 12*: 3–69.

Ionin, Tania, Maria Luisa Zubizarreta, and Salvador Bautista Maldonado. 2008. Sources of linguistic knowledge in the second language acquisition of English articles. *Lingua 118* (4): 554–576.

Jain, Ritu, and Lionel Wee. 2015. Multilingual education in Singapore: Beyond language communities? In Androula Yiakoumetti (ed.), *Multilingualism and language in education: Sociolinguistic and pedagogical perspectives from Commonwealth countries*. Cambridge: Cambridge University Press, pp. 67–85.

Jarvis, Scott. 2002. Topic continuity in L2 English article use. *Studies in Second Language Acquisition 24*: 387–418.

Jaszczolt, K. M. 2009. *Representing time: An essay on temporality as modality*. Oxford: Oxford University Press.

Jenkins, Jennifer. 2003. *World Englishes*. London: Routledge.

Jespersen, Otto. 1933. *Essentials of English grammar*. London: Allen and Unwin.

John, Binoo K. 2007. *Entry from backside only: Hazaar fundas of Indian-English*. New Delhi: Penguin.

Johnson, Daniel Ezra. 2009. Getting off the GoldVarb standard: Introducing Rbrul for mixed-effects variable rule analysis. *Language and Linguistics Compass 3*: 359–383.

Kachru, Braj B. 1965. The Indianness of Indian English. *Word 21*: 391–410.

Kachru, Braj B. 1976. Models of English for the Third World: White man's linguistic burden or language pragmatics? *TESOL Quarterly 10*: 221–239.

Kachru, Braj B. 1983. *The Indianization of English: The English language in India*. Oxford: Oxford University Press.

Kachru, Braj B. 1986. *The alchemy of English: The spread, functions, and models of non-native Englishes*. London: Pergamon Press.

Kachru, Braj B. 1991. Liberation linguistics and the Quirk concern. *English Today 7* (1): 3–13.

Kachru, Braj B. 1992 [1982]. *The other tongue: English across cultures*. Urbana: University of Illinois Press.

Kachru, Braj B. 1994. English in South Asia. In R. Burchfield (ed.), *The Cambridge history of the English language*. Cambridge: Cambridge University Press, pp. 497–626.

Kachru, Braj B. 2005. *Asian Englishes: Beyond the canon*. Hong Kong: Hong Kong University Press.

Kachru, Yamuna. 2003. On definite reference in world Englishes. *World Englishes 22*: 497–510.

Kachru, Yamuna. 2006. Speaking and writing in world Englishes. In B. B. Kachru, Y. Kachru, and C. L. Nelson (eds.), *The handbook of world Englishes*. Oxford: Blackwell, pp. 366–386.

Kandiah, Thiru. 1991. South Asia. In J. Cheshire (ed.), *English around the world: Sociolinguistic perspectives*. Cambridge: Cambridge University Press, pp. 271–287.

Kandiah, Thiru. 1998. Epiphanies of the deathless native users' manifold avatars: A post colonial perspective on the native-speaker. In R. Singh (ed.), *The native speaker: Multilingual perspectives*. New Delhi: Sage, pp. 75–110.

Katenina, T. E. 1960. *Jazyk Chindi*. Moscow: Nauka.

Kenny, A. 1963. *Action, emotion and will*. London: Routledge and Kegan Paul.

Kerswill, Paul, and Ann Williams. 2000. Creating a new town koine: Children and language change in Milton Keynes. *Language in Society 29*: 65–115.

Khan, Farhat. 1991. Final consonant cluster simplification in a variety of Indian English. In J. Cheshire (ed.), *English around the world*. Cambridge: Cambridge University Press, pp. 288–298.

Kher, B. G. 1957. *Report of the Official Indian Language Commission, 1956*. New Delhi: Government of India Press.

Khilnani, Sunil. 2003. Gandhi and Nehru: The uses of English. In: A. K. Mehrotra (ed.), *A history of Indian literature in English*. London: Hurst and Company, pp. 135–156.

Khubchandani, Lachman M. 1978. Language planning processes for pluralistic societies: A critical review of the Indian scene. *Language Problems and Language Planning 2/3*: 141–161.

Klecha, Peter, Joe Jalbert, Alan Munn, and Cristina Schmitt. 2008. Explaining why *gonna* precedes will in acquisition. In H. Chain, H. Enkeleida, and H. Jacob (eds.), *Supplement of the proceedings of the 32nd Annual Boston University Conference on Language Development*. Available at: https://www.bu.edu/bucld/proceedings/supplement/vol32/.

Klein, Flora. 1980. A quantitative study of syntactic and pragmatic indications of change in the Spanish of bilinguals in the U.S. In W. Labov (ed.), *Locating language in time and space*. New York: Academic Press, pp. 69–82.

Klein, Wolfgang, and Clive Perdue. 1992. *Utterance structure: Developing grammars again*. Amsterdam: Benjamins.

Kortmann, Bernd. 2013. How powerful is geography as an explanatory factor of variation? Areal features in the anglophone world. In P. Auer, M. Hilpert, A. Stukenbrock, and B. Szmrecsanyi (eds.), *Space in language and linguistics: Geographical, interactional, and cognitive perspectives*. Berlin: Walter de Gruyter, pp. 165–194.

Kortmann, Bernd, and Lunkenheimer, Kerstin, eds. 2013. The electronic world atlas of varieties of English (eWAVE). Leipzig: Max Planck Institute for Evolutionary Anthropology.

Kortmann, Bernd, and Benedikt Szmrecsanyi. 2004. Global synopsis—morphological and syntactic variation in English. In B. Kortmann, K. Burridge, R. Mesthrie, and E. Schneider (eds.), *A handbook of varieties of English, vol. 2: Morphology and syntax*. Berlin: Mouton de Gruyter, pp. 1122–1182.

Kothari, Rita, and Rupert Snell. 2011. *Chutnefying English: The phenomenon of Hinglish*. New Delhi: Penguin.

Kratzer, Angelica. 1991. Modality. In A. von Stechow and D. Wunderlich (eds.), *Semantics: An international handbook of contemporary research*. Berlin: de Gruyter, pp. 639–650.

Krishnaswamy, Subashree. 2009. "Mind it! We are in Chennai, Machan!" Paper presented at Chutnefying English conference, January 2009, Mumbai, India.

Kurzon, Dennis. 2004. *Where east looks west: Success in English in Goa and on the Konkan coast*. Clevedon, UK: Multilingual Matters.

Labov, William. 1969. Contraction, deletion, and inherent variability of the English copula. *Language 45*: 715–762.

*References* [273]

Labov, William. 1972. *Sociolinguistic patterns*. Philadelphia: University of Pennsylvania Press.

Labov, William. 1993. "The unobservability of structure and its linguistic consequences." Paper presented at the 22nd New Ways in Analyzing Variation conference, University of Ottawa, October 22–25.

Labov, William. 1994. *Principles of linguistic change: Internal factors*. Cambridge, MA: Blackwell Publishers.

Lado, R. 1957. *Linguistics across cultures: Applied linguistics for language teachers*. Ann Arbor: University of Michigan Press.

Lambrecht, Knud. 1994. *Information structure and sentence form*. Cambridge: Cambridge University Press.

Lange, Claudia. 2007. Focus marking in Indian English. *English World-Wide 28* (1): 89–118.

Lange, Claudia. 2012. *The syntax of spoken Indian English*. Amsterdam: Benjamins.

Lapidus, N., and Otheguy, R. 2005. Contact induced change? Overt nonspecific *ellos* in Spanish in New York. In L. Sayahi and M. Westmoreland (eds.), *Selected proceedings of the second workshop on Hispanic sociolinguistics*. Somerville, MA: Cascadilla Press, pp. 157–174.

Lardiere, Donna. 2009. Some thoughts on the contrastive analysis of features in second language acquisition. *Second Language Research* 25 (2): 173–227.

Larrañaga, P., J. Treffers-Daller, F. Tidball, and M.-c. Gil Ortega. 2012. L1 transfer in the acquisition of manner and path in Spanish by native speakers of English. *International Journal of Bilingualism 16* (1): 117–138.

Lee, Nala H., Ai Ping Ling, and Hiroki Nomoto. 2009. Colloquial Singapore English *got*: Functions and substratal influences. *World Englishes 28*: 293–318.

Lee, Tong King. 2021. Writing Singapore: Choreographed and emergent practices. *Social Semiotics 31* (1): 36–60.

Leech, Geoffrey. 2003. Modality on the move: The English modal auxiliaries 1961–1992. In R. Facchinetti, M Krug, and F. Palmer (eds.), *Modality in contemporary English*. Berlin: Mouton de Gruyter, pp. 233–240.

Lefebvre, Claire. 1998. *Creole genesis and the acquisition of grammar: The case of Haitian Creole*. Cambridge: Cambridge University Press.

Leimgruber, Jakob. 2008a. From post-creole continuum to diglossia: The case of Singapore English. In M. Kokkonidis et al. (eds.), *Proceedings of LingO 2007*. Oxford: Faculty of Linguistics, Philology, and Phonetics, pp. 149–156.

Leimbgruber, Jakob. 2008b. English in Singapore: Diglossia or continuum? In J. Angouri et al. (eds.), *LangUE 2007: Proceedings of the second language at the University of Essex postgraduate conference*. Colchester, UK: Department of Language and Linguistics.

Leimgruber, Jakob. 2011. Singapore English. *Language and Linguistics Compass 5* (1): 47–62.

Leimgruber, Jakob. 2013. *Singapore English: Structure, variation and usage*. Cambridge: Cambridge University Press.

Le Page, Robert, and Andre Tabouret-Keller. 1985. *Acts of identity: Creole-based approaches to language and ethnicity*. Cambridge: Cambridge University Press.

Leitner, Gerhard. 1991. The Kolhapur Corpus of Indian English—intra-varietal description and/or intervarietal comparison. In S. Johansson and A-B. Stenström (eds.), *English computer corpora: Selected papers and research guide*. New York: Mouton de Gruyter, pp. 215–232.

[274]   *References*

Leuckert, Sven. 2019. *Topicalization in Asian Englishes: Forms, functions, and frequencies of a fronting construction*. London: Routledge.

Levon, Erez, and Isa Buchstaller. 2015. Perception, cognition and linguistic structure: The effect of linguistic modularity and cognitive style on sociolinguistic processing. *Language Variation and Change* 27: 319–348.

Lewis, Ivor. 1991. *Sahibs, nabobs and boxwallahs: A dictionary of words of Anglo-India*. Oxford: Oxford University Press.

Li, Charles N., and Sandra Thompson. 1981. *Mandarin Chinese: A functional reference grammar*. Berkeley: University of California Press.

Li, Wei, Lesley Milroy, and Sin Ching Pong. 1992. A two-step sociolinguistic analysis of code-switching and language choice. *International Journal of Applied Linguistics* 2 (1): 63–86.

Lim, Lisa. 2004. *Singapore English: A grammatical description*. Amsterdam, NL: John Benjamins Publishing Company.

Lim, Lisa. 2007. Mergers and acquisitions: On the ages and origins of Singapore English particles. *World Englishes* 26 (4): 446–473.

Lim, Lisa. 2009. Revisiting English prosody: (Some) New Englishes as tone languages? *English World-Wide 30* (2): 97–118.

Lim, Lisa. 2010a. Migrants and "mother tongues": Extralinguistic forces in the ecology of English in Singapore. In L. Lim, A. Pakir, and L. Wee (eds.), *English in Singapore: Modernity and management*. Hong Kong: Hong Kong University Press, pp. 19–54.

Lim, Lisa. 2010b. Peranakan English in Singapore. In D. Schreier, P. Trudgill, E. W. Schneider, and J. P. Williams (eds.), *The lesser-known varieties of English: An introduction*. Cambridge: Cambridge University Press, pp. 327–347.

Lim, Lisa. 2011. Revisiting English prosody: (Some) New Englishes as tone languages? In N. Gisborne and L. Lim (eds.), *The typology of Asian Englishes*. Amsterdam: John Benjamins, pp. 97–118.

Lim, Lisa, and Joseph A. Foley. 2004. English in Singapore and Singapore English: Background and methodology. In L. Lim (ed.), *Singapore English: A grammatical description*. Amsterdam: John Benjamins, pp. 1–18.

Lim, Lisa, Anne Pakir, and Lionel Wee. 2010. English in Singapore: Policies and prospects. In L. Lim, A. Pakir, and L. Wee (eds.), *English in Singapore: modernity and management*. Hong Kong: Hong Kong University Press, pp. 3–8.

Low, Ee Ling, and Adam Brown. 2005. *English in Singapore: An introduction*. Singapore: McGraw-Hill.

Lowenberg, Peter. 1986. Non-native varieties of English: Nativization, norms, and implications. *Studies in Second Language Acquisition 8*: 1–18.

Lyons, Christopher. 1999. *Definiteness*. Cambridge: Cambridge University Press.

Maher, James Reginald. 2007. *These are the Anglo Indians*. London: Simon Wallenberg Press.

Mair, Christian. 2003. Kreolismen und verbales Identitätsmanagement im geschriebenen jamaikanischen Englisch. In E. Vogel, A. Napp, and W. Lutterer (eds.), *Zwischen Ausgrenzung und Hybridisierung*. Würzburg, Germany: Ergon, pp. 79–96.

Marckwardt, Albert. 1958. *American English*. Oxford: Oxford University Press.

Masica, Colin P. 1991. *The Indo-Aryan languages*. Cambridge: Cambridge University Press.

Matras, Yaron. 2009. *Language contact*. Cambridge: Cambridge University Press.

Matras, Yaron, and Jeanette Sakel. 2007. Investigating the mechanisms of pattern replication in language convergence. *Studies in Language 31*: 829–865.

Matthews, Stephen, and Virginia Yip. 1994. *Cantonese: A comprehensive grammar*. London: Routledge.

Maxwell, Olga, and Janet Fletcher. 2010. The acoustic characteristics of diphthongs in Indian English. *World Englishes 29* (1): 27–44.

Maxwell, Olga, Elinor Payne, and Rosey Billington. 2018. Homogeneity vs. heterogeneity in Indian English: Investigating influences of L1 on f0 range. In B. Yegnanarayana, C. Chandra Sekhar, Shrikanth Narayanan, S. Umesh, S. R. M. Prasanna, Hema A. Murthy, Preeti Rao, Paavo Alku, and Prasanta Kumar Ghosh (eds.), *Proceedings of Interspeech 2018*. Hyderabad, India: International Speech Communication Association, pp. 2191–2195.

McMahon, April. 1994. *Understanding Language Change*. Cambridge: Cambridge University Press.

McWhorter, John H. 1999. The Afrogenesis hypothesis of plantation creole origin. In M. Huber and M. Parkvall (eds.), *Spreading the word: The issue of diffusion among the Atlantic Creoles*. London: University of Westminster Press, pp. 111–152.

Mehrotra, Arvind Krishna, ed. 2003. *A History of Indian literature in English*. London: Hurst and Company.

Mehrotra, Raja Ram. 1982. Indian English: A sociolinguistic profile. In John B. Pride (ed.), *New Englishes*. Rowley, MA: Newbury House, pp. 150–173.

Mehrotra, Raja Ram. 1998. *Indian English*. Amsterdam: John Benjamins.

Melchers, Gunnel, and Philip Shaw. 2003. *World Englishes: An introduction*. London: Arnold.

Meriläinen, Lea, and Heli Paulasto. 2014. Embedded inversion as an Angloversal: Evidence from inner, outer, and expanding circle Englishes. In M. Filppula, J. Klemola, and D. Sharma. (eds.), *The Oxford handbook of world Englishes*. Oxford: Oxford University Press, pp. 191–216.

Mesthrie, Rajend. 1992. *English in Language Shift*. Cambridge: Cambridge University Press.

Mesthrie, Rajend. 2001. Male workers' English in the Western Cape—interlanguage, code-switching and pidginisation. In S. Ridge, E. Ridge, and S. Makoni (eds.), *Freedom and discipline: Essays in applied linguistics from Southern Africa*. New Delhi: Bahri, pp. 85–104.

Mesthrie, Rajend, and Rakesh M. Bhatt. 2008. *World Englishes: The study of new linguistic varieties*. Cambridge: Cambridge University Press.

Meyerhoff, Miriam, and Nancy Niedzielski. 2003. The globalisation of vernacular variation. *Journal of Sociolinguistics 7* (4): 534–555.

Meyerhoff, Miriam, and Walker, James. 2013. An existential problem: The sociolinguistic monitor and variation in existential constructions on Bequia (St. Vincent and the Grenadines). *Language in Society 42*: 407–428.

Mishra, Arpita. 1982. Discovering connections. In John Gumperz (ed.), *Language and social identity*. Cambridge: Cambridge University Press, pp. 57–71.

Mithun, Marianne. 1986. On the nature of noun incorporation. *Language 62* (1): 32–37.

Mithun, Marianne. 1995. Morphological and prosodic forces shaping word order. In P. Downing and M. Noonan. (eds.), *Word order in discourse*. Amsterdam: Benjamins, pp. 387–423.

Mohanan, Tara. 1994. *Argument structure in Hindi*. Stanford, CA: CSLI Publications.

Montrul, Silvina. 2004. Subject and object expression in Spanish heritage speakers: A case of morphosyntactic convergence. *Bilingualism: Language and Cognition 7*: 125–142.

Mougeon, Raymond, and Édouard Beniak. 1996. Social class and language variation in bilingual speech communities. In D. Schiffrin, G. Guy, J. Baugh, and C. Feagin (eds.), *Towards a social science of language: A Festschrift for William Labov*, vol. 1. Amsterdam: John Benjamins, pp. 69–99.

Mourelatos, A. P. D. 1978. Events, processes and states. *Linguistics and Philosophy 2* (3): 415–434.

Mufwene, Salikoko S. 1994. New Englishes and criteria for naming them. *World Englishes 13*: 21–31.

Mufwene, Salikoko. 1996. The Founder Principle in creole genesis. *Diachronica 13*: 83–134.

Mufwene, Salikoko. 2001. *The ecology of language evolution*. Cambridge: Cambridge University Press.

Mukherjee, Joybrato. 2007. Steady states in the evolution of new Englishes: Present-day Indian English as an equilibrium. *Journal of English Linguistics 35* (2): 157–187.

Mukherjee, Joybrato, and Marianne Hundt, eds. 2011. *Exploring second-language varieties of English and learner Englishes: Bridging a paradigm gap*. Amsterdam: Benjamins.

Müller, Natascha, and Aafke Hulk. 2001. Crosslinguistic influence in bilingual language acquisition: Italian and French as recipient languages. *Bilingualism: Language and Cognition 4*: 1–22.

Myhill, John. 1995. The use of features of present-day AAVE in the ex-slave recordings. *American Speech 70* (2): 115–147.

Nagarajan, Rema. 2015. Number of children studying in English doubles in 5 years. *The Times of India*, September 28.

Nayak, Shrishti, Inder Singh, and Catherine Caldwell-Harris. 2016. Familiarity, comprehension and use of Indian English *only*: L1 Indian English speakers' psycholinguistic judgments and interview responses. *English World-Wide 37* (3): 267–292.

Newbrook, Mark, ed. 1987. *Aspects of the syntax of educated Singaporean English*. Frankfurt: Peter Lang.

Newbrook, Mark, and Chinniah, Y. A. 1987. Aspects of the Singaporean English verb phrase: Norms, claims and usage. In Mark Newbrook (ed.), *Aspects of the syntax of educated Singaporean English*. Frankfurt: Peter Lang, pp. 339–379.

Newman, Michael. 2010. Focusing, implicational scaling, and the dialect status of New York Latino English. *Journal of Sociolinguistics 14* (2): 207–239.

Ng, E-Ching. 2008. "English meets Malay meets Chinese: Colloquial Singaporean English." Presented at the Workshop on Interdisciplinary Approaches to Transfer, Crosslinguistic Influence and Contact-Induced Change, University of the West of England, Bristol, July 2008.

Ng, E-Ching. 2011. Reconciling stress and tone in Singaporean English. In L. J. Zhang, R. Rubdy, and L. Alsagoff (eds.), *Asian Englishes: Changing perspectives in a globalised world*. Singapore: Pearson Longman, pp. 76–92.

Nihalani, Paroo, R. K. Tongue, and Priya Hosali. 1979. *Indian and British English: A handbook of usage and pronunciation*. Delhi: Oxford University Press.

O'Rourke, Bernadette, and Joan Pujolar. 2013. From native speakers to "new speakers" - problematizing nativeness in language revitalization contexts. *Histoire Épistémologie Langage 35* (2): 47–67.

Orsini, Francesca. 2015. *Dil Maange more*: Cultural contexts of Hinglish in contemporary India. *African Studies 74* (2): 199–220.

Paikeday, Thomas, 1985. *The native speaker is dead!* Toronto: Paikeday Publishing Company.

Pakir, Anne. 1991. The range and depth of English-knowing bilinguals in Singapore. *World Englishes 10*: 167–179.

Pakir, Anne. 1994. English in Singapore: The codification of competing norms. In Saravanan Gopinath, Anne Pakir, Ho Wah Kam, and Vanithamani Saravanan (eds.), *Language, society, and education in Singapore: Issues and trends*. Singapore: Times Academic Press, pp. 65–84.

Pandey, P. K. 1994. On a description of the phonology of Indian English. In R. K. Agnihotri and A. L. Khanna (eds.), *Second language acquisition: Socio-cultural and linguistic aspects of English in India*. New Delhi: Sage, pp. 198–207.

Pandharipande, Rajeshwari. 2007. Defining politeness in Indian English. *World Englishes 11* (2): 241–250.

Paolucci, Henry. 1984. Italian and English "Models" for the modern vernacular literatures of India. In A. Scaglione (ed.), *The Emergence of National Languages*. Ravenna: Longo Editore, pp. 209–231.

Parasher, S. V. 1983. Indian English: Certain grammatical, lexical and stylistic features. *English World-Wide 4* (1): 27–42.

Parkvall, Mikael. 2000. Reassessing the role of demographics in language restructuring. In Ingrid Neumann-Holzschuh and E. W. Schneider (eds.), *Degrees of restructuring in Creole languages*. Amsterdam: Benjamins, pp. 185–213.

Parshad, Rana D., Suman Bhowmick, Vineeta Chand, Nitu Kumari, and Neha Sinhad, 2016. What is India speaking? Exploring the "Hinglish" invasion. *Physica A: Statistical Mechanics and Its Applications 449*: 375–389.

Parviainen, Hanna. 2012. Focus particles in Indian English and other varieties. *World Englishes 31* (2): 226–247.

Pathak, Maulik. 2013. India becoming graveyard of languages: Ganesh Devy. *Live Mint*. Accessed December 10, 2019. Retrieved from http://www.livemint.com/.

Paulasto, Heli. 2014. Extended uses of the progressive form in L1 and L2 Englishes. *English World-Wide 35* (3): 247–276.

Pennycook, Alastair. 1994. *The cultural politics of English as an international language*. London: Routledge.

Pennycook, Alastair. 2010. Rethinking origins and localization in Global Englishes. In M. Saxena and T. Omoniyi (eds.), *Contending with globalization in world Englishes*. Clevedon, UK: Multilingual Matters, pp. 196–210.

Phillipson, Robert. 1992. *Linguistic imperialism*. Oxford: Oxford University Press.

Pienemann, Manfred, and Alison Mackey. 1993. An empirical study of children's ESL development and rapid profile. In P. McKay (ed.), *ESL development: Language and literacy in schools*, vol. 2. Melbourne: Commonwealth of Australia and National Languages and Literacy Institute of Australia, pp. 115–259.

Pillai, N. Nadaraja. 1992. *A syntactic study of Tamil verbs*. Mysore, India: Central Institute of Indian Languages.

Pinker, Steven. 1984. *Language learnability and language development*. Cambridge: Harvard University Press.

Pinker, S. 1989. *Learnability and cognition: The acquisition of argument structure*. Cambridge: MIT Press.

Platt, John. 1977. A model for polyglossia and multilingualism (with special reference to Singapore and Malaysia). *Language in Society 6*: 361–378.

Platt, John. 1979. Variation and implicational relationships: Copula realization in Singapore English. *General Linguistics 19* (1):1–14.

Platt, John, Heidi Weber, and Mian Lian Ho. 1983. *Singapore and Malaysia*. Amsterdam: John Benjamins.

Platt, John, Heidi Weber, and Mian Lian Ho. 1984. *The new Englishes*. London: Routledge.

[278] *References*

Polinsky, Maria, and Greg Scontras. 2019. Understanding heritage languages. *Bilingualism: Language and Cognition 23* (1): 4–20.

Prentice, D. J. 1990. Malay (Indonesian and Malaysian). In B. Comrie (ed.), *The world's major languages*. Oxford: Oxford University Press, pp. 913–935.

Preston, Dennis. 1996. Whaddayaknow? The modes of folk linguistic awareness. *Language Awareness 5*(1): 40–74.

Prince, Ellen. 1981. Toward a taxonomy of given-new information. In P. Cole (ed.), *Radical pragmatics*. New York: Academic Press, pp. 223–254.

Punnoose, Reenu. 2017. Indian English at sociolinguistic crossroads: Impact of the tripartite relationship between schooling, social class and English in urban India. *Journal of Advanced Linguistic Studies 6* (1–2): 189–214.

Quirk, Randolph. 1990. Language varieties and standard language. *English Today 21*: 3–10.

Quirk, Randolph, Sidney Greenbaum, Geoffrey Leech, and Jan Svartvik. 1985. *A comprehensive grammar of the English language*. London: Longman.

Rahman, Jacquelyn. 2002. "Black Standard English: Its role in the lives of African American students and staff." *NWAV 31 Presentation*, Stanford University, California, October 2002.

Rai, Rajesh. 2007. Singapore. In B. V. Lal, P. Reeves, and R. Rai (eds.), *The Encyclopedia of the Indian Diaspora*. Honolulu: University of Hawai'i Press, pp. 176–188.

Ramanathan, Vaidehi. 2006. Gandhi, non-cooperation, and socio-civic education in Gujarat, India: Harnessing the vernaculars. *Journal of Language, Identity, and Education 5* (3): 229–250.

Rampton, Ben. 1990. Displacing the "native speaker": Expertise, affiliation, and inheritance. *ELT Journal 44* (2): 97–101.

Rautionaho, Paula. 2014. *Variation in the progressive: A corpus-based study into world Englishes*. Tampere, Finland: Tampere University Press.

Reichenbach, Hans. 1947. *Elements of symbolic logic*. New York: The Macmillan Company.

Rickford, John R. 1987. *Dimensions of a creole continuum*. Stanford, CA: Stanford University Press.

Rickford, John R. 2002. Implicational scales. In J. Chambers, P. Trudgill, and N. Schilling-Estes (eds.), *Handbook of language variation and change*. New York: Blackwell Press, pp. 142–167.

Rickford, John R. 2006. Down for the count? The Creole Origins Hypothesis of AAVE at the hands of the Ottawa Circle, and their supporters. *Journal of Pidgin and Creole Languages 21*: 97–155.

Rickford, John R., and Russell J. Rickford. 2000. *Spoken soul: The story of Black English*. New York: John Wiley and Sons Inc.

Rickford, John R., and Christine Théberge Rafal. 1996. Preterite *had* + V-ed in the narratives of African-American adolescents. *American Speech 71* (3): 227–254.

Robertson, Daniel. 2000. Variability in the use of the English article system by Chinese learners of English. *Second Language Research 16*: 135–172.

Robison, Richard. 1990. The primacy of aspect: Aspectual marking in English interlanguage. *Studies in Second Language Acquisition 12*: 315–330.

Rousseau, Pascale, and David Sankoff. 1978. Advances in variable rule methodology. In D. Sankoff (ed.), *Linguistic variation: Models and methods*. New York: Academic Press, Inc., pp. 57–69.

Roy, Anjali Gera. 2013. The politics of Hinglish. In L. Wee, R. B. H. Goh, and L. Lim (eds.), *The politics of English: South Asia, Southeast Asia and the Asia Pacific*. Amsterdam: Benjamins, pp. 21–36.

Rubdy, Rani 2001. Creative destruction: Singapore's Speak Good English Movement. *World Englishes 20*(3): 341–355.

Rushdie, Salman. 1995. *The moor's last sigh*. New York: Random House.

Sadaf, Shazia. 2007. *Sahib's English: A study of the peculiarities in the use of Indian loan vocabulary amongst the British ruling class in India*. PhD diss., Senate House, London.

Sahgal, Anju. 1991. Patterns of language use in a bilingual setting in India. In J. Cheshire. (ed.), *English around the world*. Cambridge: Cambridge University Press, pp. 299–307.

Sahgal, Anju, and R. K. Agnihotri. 1985. Syntax—the common bond: Acceptability of syntactic deviances in Indian English. *English World-Wide 6* (1): 117–129.

Sahgal, Anju, and R. K. Agnihotri. 1988. Indian English phonology: A sociolinguistic perspective. *English World-Wide 9* (1): 51–64.

Sailaja, Pingali. 2009. *Indian English*. Edinburgh: Edinburgh University Press.

Salaberry, M. R. 1999. The development of past tense verbal morphology in classroom L2 Spanish. *Applied Linguistics 20*: 151–178.

Sand, Andrea. 2004. Shared morpho-syntactic features in contact varieties of English: Article use. *World Englishes 23* (2): 281–298.

Sankoff, Gillian. 1983. Comments on Valdman's "Creolization and second language acquisition." In R. Andersen (ed.), *Pidginization and creolization as second language acquisition*. Rowley: Newbury House Publishers, pp. 235–240.

Sankoff, Gillian. 2002. Linguistic outcomes of language contact. In J. Chambers, P. Trudgill, and N. Schilling-Estes (eds.), *The handbook of language variation and change*. Oxford: Blackwell, pp. 638–668.

Sankoff, Gillian, and Claudia Mazzie. 1991. Determining noun phrases in Tok Pisin. *Journal of Pidgin and Creole Languages 6*: 1–24.

Sanyal, Jyoti. 2007. *Indlish - the book for every English-speaking Indian*. New Delhi: Viva Books.

Sarkar, Anoop. 1998. The conflict between future tense and modality: The case of *will* in English. *University of Pennsylvania Working Papers in Linguistics 5* (2). https://repository.upenn.edu/pwpl/vol5/iss2/6.

Schiffman, Harold. 1999. *A reference grammar of Spoken Tamil*. Cambridge: Cambridge University Press.

Schilk, Marco. 2011. *Structural nativization in Indian English lexicogrammar*. Amsterdam: Benjamins.

Schilling-Estes, Natalie. 1998. Investigating "self-conscious" speech: The performance register in Ocracoke English. *Language in Society 27* (1):53–83.

Schneider, Edgar. 2003. The dynamics of New Englishes: From identity construction to dialect birth. *Language 79*: 233–281.

Schneider, Edgar. 2007. *Postcolonial English: Varieties around the world*. Cambridge: Cambridge University Press.

Schröter, Verena. 2010. *Stylistic variation in Singapore English: A corpus-based analysis of be deletion and subject omission*. Masters diss., Freiburg, Germany: Albert Ludwigs Universität.

Schwartz, B. D. and R. A. Sprouse. 1994. Word order and nominative case in nonnative language acquisition: A longitudinal study of (L1 Turkish) German interlanguage. In T. Hoekstra and B. D. Schwartz (eds.), *Language acquisition studies in generative grammar*. Amsterdam: John Benjamins. pp. 317–368.

Sedlatschek, Andreas. 2009. *Contemporary Indian English: Variation and change*. Amsterdam: John Benjamins.

Selinker, Richard. 1974. Interlanguage. In J. Richards (ed.), *Error analysis: Perspectives on second language acquisition*. London: Longman, pp. 209–231.

Serratrice, Ludovica, Antonella Sorace, and Sandra Paoli. 2004. Subjects and objects in Italian-English bilingual and monolingual acquisition. *Bilingualism: Language and Cognition* 7: 183–206.

Sharma, Devyani. 2001. The pluperfect in native and non-native English: A comparative corpus study. *Language Variation and Change* 13 (3): 343–375.

Sharma, Devyani. 2003. *Structural and social constraints on non-native varieties of English*. PhD diss., Stanford University, Stanford, CA.

Sharma, Devyani. 2005a. Dialect stabilization and speaker awareness in non-native varieties of English. *Journal of Sociolinguistics* 9 (2): 194–225.

Sharma, Devyani. 2005b. Language transfer and discourse universals in Indian English article use. *Studies in Second Language Acquisition* 27 (4): 535–566.

Sharma, Devyani. 2009. Typological diversity in New Englishes. *English World-Wide* 30 (2): 170–195.

Sharma, Devyani. 2012. Shared features in new Englishes. In R. Hickey (ed.), *Areal features of the Anglophone world*. Berlin: Mouton de Gruyter, pp. 211–232.

Sharma, Devyani. 2014. Transnational flows, language variation, and ideology. In M. Hundt and D. Sharma (eds.), *English in the Indian diaspora*. Amsterdam: Benjamins, pp. 215–242.

Sharma, Devyani. 2017. "A dynamic typology of syntactic change in Postcolonial Englishes." Plenary lecture, *Societas Linguistica Europaea 50*, 12 September, University of Zurich.

Sharma, Devyani. 2018. Style dominance: Attention, audience, and the "real me." *Language in Society* 47 (1): 1–33.

Sharma, Devyani, and Ashwini Deo. 2010. A new methodology for the study of aspect in contact: Past and progressive in *Indian* English. In J. Walker (ed.), *Aspect in grammatical variation*. Amsterdam: Benjamins, pp. 111–130.

Sharma, Devyani, and John Rickford. 2009. AAVE/Creole copula absence: A critique of the imperfect learning hypothesis. *Journal of Pidgin and Creole Languages* 24 (1): 53–90.

Sharma, Devyani, and Lavanya Sankaran. 2011. Cognitive and social forces in dialect shift: Gradual change in London Asian speech. *Language Variation and Change* 23: 399–428.

Sharma, Richa. 2010. *Phonetic realizations of vowels in Indian English*. MPhil diss., University of Delhi.

Shastri, S. V. 1992. Opaque and transparent features of Indian English. In G. Leitner (ed.), *New directions in English language corpora: Methodology, results, software developments*. New York: Mouton de Gruyter, pp. 263–275.

Shastri, S. V. 1996. Using computer corpora in the description of language with special reference to complementation in Indian English. In R. J. Baumgardner (ed.), *South Asian English: Structure, uses, and users*. Urbana: University of Illinois Press, pp. 70–81.

Shatz, Marilyn, and Sharon Wilcox. 1991. Constraints on the acquisition of English modals. In S. Gelman and J. Byrnes (eds.), *Perspectives on language and thought: Interrelations in development*. Cambridge: Cambridge University Press, pp. 319–353.

Shirai, Yasuhiro. 1991. *Primacy of aspect in language acquisition: Simplified input and prototype*. PhD diss., University of California, Los Angeles.

Shirai, Yasuhiro, and Atsuko Kurono. 1998. The acquisition of tense-aspect marking in Japanese as a second language. *Language Learning 48*: 245–279.

Sidnell, Jack. 1999. Gender and pronominal variation in an Indo-Guyanese creole-speaking community. *Language in Society 28*(3): 367–399.

Siebers, Lucia. 2007. *Investigating Black South African English: The case of Xhosa English.* PhD diss., University of Duisburg-Essen, Germany.

Siemund, Peter. 2013. *Varieties of English. A typological approach.* Cambridge: Cambridge University Press.

Silva-Corvalán, Carmen. 1994. *Language contact and change: Spanish in Los Angeles.* Oxford: Oxford University Press.

Silverstein, Michael. 2001. The limits of awareness. In A. Duranti (ed.), *Linguistic anthropology: A reader.* Malden, MA: Blackwell, pp. 382–401.

Simons, Gary F., and Charles D. Fennig, eds. 2018. *Ethnologue: Languages of the world.* 21st ed. Dallas: SIL International.

Singapore Census of Population. 2020. *Statistical release 1: Demographic characteristics, education, language and religion.* Singapore: Department of Statistics, Ministry of Trade and Industry, Republic of Singapore.

Singh, Rajendra. 1972. Syntactic interference: A case study. In D. Hays and D. Lance (eds.), *From soundstream to discourse.* Columbia: University of Missouri Press, pp. 214–223.

Singh, Rajendra. 1994. Indian English: Some conceptual issues. In R. K. Agnihotri and A. L. Khanna (eds.), *Second language acquisition.* Thousand Oaks, CA: Sage Publications, pp. 369–81.

Singh, Rajendra. 1996. *Lectures against sociolinguistics.* New York: Peter Lang.

Singh, Rajendra. 2007. The nature, structure, and status of Indian English. In R. Singh (ed.), *Annual Review of South Asian Languages and Linguistics.* Berlin: Mouton de Gruyter, pp. 33–46.

Singh, Rajendra. 2012. Reflections on Indian English and English in India. In R. K. Agnihotri and R. Singh (eds.), *Indian English: Towards a new paradigm.* Hyderabad, India: Orient Blackswan, pp. 15–46.

Singler, John. 1998. What's not new in AAVE. *American Speech 73* (3): 227–256.

Skinner, John. 1998. *The stepmother tongue: An introduction to new Anglophone fiction.* New York: St. Martin's Press.

Slabakova, Roumyana. 2008. *Meaning in the second language.* Berlin: Walter de Gruyter.

Smith, Jennifer, Mercedes Durham, and Liane Fortune. 2007. "Mam, my trousers is fa'indoon!": Community, caregiver, and child in the acquisition of variation in a Scottish dialect. *Language Variation and Change 19* (1): 63–99.

Smith, Neil, and Ianthi Maria Tsimpli. 1995. *The mind of a savant: Language learning and modularity.* Oxford: Blackwell.

Snell, Julia. 2013. Dialect, interaction and class positioning at school: From deficit to difference to repertoire. *Language and Education 27* (2): 110–128.

Snell, Rupert, and Simon Weightman. 2003. *Teach yourself Hindi.* London: Hodder and Stoughton.

Sorace, Anotenella. 2011. Pinning down the concept of "interface" in bilingualism. *Linguistic Approaches to Bilingualism 1*: 1–33.

Sorace, Anotenella. 2012. Pinning down the concept of "interface" in bilingualism: A reply to peer commentaries. *Linguistic Approaches to Bilingualism 2*: 209–216.

Sorace, Antonella, and Filiaci, Francesca. 2006. Anaphora resolution in near-native speakers of Italian. *Second Language Research 22*: 339–368.

Sorace, A., and Serratrice, L. 2009. Internal and external interfaces in bilingual language development: Beyond structural overlap. *International Journal of Bilingualism 13*: 1–16.

Sridhar, K. K. 1985. Sociolinguistics of non-native English. *Lingua 68*: 39–58.

Sridhar, K. K. 1991. Speech acts in an indigenised variety: Sociocultural values and language variation. In J. Cheshire (ed)., *English around the world*. Cambridge: Cambridge University Press, pp. 308–318.

Sridhar, Kamal K., and S. N. Sridhar .1986. Bridging the paradigm gap: Second-language acquisition theory and indigenized varieties of English. *World Englishes 5* (1): 3–14.

Sridhar, K. K., and S. N. Sridhar. 1992. Bridging the paradigm gap: Second-language acquisition theory and indigenized varieties of English. In B. Kachru (ed.), *The other tongue*. Urbana: University of Illinois Press, pp. 91–108.

Sridhar, S. N. 1990. *Kannada*. New York: Routledge.

Starr, Rebecca Lurie. 2019. Attitudes and exposure as predictors of -t/d deletion among local and expatriate children in Singapore. *Language Variation and Change 38* (4): 630–643.

Starr, Rebecca Lurie, and Brinda Balasubramaniam. 2019. Variation and change in English /r/ among Tamil Indian Singaporeans. *World Englishes 38* (4): 630–643.

Stassen, Leon. 1994. Typology versus mythology: The case of the zero-copula. *Nordic Journal of Linguistics 17*: 105–126.

Steel, Flora Annie. 1900. *Voices in the night*. Montana: Kessinger.

Stephany, Ursula. 1986. Modality. In P. Fletcher and M. Garman (eds.), *Language acquisition*. Cambridge: Cambridge University Press, pp. 375–400.

Sun, Chaofen. 2006. *Chinese: A linguistic introduction*. Cambridge: Cambridge University Press.

Svalberg, Agneta, and Hajah Fatimah binti Haji Awang Chuchu. 1998. Are English and Malay worlds apart? Typological distance and the learning of tense and aspect concepts. *International Journal of Applied Linguistics 8* (1): 27–60.

Szmrecsanyi, Benedikt. 2009. Typological parameters of intralingual variability: Grammatical analyticity versus syntheticity in varieties of English. *Language Variation and Change 21* (3): 319–353.

Szmrecsanyi, Benedikt, and Bernd Kortmann. 2009. Vernacular universals and anglo-versals in a typological perspective. In M. Filppula, J. Klemola, and H. Paulasto (eds.), *Vernacular universals and language contacts: Evidence from varieties of English and beyond*. London: Routledge, pp. 33–53.

Tagliamonte, Sali. 2002. Comparative sociolinguistics. In J. Chambers, P. Trudgill, and N. Schilling-Estes (eds.), *Handbook of language variation and change*. Oxford: Blackwell, pp. 729–763.

Tan, Angela. 2010. *Right* in Singapore English. *World Englishes 29* (2): 234–256.

Tan, Peter. 2012. English in Singapore. *International Journal of Language, Translation and Intercultural Communication 1* (1): 123–138.

Tan, Peter K. W., and Daniel K. H. Tan. 2008. Attitudes towards non-standard English in Singapore. *World Englishes 27* (3): 465–479.

Tarone, Elaine, and Betsy Parrish. 1988. Task-related variation in interlanguage: The case of articles. *Language Learning 38*: 21–45.

Thomason, Sarah G., and Terence Kaufman. 1988. *Language contact, creolization, and genetic linguistics*. Berkeley: University of California Press.

Tickoo, Makhan L. 1996. Fifty years of English in Singapore: All gains, (a) few losses? In J. A. Fishman, A. W. Conrad, and A. Rubal-Lopez (eds.), *Post-imperial English: Status change in former British and American colonies, 1940–1990*. Berlin: Mouton de Gruyter, pp. 431–456.

Tongue, Ray K. 1979. *The English of Singapore and Malaysia*. 2nd ed. Singapore: Eastern Universities Press.

Toribio, Almeida Jacqueline. 2004. Convergence as an optimization strategy in bilingual speech: Evidence from codeswitching. *Bilingualism: Language and Cognition* 7: 165–173.

Treffers-Daller, Jeanine. 1999. Borrowing and shift-induced interference: Contrasting patterns in French–Germanic contact in Brussels and Strasbourg. *Bilingualism: Language and Cognition 2* (1): 1–22.

Trenkic, Danijela. 2001. *Establishing the definiteness status of referents in dialogue in languages with and without articles. Working Papers in English and Applied Linguistics*, University of Cambridge.

Trenkic, Daniella. 2007. Variability in L2 article production: Beyond the representational deficit vs. processing constraints debate. *Second Language Research* 23: 289–327.

Trenkic, Daniella. 2009. Accounting for patterns of article omissions and substitutions in second language production In M. P. Garcia Mayo and R. Hawkins (eds.), *Second language acquisition of articles: Empirical findings and theoretical implications*. Amsterdam: Benjamins, pp. 115–143.

Trenkic, Danijela, and Nattama Pongpairoj. 2013. Referent salience affects second language article use. *Bilingualism: Language and Cognition 16* (1): 152–166.

Trousdale, Graeme. 2008. Constructions in grammaticalization and lexicalization: Evidence from the history of a composite predicate construction in English. In G. Trousdale and N. Gisborne (eds.), *Constructional approaches to English grammar*. Berlin: Mouton de Gruyter, pp. 33–67.

Trudgill, Peter. 1986. *Dialects in contact*. Oxford: Blackwell.

Trudgill, Peter. 2004. *New-dialect formation: The inevitability of colonial Englishes*. Edinburgh: Edinburgh University Press.

Trudgill, Peter, and Jean Hannah. 2008. *International English: A guide to varieties of Standard English*. 5th ed. Oxford: Oxford University Press.

Tsimpli, Ianthi Maria, and Maria Dimitrakopoulou. 2007. The Interpretability Hypothesis: evidence from wh-interrogatives in second language acquisition. *Second Language Research 23* (2): 215–242.

Tsimpli, I. M., Sorace, A., Heycock, C., and Filiaci, F. 2004. First language attrition and syntactic subjects: A study of Greek and Italian near-native speakers of English. *International Journal of Bilingualism 8*: 257–277.

Vaid, D. D. 1977. *Improve your English*. Delhi: Orient.

Vallduvi, Enric. 1992. *The informational component*. New York: Garland.

van Osch, Brechje, Aafke Hulk, Petra Sleeman, and Pablo Irizarri van Suchtelen. 2014. Gender agreement in interface contexts in the oral production of heritage speakers of Spanish in the Netherlands. *Linguistics in the Netherlands 31* (1): 93–106.

van Rooy, Bertus. 2006. The extension of the progressive aspect in Black South African English. *World Englishes 25* (1): 37–64.

van Rooy, Bertus. 2011. A principled distinction between error and conventionalized innovation in African Englishes. In J. Mukherjee and M. Hundt (eds.), *Exploring second-language varieties of English and learner Englishes: Bridging a paradigm gap*. Amsterdam: John Benjamins, pp. 189–208.

van Rooy, Bertus, and Caroline Piotrowska. 2015. The development of an extended time period meaning of the progressive in Black South African English. In P. Collins (ed.), *Grammatical change in English world-wide*. Amsterdam: Benjamins, pp. 465–484.

van Rooy, Bertus, Lize Terblanche, Christoph Haase, and Josef J. Schmied. 2010. Register differentiation in East African English: A multidimensional study. *English World-Wide 31* (3): 311–349.

Vendler, Zeno. 1967. Verbs and time. In Z. Vendler (ed.), *Linguistics in philosophy*. Ithaca, NY: Cornell University Press, pp. 97–121.

Verkuyl, Henk J. 1972. *On the compositional nature of the aspects*. Dordrecht, the Netherlands: Springer.

Vohra, Paromita. 2015. "Falling in and out of love with Hinglish: Advertising and the domestication of Hinglish." Paper presented at Workshop on Hinglish: Social and Cultural Dimensions of Hindi-English Bilingualism in Contemporary India, School of Oriental and African Studies, London, May 28, 2015.

Wahid, Ridwan. 2009. *The use of articles in inner and outer circle varieties of English: A comparative corpus-based study*. PhD diss., University of New South Wales, Sydney, Australia.

Wee, Lionel. 1998. The lexicon of Singapore English. In J. Foley et al. (eds.), *English in new cultural contexts: Reflections from Singapore*. Singapore: Oxford University Press, pp. 175–200.

Wee, Lionel. 2003. The birth of a particle: *Know* in Colloquial Singapore English. *World Englishes 22* (1): 5–13.

Wee, Lionel. 2004. Reduplication and discourse particles. In L. Lim (ed.), *Singapore English: A grammatical description*. Amsterdam: Benjamins, pp. 105–126.

Wee, Lionel. 2005. Intra-language discrimination and linguistic human rights: The case of Singlish. *Applied Linguistics 26*: 48–69.

Wee, Lionel. 2006. The semiotics of language ideologies in Singapore. *Journal of Sociolinguistics 10*: 344–361.

Wee, Lionel. 2010. The particle *ya* in Colloquial Singapore English. *World Englishes 29* (1): 45–58.

Wee, Lionel. 2014. Linguistic chutzpah and the Speak Good Singlish movement. *World Englishes 33* (1): 85–99.

Wee, Lionel. 2018. *The Singlish controversy: Language, culture and identity in a globalizing world*. Cambridge: Cambridge University Press.

Wee, Lionel, and Umberto Ansaldo. 2004. Nouns and noun phrases. In L. Lim (ed.), *Singapore English: A grammatical description*. Amsterdam: Benjamins, pp. 57–74.

Wee, Lionel, Robbie B. H. Goh, and Lisa Lim, eds. 2013. *The politics of English: South Asia, Southeast Asia, and the Asia Pacific*. Amsterdam: John Benjamins.

Weinreich, Uriel. 1953. *Languages in contact: Findings and problems*. New York: Linguistic Circle of New York.

Weinreich, Uriel, William Labov, and Marvin Herzog. 1968. Empirical foundations for a theory of language change. In W. Lehmann and Y. Malkiel (eds.), *Directions for historical linguistics: A symposium*. Austin: University of Texas Press, pp. 95–195.

Wells, J. C. 1982. *Accents of English, volume 1: An introduction*. Cambridge: Cambridge University Press.

Wexler, K., and Manzini, R. 1987. Parameters and learnability in binding theory. In T. Roeper and E. Williams (eds.), *Parameter setting*. Dordrecht, the Netherlands: Reidel, pp. 41–76.

White, Lydia. 1989. *Universal grammar and second language acquisition*. Amsterdam: John Benjamins.

Widdowson, H. G. 1979. *Explorations in applied linguistics*. Oxford: Oxford University Press.

Williams, Jessica. 1987. Non-native varieties of English: A special case of language acquisition. *English World-Wide 8*: 161–199.

Wiltshire, Caroline. 2014. New Englishes and the emergence of the unmarked. In E. Green and C. Meyer (eds.), *The variability of current world Englishes*. Berlin: Mouton de Gruyter, pp. 13–40.

Wiltshire, Caroline, and James Harnsberger. 2006. The influence of Gujarati and Tamil L1s on Indian English: A preliminary study. *World Englishes 25*(1): 91–104.

Wiltshire, Caroline, and Russell Moon. 2003. Phonetic stress in Indian English vs. American English. *World Englishes 22* (3): 291–303.

Winford, Donald. 2003. *An introduction to contact linguistics*. Oxford: Blackwell.

Winford, Donald. 2009. The interplay of "universals" and contact-induced change in the emergence of New Englishes. In M. Filppula, J. Klemola, and H. Paulasto (eds.), *Vernacular universals and language contacts: Evidence from varieties of English and beyond*. London: Routledge, pp. 206–230.

Wolfram, Walt. 1969. *A sociolinguistic description of Detroit Negro speech*. Washington, DC: Center for Applied Linguistics.

Wolfram, Walt. 1985. Variability in tense marking: A case for the obvious. *Language Learning 35*: 229–253.

Wolfram, Walt, and Erik R. Thomas. 2002. *The development of African American English*. Oxford: Blackwell.

Wong, Bee Eng, and Soh Theng Quek. 2007. Acquisition of the English definite article by Chinese and Malay ESL learners. *Electronic Journal of Foreign Language Teaching 4* (2): 210–234.

Wong, Jock. 2004. The pragmatic particles of Singapore English: A semantic and cultural interpretation. *Journal of Pragmatics 36*: 739–793.

Wong, Jock. 2014. *The culture of Singapore English*. Cambridge: Cambridge University Press.

Xiao, Richard. 2009. Multidimensional analysis and the study of world Englishes. *World Englishes 28* (4): 421–450.

Yao, Xinyue. 2016. Cleft constructions in Hong Kong English. *English World-Wide 37* (2): 197–220.

Yao, Xinyue, and Peter Collins. 2012. The present perfect in world Englishes. *World Englishes 31* (3): 386–403.

Yip, Po-Ching, and Don Rimmington. 2004. *Chinese: A comprehensive grammar*. London: Routledge.

Yip, Virginia, and Stephen Matthews. 2007. *The bilingual child: Early development and language contact*. Cambridge: Cambridge University Press.

Young, R. 1996. Form-function relations in articles in English interlanguage. In R. Bayley and D. Preston (eds.), *Second language acquisition and linguistic variation*. Amsterdam: John Benjamins, pp. 135–175.

Yule, Henry, and A. C. Burnell. 1994 [1886]. *Hobson-Jobson: Glossary of colloquial Anglo-Indian words and phrases*. Kent, UK: Linguasia.

Zastoupil, L., and M. Moir, eds. 1999. *The great Indian education debate: Documents relating to the Orientalist-Anglicist controversy, 1781–1843*. London: Curzon Press.

Zentella, Ana Celia. 1997. *Growing up bilingual: Puerto Rican children in New York*. Oxford: Blackwell.

Ziegeler, Debra. 1996. Diachronic factors in the grammaticalization of counterfactual implicatures in Singaporean English. *Language Sciences 17* (4): 305–328.

Ziegeler, Debra. 2015. *Converging grammars: Constructions in Singapore English.* Berlin: Mouton de Gruyter.

Zipp, Lena, and Volker Dellwo. 2012. "The sociophonetics of prosodic parameters and identity construction in the London Indian diaspora." Paper presented at Sociolinguistics Symposium 19, Berlin, Germany, August 23.

# INDEX

*For the benefit of digital users, indexed terms that span two pages (e.g., 52–53) may, on occasion, appear on only one of those pages.*
Tables are indicated by t following the page number

accent, 135, 137–42, 146–50, 229, 231
accommodation, 48, 136–37, 143, 144
acquisition-like factors, 73–74. *See also*
    child language acquisition; second
    language acquisition (SLA)
acrolects, 31, 59, 60, 75, 120, 162, 169,
    172, 227
actuation question, 6
adjectives, and article omission, 102
adverbials, 123–24, 184, 185
advertising, 234
African-American English, 46, 111, 151,
    190, 209, 210, 213
age, as social factor in IndE usage
    cline, 73
agentive exploitation, 104
agglutinative substrates, 163–64
Agha, Asif, 225
Agnihotri, Rama Kant, 39, 63, 102, 139,
    150, 215, 217
Allen, Charles, 27, 28
*already*, 184, 223
Alsagoff, Lubna, 160, 166, 167, 185,
    223, 224–25
*also*, 223
American English, 258n.2
    accent as identity, 139–42
    article omission, 85
    attitudinal factors, 143–46
    contact with Indian English, 135,
        137, 217
    corpora, 13
    datasets, 11

discourse pragmatics, 38
loanwords, 218
modals, 131
multilingual style repertoires, 230
past perfect, 126
prestige, 34
rhoticity, 34, 36, 39, 140
style variation, 214
    as target norm for Indian English, 235
    as target norm for Singapore
        English, 236
analogy, 44
anchored new information, 90
Andersen, Roger, 111, 116–18, 184, 192
Andreasson, Anne-Marie, 136
Anglicism, 21, 22, 23, 29
Anglo-Indian communities, 20–21, 25
Anglo-Indian English, 25, 36, 47–48, 50,
    163, 211
Angloversals, 174–75, 180, 189–90,
    195, 207
Ansaldo, Umberto, 14, 158, 177, 179,
    180–81, 192, 195
Anstey, Frank, 27
anteriority, 108–9
archaisms, 165, 214, 217
areal convergence, 195
argument omission, 41
Ariel, Mira, 89–90
articles
    article insertion, 85–86
    Indian English article omission, 65,
        69, 70–71, 79–105

articles (*cont.*)
  Interface Hypothesis, 206–7
  proficency, 198
  Singapore English article
    omission, 176–79
  Subset Principle, 204
  universals, 173, 176–80
aspect, 107, 110, 116–18, 181–83. *See
  also* imperfective aspect; perfective
  aspect; progressive
aspiration, 139–42
attitudinal change, 212–40, 245
audio recordings, 11
Austronesian languages, 163–
  64, 165–67
auxiliaries, 37
Ayoun, Dalila, 201

Baba Malay, 159, 160, 164
Babas/Peranakan Chinese, 159, 163
Babu English, 26, 27, 38, 47–48, 50–
  51, 156
Baker, Philip, 61
Baker, Wendy, 150
balanced bilingualism, 11–12, 34, 35, 38,
  39, 192, 198, 205
Balasubramanian, Chandrika, 39–40, 44,
  47, 50, 102, 120, 123–24, 130–31,
  187, 215–16
Bamgbose, Ayo, 5, 6, 72
Bandra district, Mumbai, 26
Bao, Zhiming, 6, 75, 123, 131, 132, 136,
  160, 162, 166, 167, 175, 184, 185,
  186, 187, 192, 195, 209, 223, 236,
  239, 246, 247–48
basilects, 46, 75, 162, 164, 169, 170,
  180, 191, 227, 229
BATH lexical set, 36, 38, 44, 165
Bautista, Maria Lourdes, 168
Bazaar Malay, 159, 160, 164
*bearer*, 21
Bearer English, 21
*be* deletion, 173, 190–92, 198–99, 210
Bengali, 39, 157–58
Bentinck, Lord, 23, 24
Bernaisch, Tobias, 235, 239
Berwick, R. C., 201
Bhatia, V. K., 150
Bhatt, Rakesh, 34, 42, 46, 110, 173–74,
  194, 212

Biber, Douglas, 123–24
Bickerton, Derek, 84, 94, 95, 103,
  119, 183
bilingual clines, 4, 10, 62, 213
bilingual continua, 9, 62, 74–78, 222–
  24, 248
bilingualism and early colonial contact in
  India, 21
Binnick, Robert, 108–9
Black South African English, 58–59
Blom, Jan-Petter, 225
Bombay Hinglish, 34
boundedness, 108
British English
  article omission, 85
  British working class dialects, 28
  copulas, 194
  corpora, 13
  divergence from, 216–17
  elements of 19th century British
    dialects in Indian English, 25
  loanwords, 218
  modals, 131
  past perfect, 126
  prestige, 34
  retention in Indian English, 35–38
  and Singapore English, 158, 163, 165
  style variation, 214
  Subset Principle, 203
  as target for convergence, 48
  as target norm for Indian English, 64–
    65, 136, 149, 234–35
  upper class Indian varieties, 216
  usage cline, 73–74
British India, history of, 20–31
British Raj period, 21–29
"brokenness," 212
Brown, Adam, 160
Brown, Penelope, 128
Brown, Roger, 80
Brown Corpus, 13, 112, 125, 214
bureaucratic English, 26, 37, 217
Burnell, A. C., 27–28
Burt, Marina K., 69
Butler English, 21, 27, 35, 47–48, 49,
  50–51, 249
Bybee, Joan, 108–9, 174, 189

California speaker data, 11, 137–39
calques, 39–40, 167

[290]  *Index*

Canagarajah, Suresh, 4
Cannadine, David, 27, 48
Cantonese, 14–15, 160, 161, 172–73, 182
Catholic church, 26
Cavallaro, Francesco, 239
Chambers, Jack, 173–74
Chand, Vineeta, 36, 39, 44, 60, 139–40, 150, 213, 216, 233, 234
Charter Act (1813), 23
Chaudhary, Rakesh, 219
Chaudron, Craig, 84, 85
"Chee-Chee" English, 25
child language acquisition, 128, 131, 192, 202, 246
Chinese-medium education, 159
Chinniah, Y. A., 258–59n.10
Christianity, 22, 25–26, 50, 156, 157
civil service English in India, 24
clausal aspect, 183
clausal topicality, 87
clause position, 87, 91
Clements, J. Clancy, 213
clerical English, 26
cline of bilingualism, 4, 10, 62, 213
cliticized auxiliaries, 37
clusters of varieties, 47
co-construction in creoles, 61
code-switching, 45, 218–19, 222, 225–27
codification, 246
Coelho, Gail, 25, 36
coinage, 45, 167
Collins, Peter, 120, 124, 131
Colloquial Singapore English (CSE), 158–59, 180, 222, 223, 224–25, 229, 236, 238
colonialism
    archaisms, 165
    British Raj period, 21–29, 36
    early colonial contact in India, 20–21
    shared past of India and Singapore, 227, 241
    Singapore, 160, 164, 169
"colonial lag," 35–36, 37
comparative analysis methods, 172–73
complementizer phrases, 90
completion, marking of, 108
computational methods, 60
Comrie, Bernard, 107, 108–9, 121–23

conjunctions (*and that too*), 37
conservatism, 37, 38, 77, 136, 150, 151, 159, 214–15, 249, 250–51
consonant cluster simplification, 185
contrastive analysis methods, 8, 57
convent schools, 24, 25
conversational genre, 85
copulas
    comparative studies Indian and Singaporean English, 172, 190–92
    copula omission, 65, 69, 190, 210
    Creole studies, 190
    Indian English, 65, 69
    pidginized English, 21
    proficency, 198
    Singapore English, 186
Corder, S. P., 57
Corne, Chris, 103
Cornwallis, Charles, 22
corpus methods, 9, 12–13, 14
corpus studies, 59–60, 113
"correctness," 55, 148–49, 215, 231–35, 246, 250–51
Council for Secondary Education, 32–33
covert prestige, 25, 75, 136, 224, 239
Cowie, Claire, 44, 73, 139–40, 230
Creole continua, 74–75
Creole studies, 8–9, 10, 46, 62, 63, 103, 159, 190
creolization, 61–62, 162
Croft, William, 4–5
cultural orientation model, 223
cultural variation in lexicon, 40

Dahl, Östen, 109
Dasgupta, Probal, 34, 47, 52
datasets
    Indian English, 10–13
    Singapore English, 14–15
Davydova, Julia, 175, 200–1
de-bleaching, 45
DeCamp, David, 75
decreolization, 46
deficit versus dialect models, 4, 5, 242
definite articles. *See also* articles
    comparative studies Indian and Singaporean English, 177
    Indian English, 65, 69, 80, 91, 92, 100–1
    Interface Hypothesis, 207
    universals, 179

*Index* [291]

definiteness, 80, 81, 83, 84, 86
defocusing, 48–49, 51
degrees of nativeness, 55
deixis, 95, 108–9
DeKeyser, Robert, 210
Deleuze, Gilles, 19, 48
Delhi datasets, 11–12
Delhi Hinglish, 34
Dellwo, Volker, 150
demonstratives, 42
Deo, Ashwini, 106, 112, 115, 116–
    18, 258n.2
Deterding, David, 166, 185, 192,
    198, 209
determiners, 85–86, 98, 179
Deuber, Dagmar, 131, 192–93,
    260n.10
diachronic studies, 200
dialect confidence, 55
dialect continua, 74–77
dialect focusing, 5
dialect identity, 135–52, 170, 227,
    243, 246
differentiation phase (Phase 5), 26, 50,
    158–59, 169, 212–13
"difficulty" metrics, 208
diglossia, 59, 75, 169, 222–24, 228
discourse disambiguation, 96
discourse-driven restructuring, 104–5
discourse familiarity, 82–83, 87
discourse markers, 43, 219
discourse organization universals, 180
discourse particles, 167, 225
discourse pragmatics, 37–38, 42–43
discourse prominence, shift to, 80,
    91, 104
discourse recoverability, 85
discourse status, 84–85, 94–105
distance, measures of, 89–90
distributive meaning, 42
Dixon, R. M. W., 3
Domange, Raphael, 36, 44, 60, 73,
    213, 216
domestic staff, 21, 27
Domínguez, Laura, 208–9
domino effects, 209
Dowty, David, 113–14
Dravidian languages
    articles, 81
    aspect, 258n.1

demonstratives, 42
focus marking, 43
morphological richness, 157
perfect tense, 109
phonetics and phonology, 39
politics in India, 32
"sprachbunds," 38
DRESS lexical sets, 44
Dulay, Heidi C., 69
dynamic learners, 211
Dynamic Model, 4, 56, 248. *See also*
    differentiation phase (Phase 5);
    endonormative stabilization (Phase
    4); Schneider, Edgar

East India Trading Company, 20, 21, 22,
    159, 162, 214
Eckert, Penelope, 62
education. *See also* English-medium
    education; Hindi-medium
    education; mother tongue
    education
    convent schools, 24, 25
    education levels as social factor in
        usage cline, 72
    English in Singapore, 161
    missionary schools, 20
    modes of acquisition, 162
    mother tongue education, 29, 32–33
    three-language formula in
        India, 32–33
Eersel, Christian, 151
Eggington, William, 150
elaborate written styles, 37–38
elicitation studies, 8–9, 11
elites, 46–47, 49, 50, 59, 132, 163
ellipsis, 90
endonormative stabilization (Phase 4)
    Indian English, 31, 50, 60
    Indian English dialect identity, 135,
        150, 151
    learner input, 199–201
    Singapore English, 169, 236, 239
    style variation, 212–13, 215–
        16, 231–32
English
    modals, 127–28
    pidginized English, 21, 27, 47–48,
        162, 169, 249
    style range, 227–29

[292]   *Index*

tense, modality and aspect, 107–10, 181–83
English as a Second Language (ESL), 56, 58, 213, 234
English in India
  banishment of, 32
  British Raj period, 21–29
  comparative history with Singaporean English, 156–58
  constitution, 30–31
  current number of speakers, 34
  early colonial contact, 20
  independence movement, 29–31
  informal genres, 35
  official status languages, 31
  prestige, 34
English in Singapore, 158–64
English-medium education
  India generally, 20–21, 156, 157
  India post-independence, 31, 33
  India British Raj period, 23–24
  Singapore, 159, 162, 236
  in universities, 33
English teaching industry, 234
enregistered styles, 26, 50–51, 76–77, 218–19, 224, 225
equatives, 90
error analysis methods, 8, 57
evangelical movement, 22, 23
Evans, Stephen, 50, 170, 231, 248
Event X, 50, 167, 241
existential *got*, 225

factives, 87
familiarity, 84–85, 94–99, 103
feature pervasiveness, 175–76
feedback loops, 245–46
Ferguson, Charles A., 222
Filiaci, Francesca, 205
Filppula, Markku, 6, 44, 175, 194–95, 259n.1
Fishman, Joshua, 59
fixed constructions, 90, 96
florid phrasings, 38
focus marking, 43, 65, 71–72, 167, 231–32
Fodor, Janet D., 80
Foley, Joseph A., 61, 161, 162, 163–64, 213, 236
Fong, Vivienne, 167, 185

FORCE lexical set, 25, 36
"foreigner talk," 222
formal registers, 214–15, 216, 218
fossilized variation, 76
Foucault, Michel, 10, 19
founder effects, 25–26, 44, 49, 157, 163
French learners and the Subset Principle, 202
French TAM system, 109, 111, 121, 123, 124
"frontier languages," 27–28
fronting of topicalized constitutents, 40
Fuchs, Robert, 37, 166, 189–90
Full Transfer/ Full Access, 210
function transfer, 92
future tense, 127, 129, 131

Gal, Susan, 63
Gandhi, Mahatma, 29, 30
Gargesh, Ravinder, 35, 76
gender, as social factor in IndE usage cline, 73
genericity, 87, 94, 177
George, Stephen, 102, 180, 207
Gil, David, 179
givenness, degrees of, 85, 88, 89, 95–98, 99, 103
Givón, Talmy, 95, 103, 257n.9
glide epenthesis, 39
Goa/Karanataka, 25–26
Goldvarb, 99, 137
Gonzalez, Andrew, 168
*got*, 166
grammar acquisition, 137–39
grammar awareness, 146–48
Grammar of Spoken Singapore English corpus (GSSEC), 14, 180
grammaticalization, 95, 109, 189
grammatical universals, 171–96
Grant, Charles, 22
Guattari, Félix, 19, 48
Gujarati, 30, 108
Gumperz, John, 225
Gupta, Anthea Fraser, 75, 159, 160–61, 163, 193, 223
Gut, Ulrike, 184, 185, 189–90, 209

habitual meaning, 114, 116, 118, 119, 120, 129, 185, 192–93
Hakka, 160

*Index* [293]

Halliday, Michael A. K., 80
hartal, 31
Hastings, Warren, 22
*having*, 187–88
Hawkins, John, 80, 95, 257n.5
h-dropping, 25, 36
Hickey, Raymond, 49, 75, 216, 217
Hicks, Glyn, 208–9
Hilbert, Michaela, 42, 58, 260n.4
Hindi
  argument omission, 41
  articles, 80–81
  discourse markers, 43
  focus marking, 43
  and identity, 170
  imperative suffix *-o*, 29, 37
  imperfective aspect, 189
  lingua franca, 32, 35, 157–58
  loans into Indian English, 29
  newspaper production, 33–34
  number of speakers, 34
  official status languages, 31
  opposition to use of, 32
  past tense, 181
  perfective aspect, 116–18
  progressive, 110–11, 118–20, 121–23
  question formation, 42
  rhoticity, 39
  role in contemporary India, 31
  semantic transfer, 168
  settler varieties of Indian English, 27–28
  tag questions, 43
  tense, modality and aspect, 107–10
  use of Hindi as "other" code, 29
  vernacularization of Indian English forms, 216
Hindi-medium education, 31, 32–33
Hindi speakers (participant details), 11–12
*Hindu, The*, 31
Hinglish, 34, 45, 218–19, 222, 234, 261n.3
Hiramoto, Mie, 166
Hirson, A., 39
historical linguistics, 6, 19–51, 197, 206
Ho, Mian Lian, 8–9, 14, 57, 63, 160, 162, 180–81, 185, 186, 188, 191, 192, 193, 227, 228, 238

Ho Chee Lick, 166, 167, 224
Hohenthal, Annika, 235
Hokkein, 14–15, 159, 160, 164, 172–73, 182, 192–93
Hong Huaqing, 75, 223
Hong Kong English, 50, 231
honorific markers, 38, 131–32
Hoover, Mary, 151
Hosali, Priya, 21, 26
Housen, Alex, 200–1
Huebner, Thomas, 84, 85–86
Hum Chong Kai, Darren, 239
Hundt, Marianne, 35–36, 102, 121–23, 150, 180, 187, 199–200, 207
Hunter Commission (1883), 24
hypercorrection, 44, 131, 228, 235

ICAME (International Computer Archive of Medieval and Modern English), 258n.3
ICE (International Corpus of English), 9
ICE-India, 13, 14, 120, 187
ICE-Singapore, 14, 172, 178–79, 180, 187, 198, 225, 260n.10
identifiability, 95
identity
  dialect identity, 135–52, 170, 227, 243, 246
  identity shift, 76, 230, 245, 249
  identity work, 249
  implications for theory, 248
  multilingual style repertoires, 230
ideologies of New Englishes, 2, 3–5, 21, 22, 72, 136, 230–39, 245, 250
idiomatic constructions, 45, 165, 168
imperative suffix *-o*, 29, 37
imperfective aspect
  comparative studies Indian and Singaporean English, 181–82, 183–84, 185–90
  Indian English, 107–10, 113–14, 118, 121, 132–34
  Subset Principle, 203
implication scaling, 8–9, 10, 62–78, 134, 213
incipient dialect confidence, 231–35
indefinite articles, 65, 69, 86, 91, 92, 93–94, 96, 100–1. *See also* articles
independence movement, 29–31

[294]  *Index*

independent innovations, 167–68
indexicality, 223, 236
Indian Constitution, 30–31
Indian English
  acceptance of, 136
  article omission, 79–105
  as cluster of varieties, 47
  common features, 35–46
  comparative history with Singaporean
    English, 155–70
  comparative studies Indian and
    Singaporean English, 227–39
  conservatism, 37, 38, 77, 136, 150,
    151, 159, 214–15, 249, 250–51
  "correctness," 55, 148–49, 215, 231–
    35, 246, 250–51
  datasets, 10–13
  as "decreasingly imperfect," 46–49
  influence on Singapore English, 163
  public understanding, implications
    for, 250
  style variation, 213–22
  Subset Principle, 201–5
  supraregionalization, 215–19
  verbal system, 106–34
  vernacularization, 215–19
"Indianization," 21
Indian Mutiny (1857), 20, 21
indigenization
  Indian English, 35, 40, 44–46, 136,
    217, 222, 234
  lexical indigenization, 167, 217
  Singapore English, 167
individual cognition, 244
Indo-Aryan languages
  articles, 81, 99, 177
  aspect, 107–8
  copula omission, 191
  modals, 110, 130, 133
  morphological richness, 157
  Orientalism, 22
  past perfect, 123–27
  perfective aspect, 116, 195
  phonetics and phonology, 38
  positional marking of discourse
    familiarity, 82–83
  semantic transfer, 111
  specificity marking, 83
  "sprachbunds," 38
inferable new information, 90, 98

informal registers, 96, 162. *See also* style
  variation
information structure, 41, 81, 211
Ingham, Richard, 206
input, role of, 197
input demand, 200, 204, 211, 244
intensity of contact, 120
Interface Hypothesis, 200, 205–7
intergenerational transmission, 245
interlanguage, 57
intermarriage, 20–21, 25
international intelligibility, 234
interrogative inversion, 42, 58
invariant tags, 42
Ionin, Tania, 84, 174
Irish English, 37, 75, 246
irrealis, 90, 127–28, 129
IT industry, 33

Jamaican Creole, 75
Jarvis, Scott, 85, 103, 105
Jenkins, Jennifer, 173–74
Jones, William, 22

Kachru, Braj, 4, 8, 10, 21, 32, 39–40, 50,
  57, 59, 62, 74–75, 150, 151, 213,
  234, 238
Kachru, Yamuna, 59, 95, 131–32
Kannada, 33, 257n.4
Karnataka state, 33
Kaufman, Terence, 59, 61, 248–49
*keep*, 168
*kena* passive, 167
Khanna, A. L., 63, 102, 139
Kher, B. G., 32
Khilnani, Sunil, 30–31
Kitchen English, 21
Klecha, Peter, 131
Klein, Flora, 103
*know*, 167
*knowing*, 187–88
Koch, Christopher, 235, 239
Kolhapur Corpus of Indian English, 13,
  112, 125, 214
Konkani, 25–26
Kortmann, Bernd, 6, 44, 58–59, 173–75,
  200–1, 207, 209
Krishnaswamy, Subashree, 40, 45,
  219, 229
Kurzon, Dennis, 25–26

*Index* [295]

L1 (child) language acquisition, 128, 131, 192, 202, 246
L1 interference, 77
Labov, William, 146, 147, 220, 228
Lado, R., 57
Lambrecht, Knud, 89–90
Lancaster-Oslo/ Bergen (LOB) Corpus, 13, 112, 125, 214
Lange, Claudia, 41, 43, 50, 80, 82, 91, 104, 180, 195, 211, 247–48
language contact studies, 9, 61–62, 136–37, 248–49
language evolution, 155
language policies, 158, 164, 168–70
language riots, 32
language shift, 34, 49, 56, 156, 161, 162, 249
languages in contemporary India, 31–35
language transfer. *See also* substrate influences; transfer from Indian languages
  Indian English, 38–43
  historical language transfer, 57
  methods, 8
Larrañaga, P., 202
late L2 acquisition features, 71
Latinizations, 38
laws, English as language of, 31
learner features, 69–70, 72
learner grammars, 204
learner input, 190, 197
lectal continua, 223
Lee, Nala, 166
Lee, Tong King, 239
Lefebvre, Claire, 121
Leimgruber, Jakob, 14, 75, 161, 162, 168, 223, 225
Leitner, Gerhard, 123
Le Page, Robert, 5, 47
Levinson, Stephen, 128
Lewis, Ivor, 27–28
lexical aspect, 114, 115, 116–18, 258n.2
lexical indigenization, 167, 217
lexical innovations/coinages, 45, 167
lexical retentions from British English to Indian English, 36
lexical semantics
  article omission, 90
  progressivity, 120
lexical transfer principles, 179, 217

Lim, Lisa, 14, 159, 160–61, 162, 163–64, 165, 167, 180–81, 213, 236, 239
limited style ranges, 220–22
lingua francas
  Baba Malay, 159, 164
  Bazaar Malay, 160, 164
  English in India, 157–58
  English in Singapore, 160, 161, 164
  Hindi, 32, 35, 157–58
  Hokkein, 159, 164
  other Indian languages, 157–58
  Singapore, 160
linguistic convergence, 38, 44, 48, 53, 54
linguistic ecologies, 10, 56, 131–32, 155, 160, 168–70, 244–45
linguistic schizophrenia, 151
literature in Indian English, 218
Li Wei, 63
loan translations/calques, 39–40, 167
loanwords, 29, 31, 39–40, 167, 218
locatives, 90
Low, Ee Ling, 160
Lowenberg, Peter, 45
Lunkenheimer, Kerstin, 175–76, 209
l-velarization, 139–42

Macaulay, Thomas Babington, 23, 29, 32
macrosocietal change, 248
Maher, James Reginald, 157
Malay
  agglutinative substrates, 163–64
  article use, 176–77
  colonialism in Singapore, 159
  copulas, 191
  linguistic ecologies, 160
  loanwords, 167
  official status languages, 161
  progressive, 188
  substrate influences, 14–15, 172–73, 189
  tense, modality and aspect, 182, 184
Malayalam, 39
Mandarin
  article use, 176–77, 179
  colonialism in Singapore, 160
  copulas, 190
  language contact studies, 172–73
  lingua franca, 164
  modals, 192–93
  past tense, 181

semantic transfer, 168
shift to, 160, 161, 238
Singapore Mandarin, 14–15
Marckwardt, Albert, 35–36
Masica, Colin P., 108
mass/count distinctions, 45, 168
matched-guise studies, 239
Matras, Yaron, 43, 247–48
Maxwell, Olga, 44, 216
Mazzie, Claudia, 87, 95, 103
McMahon, April, 6, 197
media and television, 234. *See also* newspapers
medium for interethnic communication (MIC), 61
medium of instruction. *See also* English-medium education
  Chinese-medium education, 159
  India post-independence, 31
  Hindi-medium education, 31, 32–33
  mother tongue education, 29, 32–33
  universities, 33
  vernacular-medium education, 29, 32–33
Mehboob, A., 34
Mehrotra, Arvind Krishna, 30–31
Mehrotra, Raja Ram, 29, 31, 33–34, 38
Meriläinen, Lea, 199–200
mesolects, 14, 172, 177, 180
Mesthrie, Rajend, 8–9, 46, 58–59, 84, 173–74, 191, 194, 212
metalinguistic awareness, 146–48
metalinguistic commentaries, 145, 148–50, 231–35
metaphorical code-switching, 225
metapragmatic commentary, 231, 247
methods, 8–10, 52, 55–62, 247
Meyerhoff, Miriam, 217
middle classes, 26, 27, 49, 216, 228
migration, 157, 159, 163, 170
military language, 20
*Minute on Indian Education* (Macaulay), 23, 29, 30, 32
Mishra, Arpita, 96
missionaries, 20
Mithun, Marianne, 91
mixed methods, 247
modals
  comparative studies Indian and Singaporean English, 192–94

Indian English, 65, 71–72, 110, 111, 115, 127–32
  proficency, 198
  universals, 173
Moir, M., 22, 23–24
monolingual dialect birth, 249
monopthongization, 141
mother tongue education, 29, 32–33
Mufwene, Salikoko, 25, 46, 61, 155
Mukherjee, Joybrato, 50, 55, 77, 102, 136, 151, 199–200, 215–16, 219, 234, 246
multilingual hierarchies, 31
multilingual repertoires, 11, 228, 229–30, 250
multiple genealogies, 10
multivariate analysis, 10, 63, 98–99, 116
music, 40

National Swadeshi Movement, 29
native dialect variation, 59–61
nativeness, 5, 53–55
native targets, 57, 59
nativization, 26, 136, 212, 213, 230, 236, 243
naturalistic speech data, 11, 85, 112, 247
Nayak, Shrishti, 43, 71–72, 231–32
Nehru, Jawaharlal, 30
Newbrook, Mark, 161, 258–59n.10
New Englishes, use of term, 255n.2
Newman, Michael, 63, 75
newness of referent, 84–85, 95–98
newspapers, 33–34, 35, 217
Ng, Bee Chin, 239
Ng, E-Ching, 160
Niedzielski, Nancy, 217
nominalizations, 37
nonrhoticity, 25, 36, 39, 139, 165, 216
NORTH lexical set, 25, 36
noun phrase omission, 166
noun reduplication, 21
null copulas, 21, 65, 69
null definite articles, 65, 69. *See also* articles; definite articles
null indefinite articles, 65, 69. *See also* articles; indefinite articles

official status languages
  India, 31, 156, 158
  Singapore, 161, 164

*Index* [297]

*one*, 81, 83, 92, 166, 176–77
*only*, 43, 65, 71–72, 167, 231–32
Orientalism, 21, 22, 23–24
overgeneralizations/overextensions,
110–11, 118, 119, 128, 130, 131,
186, 188, 193

Paikeday, Thomas, 55
Pakir, Anne, 75, 151, 223
Pande, Anna, 230
Pandharipande, Rajeshwari, 131–32
Parker, Kate, 84, 85
Parkvall, Mikael, 61–62
Parrish, Betsy, 85–86
Parshad, Rana D., 218–19
participant details, 11, 12*t*, 13*t*
Partition of Bengal, 20
Parviainen, Hanna, 43, 163
passive voice, 37, 167
past perfect, 13, 108–9, 111,
115, 123–27
past tense
comparative studies Indian and
Singaporean English, 172, 180–85
Indian English, 65, 69, 111, 115, 116–
18, 123
input, 209
omission, 173, 183–85
proficency, 198
Subset Principle, 203
universals, 173
Pathak, Maulik, 34
Paulasto, Heli, 120, 187, 189–90,
199–200
pedagogical/corrective stances on New
Englishes, 57. *See also* "correctness"
Pennycook, Alastair, 4, 22, 23–24
Peranakan Chinese, 159, 163
Peranakan English, 165
perception experiments, 231–32
Perdue, Clive, 103
perfective aspect, 107–10, 111, 113–14,
123–27, 132–34, 181, 182, 183–
84, 203
perfect tense, 108–9. *See also* past
perfect
personal factors in dialect contact, 143–
46, 227
pervasive features, 175–76
Phillipson, Robert, 34

phonetics and phonology. *See also*
rhoticity
[oː/ ɔː] lexical distinction, 25
accent, 135, 137–42, 146–50,
229, 231
accent as identity, 139–42
Colloquial Singapore English, 224–25
consonant cluster simplification, 185
morphological change, 185
past tense omission, 210
retention of British English features in
Indian English, 36
Singapore English, 163, 165, 166
transfer from Indian languages, 38–39
phonological awareness, 146–48
phonotactic transfer from Indian
languages, 38
phrasal verbs, 44
pidginized English, 21, 27, 47–48, 162,
169, 249
pidgin studies, 61
Platt, John, 8–9, 14, 56, 57, 63, 79, 92,
160, 162, 172, 180–81, 186, 188,
190, 191, 192, 193, 223, 227, 228
plural markings (lack of), 21
pluricentricity, 4
politeness markers, 38, 42–43, 128, 131,
192, 193
polyglossia, 223
Portuguese, 256n.7
positional marking of discourse
familiarity, 82–83, 91
pragmatics
article omission, 96, 99–105
definiteness, 80
discourse pragmatics, 37–38, 42–43
Interface Hypothesis, 205, 206–7
modals *will* and *would*, 127–28
pragmatic inferencing, 179
retention of British English features in
Indian English, 37–38
Singapore English, 167
substrate influences, 195
transfer from Indian languages, 42–43
universals, 180
prepositions, 90
prescriptivism, 7, 34, 38, 170, 212, 217,
231–32, 236, 242–43
press registers, 214
prestige. *See also* elites

[298] *Index*

British versus American English, 34
Colloquial Singapore English, 224
covert prestige, 25, 75, 136, 224, 239
grammar and correctness
    attitudes, 148–49
hypercorrection, 44
indigenization of Indian English, 136
linguistic convergence, 48–49
and politeness, 131–32
rhoticity, 36, 39
Singapore English, 170, 237
style variation, 75, 212
substrate influences, 196
Prince, Ellen, 85, 88–89, 95, 99, 257n.9
prior knowledge, 90
process versus product, 199–201
prodrop, 41
proficency
    and accent as identity, 139–42, 151
    article omission, 198
    copulas, 198
    dialect continua, 76
    implication scaling, 64
    inclusion of less proficient speakers,
        54, 60–61
    modals, 198
    and nativeness, 54
    past tense, 198
    personal factors in dialect contact, 146
    proficiency cline, 137–39
    progressives, 198
    sharing of new dialect features, 71
    style shifting, 213
progressive
    comparative studies Indian and
        Singaporean English, 185–90
    habitual meaning, 21
    Indian English, 65, 108, 110–11, 114,
        121–23, 127
    pragmatics, 118–20
    proficency, 198
    progressive -ing, 110–11, 118–20,
        121–23, 132–34, 185–90
    Singapore English, 204
    stabilization of, 198
    Subset Principle, 203
    universals, 173
"properness," 212. See also "correctness"
prosody, 38, 44, 81, 82, 96, 147–48, 150,
    166, 181–82, 216

public understanding, implications
    for, 250–51
punctual reference, 184
Punjabi, 108, 157
Punnoose, Reenu, 34, 49, 213, 250

quantification, 88, 102
quantitative sociolinguistics, 8–9,
    10, 79–80
question formation, 42, 43
*qui-his*, 27–28
Quirk, Randolph, 3, 4, 76

Rahman, Jacquelyn, 151
Rampton, Ben, 55, 64
real actuation question, 6
recoverability principle, 179
redundancy effects, 178
reduplication, 21, 39–40, 42
referents, specificity of, 80, 89
refocusing, 48–49, 51
regional languages, 31, 32–33, 34, 157–
    58, 170, 243. *See also* substrate
    influences
regional variation
    lexicon, 40
    syntax, 42
regression analysis, 137, 141–42
regularization features in New Englishes,
    common, 44–46
Reichenbach, Hans, 115
relative clauses, 90, 166
relexification, 121
resumption, 40
retroflexion, 141
"rhizome" development, 19, 48, 242–43
rhoticity
    accent as identity, 139–42
    American English, 34, 36, 39, 140
    Anglo-Indian English, 25
    Asian identity, 39
    global influences on, 44
    nonrhoticity, 36, 39, 139, 165, 216
    retention of British English features in
        Indian English, 36
    transfer from Indian languages, 39
    women, 39
Rickford, John R., 63, 64, 68, 75, 151,
    175, 260n.9
*right*, 167

*Index* [299]

Rimmington, Don, 181–82
Robertson, Daniel, 179, 207
Roy, Anjali Gera, 219
Roy, Raja Rammohun, 23–24
Rushdie, Salman, 32, 218

Sadaf, Shazia, 29, 256n.4
Sag, Ivan, 80
Sahgal, Anju, 39, 150, 215, 217, 234–35
*sahib*, 21
Sailaja, Pingali, 20, 27, 34, 38, 139, 213, 222
Sakel, Jeanette, 43, 247–48
Sand, Andrea, 80, 102–3, 174–75, 176
Sankaran, Lavanya, 60, 142
Sankoff, Gillian, 3, 87, 95, 103, 104
Sanskrit, 33, 108
Sanyal, Jyoti, 214
Sato, Yosuke, 166
Save Our Singlish, 238
Scale of Assumed Familiarity, 88–89, 95, 96, 99
Schiffman, Harold, 258n.1
"schizoglossia," 151
Schneider, Edgar, 4, 26, 27–28, 31, 49–51, 135, 150, 158–59, 160, 170, 212–13, 215–16, 230–31, 234–35, 241, 245, 248, 256n.2, 261n.6
Schröter, Verena, 192
Schwartz, B. D., 210
second language acquisition (SLA)
    Creole studies, 46
    feedback loops, 245
    implication scaling, 62, 63
    implications for theory, 248
    input as a core factor, 207–9
    Interface Hypothesis, 205–7
    methods, 8
    and New Englishes, 4–5, 8, 56–59
    process versus product, 199–201
    Subset Principle, 201–5
    varioversals, 174–75
second-person plural pronouns, 25
Sedlatschek, Andreas, 102, 180, 207, 216, 217, 218
self-corrections, 147, 148
Selinker, Richard, 57, 76
semantic broadening, 168
semantic conflation, 131
semantics and modality, 127–28

semantic shift, 45, 168
semantic transfer, 83, 111, 113
semantic transparency, 44, 45
semiautonomous models, 55, 234
sentence length, 214
Serratrice, Ludovica, 205, 207
settler varieties, 27–28
Sharma, Devyani, 39, 60, 63, 73–74, 79–80, 102, 106, 112, 115, 116–18, 123–24, 142, 164, 175, 180, 189–90, 192–93, 207, 210, 217, 233, 235, 258n.2, 258n.9, 260n.9
Shastri, S. V., 113
Shatz, Marilyn, 128, 131
Shirai, Yasuhiro, 111, 116–18, 184
Siemund, Peter, 192
Singapore English
    code-switching, 225–27
    common features, 164–68
    comparative history with Indian English, 155–70
    comparative studies Indian and Singaporean English, 227–39
    datasets, 14–15
    dialect confidence, 236–39
    diglossia, 75
    historical language transfer, 57
    nativization, 213
    past tense, 209
    social histories of English, 158–64
    style variation, 222–27
    Subset Principle, 204
    *will*, 258–59n.10
Singapore Mandarin, 14–15
Singh, Rajendra, 53–54, 55, 72–73
Singlish, 238
Sinitic languages, 163–64, 165–67, 177
Snell, Julia, 4
social class. *See also* elites
    class inequalities, 34
    Indian English, 34, 36, 47–48
    middle classes, 26, 27, 49, 216, 228
    rhoticity, 39
    style variation, 216, 219
    working classes, 28, 29, 49, 73–74, 228
social factors and Indian English, 72–74
social histories
    conclusions on, 243
    English in India, 20–35

[300]  *Index*

English in Singapore, 158–64
sociolects, 228
sociolinguistic interviews, 11
Sohail, N., 39
Sorace, Anotenella, 205, 207
South African Indian English, 84, 191
Speak Good English Movement,
236, 237
Speak Mandarin Campaign, 161
specificity, 80, 81, 83, 87, 92–93, 103–4, 177
speech communities, 47, 135–52, 172
"sprachbunds," 38, 104
Sprouse, R. A., 210
Sridhar, K.K., 4–5, 8–9, 42–43, 57, 58, 81, 109, 131–32
Sridhar, S.N., 4–5, 57, 58
stable bilingualism, 163–64
stable multilingualism, 157–58, 170
stable norms, 60
Staicov, Adina, 150
Starr, Rebecca Lurie, 44
state languages. *See* official status languages
stative meanings, 65, 71–72, 111, 114, 115, 118, 119, 120, 183, 185, 187, 193
*stay*, 168
steady state, 77, 136, 151
Steel, Flora Annie, 27, 28
Stephany, Ursula, 128
stereotypes, 146, 147–48, 214
St. George's Anglo-Indian School and Orphanage, 20–21
stress, 44, 166. *See also* prosody
style variation, 75, 145, 147, 212–40, 249
subject-verb agreement, 65, 69
Subset Principle, 190, 200, 201–5
substrate influences. *See also* transfer from Indian languages
article use, 176–80
conclusions on, 243
copula omission, 190
imperfective aspect, 123, 185–90
implications for theory, 247–48
indirect substrate influence, 171, 177, 229, 243
individual cognition, 244
versus input, 208–9

lexical transfer from Indian languages, 39–40
modals, 128, 133
past perfect, 124
past tense, 181–83
progressivity, 120
Singapore English, 14–15, 160, 161, 163, 165–67, 172–73
style variation, 229
substrate-superstrate interaction, 189
transfer from Indian languages, 38–43
typology, 194–96, 210
versus universals, 6, 171–96
Sun, Chaofen, 181–82
Superficial English, 21
supersets, 203, 204
superstrate influences, 121, 123, 126, 131, 132, 188, 189, 195
supraregionalization, 49, 215–19
syllable timing, 166
syntactic awareness, 146–48
syntax
articles, 79–105
code-switching, 219
retention of British English features in Indian English, 37
Singapore English, 166
transfer from Indian languages, 40–42
verbal system, 106–34
syntax of discourse, 195
syntax-pragmatics interface, 205, 211
Szmrecsanyi, Benedikt, 6, 44, 58–59, 152, 173–75, 200–1, 207

Tabouret-Keller, Andre, 5, 47
Tagliamonte, Sali, 152, 175
tag questions, 43
Talking Cock, 224
Tamil, 39, 40, 43, 157–58, 161, 170, 190, 191, 219, 229, 257n.4
Tamil Nadu, 32
Tamlish, 40
Tan, Daniel K. H., 239
Tan, Peter K. W., 239
Tarone, Elaine, 85–86
Telangana state, 33
Telegu, 33
telicity, 107, 111, 114, 183
temporary result states, 181–82

*Index* [301]

tense, modality and aspect, 106–34, 181–83, 203, 209, 210
tense-to-aspect shift, 120–23
Teochew, 160, 172–73, 182
theme/rheme, 81
third grammars, 77–78, 79, 100–1, 121, 123, 171, 195, 243
Thomason, Sarah G., 59, 61, 248–49
three circles model, 4
*Times of India, The,* 33–34
Tok Pisin, 257n.9
tone languages, 166
topicality marking, 41, 81, 82–83, 91, 104, 205
topic continuity, 85
transfer from Indian languages
   article omission, 92–94, 99
   dialect-like features, 77
   Indian English, 79
   discourse-driven restructuring, 104–5
   discourse pragmatics, 38–43
   tense, modality and aspect, 110–12
TRAP/BATH lexical sets, 36, 44, 165
Treffers-Daller, Jeanine, 248–49
Trenkic, Danijela, 85, 95, 103, 180
Trudgill, Peter, 136–37, 143, 146–47, 173–74

Universal Grammar, 61, 174
universals
   article omission, 84, 94, 95
   aspect, 111
   conclusions on, 243
   definiteness, 84
   grammatical universals, 171–96
   individual cognition, 244
   and L1 transfer, 79–80
   modals, 128, 133
   progressivity, 118
   versus substrate influence, 6, 171–96
universities (English-medium education), 33
urban varieties
   code-switching, 45
   feedback loops, 76–77
   high-prestige varieties, 157
   nonrhoticity, 216
   refocusing, 48–49
   rhoticity, 39

style range, 228–29
vernacularization, 218
Urdu, 35, 157–58
usage cline, 52–53, 62–78, 242
utilitarianism, 22

van Rooy, Bertus, 4–5, 58–59, 175, 189–90
variationist sociolinguistics, 9, 10, 55–62, 79–80, 216
varioversals, 174–75
velarization, 139–42
Vendler, Zeno, 114
vernacularization, 49, 170, 215–19, 222, 228, 229, 234, 236
vernacular-medium education, 29, 32–33
Vogel, Katrin, 121–23, 187

Wee, Lionel, 14, 167, 168, 170, 177, 179, 180, 198, 236, 239
Weinreich, Uriel, 57, 197
Wells, J. C., 256n.6
White, Lydia, 201
whole dialect approaches, 247
wh-questions, 42
'Why this Kolaveri, Di?' 40
Widdowson, H. G., 26
Wilcox, Sharon, 128, 131
*will,* 71–72, 111, 115, 127–32, 133, 192, 208
Wiltshire, Caroline, 194–95, 213
Winford, Donald, 58, 61, 210
Wolfram, Walt, 210
women, 20–21, 39
Wong, Jock, 167
word order, 40, 81, 82–83
working classes, 28, 29, 49, 73–74, 228
*World Atlas of Variation in English* (Kortmann and Lunkenheimer 2013), 175–76
World Englishes, 4, 8–9, 52, 53
*would,* 65, 71–72, 111, 115, 127–32, 133, 192, 193, 208
written corpora, 102
written Indian English, 37

Xiao, Richard, 214

Yao, Xinyue, 124, 206

Yip, Po-Ching, 181–82
*you-all/y'all*, 25
Young, R., 83, 85–86, 87
Yule, Henry, 27–28

Zastoupil, L., 22, 23–24
Zentella, Ana Celia, 63
Ziegeler, Debra, 193, 210
Zipp, Lena, 150